THE MORAL STATUS OF CHILDREN

THE MORAL STATUS OF CHILDREN

Essays on the Rights of the Child

by

MICHAEL FREEMAN

Professor of English Law
University College London

MARTINUS NIJHOFF PUBLISHERS

Published by Kluwer Law International
P.O. Box 85889
2508 CN The Hague, The Netherlands

Sold and distributed in the USA and Canada by
Kluwer Law International
675 Massachusetts Avenue
Cambridge, MA 02139, USA

Sold and distributed in all other countries by
Kluwer Law International
Distribution Centre
P.O. Box 322
3300 AH Dordrecht, The Netherlands

A C.I.P. Catalogue record for this book is available from the Library of Congress

Picture on cover: Boys Playing on the Shore, 1884
by Albert Edelfelt
owner: Ateneum, Helsinki
photo: The Central Art Archives/ Hannu Aaltonen

Printed on acid-free paper

Cover design: Robert Vulkers BNO

ISBN 90 411 0377 5

© 1997 Kluwer Law International

Kluwer Law International incorporates the publishing programmes of Graham & Trotman Ltd, Kluwer Law and Taxation Publishers and Martinus Nijhoff Publishers

This publication is protected by international copyright law.
All rights reserved. No part of this publication may be reproduced, stored in a retrieval system, or transmitted in any form or by any means, electronic, mechanical, photocopying, recording or otherwise, without the prior permission of the publisher.

TO THE MILLION AND A HALF
CHILDREN OF THE HOLOCAUST,
THE MOST EGREGIOUS VICTIMS
OF THE DENIAL OF THE
MORAL STATUS OF CHILDREN
THIS CENTURY (OR PERHAPS ANY).

Table of Contents

PREFACE ix

CHAPTER 1. THE MORAL STATUS OF CHILDREN 1

CHAPTER 2. TAKING CHILDREN'S RIGHTS MORE SERIOUSLY 19

CHAPTER 3. LAWS, CONVENTIONS AND RIGHTS 47

CHAPTER 4. BEYOND CONVENTIONS–TOWARDS EMPOWERMENT 63

CHAPTER 5. THE LIMITS OF CHILDREN'S RIGHTS 83

CHAPTER 6. ENGLISH LAW AND THE UNITED NATIONS CONVENTION ON THE RIGHTS OF THE CHILD 105

CHAPTER 7. CHILDREN'S RIGHTS AND CULTURAL PLURALISM 129

CHAPTER 8. CONTACT WITH ABSENT PARENTS: AN EMERGENT CHILD RIGHT 149

CHAPTER 9. DO CHILDREN HAVE THE RIGHT NOT TO BE BORN? 165

CHAPTER 10. THE RIGHTS OF THE ARTIFICIALLY PROCREATED CHILD 185

CHAPTER 11. CAN CHILDREN DIVORCE THEIR PARENTS? 213

CHAPTER 12. THE JAMES BULGER TRAGEDY: CHILDISH INNOCENCE AND THE CONSTRUCTION OF GUILT 235

CHAPTER 13. CLEVELAND, BUTLER-SLOSS AND BEYOND: HOW ARE WE TO REACT TO THE SEXUAL ABUSE OF CHILDREN? 255

CHAPTER 14. IN THE CHILD'S BEST INTERESTS? READING THE CHILDREN ACT CRITICALLY 305

CHAPTER 15.   REMOVING RIGHTS FROM ADOLESCENTS 345

CHAPTER 16.   STERILIZING THE MENTALLY HANDICAPPED 357

CHAPTER 17.   AFTERWORD 389

INDEX 397

Preface

I have been writing on children's issues since the late 1960s. The focus was not then on the rights of children, at least not in the way in which we view rights today. In the 1970s I wrote widely on child law (including a book on the English Children Act of 1975) and on child abuse, culminating in *Violence in the Home—A Socio-Legal Study*, which Saxon House published in 1979.

In 1979, the International Year of The Child, in a major public lecture that I gave at my own college, I focused my attention for the first time directly on children's rights. The lecture, published as 'The Rights of the Child in the International Year of The Child' in *Current Legal Problems* identified 'rightlessness' as a root cause of child abuse. The article also contained a critique of the child liberationist philosophy associated with John Holt and Richard Farson whose views were then very much to the fore. These writers deserve a reassessment, as I say in chapter 1 of this book, but I reserve this for a future occasion.

In 1983 I published *The Rights and Wrongs of Children* (Frances Pinter). In this I identified a *via media* between child protection and child liberation: I wrote of the value but also the limits of each. Re-reading the book now it is clear to me that I underestimated the importance of giving children participatory rights. This is a subject taken up in a number of the chapters of this book, notably in chapters 1 and 4.

The Rights and Wrongs of Children has been out of print for some time. It is still widely used; indeed, to judge from quotation and citation, perhaps more so now than when it was first published. It would have been tempting to write a second edition. Most of the issues explored in the book remain current, but the contours of the subject have shifted—the United Nations Convention on the Rights of the Child being a profound influence—so that the focus in a new edition would have been very different. With hindsight the *Rights and Wrongs* was written too early. A paradigm shift in thinking about children occurred in the late 1980s and early 1990s. The book, if published then, might have had a greater impact.

Since 1983 I have been engaged in children's issues on a number of fronts. I wrote a number of articles on English child law. I was at the outset of the campaign to make it unlawful to hit children. I spoke regularly at conferences, national and international, about the theory and practice of children's rights. By 1987 my ideas seemed to strike a chord with the media and I found them being discussed in the newspapers, as well as on radio and television. I was both applauded and attacked (Barbara Amiel's 'Smack of Statism' in *The Times* sticks in the memory).

The media were particularly interested in the Brian Jackson Memorial Lecture I gave at Huddersfield Polytechnic in November 1987. I spoke of the importance of regarding children as persons rather than as objects of concern. This adage is now part of common currency, though it is usually identified with the report of the Cleveland Inquiry, where it also features. The lecture, entitled 'Taking Children's Rights Seriously' was published in *Children and Society*. A later version of this, the word 'More' inserted to take account of the passing of the United Nations Convention, was the basis of a lecture delivered at an international conference at the Australian National University in Canberra in July 1991 (and also at the University of Otago in New Zealand). It is reproduced here as chapter 2.

What is now chapter 5 has its source in a paper delivered to a conference on the 'ideologies' of children's rights at the Hebrew University of Jerusalem in December 1990, and subsequently published in *The Ideologies of Children's Rights* by Martinus Nijhoff. It was at this conference that the *International Journal of Children's Rights* was born. The journal commenced publication in 1993 with myself as one of the editors. The journal has stimulated, and will continue to stimulate, thinking about children's rights world-wide. One special issue—there have already been three—was on cultural pluralism. I contributed the introductory essay to this, entitling it 'The Morality of Cultural Pluralism'. I delivered this also as a public lecture in the Lunch Hour Lecture series at University College London in October 1994, and subsequently it formed the basis of a paper given to the U.S. Law and Society Association Conference in Glasgow in July 1996. It is included in this collection as chapter 7. The subject continues to occupy my research time and a monograph on the subject has been commissioned by Dartmouth for a series which Geraldine van Bueren is editing.

In January 1992 I gave the keynote address at a children's ombudswork conference in Amsterdam. My lecture 'Beyond Conventions—Toward Empowerment' contains some of my most significant thoughts on the status of children in particular as regards a re-thinking of the culture of childhood. A revised version of the lecture was published in a slim volume of essays entitled *Towards The Realization of Human Rights of Children*,

Preface xi

which Defence for Children International—Netherlands put together. It is re-published in this collection (see chapter 4) in the hope that it will attract a wider audience.

In 1993 I spoke at the First World Congress on Family Law and Children's Rights which was held in Sydney on a child's right to access with parents and other family members. This was a law conference and my presentation reflected this. A version of the lecture was published in the conference proceedings: chapter 8 of this book is a major revision of the theme, though it retains its essentially legal (and comparative) framework.

The James Bulger killing in February 1993 and in particular the subsequent trial of two 11-year-olds in November of that year has provoked a lot of literature. I gave public lectures on the subject in 1994 at a number of American universities, including Wisconsin, Illinois and Tulane. I also used the case to focus on children's representation issues at a conference arranged by DCI - International - Israel at Tel-Aviv University in March 1995. Chapter 12 draws on these lectures and on the paper I presented to a panel on 'governing childhood' at the U.S. Law and Society Conference held in Toronto in June 1995.

In 1995 I was also invited to deliver the so-called 'Mini-Hamlyn' lectures. Two lectures were given in April at the University of Essex and in May at the University of East Anglia. It was not clear to me in what sense they were 'mini', save in that the exposure they receive is minuscule! There is a promise to publish these in a volume entitled *Frontiers of Family Law*. That may happen: in the meanwhile versions of both lectures are contained in this volume, as chapters 9 and 10 respectively. Both chapters explore neglected subjects and chapter 9 also makes some preliminary investigations into the conception of responsible parenthood. This is also alluded to in chapter 1. It is, of course, a subject which strikes a chord on both sides of the Atlantic. Though I would wish to distance myself from the 'Moral Right', it is a subject of importance and one to which I intend to return.

The title of the book is drawn from the keynote opening address at a summer school organized by the University of Gent in June 1996. The lecture itself is reproduced as chapter 1. The essay draws on a number of concerns: the virtual non-existence of 'children's studies' as a discipline, the absence of communication between the different academic disciplines with a concern for children (do sociologists of childhood and international human rights lawyers even realize their common or at least contiguous interests?), the implications of the backlash against rights for children's rights (a subject I addressed also in a public lecture at the University of Wisconsin in March 1994).

Two other chapters of this originate in lectures delivered in University College London's *Current Legal Problems* series. The essay on the Cleveland affair is adapted from a lecture given in December 1988 and that on England's innovative Children Act 1989 coincided with the implementation of the Act in October 1991. Chapters 13 and 14 reproduce the texts of these lectures, already published in *Current Legal Problems*, with a number of changes. 'Removing Rights From Adolescents' addresses the backlash against the emphasis on a child's autonomy represented in the famous *Gillick* decision. Its source is a lecture to the British Agencies for Adoption and Fostering delivered in Newcastle-upon-Tyne in November 1991 and subsequently published in *Adoption and Fostering*.

'Laws, Conventions and Rights' was commissioned by the National Children's Bureau for its thirtieth anniversary and published in *Children and Society*. It appears here, as chapter 3, updated to take account of the European Convention on the Exercise of Children's Rights. Earlier versions of chapter 6 have been published in Bob Franklin's *Handbook of Children's Rights* and in my *Children's Rights: A Comparative Perspective*. 'Can Children Divorce Their Parents?'—an essay that can be traced to a seminar I gave at the University of Minnesota in February 1994—was previously published in another edited collection of mine *Divorce—Where Next?* 'Sterilising The Mentally Handicapped', a critical assessment of the notorious 'Jeanette' decision, was previously published by Stevens in a volume called *Medicine, Ethics and the Law*, which I edited. It is included here, though it takes no account of the many later cases, because it contains a sustained defence of, what has come to be called, pejoratively, 'rights-talk', and because it analyses one of the most oppressive forms of the social control of children produced in the twentieth century.

I am grateful to the Oxford University Press and the International Journal of Law and the Family for permission to republish chapter 2; to Whiting and Birch and the National Children's Bureau for permission to republish chapter 3; to DCI—Netherlands for permission to republish chapter 5; to Routledge for permission to republish chapter 6; to Dartmouth for permission to republish chapters 6 and 9; to Stevens for permission to republish chapters 13 and 16; to the British Agencies for Adoption and Fostering for permission to reproduce chapter 15 and to Oxford University Press for permission to reproduce chapter 14.

Although most of this book has been previously published, I believe that there is justification for a collection of this nature and also that the essays, though disparate in origin, form a coherent whole. Indeed, in some ways, *The Moral Status of Children* is a second edition to *The Rights and Wrongs of Children*. This book states the case for children's rights (see particularly chapters 1, 2, 4), traces the history of the development of the idea (see chapter 3) and exposes the limits in chapter 5. Chapter 6 is an attempt to measure the commitment of one legal system and institutional complex to children's rights. Chapter 7 raises questions about the universalism of a code of rights such as that found in the United Nations Convention on the Rights of the Child and also in International Labour Office conventions. Chapter 8 through 11, and also 15 and 16, are case studies of children's rights. Each of the studies in chapters 8 to 11 look at relatively new concerns: little has been written on any of the four subjects of these chapters, in particular from a children's rights perspective. Chapters 12 to 14 are studies of children's rights issues situated within wider problems (the problem of young delinquency, crime panics, law and order policies and victims' rights in chapter 12, the rights of innocent parents in chapter 13, the interests and values of children's legislation as well as rights to parental autonomy in chapter 14). Throughout there is a commitment to upholding the personality, integrity and moral status of children and a vision of a better future where these qualities are recognized.

It remains for me to thank those who over the years have helped my think about children: Philip Alston, Cynthia Price Cohen, John Eekelaar, Kate Federle, Målfrid Flekkøy, Penelope Leach, Gerison Lansdown, Catherine Lowy, Christina Lyon, Mary Ann Mason, Neil MacCormick, Anne McGillivray, Gary Melton, Peter Newell, Ludwig Salgo, Geraldine van Bueren, Philip Veerman, Eugeen Verhellen and Olga Zhakova. I am grateful also to my secretary Rebekah Williams, without whom this collection would not have seen the light of day and to others who in earlier days laboured in the same cause, in particular the late Edith Ray and Anna Mochan. The encouragement of Lindy Melman at Kluwer is also gratefully acknowledged.

Michael Freeman
25 September 1996

CHAPTER 1

The Moral Status of Children

For anyone interested in children a trip to a major bookshop is an amusing and an instructive experience. Tell them your interest at the information desk and likely as not you will be guided to shelves full of Louisa M. Alcott, Enid Blyton and Christopher Milne. Your world may be Sophie's, but *Sophie's World* is far more likely to be found amongst the adult novels.[1] Further enquiries may send you to the child welfare section where you—now adult—will discover how to recover from sexual abuse or to adopt. If they perceive your interest to be legal—they don't find this difficult—you may be sent to sift through the section on family law where books on child support, child abuse or even children's rights may greet you. If they think your interest is sociological—equally easy to detect—there will be a well-stocked selection of books on family sociology and all sorts of books wherein one may read about the socialization of children,[2] their education, punishment patterns and so on. Why, given the same shops have well-stocked individual sections on women's studies, gay and lesbian studies, black studies, are there no sections devoted to children's studies? In Europe's largest city at its main university bookshop it was impossible to purchase any of the ten significant books on children that I identified prior to a visit.[3] All are recent publications. Nor is this a reflection of an ab-

---

[1] See Jostein Gaarder, *Sophie's World* (London: Phoenix House, 1995).

[2] The themes of dominant family sociological works such as those of Talcott Parsons and Kingsley Davis. To Parsons children were the 'barbarian invasion'. An example of this tradition is O. W. Ritchie and M. R. Kollar, *The Sociology of Childhood*, (New York: Appleton-Century-Crofts, 1964). For its influence on pedagogy see P. H. Hirst and R. S. Peters, *The Logic of Education*, (London: R.K.P., 1970).

[3] The books I identified were:
C. Jenks, *Childhood* (London: Routledge, 1996)
J. Qvortrup et al, *Childhood Matters* (Aldershot: Avebury, 1994)
B. Mayall, *Children's Childhoods Observed and Experienced* (London: Falmer, 1994)
N. Postman, *The Disappearance of Childhood* (New York: Vintage, 1994)
C. J. Somerville, *The Rise and Fall of Childhood* (New York: Vintage, 1990)

sence of an inquisitive interest in children: a recent research initiative in the United Kingdom entitled 'Children 5–16' attracted nearly three hundred applications.[4]

All this is despite an international year devoted to children,[5] a widely-acclaimed and almost universally endorsed convention,[6] a world summit on children[7] and with children—as victims of sexual abuse,[8] murderers,[9] targets of educational policies[10] or health cuts[11]—rarely off the front pages. On one level it would be comforting, on another discomforting, to think this was some kind of English malaise. It is in England, after all, that Lloyd de Mause's 'nightmare'[12] was, perhaps still is, most graphically experienced. But we know that the marginalization to which I refer is not unique to one country. Even now with the focus there is on children, it is on children seen through the prism of an adult lens. And this allows children to be seen but not heard: the saying so accurately reflects the truth that it is worth repeating.

But work on children has moved on, even if you would be hard-pushed to guess this from a visit to a bookshop. Where once children were studied as passive beings structured by the social context of the family or the

---

A. James and A. Prout, *Constructing and Reconstructing Childhood* (Basingstoke: Falmer, 1990)

J. Ennew, *The Sexual Exploitation of Children* (Cambridge: Polity Press, 1986)

J. Hockey and A. James, *Growing Up and Growing Old* (London: Sage, 1993)

J. Boswell, *The Kindness of Strangers* (Harmondsworth: Penguin, 1991)

L. Purdy, *In Their Best Interest?* (Ithaca, Cornell University Press, 1992)

[4] Under E.S.R.C. auspices. Twenty-two applications were successful.

[5] In 1979. See Judith Stone, *The International Year of The Child: A Continuing Challenge* (London: IYC Trust, 1981).

[6] On which see Geraldine van Bueren, *The International Law On The Rights of The Child* (Dordrecht: Martinus Nijhoff, 1995).

[7] Children being proclaimed by Margaret Thatcher as 'our sacred trust'.

[8] From Cleveland in 1987 (see the Butler-Sloss report, Cm. 412) to Clwyd in 1996, where demands to publish the report revealing widespread abuse of children in homes was resisted because it would lead to the local authority (or its insurers) having to pay huge sums of damages. A public judicial inquiry began in January 1997.

[9] See Stewart Asquith, 'When Children Kill Children', *Childhood*, 3, 99 (1996).

[10] Note the way that the test for testing children's educational attainments is constantly lowered. England is now to test 5-year-olds. The government's policies have been said by Sir Claus Moser, founder of the National Commission on Education, to ignore children's needs. See *The Independent*, 18 April 1996.

[11] See Zarrina Kurtz's 'Milroy Lecture' of 1995, 'Do Children's Rights To Health Care in the U.K. Ensure Their Best Interests?', *Journal of The Royal College of Physicians of London*, 29, 508, (1995).

[12] See *The History of Childhood* (London: Souvenir Press, 1976), p. 1.

school, now research focuses on children's agency, on the ways they construct their own autonomous social worlds. Hardman, in an important article published in 1973 but, I think, too often overlooked by those interested in children's rights, put the case for children to be seen as 'people to be studied in their own right, and not just as receptacles of adult teaching.'[13] And this has been grasped by international legislators: Article 12 of the United Nations Convention on the Rights of the Child is an obvious manifestation[14] and there are examples, through also pockets of resistance, in national legislation and case law too.[15]

The children's rights movement has achieved much, not least a convention which nearly every country in the world has accepted.[16] A generation ago who would have thought this was possible. That children's rights could find a place in a country's constitution was unimaginable, as inconceivable as that country would be South Africa rid of the disease of apartheid.[17] Visits to bookshops are salutary experiences, for it would be all too easy to sink into a complacent euphoria. We must not do this for a number of reasons.

First, we all know from the experiences of our own countries that the status of children remains low. In most there are status offences. In Britain[18] and in New Zealand[19] there have been recent proposals to follow the American example[20] and curfew children. That these proposals have been

---

[13] See C. Hardman, 'Can There Be an Anthropology of Children?', *Journal of the Anthropological Society of Oxford*, 4 (1), 85 (1973).

[14] States Parties shall assure to the child who is capable of forming his or her own views the right to express those views freely in all matters affecting the child, the views of the child being given due weight in accordance with the age and maturity of the child.

For this purpose, the child shall in particular be provided the opportunity to be heard in any judicial and administrative proceedings affecting the child, either directly, or through a representative or an appropriate body, in a manner consistent with the procedural rules of national law.

On interpretation of this see Marie-Françoise Lücker-Babel, *International Journal of Children's Rights*, 3, 391 (1995).

[15] On the United Kingdom's experience see Gerison Lansdown, *Taking Part: Children's Participation in Decision Making* (London: IPPR, 1995).

[16] As of March 1995 there were 170 ratifications and 8 further signatures.

[17] See Constitution of the Republic of South Africa and Bill of Rights 1996, s.28 (1996).

[18] See *The Guardian*, 3 June 1996 and its leading article the same day, 'A Curfew on Common Sense.'

[19] This was widely reported in the New Zealand media on 19 April 1996.

[20] On which see Katherine Hunt Federle, 'Children, Curfews and the Constitution', *Washington University Law Quarterly*, 73, 1315 (1995).

generally welcomed,[21] that in Britain they emanate from the supposed left[22] speaks volumes. In all but a handful of countries children remain the only members of society against whom violence is sanctioned.[23] In few countries do children, despite Article 12 of the U.N. Convention, have genuine participatory rights.[24] We can all catalogue the ills, the indignities children suffer. The emphasis may differ from country to country, a reflection often of culture and socio-economic conditions, but the myth of a golden age of childhood[25] remains firmly entrenched in our consciousness to be just occasionally disturbed when a child is abducted to her death,[26] when there is a 'Dunblane'[27] or when we notice a news item about sex tourism,[28] child slave labour[29] or state-run extermination squads,[30] of course in faraway countries. And we rarely notice because such news is usually tucked away in the inside pages of 'foreign' news. Conventions, like laws generally, need to be more than exercises in symbolic politics.[31]

---

[21] For example, see 'Putting Back Barriers', *The Times*, 4 June 1996.

[22] Their architect is Jack Straw (once a student of mine!), the 'New Labour' Home Affairs spokesman and likely to be Home Secretary in 1997.

[23] Only Sweden, Norway, Finland, Austria and Cyprus have made the hitting of children unlawful.

[24] In general see Roger A. Hart, *Children's Participation: From Tokenism to Citizenship*, (Florence: UNICEF, 1992).

[25] John Holt referred to the myth of a 'walled garden of "Happy, Safe, Protected, Innocent Childhood"' (see *Escape from Childhood*, Harmondsworth: Penguin, 1975).

[26] The abduction of 7-year-old Sophie Hook from a tent in her uncle's garden in which she was staying on July 30 1995 caused a widespread panic. She was raped and killed by a paedophile, Howard Hughes. He was sentenced to life imprisonment in July 1996. See also the article by Polly Toynbee, 'The Age of Innocence is Dead, Killed by Suspicion', *The Independent*, 1 May 1996.

[27] Where a whole class and their teacher were gunned down by a paedophile. Yet months later the House of Commons Select Committee resisted a demand for a ban on handguns.

[28] The government in Britain has belatedly moved to punish organizers of foreign child-sex trips, at the same time resisting demands that individuals who abuse and exploit children abroad be prosecuted on their return to this country. See *The Independent*, 9 December 1995; *The Guardian*, 9 December 1995. It has now relented and prosecutions may take place.

[29] See Judith Ennew, *Learning Or Labouring: A Compilation of Key Texts on Child work and Basic Education* (Florence: UNICEF, 1995).

[30] For example see *Report to the UN Committee Against Torture on the Torture of Guatemalan Street Children 1990–1995* (Casa Alianza, San Jose, Costa Rica, 1996). See also Martha K. Huggins and Myriam Mesquita P. de Castro, 'Youth Murders In Brazil,' *Childhood*, 3, 77 (1996).

[31] See Murray Edelman, *Political Language: Words That Succeed and Policies That Fail* (New York: Academic Press, 1977).

This has been said before. There are, however, two other reasons I wish to identify which need to be addressed by those concerned with the moral status of children. Both feature prominently in the literature, but neither has been addressed in the now vast literature on children's rights.

The first of these questions is unique to the debate on children: it focuses on the supposed disappearance of childhood. What are the implications of the thesis of Neil Postman[32] and others[33] for the moral status of children and, in particular, their rights.

The second addresses rights generally. In liberal discourse rights are salient markers, supposed guarantees of citizenship and legal subjecthood. But they have now been challenged within critical thought.[34] This could, of course, lead to children's rights being questioned, and not from more conventional conservative sources.[35] These we are used to: the new attacks are more sophisticated. The implications of this critical thinking for the children's rights movement must be assessed. There could yet be a backlash against children's rights.

It is to these new features of the debate that I now turn.

THE DISAPPEARANCE OF CHILDHOOD

It is more than a striking coincidence, perhaps even a paradox, that with the growing institutional recognition that children have rights has come the belief that childhood is a disappearing phenomenon.

Indeed, Postman, one of those to look into an apocalyptic future and see no 'children', believes that it is because of this that there exists a movement to recast the legal rights of children so that they are, as he sees it, more or less the same as adults.[36] He cites Richard Farson's *Birthrights*,[37] though he could equally have referred to the work of John Holt, particularly his *Escape From Childhood*,[38] or indeed the texts and docu-

---

[32] *The Disappearance of Childhood* (New York: Vintage Books, 1994, originally published in 1982).
[33] C. John Sommerville, *The Rise and Fall of Childhood* (New York: Vintage Books, 1990).
[34] Earlier this had been the orthodox Marxist position. See Steven Lukes, 'Marxism, Morality and Justice' in (ed.) G.H.R. Parkinson, *Marx and Marxism* (Cambridge: Cambridge University Press, 1982, p. 177).
[35] As in the writings of Joseph Goldstein, Anna Freud and Albert Solnit (see *Before The Best Interests of The Child*, New York: Free Press, 1979).
[36] *Op. cit.*, note 32, p. 4.
[37] Harmondsworth: Penguin Books, 1978 (first published in 1974).
[38] Harmondsworth: Penguin Books, 1975 (first published in 1974).

ments that emanated from a number of sources in the 1970s.[39] These were important statements in their day, and the 'liberation' movements of the 1970s deserve a critical reappraisal. One wonders whether Farson or Holt are still read[40] (the books of neither[41] were obtainable on my bookshop trip). Important though this strand of writing is, it does not represent the current state of thinking about children and their rights.[42] Postman can be forgiven for making this identification in 1982: it is less acceptable that he felt equally happy with it in 1994, when *The Disappearance of Childhood* was re-issued with a new preface by the author.

For Postman the evidence for the disappearance of childhood comes from several sources. I quote:

> There is, for example, the evidence displayed by the media themselves, for they not only promote the unseating of childhood through their form and context but reflect its decline in their content. There is evidence to be seen in the merging of the taste and style of children and adults, as well as in the changing perspectives of relevant social institutions such as the law, the schools and sports. And there is evidence of the "hard" variety—figures about alcoholism, drug use, sexual activity, crime etc., that imply a fading distinction between childhood and adulthood.[43]

It would be idle to pretend that these trends cannot be detected, whether in the form of twelve-year-old waif-like models exploited by the advertising industry,[44] or in the horrific examples of murder by young children of young children of which the *Bulger* case is the most graphic.[45] But the Postman thesis is facile. Childhood was no more created by the printing

---

[39] For example, Howard Cohen, *Equal Rights For Children* (Totowa, NJ: Littlefield, Adams, 1980).

[40] There is an assessment in Philip E. Veerman, *The Rights of the Child and the Changing Image of Childhood* (Dordrecht: Martinus Nijhoff, 1992), ch. ix. But Penelope Leach's *Children First* (London: Michael Joseph, 1994) ignores these distinguished predecessors.

[41] Such as *How Children Fail*.

[42] As, for instance, in David Archard, *Children: Rights and Childhood* (London: Routledge, 1993) or Laura Purdy, *In Their Best Interest?* (Ithaca: Cornell University Press, 1992).

[43] *Op. cit.*, note 32, p. 120.

[44] The English media in June 1996 was saturated by examples of this, though there was articulated rarely a concern for the problem it represented.

[45] See Colin Hay, 'Mobilization through Interpretation: James Bulger, Juvenile Crime and the Construction of a Moral Panic', *Social and Legal Studies*, 4, 197 (1995).

press,⁴⁶ though this may have contributed to the construction of modern childhood, than it will be 'disappeared' by the spread and intrusion of electronic media.

It is almost as if Postman would wish to create yet another status offence: children playing with adult 'toys.' Many of the trends Postman detects are anyway not new: we may know more about them now, or have greater concerns for the effect on adult society of criminal activity, drug use etc. by the young. But, anyone with an insight into 'Victorian values', or anyone who has read Charles Dickens (or Zola or Gogol) will know that much to which Postman refers as evidence of the decline of childhood is there to be seen in the pre-electronic age. What Postman also seems to overlook is the effect of the communication revolution on adult society too.

Postman is, however, right to point out that childhood is a social artefact.⁴⁷ As Turner has noted age, like sex and race, are not 'facts about being...there is no necessary reason why persons should be described in terms of age, gender and race.'⁴⁸ Nor should we ignore the significance of using an ascriptive category: in the case of age it is an association with incapacity, incompetence, immaturity, irresponsibility, characteristics which are informed by a postulate about the paramount importance of adulthood.⁴⁹

Childhood has changed and will continue to do so. But those who toll the knell of its passing, often interpreting, what they consider to be, its demise to moral decadence, oversimplify, exaggerate and, in making the link with the children's rights movement, dangerously distort.

Childhood has not disappeared and it will not do so. A childhood in which children are granted a moral status, in which their rights are taken seriously, will be a better childhood, not a worse one. What we should take from Postman's thesis is not his prognosis. It is his implication, which others have more clearly shown, that childhood is a social construction. What consequences follow from this?

---

⁴⁶ See, *op. cit.*, note 32, chs. 2 and 3. See, more generally, Elizabeth Eisenstein, *The Printing Press As an Agent of Change* (Cambridge: C.U.P., 1979).

⁴⁷ See C. Jenks, *The Sociology of Childhood* (London: Batsford, 1982); J. Qvortrup, *Childhood As a Social Phenomenon* (Vienna: European Centre, 1993).

⁴⁸ 'Personhood and Citizenship', *Theory, Culture and Society*, 3 (1), 1, 12 (1986).

⁴⁹ See, for agreement, Jens Qvortrup, 'Childhood Matters: An Introduction' in (eds.) J. Qvortrup, M. Bardy, G. Sgritta and H. Wintersberger, *Childhood Matters* (Aldershot: Avebury, 1994), p. 4.

One which does not flow is the denial that children have rights. Rather this understanding of childhood should lead to a further recognition that childhood cannot be understood outside the context of other variables such as class, gender[50] and ethnicity, or, for obvious reasons, culture. If childhood is a social construction, then there are 'childhoods' rather than a single, universal, cross-cultural phenomenon.[51] And, it has to be said, the implications of this for a universal code of children's rights, such as the United Nations Convention, have been barely grasped.[52]

It also follows that greater attention should be given to how childhoods are constructed. And this means looking beyond the obvious institutions which structure and restructure childhood—the law, culture, religion, the economy, the media, social work, educational institutions and practices—to the part played by children themselves in the construction of their own social lives, the lives of others with whom they interact and the societies in which they live.

The question has been asked more than once whether the United Nations Convention would have looked very different if children had had an input into it. It remains a question worth asking. The law-making network that forged the Convention was broad-based with a plethora of committed non-governmental organizations, but these did not include children.[53] Children should not be 'just passive subjects of social structural determinations', James and Prout remind us.[54] It has become commonplace to parrot the aphorism in the Butler-Sloss report into sexual abuse in Cleveland that children are social actors, subjects in their own right, not merely objects of social concern or the targets of adult intervention.[55] But the implications of this, even after Article 12, have not been properly thought through. The dissonance between children's own experiences of being a child and the insti-

---

[50] On which see B. Thorne and L. Zella, 'Sexuality and Gender in Children's Daily Worlds', *Social Problems*, 33 (3), 176 (1986).

[51] See A. James and A. Prout, *Constructing and Reconstructing Childhood* (Basingstoke: Falmer, 1990), p. 4 (see also the chapters in this by M. Woodhead and J. Boyden).

[52] Article 24 (3)'s reference to 'traditional practices prejudicial to the health of children' stands out as the solitary recognition of multi-cultural issues. See, further, M. Freeman, *Cultural Pluralism and The Rights of the Child* (Aldershot: Dartmouth, forthcoming 1998).

[53] See C. P. Cohen, 'The Role of Non Governmental Organizations in The Drafting of The Convention on The Rights of The Child', *Human Reports Quarterly*, 12, 137 (1990).

[54] *Op. cit.*, note 51, p. 4. See also their 'Strategies and Structures: Toward A New Perspective on Children's Experiences of Family Life' in (eds.) J. Brannen and M. O'Brien, *Children In Families* (London: Falmer Press, 1996), p. 41.

[55] See *Report of Inquiry into Child Abuse in Cleveland* (London: H.M.S.O. 1988), Cm. 412.

tutional form which childhood takes is paralleled by a mismatch between the different understandings of childhood now emerging in the writings of sociologists, anthropologists and historians and what so often finds its way into laws, institutions, policies and practices on children.

We have created a childhood which is essentially a protectionist experience.[56] Jenks in his recent text explains the consequences of this:

> Routinely, children find their daily lives shaped by statutes regulating the pacing and placing of their experience. Compulsory schooling, for example, restricts their access to social space and gerontocratic prohibitions limit their political involvement, sexual activity, entertainment and consumption. Children are further constrained not only by implicit socializing rules which work to set controls on behaviour and limits on the expression of unique intent, but also by customary practices which, through the institution of childhood, articulate the rights and duties associated with "being a child".[57]

Ideas of childhood are frequently utilized as control mechanisms. And 'our' ideas with childhood conceived 'as a period of lack of responsibility, with rights to protection and training but not to autonomy'[58] may be even more suspect where such notions are culturally irrelevant. Judith Ennew talks of countries where a high proportion of children work alongside adults from an early age, or leave home to seek waged work from the age of eight or ten years old.[59]

There is a dominant discourse on childhood and it has created a model of what Ennew calls 'correct childhood'.[60] And this is used not only to judge different family forms and parenting practices but to do so upon the basis of an ahistoric and false universalism. What we know to be an image, an interpretation, a social construction passes as a final judgment. Variation from the norms of dominant discourse is characterized as failure.

Hockey and James in their *Growing Up and Growing Old*[61] explain the supposed intrinsic characteristics of 'the child' from which this discourse

---

[56] See B. Mayall, *Children's Childhoods Observed and Experienced* (London: Falmer Press, 1994).
[57] *Childhood* (London: Routledge, 1996).
[58] *Per* Judith Ennew, *The Sexual Exploitation of Children* (Cambridge: Polity Press, 1986), p. 21.
[59] *Idem.*
[60] *Idem.*
[61] *Growing Up and Growing Old: Ageing and Dependency in the Life Course*, (London: Sage, 1993).

emerges as fourfold. First, the temporal setting apart of the child, difference resting upon a calculation of age. Secondly, the deeming of the child to have a special nature, itself determined by Nature. Thirdly, the concept of the child as innocent, as *tabula rasa*, And, fourthly, the notion of the child as vulnerably dependent.

The first and last of these characteristics centre on the child's capacity: the second and third on questions of the child's morality. Both capacity and morality are issues at the centre of debates about child policy and children's welfare. And they may by equally important to perceptions about the moral status of children, and, accordingly, to the children's rights debate.

CAPACITY AND RIGHTS

It is the issue of capacity,[62] however, that I wish to address here. Kate Federle, in a series of important articles,[63] has pointed to the problems which 'capacity' has caused those who with to construct a case for children's rights. She argues:

> Having a right means having the power to command respect, to make claims and to have them heard. But if having a right is contingent upon some characteristic, like capacity, then holding the right becomes exclusive and exclusionary; thus, only claims made by a particular group of (competent) beings will be recognized. The confining effects of this kind of rights talk is apparent when the obverse is considered: claims made by those without the requisite characteristics of a rights holder need not be recognized, although specific claims which reinforce existing hierarchies may be acknowledged. There is historicity to the claim that rights for excluded groups evolve from paternalistic notions of the need to protect the weak and ignorant to recognition of capacity and autonomy, for this has been the experience of women and people of color. Children, however, have been unable to redefine themselves

---

[62] Classical political philosophical literature, Kant for example, ties rights to capacity.

[63] 'On the Road to Reconceiving Rights for Children: A Postfeminist Analysis of The Capacity Principle', (1993) *De Paul Law Review*, 42, 983; 'Looking For Rights in All The Wrong Places: Resolving Custody Disputes in Divorce Proceedings', (1994) *Cardozo Law Review* 15, 1523; 'Rights Flow Downhill', (1994) *International Journal of Children's Rights*, 2, 343.

as competent beings; thus, powerful elites decide which, if any, of the claims made by children they will recognize.[64]

Federle offers a searing indictment of classical and modern rights theories which, she shows, link having and exercising rights to capacity. She appears, initially at least, to find greater promise in feminist theory which de-emphasizes 'the significance of competency in rights talk by focusing on individual relationships between children and adults'.[65] But it is to the writings of Martha Minow[66] that she turns, and she is right to find shortcomings in these.[67] As Federle says, 'the emphasis on relationships presupposes a connection between adults and children that merely underscores children's dependencies rather than rendering them irrelevant'.[68] And, more significantly, she notes that 'when our rights talk speaks of children's rights in relationships, it forecloses an honest assessment of the power we have over our children.'[69] Thus, tying rights to relationships is nothing more than a 'sophisticated' version of the argument that 'children should have rights because of their incompetencies.'[70]

It is Federle's conclusion that there is a need to re-conceptualize the meaning of having and exercising rights. The kind of rights she envisions 'are not premised upon capacity but upon power, or more precisely, powerlessness.'[71] She sees rights more as inhibitions on the ability of those with power. This, she says, creates 'zones of mutual respect for power that limit the kinds of things that we may do to one another.'[72] And, this has, so she claims, 'a transformative aspect as well, for the empowering effects of rights would reduce the victimization of children because we would no longer see them as powerless beings'.[73]

This is an intriguing argument, and the message that 'rights flow downhill',[74] if true, would be of great comfort to the disadvantaged everywhere.

---

[64] 'Rights Flow Downhill', (1994) *International Journal of Children's Rights*, 2, 343, 344.
[65] *Ibid.*, p. 354.
[66] 'Rights for the Next Generation: A Feminist Approach To Children's Rights', *Harvard Women's Journal*, 9, 1 (1986).
[67] See *op. cit.*, note 64, pp. 356–357.
[68] *Ibid.*, p. 356.
[69] *Idem.*
[70] *Idem.*
[71] *Ibid.*, p. 366.
[72] *Idem.*
[73] *Idem.*
[74] *Ibid.*, p. 365.

But, even aside from the problem Federle acknowledges, namely, how do children actually claim rights violations within the conceptual structure she depicts, there are difficulties with this thesis. How, for example, does this carefully-constructed case transcend the oft-cited objection to rights that what is on offer is formal acknowledgement rather than anything of substantive value? Further, the thesis as posited should give certain children—ppoor children, children with special needs are two examples—more rights than other children if there is to be any equalization. Is this intended? Is it morally right? There is also the problem that the same formal right accorded two different children, one of whom was already endowed with some 'power' (by reason of education, social status or just genetic inheritance) would not be of the same value to each. Just as there are different childhoods, so there are differently situated subjects. Different children might 'need' different rights, might wish to claim different rights, or ought to have different rights claimed on their behalf. Is this not a recognition that the having or the exercising of rights is tied to competence? That rights and power are linked? Federle's thesis may also oversimplify power. That children lack rights is not necessarily an indication that others have power or power over them. And power can often be fragmented and diffuse.[75]

Federle could have sought inspiration in another corpus of feminist thought. The writings of the French feminist, Luce Irigaray,[76] offer a hint of how to reconstruct rights. She has put forward a radical argument for intersubjective rights which express and confirm genuine relations among persons, rather than seeing rights, as orthodox discourse does, as a quasi-proprietary form. She writes of rights of being rather than of having.[77]

Irigaray's goal is to advance thinking about the status of women. Her analysis is targeted at the problematic way in which dominant discourse represses difference and in particular, the way in which it excludes the feminine from subject status. Her argument is that a relational conception of rights would have to be premised on the recognition of irreducibly different subjectivities which relate in an intransitive way to one another. As Nicola Lacey puts it: 'until women…are recognised as full subjects those…with female bodies will never be either citizens or rights bearers.'[78] Irigaray is led

---

[75] On which see Steven Lukes, *Power: A Radical View* (London: Macmillan, 1974).

[76] See her *J'Aime A Toi* (Paris: Grasset, 1992); *Je, Tu, Nous: Toward A Culture of Difference* (transl. Alison Martin) (London: Routledge, 1993); *Thinking The Difference* (transl. Karin Montin) (London: Athlone, 1994).

[77] See *Thinking The Difference, op. cit.*, note 76, ch. 3 (the idea can be traced in the other two books referred to in note 76 as well).

[78] *Per* Nicola Lacey, 'Normative Reconstruction in Socio-Legal Theory', (1996) *Social and*

to some strange conclusions, including a package of special rights for women.[79] These have been criticized,[80] and rightly so. But a package of special rights for children, so long as these are additional, rather than in necessary substitution for rights which others have, looks to have an arguable case. And, of course, to some extent this is recognized, not least in the United Nations Convention.[81] But what of a right, by virtue of being a child, to responsible parents?[82] To a challenging education? To have a 'say' in what rights they should enjoy? Whereas 'having rights' is about distributive justice,[83] rights conceived in terms of 'being' is as much concerned with the values of dignity[84] and decency.[85] These are important, if neglected, values because they offer defences against dehumanization,[86] the reduction of persons to animal status, to being treated as machines or as property. And at times in history, even recent history, children have been treated in this way. Sometimes they still are.

But Why Rights?

But is the moral status of children enhanced by giving them rights? Can struggles around rights, the sort we witnessed as the U.N. Convention was formulated or we see in daily practice (did the boy in the so-called 'Zulu' case have right to remain with his 'adoptive' mother or the right to be reunited with his family[87]? Did Jaymee Bowen have the right to expensive

---

Legal Studies, 5, 131 at 147.

[79] See *Je, Tu, Nous: Toward A Culture of Difference*, op. cit. note 76, pp. 86–87.

[80] By Nicola Lacey, 'Feminist Legal Theory Beyond Neutrality', *Current Legal Problems*, 48, 1, 31–36 (1995).

[81] For example, the 'right' to a family, the right to education, the rights of children with special needs, the right of children in armed conflicts.

[82] The Children Act 1989 attempts to do this, but largely by imputing responsibility even where it is absent. And see John Eekelaar 'Parental Responsibility: State of Nature or Nature of the State?' (1991) *Journal of Social Welfare and Family Law*, 37. See also the Child Support Act 1991, another bungling attempt.

[83] See, further, Michael D. A. Freeman, 'Taking Children's Rights More Seriously' in (eds.) P. Alston *et al*, *Children, Rights and The Law* (Oxford: Clarendon Press, 1992), p. 52, and ch. 2.

[84] A concept curiously neglected, despite figuring so predominately in Kant.

[85] See Avishai Margalit, *The Decent Society* (Cambridge: Harvard University Press, 1996).

[86] See Avishai Margalit and Gabriel Motzkin, 'The Uniqueness of The Holocaust', *Philosophy and Public Affairs*, 25, 65 (1996).

[87] An instructive test-case for an interesting conflict of rights: did the child have a right to be reunited with his biological family in South Africa or to stay in England with the Afri-

cancer treatment on the N.H.S.?[88] Do children have the right not to be hit?[89]) advance the interests of children? To those of us who believe that rights are 'valuable commodities',[90] the answer is self-evident. But not everyone believes this.

Critical theorists present existing legal discourse and the legal system as the central elements in the process of hegemony: the main instruments through which the dominant ideology is able to permeate the popular consciousness.[91] To Robert Gordon, a leading American Critical Legal theorist:

> The most effective kind of domination takes place when both the dominant and dominated classes believe that the existing order, with perhaps some marginal changes is satisfactory, or at least represents the most that anyone could expect, because things pretty much have to be the way they are.[92]

Instead, therefore, of using a rights strategy to effect social change, such theorists see their task as the deconstruction of existing legal discourse and ideology.[93] Indeed, any engagement with existing legal discourse should be rejected since this 'reinforces not only the discourse itself, but also the society and the work that it embodies'.[94] We have, so it has been argued, been taken in by 'the myth of rights.'[95] Rights are characterized as

---

kaner woman who had brought him up for several years? Though criticized for so doing, the Court of Appeal was probably right to come down in favour of the first right.

[88] See *R v. Cambridge District Health Authority ex parte B* [1995] I F L R 1055. She died about 15 months later (see Carol Midgley, 'She Wanted To Come Back As A Butterfly', *The Times*, 23 May 1996).

[89] See Report of the Commission on Children and Violence by Gulbenkian Foundation, *Children and Violence* (London: Calouste Gulbenkian Foundation, 1995).

[90] See, for example, John Eekelaar, 'The Importance of Thinking That Children Have Rights', in (eds.) P. Alston *et al*, *Children, Rights and The Law* (Oxford: Clarendon Press, 1992), p. 221.

[91] This analysis uses explicitly the ideas of the Italian Marxist, Antonio Gramsci (see his *Selections from The Prison Notebooks*, ed. transl. Q. Hoare and G. Nowell Smith (London: Lawrence and Wishart, 1971).

[92] 'New Developments in Legal Theory' in (ed.) David Kairys, *The Politics of Law* (New York: Pantheon Books, 1982), p. 281).

[93] See Robert Gordon, 'Law and Ideology', *Tikkun* 3 (1) (1988) (and see Lloyd's *Introduction To Jurisprudence* (6th ed. by M. D. A. Freeman) (London: Sweet and Maxwell, 1994), p. 950).

[94] *Per* Kimberlé Crenshaw, 'Race, Reform and Retrenchment: Transformation and Legitimization in Anti-Discrimination Law', Harvard Law Review, 101, 1331 (1988), at p. 1365.

[95] *Per* Stuart Scheingold, *The Politics of Rights: Lawyers, Public Policy and Political*

vacuous, competitive and abstract. According rights to individuals serves to atomize social struggles. For Duncan Kennedy rights discourse is a 'trap', 'because it is logically incoherent and manipulable, traditionally individualist and wilfully blind to the realities of substantive inequality'.[96]

This attack cannot be ignored. Nor can it be overlooked that the best defences of the rule of law and the rights strategy are to be found within the writings of critical legal thought. It was E. P. Thompson who, in *Whigs and Hunters*, was one of the first critical thinkers to recognize that law can restrain oppression. 'The essential precondition for the effectiveness of law, in its function as ideology,' he wrote, 'is that it shall display an independence from gross manipulation and shall seem to be just.'[97] In societies that make rights the coin of the realm, a critique of rights that reduces the availability of rights does nothing to assist the excluded or the disadvantaged.

Mari Matsuda asks:

How can anyone believe both of the following statements?

1. I have a right to participate equally in society with any other person.

2. Rights are whatever people in power say they are.

One of the primary lessons [critical legal scholars] can learn from the experience of the bottom is that one can believe in both of these statements simultaneously, and that it may well be necessary to do so.[98]

It is significant that some of the best restatements of the case for rights have come from minority scholars, like Matsuda and Kimberlé Crenshaw,[99] or from those arguing the case of the excluded, like Martha Minow.[100] For Crenshaw, as also for Alan Hunt,[101] adopting a rights-based discourse is a vehicle in which social movements can enter a debate into

---

Change (New Haven: Yale University Press, 1974). See also Valerie Kerruish, *Jurisprudence as Ideology* (London: Routledge, 1991), ch. 5.

[96] 'Legal Education as Training for Hierarchy' in Ian Grigg-Spall and Paddy Ireland (eds.), *Critical Lawyers' Handbook* (London: Pluto Press, 1992), p. 51 at 57.

[97] *Whigs and Hunters: The Origins of The Black Act* (Harmondsworth: Penguin Books, 1975), p. 263.

[98] 'Looking To The Bottom: Critical Legal Studies and Reparations', *Harvard Civil Rights—Civil Liberties Law Review*, 22, 338 (1987).

[99] See, *op. cit.*, note 94.

[100] See *Making All The Difference* (Ithaca: Cornell University Press, 1990).

[101] 'Rights and Social Movements: Counter-Hegemonic Strategies', *Journal of Law and Society*, 17, 309 (1990).

the validity of the dominant ideology as part of a counter-hegemonic strategy. For Hunt, 'rights…have the capacity to be elements of emancipation, but they are neither a perfect nor exclusive vehicle for the emancipation. [They] can only be operative as constituents of a strategy for social transformation as they become part of an emergent common sense and are articulated within social practices.'[102]

Where the law has been silent, this has all too often meant not an absence of power, but the absence of a means to challenge private power: often the power of husbands and fathers. In areas like domestic violence and sexual abuse the public violence of law has been invoked to challenge private violence.[103] Can the lessons of other minority groups be an example to children? Can children too take action to further their own self-defined interests? There have been school strikes,[104] unionization by school-children[105] and young people in care,[106] attempts by children to 'divorce' parents.[107] Children are more likely to use self-help than invoke the law. But as rights for children seep further into their consciousness, we can expect, even applaud litigation by children in pursuit of their self-perceived interests.

In the past it has been common to use liberal arguments to buttress the case of children's rights. The language of Joel Feinberg[108] and others of his ilk[109] still has a fine ring to it. Who would wish to beg or grovel, to be the recipient of *noblesse oblige* or charity when they can demand what is their

---

[102] *Ibid.*, p. 325. Similarly, Crenshaw, *op. cit.*, note 94, argues that social groups 'can only make demands for change that reflect the logic of the institutions they are trying to challenge' (p. 1367).

[103] On law as violence see Robert Cover, 'Violence and the Word', *Yale Law Journal*, 95, 1601 (1986).

[104] Those in England in 1911 and South Africa in 1976 are well-documented. See, for example, in England Bertram Edwards, *The Burston School Strike* (London: Lawrence and Wishart, 1974). Martin Hoyles, *Changing Childhood* (London: Writers and Readers Publishing Co-operative, 1979, ch. 4) is a useful collection of materials.

[105] See Graham Kennedy in (ed.) M. Hoyles, *op. cit.*, note 104, p. 255.

[106] By NAYPIC.

[107] In effect to decide where they live: see M. Freeman, Can Children Divorce Their Parents? in (eds.) M. Freeman, *Divorce: Where Next?* (Aldershot: Dartmouth, 1996), p. 159, and ch. 11.

[108] He described rights as 'indispensably valuable possessions' and wrote that a world without them would 'suffer an immense moral impoverishment', 'Duties, Rights and Claims', *American Philosophical Quarterly*, 3 (2), 1, at p. 8 (1966).

[109] For example Bertram Bandman, 'Do Children Have Any Natural Rights?', *Proceedings of the 29th Annual Meeting of Philosophy of Education Society* (1973), p. 234 at p. 236.

due? Rights are entitlements; they are trumps[110]; they are valuable commodities. But they are also, we now learn, weapons to undermine power. We should, of course, have realized this : think how many landmarks in the progress of the rights of the disadvantaged are identified by case names and legal victories.[111] Nor should it be forgotten that the language of rights can make new stories be heard in public.[112] Justice, Martha Minow reminds us, is 'partial',[113] in both senses of that term. A rights strategy is one way in which the hitherto excluded can be included, within the community and within the political structure. Inclusion within bookshops may take a little longer!

---

[110] See Ronald Dworkin, *Taking Rights Seriously* (London: Duckworth, 1977).

[111] *Re Gault* 387 U.S. 1 , *Gillick* v. *West Norfolk and Wisbech A.H.A.* [1986] A.C. 112 are two of the most obvious examples.

[112] 'Each time we let in a new excluded group, …each time we listen to a new way of knowing, we learn more about the limits of our current way of seeing' *per* Carrie Menkel-Meadow, 'Excluded Voices: New Voices in the Legal Profession Making New Voices In The Law', *University of Miami Law Review*, 42, 52 (1987). And see Kate Wilson and Anne Ridler, 'Children and Literature', *British Journal of Social Work*, 26, 17 (1996).

[113] See 'Partial Justice: Law and Minorities' in (eds.) Austin Sarat and Thomas R. Kearns, *The Fate of Law* (Ann Arbor: the University of Michigan Press, 1991), p. 15. See also Cass R. Sunstein, *The Partial Constitution* (Cambridge, Mass: Harvard University Press, 1993).

CHAPTER 2

Taking Children's Rights More Seriously

INTRODUCTION

We have begun to take children's rights more seriously—at least on one level.

The international community has framed its much-lauded convention on the rights of children (United Nations, 1989). It has convened a World Summit on the subject (UNICEF, 1991). There are regional conventions too (Thompson, 1992; Killerby, 1995). Legislators and judges, in the Western industrialized world at least, have become conscious of the need to recognize the individuality and autonomy of older children. Institutions, including Ombudsmen, have been established in a few countries, Norway, Sweden, New Zealand, Costa Rica and Israel (Flekkøy, 1991; Koren, 1995).

England has its *Gillick*[1] decision and implemented in 1991 children's legislation (The Children Act 1989), which is not only more child-centred, but the clearest recognition yet of the decision-making capacities of children.[2] But, despite Government protestations to the contrary,[3] the law of the United Kingdom still falls far short of the ideals of the United Nations' Convention, a fact recognized by the United Nations Committee on the Rights of the Child.[4] Although the British Prime Minister of the 1980s could state: '...children come first because children are our most sacred trust',[5] she presided over a steep rise in child poverty and deprivation

---

[1] *Gillick* v. *West Norfolk and Wisbech Area Health Authority*, [1986] AC 112. But see now *Re R* [1991] 4 All ER 177. See also ch. 15.
[2] Children Act 1989. See in particular, ss.1(3)(a); 4 (3)(b); 6 (7)(b); 10 (8); 20 (11); 22 (4)(a), (5); 26 (3); 34 (2), (4); 38 (6); 43 (8); 44 (7); 64 (2)(a).
[3] Notably, those of the then Minister of Health, Virginia Bottomley. See for example, her statement, reported in *Community Care*, 850, 4 (7 February 1991).
[4] For a detailed exposition of the shortcomings see Newell (1991). A similar exposé of US laws and practices is Cohen and Davidson (1990). And see ch. 6.
[5] She said this at the George Thomas Society Inaugural Lecture on 17 February 1990.

(Bradshaw, 1990; Oppenheim and Harker, 1996). The same government, which proudly vaunts its commitment to children by pointing to the Children Act 1989, could also boast (though it would prefer the evidence was discretely veiled) that the number of children living in poverty (defined as below 50 per cent of average income after housing costs) more than tripled between 1979 and 1992/3.[6] The number of homeless households has more than doubled since 1979.[7] The impact of this on children is inestimable: it has, for example, deleterious effects on children's education (Power *et al*, 1995). There has been a dramatic increase in the number of young people who are homeless and living rough on the streets of large cities.[8] Though there has been a decline in infant mortality, rates have declined more slowly than in some other comparable countries, and are still high in comparison with, for example, France, Italy and Sweden. And 'causes of death which can be regarded as "preventable"...cause infant deaths in Social Class V at about three times the rate for Social Class 1.

Children in manual social class families are likely to have more illnesses: the General Household Survey shows that children aged 0–15 with a father in Social Class V have 1.85 times the rate of long-standing illness than those in Social Class 1. Children's development in terms of birth weight and height at primary school age is worse in deprived areas (Holtermann, 1995). *The Health of Our Children, Decennial Supplement* (OPCS, 1995), suggests there is some evidence that children's psychological health may be indirectly related to socio-economic conditions: for example, behavioural difficulties are more associated with children in poorer social groups.

These examples could be multiplied. But, whatever the state of deprivation of children in relatively prosperous Britain, it is nothing as compared with much of the rest of the world, with children the legitimate objects of extermination squads in Brazil and Guatemala, dying of starvation in much of Africa and of radiation in parts of the Ukraine, used as slave labour in much of Asia, and living in shanties, refugee camps and as pros-

---

[6] 33 per cent of all children were living around this standard. This figure is derived from official Department of Social Security statistics.

[7] This figure is extrapolated from National Children's Home Statistics, in particular annual 'Factfiles' entitled 'Children in Danger.' See also Bradshaw (1990: 40) and Oppenheim and Harker (1996: 82–7).

[8] It has been estimated that over 150,000 experience homelessness every year as a result of leaving home or care and being unable to find or afford accommodation. See Gosling and Diarists (1989). Changes in social security rules that removed entitlement for 16- and 17-year-olds and reduced it for other young people have aggravated the situation. See Craig and Glendinning (1990).

titutes for Western tourists in many countries of the third world (UNICEF, 1991; Bruce, 1995).

It would be idle to pretend that the answer to all this lies in theory or, indeed, that deliberations at academic conferences will have any immediate impact on the lives of children. But we can and must believe that the state of childhood will be improved if we are prepared to take children's rights more seriously, to transcend the rhetoric of international documents and domestic legislation and tease out the moral argument for the recognition of children's rights (Worsfold, 1974; MacCormick, 1982; Lucy, 1990; Federle, 1994). It was Oliver Wendell Holmes, the jurist and judge, who commented that the world to-day was governed more by Kant than Bonaparte (Holmes, 1897). Rights, of course, are never given but are fought for.[9] In searching out the moral grounds for the recognition of children's rights we must believe that this fight will be strengthened and that, ultimately, the condition of childhood will be ameliorated. And this it may achieve if it can transcend the impoverishment of political discourse with the inconsistencies and hypocrisies all too commonly found therein.

THE IMPORTANCE OF RIGHTS

Ubi ius, ibi remedium. Where rights exist redress is possible. This is lawyers' discourse and its roots go deep into legal culture. Lawyers have not articulated the reason why this correlativity should be so important. Perhaps to them it has been obvious. Philosophers and jurists have, however, sought out the justification. Rights are 'valuable commodities' (Wasserstrom, 1964).

It is useful to reflect upon what a society without rights would look like. Such a society would be morally impoverished. It might well be a benevolent society in which people were treated well, but they would have no cause for complaint if standards were to fall. A world with claim-rights is, as Joel Feinberg has put it, 'one in which all persons...are dignified objects of respect'. And he adds: 'No amount of love and compassion, or obedience to higher authority, or *noblesse oblige*, can substitute for those values' (Feinberg, 1966). What is clearly delineated here is the close association between rights and dignity (a concept itself to which all too little attention has been given) (but *cf.* Seidler, 1986), and rights and respect, an association which, of course, is at the root of Ronald Dworkin's thinking

---

[9] See the view of Cohen, (1980) that 'rights' are a 'militant' concept. Bentham by contrast, called it 'terrorist language', thus making it very clear where he stood.

about rights.[10] In to-day's world there is little need to construct or imagine what a society without rights would look like: we only need to take a look at what countries like Romania or Albania were like to see the reality: indeed, a peep into Romanian orphanages or homes for the mentally handicapped in Albania even today tells us much about the plight of children produced in such morally impoverished environments.[11]

Children easily become victims.[12] That much is clearly recognized in the United Nations' Convention.[13] They have not been accorded either dignity or respect. They have been reified,[14] treated as objects of intervention rather than as legal subjects, labelled as a 'problem population' (Spitzer, 1973), reduced to being seen as property.[15] They complete a family rather as the standard consumer durables furnish a household (Kellmer-Pringle, 1980). Because children have lacked the moral coinage of rights it has been easy to brush their interests aside in the sweep of consequentialist thinking. Where the goal is the maximization of welfare, children do not seem to have counted or to have carried much weight. Consequentialist thought is capable of justifying rights but only as rules of thumb for maximizing welfare. But the interests upheld by rights are not just desires to seek pleasures and avoid pains, as utilitarians claim, or rank individualism, self-indulgence or egoism, as Burke, Bentham and Marx in various ways argued (Waldron, 1987). Rather, these interests are our plans and projects, our concerns and our states of mind without which our lives would be bereft of much of their meaning. The recognition and protection of these interests is that which makes human life more fully human. In this sense civilization is dependent in part upon a culture which acknowledges

---

[10] But, of course, not only Dworkin. See also Benn (1988).

[11] This is not intended to take issue with the thesis presented by Glendon (1991) on the dangers of an exaggerated rights discourse, where rights rhetoric becomes almost a 'dialect.' Nor is it the place to examine the communitarian thesis of Taylor, MacIntyre, Sandel and others, save to say that I am far from convinced that individual rights and community values are incompatible.

[12] Or an 'endangered species' as one writer Max (1990) has recently put it. On 'blaming the victim' see Ryan (1976).

[13] See in particular Articles 6, 9, 11, 16, 19, 20, 22, 23, 24, 27, 32, 33, 34, 35, 36, 37, 38, 39 and 40.

[14] Reification involves 'treating a notational device as though it were a substantive term...a construct as though it were observational' (*per* Kaplan, 1964:61). 'The "name" and the meanings assigned to it become the thing to which we react. The thing is symbolized by the name; the name takes on existence of its own' (*per* Pfuhl, 1980:28).

[15] There are many illustrations of this. One graphic recent case study is Groner (1991) an account of the *Morgan* v. *Foretich* custody/access dispute.

the integrity and personality of each individual. That is why *apartheid* was, and other forms of racial segregation are still wrong, why the marital rape immunity could not be defended (Freeman, 1985) and why the sexual abuse of children (Freeman, 1989 and see ch. 13; La Fontaine 1990), which reduces them to objects, disciplinary practices like 'pin-down', rationalized as control measures (Levy and Kahan, 1991), and corporal punishment, legitimate only in the case of children (Newell, 1990; Freeman, 1988b), are grave infringements of the interests of the human beings targeted by the practices in question.

BUT ARE RIGHTS IMPORTANT FOR CHILDREN?

Those who accept the moral importance of rights as 'trumps'[16] are often still inclined to deny the necessity of thinking in terms of rights when it comes to children. The arguments put tend to take one or more of three forms.

First, there is the argument that the importance of rights and rights-language themselves can be exaggerated. That there are other morally significant values, love, friendship, compassion, altruism, and that these raise relationships to a higher plain than one based on the observance of duty cannot be gainsaid (Kleinig, 1976). This argument may be thought particularly apposite to children's rights, particularly in the context of family relationships. Perhaps in an ideal moral world this is true. Rights may be used to resolve conflicts of interests and in an ideal world there would be harmony and these would not exist. But it is not an ideal world—certainly not for children. Children are particularly vulnerable and need rights to protect their integrity and dignity. 'Solitary, poor, nasty, brutish and short' (Hobbes, 1651) may not be a description of a state of nature (rather a construction or 'thought experiment' on Hobbes's part (Hampton, 1991) but it may come close to describing what a world without rights would look like for many children. Of course, it may be said that where children have rights this creates conflict. They complain about their treatment; they make legitimate claims; they challenge authority. Were they not able to do so life would be easier, quieter for adults (parents, teachers, social workers, police etc.). But there would still be conflict: it would simmer below the surface, occasionally boiling over. Think of our treatment of prisoners, who are endowed with few rights, and the riots which periodically erupt

---

[16] The term derives from Dworkin (1978a) where an account of rights as 'trumps' against a background of utility considerations is developed.

(Woolf, 1991). It is difficult to see how this would make the world a better place. When Kleinig asserts that 'a morality which has as its motivation merely the giving of what is due...is seriously defective'[17] he is only partly correct. Such a morality both allows for the observance of minimally decent standards and the opportunity to express and reciprocate the other morally significant values to which he refers.

The second argument is in one sense related to the first. It assumes that adults already relate to children in terms of love, care and altruism, so that the case for children's rights becomes otiose. This idealizes adult-child relations: it emphasizes that adults (and parents in particular) consider only the best interests of children. There is a tendency for those who postulate such an argument to adopt a *laisser-faire* attitude towards the family. Thus, the only right for children which Goldstein, Freud and Solnit acknowledge in *Before the Best Interests of the Child* is the child's right to autonomous parents. A policy of minimum coercive intervention by the state accords, they maintain, with their 'firm belief as citizens in individual freedom and human dignity'(1979, p. 12). But it hardly needs to be asked *whose* freedom and *what* dignity this is thought to uphold. It is difficult to see how the creation of a private space in this way can be said to protect the humanity of the child. There is a strand running through the English Children Act of 1989 which reflects very much the same philosophy.[18]

The third argument equally rests on a myth. It sees childhood as a golden age, as the best years of our life. Childhood is synonymous with innocence. It is the time when, spared the rigours of adult life, we enjoy freedom, experience play and joy. The argument runs: just as we avoid the responsibilities and adversities of adult life in childhood, so there should be no necessity to think in terms of rights, a concept which we must assume is reserved for adults. Whether or not the premise underlying this were correct or not, it would represent an ideal state of affairs, and one which ill-reflects the lives of many of to-day's children and adolescents. But for many this mythic 'walled garden of 'Happy, Safe, Protected, Innocent Childhood' (Holt, 1975) is just plain wrong, with poverty, disease, exploitation and abuse rife across the globe.

The case put forward by those who wish to deflate the importance of rights for children does not, accordingly, withstand critical scrutiny.

---

[17] Kleinig (1976: ch. 14). A revised version is Kleinig (1982: ch. 15).
[18] In particular the presumption of non-intervention is s.1(5).

Rights are important because those who lack rights are like slaves, means to the ends of others, and never sovereigns in their own right.[19] Those who may claim[20] rights, or for whom rights may be claimed, have a necessary pre-condition to the constitution of humanity, of integrity, of individuality, of personality. It is surely significant that when we wish to deny rights to those who have attained chronological adulthood, such as blacks in South Africa or the Southern States of the U.S.A. or the mentally retarded, we label them children ('boys'). To be a 'child' one does not have to be young. Foucault's aphorism that 'madness is childhood'(1967) rings very true. Childhood is, of course, a social construction, a man-made phenomenon (Jenks, 1996): it has not always 'existed', as Ariès (1962), Illich (1973) and others (James and Prout, 1990) have reminded us.[21] Those in authority determine who is a child.

BUT SHOULD WE BE LOOKING TO OBLIGATIONS RATHER THAN RIGHTS?

A more oblique attack on children's rights or rather on the appropriate way morally to justify them, is put by Onora O'Neill in 'Children's Rights and Children's Lives' (1988). She does not question the view that children's lives are a public concern, rather than a private matter. Nor does she query the aim of securing positive rights for children. What she does question is whether children's positive rights are best grounded by appeals to fundamental rights. She claims that 'children's fundamental rights are best grounded by embedding them in a wider account of fundamental obligations, which can also be used to justify positive rights and obligations'. It is her contention that 'we can perhaps go *further* to secure the ethical basis of children's positive rights if we do *not* try to base them on claims about fundamental rights'.

Her argument is closely reasoned and no summary can do it justice. The strategy of her argument, as she puts it, is: '…that theories that take rights as fundamental and those that take obligations as fundamental are not equivalent. The scope of the two sorts of theory differs and does so in ways that matter particularly for children…. (T)hat a constructivist ac-

---

[19] This is similar to Isaiah Berlin's 'positive liberty': "I wish to be an instrument of my own, not other men's acts of will, I wish to be a subject, not an object…deciding, not being decided for, self-directed and not acted upon by external nature or by other men as if I were a thing, or an animal, or a slave incapable of playing a human role, that is, of conceiving goals and policies of my own and realizing them": Berlin (1969:131).

[20] They do not have to able to exercise them at this point in time.

[21] But this should be looked at critically, if not sceptically, in the light of Pollock (1983).

count of obligations has *theoretical* advantages which constructivist accounts of rights lack, though rights-based approaches sometimes have *political* advantages which obligation-based approaches do not.... (T)hat in the specific case of children, taking rights as fundamental has political costs rather than advantages'.

She concludes 'that taking rights as fundamental in ethical deliberation about children has neither theoretical nor political advantages', and a more 'perspicuous and complete view' of ethical aspects of children's lives' can be obtained by taking obligations as fundamental'.

My differences with O'Neill are several. She cannot envisage a children's movement: I can. Indeed, there are prototypes or at least germs of children's movements already in existence. There have been school strikes and attempts at school unionization (Hoyles, 1979). There is in Britain the National Association of Young People In Care and similar organizations elsewhere. There are any number of adult writers who propagate children's rights. There are children's legal and other advisory centres and children's ombudsmen. To say that these are movements on behalf of children rather than children's movements is only a partial answer for the other rights movements were equally preceded by prototypes and led by enlightened members of the oppressing 'class'. Think of John Stuart Mill or the National Association for the Advancement of Colored People. A children's movement could emerge.

Secondly, she thinks the dependency of children is 'very different' from the dependency of other oppressed groups. 'Appeals to children's rights', she argues, ' might have political and rhetorical importance if children's dependence on others is like that of oppressed social groups whom the rhetoric of rights has served well'. There are, she believes, four ways in which children's dependence is different from the dependence of other oppressed groups. It is not artificially produced, though she concedes it can be artificially prolonged. It cannot be ended merely by social or political changes. Others are not reciprocally dependent on children whereas slave-owners, for example, need their slaves. The 'oppressors' usually want children's dependency to end. I do not deny that children's dependency is different from that of other groups, but I do not think it is quite as different as O'Neill would have us believe. To some extent it is artificially produced. The lessons of history tell us this: our own experiences and intuitions enable us to realize that many adolescents have the capacity to be less dependent than many adults. For example, if competence rather than age were the test, we could safely give the vote to many 14-year-olds and have little compunction about disenfranchising large sections of the adult population. Some (clearly not all) of it can be ended by political, if not by social, change. This may not be changes of which we approve (and I certainly would not approve) for example, encouraging children to be gainfully employed. But they are changes which would decrease dependency. The reciprocal dependency argument can also be overplayed: think of the parent who needs to be loved and shown affection by his or her child. Some child abuse can apparently be explained in this way: children who cannot, or more usually are not old enough to show affection being battered by inadequate parents.[22] Certainly, some older children perceive a parent's dependency in this way. It is not unknown for children, in the divorce setting, to think that a particular parent cannot survive their loss, with the result that their decision, if asked, as to where to live may be influenced by what they see as a parent's welfare rather than their own.[23]

A third difference I have with O'Neill follows on from the second. She perceives children as a special case. Whilst she concedes that the fact that children cannot claim rights is no reason for denying them rights, the claiming/waiving dilemma seems to be the root of her thinking. She does not discuss what she believes the theoretical underpinning of rights to be, but the references to claiming and waiving suggest she is wedded to the will theory.[24] A series of inconclusive test matches may, as Neil MacCormick (1982) put it wittily, have been played out between the will and interest theories of rights,[25] but he, I think, showed convincingly that, in the case of children's rights at least, the interest theory was more coherent and had greater explanatory power.[26] Children have interests to protect before they develop wills to assert, and others can complain on behalf of younger children when those interests are trampled upon. Questions of 'by whom' and 'how' have not been satisfactorily answered. Howard Cohen's suggestion of the 'child agent', who would 'supply information in terms which the child could understand, to make the consequences of the various courses of action a child might take clear to the child, and do what is nec-

---

[22] In saying this (for which there is some evidence) I should not be taken to be endorsing the psycho-pathological model of child abuse. (Freeman, 1983: 117–20).

[23] Therefore the view that perhaps they should have the right not to be asked to express any preference. And see *M* v. *M* (1977) 7 Fam. Law 17.

[24] See the discussion in White (1984:107–108).

[25] See the discussion in Simmonds. (1986).

[26] But *cf.* Tuck (1979: ch. 1); Lucy (1990:217). Lucy describes the debate as 'rationally irresolvable'.

essary to see that the right in question is actually exercised'[27] is appealing, if ultimately, flawed.

It cannot be right, as O'Neill states, that the child's 'main remedy is to grow up'. First this underestimates the capacities and maturity of many children. Both in moral and cognitive development, many children reach adult levels between 12 and 14, though the ability to reason improves quite obviously through adolescence. We expect adolescents to be criminally responsible at the age of 14 (indeed, we are prepared to impose criminal responsibility on them at ten, as the *Bulger* case graphically illustrated), but we are less willing to accept the correlativity of responsibility and rights. Secondly, what O'Neill ignores is the impact on adult life that parenting and socialization leave. A child deprived of the sort of rights accorded by the U.N. Convention will grow up very differently from one to whom such rights are granted.

It is then O'Neill's contention that if we care about children's lives, there are good reasons not to base our arguments on rights. These arguments are both theoretical and political. Instead she argues we should look to improve children's lives by identifying what obligations parents, teachers and indeed the wider community have towards children. 'A construction made from the agent's perspective may deliver more, though it promises less, since it does not aim at an "all or nothing" construction of ethical requirements'. But a construction of rights need not aim at absolutism either. There are very few (if any) absolute rights and these must by definition belong to children too. If there is an absolute right not to be tortured, (Gewirth, 1982), the torturing of children for whatever reason is beyond deliberation. O'Neill's concern with 'accommodation' problems seems to assume that those who construct rights are looking for 'unique' solutions. The spatial metaphor she employs is helpful to a point but is ultimately flawed because it is taken too literally and is used to explain too much. She says that when a literal interpretation is dropped, territorial metaphors lose 'sense and precision', that we lose our grip on claims that one right is larger than another or that some set of rights is maximal. For example, she questions how a rights-based theory can determine whether an older child's right to freedom of association is larger than his or her freedom of conscience and whether either of these rights is larger than the right to adequate parental care and supervision. There are no right or necessarily even best answers to these questions. Much will depend on the age of the

---

[27] It is difficult to generalize since class and gender may be crucial variables, but the evidence on moral and cognitive development suggests that many reach adult levels between twelve and fourteen.

child: older children have greater need for association rights than small children and younger children require closer parental care than more mature children do. But, at least so far as older children are concerned, which right is greater should depend upon which they, that is the recipients, perceive to be of greatest significance to them, unless, as will be argued later, the exercise of a right is destructive or irreparably debilitating. It is not a question of what 'significant others' such as parents, and teachers would accord them.[28] How this is constructed is considered in a later section of this article.

THE LIMITS OF RIGHTS

Having emphasized the importance of rights, three points must be briefly addressed.

First, crucial though it is to see children's rights recognized, we must be careful not to mistake the words for the deeds. This is particularly significant now that we have begun to take children's rights seriously. The passing of laws, the implementation of conventions, is only a beginning: it is a signal that must be taken up by governments, institutions and individuals. For some years English children's legislation had a provision, sadly now diluted,[29] that local authorities, in reaching any decision about children in their care, had to give 'first consideration' to children's welfare and 'due consideration' to the wishes and feelings of the child (see Child Care Act 1980 s.18). In practice, this was honoured more in the breach than in the observance, justifying the comment, often made, that it was mere tokenism (Gardner, 1987). But, it is worse than this, because it is easy to take the words for the act and assume that with the enactment of rights-bestowing provisions the condition of children's lives has changed. The importance of legislation as a symbol (Edelman, 1977) cannot be underestimated, but the true recognition of children's rights requires implementation in practice. Indeed, un-implemented, partially implemented or badly implemented laws may actually do children more harm than good.

---

[28] It is the case that in practice it will be adults who will impose the limits implied here and discussed in detail below. But the test of intervention is grounded in the objective standard of values of the individual parent, teacher or other adult authority.

[29] See Children Act 1989 s.22(3) where the obligation is to 'safeguard and promote' the child's welfare, rather than to give, as before, 'first consideration' to it. 'First consideration' was interpreted by Lord Brandon in *M* v. *H* [1988] 2 WLR 485 as being no different from giving 'first and paramount' consideration as then required by the Guardianship of Minors Act 1971, s.1.

Secondly, the passing of laws can have less than desirable side-effects and unintended consequences. Rights can all too easily backfire. Reform movements intended to enhance children's rights and the concomitant development of professional structures to implement such reforms can generate their own sets of problems, and these may undermine children's rights or otherwise deleteriously affect the quality of children's lives. It is not uncommon for the reforms of one era to become the problems of the next. Many examples could be given: the invention of the IQ test (in 1907 a benevolent measure by which an objective test was substituted for the injustice of the subjective method then used for placing children in institutions—now associated with the stigma of labelling); the juvenile court system (lauded as a way of 'saving' children and then conceptualized in terms of children's rights but to-day widely associated with the diminution of basic rights) are just two. Looked at in this way, can we be sure that an injection of more rights for children into the juvenile justice system would not lead to an increase in more informal 'justice without trial' (Skolnick, 1966), or that more rights for children in the divorce process would not become a method of social control of mothers and in the process harm also children, as, indeed, may be happening in régimes which are developing to control pregnant women? This is not to advocate caution in furthering children's rights, but care in so doing, and to recommend adequate surveillance of the institutional practices of those to whom the task of operationalizing children's rights is entrusted.

Thirdly, rights without services are meaningless, and services without resources cannot be provided. 'No law', wrote Monrad Paulsen (1974) in relation to mandatory child abuse legislation in the United States, 'can be better than its implementation, and implementation can be no better than resources permit'. In England the good intentions of the 1989 Children Act are foundering because of inadequate resources: local authorities are re-defining statutory definitions of 'in need' to take account of what they see as realities (Barber, 1990). There is, in other words, little point creating an improved legal framework or instituting greater rights for children, unless in addition resource allocation is addressed, and redressed. Children are not interested in symbolic politics. Ultimately, the question of rights for children resolves into questions of distributive justice.[30] If we are not prepared to accept this, we may as well give up the fight to see children's rights improved.

---

[30] See Wikler's view (1979: 377–92) that ultimately questions of rights resolve into questions of distributive justice.

WHY SHOULD WE TAKE CHILDREN'S RIGHTS MORE SERIOUSLY?

We must now seek out the moral justification for taking children's rights seriously.

Our point of departure is to ask why we believe it is morally important that adults should be regarded as rights-holders with all that this entails (Sumner, 1987). When this is answered, we can turn our attention to children and investigate whether any of the supposed reasons for discriminating against children stand up to rational scrutiny.

Why, therefore, should we take rights seriously? As the language used indicates, we cannot to-day investigate this question without taking note of the writings of Ronald Dworkin (1978). He has not addressed children's rights and much of his relevant writing has tackled specifically rights against the state (or constitutional rights). Some, but far from all, children's rights come into this category. Nevertheless, the insights offered can be generalized.

It is Dworkin's thesis that if persons have moral rights to something, they are to be accorded these rights even if a utilitarian calculation shows that utility would be maximized by denying it to them. He invokes Rawls (1972) to illuminate the moral foundations of the rights thesis. Rawls proposes a methodology of reflective equilibrium whereby we try to fashion formulations of moral principles to the cut of moral judgment until we no longer feel inclined to change our judgments to fit the theory or our theory to fit the judgments. The ideal is a perfect fit. Rawls' mechanism for this reflective equilibrium is the social contract model: it conceives of persons in the 'original position', behind a 'veil of ignorance' and thus ignorant of their identity, interests and entitlements, choosing the structure of the society in which they will live.[31] Dworkin believes that these individuals 'have a responsibility to fit the particular judgments on which they act into a coherent program of action' (1978, p. 160). Thus interpreted, Dworkin believes the contractual mechanism can be dropped. It is nothing more than a moral metaphor. Instead, he believes that we can, and should, focus on the idea that all other principles derive from the principle of equal concern and respect for each person.

---

[31] Rawls has not stood still and his articulation of the 'original position' argument has developed. The parties in the hypothetical deliberations of the original position are now identified as giving priority to the Kantian interest in the development and exercise of their moral powers of rational autonomy and fair dealing. Expressed thus the value of Rawlsian constructivism to my arguments is enhanced.

For Dworkin anyone who proposes to 'take rights seriously' must accept the ideas of human dignity and political equality. He argues in favour of a fundamental right to equal concern and respect, and against any general right to liberty. The advantage of his so doing, as John Mackie acknowledged in an important article (1984), is that the right to equal concern and respect is a final and not merely 'a *prima facie* right', in the sense that one person's possession or enjoyment of it does not conflict with another's. Dworkin puts this forward as a 'postulate of political morality' (1978, p. 272) a fundamental political right: governments must treat citizens with equal concern and respect.

But why do we have the rights we have? (Bedau, 1984). Is this by itself sufficient to explain a right-based moral theory? The question is still left open as to where rights come from. Why do we 'have' the rights we do? I am not talking here of legal rights. The answer to why we have these can be answered within the legal framework itself (the statute says...) or historically by depicting the struggles (for the vote, trade union rights etc.) that were ultimately successful.

What 'is' there then when there 'are' rights? As Jan Narveson put it, there 'must be certain features or properties of those who 'have' them such that we have *good reason to acknowledge* the obligation to refrain from interfering with, or possibly sometimes to help other bearers to do the things they are said to have the right to do, or have those things they are said to have a right to have' (1985, p. 164).

Rights then are dependent on reasoned argument, which is not always forthcoming. Thus, Nozick merely asserts peremptorily that 'individuals have rights' (1974, p. ix). Justifying principles can, and have, been sought. One common answer links rights with interests. This takes us part of the way, but not far enough. Feinberg (1966) is right to suppose that the 'sort of beings who can have rights are precisely those who have (or can have) interests'.[32] But to argue from this to a conclusion that where there is an interest there is a right is unacceptable. There is much that is in my interests but to which I can in no way make a justifiable claim. This is rather different from O'Neill's objection to finding rights where there are imperfect and non-institutionalized obligations only.[33] But it enters a caveat at

---

[32] Reasoning like this was employed in *Re B* [1987] A.C. 199, on which see Freeman (1988a).

[33] O'Neill seems to take it for granted that if there are rights they must be 'perfect' ones. 'Imperfect' rights clearly have less value than 'perfect' ones, but conceptually they make no less sense than 'imperfect' obligations.

least against the indiscriminate use of the 'manifesto' sense in which rights are sometimes used.[34]

Another argument often put forward is purely formal. It is that all persons ought to be treated alike unless there is a good reason for treating them differently. Dworkin, for one, accepts this. He envisages the right to treatment as an equal[35] as a morally fundamental idea. It is that which requires that each person be accorded the same degree of concern and respect as every other person. Though attractive, as already indicated, this reasoning alone is not without its difficulties. A problem lies in deciding what constitutes a 'good reason' for treating people differently. Gender and colour are now almost universally accepted to be indefensible distinctions but age is not yet so regarded by most policy-makers (Eekelaar and Pearl, 1989) or philosophers. Nor, on one level, should it. We cannot but accept that children, particularly young children, have needs (Kellmer-Pringle, 1980) that cannot be met by recognizing that they have rights on a par with adults.[36] That much will become clear later in this article. But, looked at generally, the principle appears more egalitarian than it is. Its potentiality for undermining egalitarianism cannot be overlooked.

An appealing argument has been advanced by William Frankena (1962). He argues that humans are 'capable of enjoying a good life in the sense in which other animals are not.... It is the fact that all men are similarly capable of enjoying a good life in this sense that justifies the *prima facie* requirement that they be treated as equals'. Superficially, this is an attractive argument. But it question begs. Are all persons, even all adults, capable of enjoying a good life? All children are capable of so doing, even if their capacities during childhood are limited. But there are dangers in using an argument like this: it can easily lead to the deprivation of rights on the grounds that it is meaningless to the person in question—the decision to allow the sterilization of mentally handicapped women has been so justified in England and elsewhere (see ch. 16). It can also be argued that, without more, it fails to show how factual similarity can be said to ground the obligation which Frankena claims. Nor is it entirely clear how factual similarity should lead to egalitarian treatment, for it would be possible to

---

[34] Where there is said to be a right wherever there is a need. This is logically fallacious and could provide a recipe for anarchy.

[35] Here the distinction is drawn between 'equal treatment' and 'treatment as an equal,' the latter being 'normatively less fundamental' (*per* Westen 1990: 102).

[36] The ambiguity of 'need' is depicted well by Woodhead (1990:69). His thesis, that we must disentangle the scientific from the evaluative, the natural from the cultural, contains important insights which repay study.

And without higher [indirect?] control to utilitarian considerations?

argue that two persons were similar, whilst supporting unequal treatment on the grounds that the value of one person's happiness is greater than that of other persons.

Space precludes the consideration of other arguments, but they are all in some way defective. Dworkin himself attempts to identify the existence of a moral right against the state when, for 'some' reason, the state would 'do wrong' to treat a person in a certain way, 'even though it would be in the general interest to do so' (1978, p. 139). It is, however, clear that what is 'wrong' for the state to do is what the state has an obligation not to do. Dworkin, in other words, is defining rights in terms of duties. But, why is it 'wrong' for the state to act in a particular way? It is because the individual has a 'right' on which state action of a particular sort would illegitimately trample. This suggests the argument is inherently circular (MacCormick, 1983).

Thus, Dworkin's arguments take us so far—but not far enough. Equality by itself cannot explain what Dworkin is trying to explain: namely, that rights as such 'trump' countervailing utilitarian considerations. Something more is needed. I suggest that this additional concept is autonomy.

A plausible theory of rights needs to take account not just of equality but also of the normative value of autonomy (Feinberg, 1986; Frankfurt, 1971; Haworth, 1986; Lindley, 1986; G. Dworkin, 1988; Young, 1986), the idea that persons as such have a set of capacities that enables them to make independent decisions regarding appropriate life choices. The deep structure of the rights thesis is equality and autonomy (Richards, 1981). Kant (1785) expressed this by asserting that persons are equal and autonomous in the kingdom of ends. (Mulholland, 1990). It is the normative value of equality and autonomy which lie at the root of the Rawlsian contractarian conception. To see people as both equal and autonomous is to repudiate the moral claim of those who would allow utilitarian calculations of the greatest happiness of the greatest number to prevail over the range of significant life choices which the rights thesis both facilitates and enhances.

Utilitarianism, by contrast, demands that the pattern of individual life choices be overridden if others are thus made better off. The result of this is that life choices become in effect the judgment of one person, the sympathetic onlooker whose pleasure is maximized only when the utilitarian principle is upheld. But such an assimilation contradicts the central theses of equality and autonomy—the fundamental tenet of ethics that people are equal and have the capacity to live as separate and independent beings. To treat persons as utilitarianism requires is to focus almost obsessively on aggregated pleasure as the only ethically significant goal and to ignore the critical fact that persons experience pleasure and that pleasure has human and moral significance only in the context of a life a person chooses to lead.

It is the rights thesis that protects the integrity of the person in leading his or her life. One of Dworkin's insights was to link Rawlsian contractarian theory to the language of rights. One of his failings was to fail to appreciate that both notions at the root of Kantian moral theory (equality and autonomy) were equally morally significant. When we take both equality and autonomy seriously, we are back to the contractarian thinking to be found in Kant and in the contemporary constructivism of Rawls. Equality is, I believe, best expressed as an original position of equal beings: autonomy as the putative choice of those beings under a 'veil of ignorance'.

To believe in autonomy is to believe that anyone's autonomy is as morally significant as anyone else's.[37] Nor does autonomy depend on the stage of life that a person has reached. Only human beings are 'persons'. A legal system may attribute 'personhood' to an inanimate entity, a corporation, an idol, a god or even to animals but these do not become 'persons' in the sense used here. What is it, then, about human beings that makes them 'persons'? Recent writers are in general agreement. For Haworth (1986) it is 'critical competence', for Lindley (1986) it is a capacity for reasoning. These tests are not unlike that constructed by Lord Scarman in the *Gillick* case. Lord Scarman offered no guidelines as to when a child reached '*Gillick*-competence' and, in terms of age, legal commentators since have assumed this was reached during adolescence.[38] It is, however, clear once criteria for personhood are examined that many children acquire critical competence considerably earlier.

A good account of the criteria is in Lindley (1986, p. 122):

Certainly consciousness is a requirement. More specifically a person is a creature which has beliefs and desires, and acts on its desires in the light of its beliefs. However, this is insufficient for personhood. What is required in addition is the capacity to evaluate and structure one's beliefs and desires, and to act on the basis of these evaluations.

He also approves Frankfurt's account of freedom of will and the concept of a person (Frankfurt, 1971). According to Frankfurt, to be a person, a creature must have 'second-order volitions', that is desires about which

---

[37] Mill (1859).
[38] See now *Re R* [1991] 4 All ER 177. Also useful is *Re C*, *The Times*, 1 October 1991.

desires she wants to become her will. As Lindley phrases it, 'people…have wills, in so far as they do not necessarily act on their strongest inclinations, but have the general ability to act on the results of their deliberation' (Lindley, 1976, pp. 122-123). He argues that a crucial requirement is possession of the concept of 'a self': someone has to be able to think of himself 'as a being with a future and a past, a subject of experiences, a possessor of beliefs and desires' (Lindley, 1976, p. 160). Of course, it is not clear exactly when children acquire these concepts, and there may be gender and class differences, but at seven it would not be uncommon and at ten it may be thought that most children have become persons in the sense depicted here. In Britain their educational attainments are now 'examined' at 7 and they are criminally responsible at 10.

To respect a child's autonomy is to treat that child as a person and as a rights-holder. It is clear that we can do so to a much greater extent than we have assumed hitherto. But it is also clear that the exercising of autonomy by a child can have an deleterious impact on that child's life chances. It is true that adults make mistakes too (and also make mistakes when interfering with a child's autonomy). Having rights means being allowed to take risks and make choices. There is a reluctance to interfere with an adult's project. This reluctance is tempered when the project pursuer is a child by the sense that choice now may harm choice later. As Lomasky (1987, p. 160) puts it: 'what counts as damage…is determined by what will likely further or diminish its eventual success in living as a project pursuer'.

This is to recognize that children are different. Many of them have lesser abilities and capacities. They are more vulnerable. They need protection. Without welfare rights being recognized, they will not be in a position to exercise autonomy. Of course, all of this is true, but it is not as true as we have come to believe. Children are different, but they are not all that different. There is a 'developmental trajectory' (Kleinig, 1989) through which we all pass. Age is often a suspect classification. If we are to apply a double standard, we must justify it. Double standards are not necessarily unjustifiable: things which appear to be alike may, on further reflection, not be as alike as they looked at first appearance. The onus lies on those who wish to discriminate. Hitherto, it has to be said that they have not discharged this burden very convincingly. How many of the structures, institutions and practices established to 'protect' children actually do so? Think of the juvenile court, the care system, observation and assessment centres, reporting systems where abuse has been identified, 'child protection' registers for children 'at risk', and ask whether the 'official' version of the truth withstands critical examination. But ask also whether, and to what extent, we are prepared to encourage children to participate in decisions regarding their life choices. It is much easier to assume abilities and capacities are absent than to take cognizance of children's choices.

If we are to make progress we have to recognize the moral integrity of children (Miller, 1987). We have to treat them as persons entitled to equal concern and respect and entitled to have both their present autonomy recognized and their capacity for future autonomy safeguarded. And this is to recognize that children, particularly younger children, need nurture, care and protection. Children must not, as Hafen (1976) put it, be 'abandoned' to their rights.

THE LIMITS OF AUTONOMY

In looking for a children's rights programme we must thus recognize the integrity of the child and his or her decision-making capacities but at the same time note the dangers of complete liberation. Too often writers on children's rights have dichotomized: there is either salvation or liberation (Margolin, 1978), either nurturance or self-determination (Rogers and Wrightsman, 1978)—in Richard Farson's pithy phrase, the one protects children, the other their rights (1978).

To take children's rights more seriously requires us to take more seriously than we have done hitherto protection of children and recognition of their autonomy, both actual and potential.

The view presented is premised on the need to respect individual autonomy and to treat persons as equals. Actual autonomy is important but it is as much the capacity for autonomy that is at the root of this thinking. Here, once again, the constructivism of Rawls's theory of justice may be prayed in aid. It is the normative value of equality and autonomy which forms the substructure of the Rawlsian conception of the social contract. The principles of justice which Rawls believes we would choose in the 'original position' are equal liberty and opportunity, and an arrangement of social and economic inequalities so that they are both to the greatest benefit of the least advantaged, and attached to offices and positions open to all under conditions of fair equality and opportunity. (See also Rawls, 1982).

These principles confine paternalism (the philosophy at the root of protection) without totally eliminating it. Those who participate in a hypothetical social contract would know that some human beings are less capable than others. They would know about variations in intelligence and strength, and they would know of the very limited capacities of small children and the rather fuller, if incomplete, capacities of adolescents. They would employ the insights of cognitive psychology (Melton, 1987). They would also bear in mind how the actions of those with limited capacities might thwart their autonomy at a future time when their capacities were no longer as limited.

These considerations would lead to an acceptance of interventions in children's lives to protect them against irrational actions. But what is to be regarded as 'irrational' must be strictly confined. The subjective values of the would-be protector cannot be allowed to intrude. What is 'irrational' must be defined in terms of a neutral theory capable of accommodating pluralistic visions of the 'good' (Rawls, 1987). Nor should we see an action as irrational unless it is manifestly so in the sense that it would undermine future life choices, impair interests in an irreversible way. Furthermore, we must tolerate mistakes, for, as Dworkin rightly observes, 'someone may have the right to do something that it is wrong for him to do' (1978, pp. 188–189). We cannot treat persons as equals without also respecting their capacity to take risks and make mistakes. We would not be taking rights seriously if we only respected autonomy when we considered the agent was doing the right thing. But we also would be failing to recognize a child's integrity if we allowed him to choose an action, such as using heroin or choosing not to attend school, which could seriously and systematically impair the attainment of full personality and development subsequently. The test of 'irrationality' must also be confined so that it justifies intervention only to the extent necessary to obviate the immediate harm, or to develop the capacities of rational choice by which the individual may have a reasonable chance of avoiding such harms.

The question we should ask ourselves is: what sort of action or conduct would we wish, as children, to be shielded against on the assumption that we would want to mature to a rationally autonomous adulthood and be capable of deciding on our own system of ends as free and rational beings? We would, I believe, choose principles that would enable children to mature to independent adulthood. One definition of irrationality would be such as to preclude action and conduct which would frustrate such a goal. Within the constraints of such a definition we would defend a version of paternalism: not paternalism in its classical sense for, so conceived, there would be no children's rights at all. Furthermore, it must be stressed that this version of paternalism is a two-edged sword in that, since the goal is

Consequentialist
Utilitarian — no to CR + even less so to DC

rational independence, those who exercise constraints must do so in such a way as to enable children to develop their capacities.

All paternalistic restrictions require moral justification. In many cases it is not difficult to adduce sufficient and convincing reasoned argument. Thus, it is not difficult to present the case for protecting children against actions which may lead to their death or to serious physical injury or mental disability. Nineteenth century legislation which made it illegal for children to go down coal-mines or up chimneys or into factories can thus readily be defended (though it may not have been passed to protect children). So can laws designed to protect children from sexual abuse and exploitation. There are clear dangers in the suggestions of writers of the 1970s like Holt (1975) and Farson (1978) that a child's right to self-determination includes a right to a sexual relationship with whomsoever he or she pleases. The 'discovery' of sexual abuse since has all but put an end to these demands (Miller, 1984; Nelson, 1987). On the other hand, 'ages of consent' as such are meaningless: the crucial factor is the presence or absence of exploitation, so that age *difference* may be of greater significance than the age of the child. A system of compulsory education, and concomitantly restrictions on employment, can also be defended, contrary to the argument of some liberationists (Duane, 1972), though the perimeters, content and goals of 'education' would be very different from those conventionally stipulated.

What should legitimize all these interferences with autonomy is, what Gerald Dworkin (1972) has called, 'future-oriented' consent. The question is: can the restrictions be justified in terms that the child would eventually come to appreciate? Looking back, would the child appreciate and accept the reason for the restriction imposed upon him or her, given what he or she now knows as a rationally autonomous and mature adult? It may readily be conceded that this is not an easy test to apply. It involves something akin to what Parfit (1984) has called 'ideal deliberation'. (See also Brandt, 1979). As Parfit puts it:

> What each of us has most reason to do is what would best achieve, not what he *actually* wants, but what he *would* want, at the time of acting, if he had undergone a process of 'ideal deliberation'—if he knew the relevant facts, was thinking clearly, and was free from distorting influences.

But what are 'relevant facts'? And how are hypothetical preferences to be considered? Can distortion of values be eliminated? The problems are real, but the effort to disentangle them remains worthwhile.

The dichotomy drawn is thus to some extent a false divide. Dichotomies and other classifications should not divert us away from the fact that true protection of children does protect their rights. It is not a question of whether child-savers or liberationists are right, for they are both correct in emphasizing part of what needs to be recognized, and both wrong in failing to address the claims of the other side.

To take children's rights more seriously requires us to take seriously nurturance and self-determination. It demands of us that we adopt policies, practices, structures and laws which both protect children and their rights. Hence the *via media* of 'liberal paternalism' which I first advocated in *The Rights and Wrongs of Children* (Freeman, 1983).

THE U.N. CONVENTION

It would be wrong to conclude without asking how the world's statement of principles matches up to the model and reasoning embodied in the 1989 U.N. Convention here set out. Certainly, it recognizes a large number of rights. Most are expressed in terms of rights (for example, freedom of expression, thought, association, social security, education), though some are conceptualized as duties upon states (for example, the provision dealing with sexual abuse). Nothing of moment hinges upon the distinction: it is certainly not a reflection of any philosophical considerations. The rights enumerated concentrate heavily on protection and on the granting to children by adults of what they think children need. But, significantly, Article 12 requires states to 'assure to the child who is capable of forming his or her own views the right to express those views freely, in all matters affecting the child, the views of the child being given due weight in accordance with the age and maturity of the child'. Whether the Convention would have looked the same had its framers consulted children on its contents is a matter upon which we can only speculate.

On the other hand, an article such as Article 29 is of great significance. The education of the child is to be directed *inter alia* towards the development of the child's personality, the development of respect for human rights, the preparation of the child for responsible life and to inculcate tolerance. As a provision which emphasizes choice and which sees education in broad terms, it is a recognition of children's rights in its widest sense. The law of England certainly falls far short of these ideals (Newell, 1991;

Freeman, ch. 6) and recent practice undermines them further.[39] So does the law of the U.S.A. (Bitensky, 1990).

The Convention is a beginning, but only a beginning. Those who wish to see the status and lives of children improved must continue the search for the moral foundation of children's rights. Without such thinking there would not have been a Convention: without further critical insight there will be no further recognition of the importance to children's lives of according them rights.

---

[39] See the editorial in the *Times Educational Supplement*, 'Keeping The Issues out of Geography,' 18 January 1991, 19 (Issue No. 3890)

References

Ariès, P. (1962), *Centuries of Childhood*, London, Jonathan Cape.
Bedau, H. (1984), 'Why do We have the Rights We do?', *Social Philosophy and Policy*, 1, 56.
Benn, S. (1988), *A Theory of Freedom*, Cambridge, Cambridge University Press.
Berlin, I. (1969), *Four Essays on Liberty*, Oxford, Oxford University Press.
Bitensky, S. (1960), 'Educating the Child for a Productive Life' in Cohen, C. and Davidson, H. (eds.) *Children's Rights in America*, Washington, American Bar Association.
Bradshaw, J. (1990), *Child Poverty and Deprivation in the U.K.*, London, National Children's Bureau.
Brandt, R. (1979), *A Theory of the Good and The Right*, Oxford, Oxford University Press.
Bruce, F. (1995), 'Child Prostitution and Pornography: The Making of International Law 1974–1995', *International Journal of Children's Rights*, 3, 469.
Cohen, C. and Davidson, H. (1990), *Children's Rights in America*, Washington, American Bar Association.
Cohen, H. (1980), *Equal Rights for Children*, Totowa, N.J., Littlefield, Adams.
Craig, G. and Glendinning, D. (1990), *The Impact of Social Security Changes: The Views of Families Using Barnado's Pre-School Services*, Barkingside, Barnado's Research and Development Section.
Duane, M. (1972), 'Freedom and The State System of Education', in Adams, P. *et al.*, *Children's Rights*, London, Panther Books.
Dworkin, G. (1972), 'Paternalism', in Wasserstrom, R. (ed.) *Morality and The Law*, California, Wadsworth.
Dworkin, G. (1988), *The Theory and Private of Autonomy*, Cambridge, Cambridge University Press.
Dworkin, R. (1978), *Taking Rights Seriously*, London, Duckworth.
Edelman, M. (1977), *Political Language; Words That Succeed and Policies That Fail*, New York, Academic Press.
Eekelaar, J. and Pearl, D. (eds.) (1989), *An Aging World—Dilemmas and Challenges for Law and Social Policy*, Oxford, Clarendon Press.
Farson, R. (1978), *Birthrights*, Harmondsworth, Penguin Books.
Federle, K. (1994), 'Rights Flow Downhill', *International Journal of Children's Rights*, 2, 343.
Feinberg, J. (1966), 'Duties, Rights and Claims', *American Philosophical Quarterly*, 3, 137.
Feinberg, J. (1986), *Harm to Self, The Moral Limits of The Criminal Law*, 3, New York, Oxford University Press.
Flekkøy, M. (1991), *A Voice For Children*, London, Jessica Kingsley.
Foucault, M. (1967), *Madness and Civilisation*, London, Tavistock.
Frankena, W. (1962), 'The Concept of Social Justice', in Brandt, R. (ed.) *Social Justice*, Englewood Cliffs, N.J., Prentice Hall

Frankfurt, H. (1981), 'Freedom of the Will and the Concept of a Person', *Journal of Philosophy*, 68, 829.
Freeman, M. (1983), *The Rights and Wrongs of Children*, London, Frances Pinter.
Freeman, M. (1985), 'Doing His Best To Sustain The Sanctity of Marriage' in Johnson, N. (ed.) *Marital Violence*, London, Routledge & Kegan Paul.
Freeman, M. (1988a), 'Sterilising the Mentally Handicapped' in Freeman, M. (ed.) *Medicine, Ethics and the Law*, London, Stevens.
Freeman, M. (1988b), 'Time to Stop Hitting Our Children', *Childright*, 51, 5.
Freeman, M. (1989), 'Cleveland, Butler-Sloss and Beyond', *Current Legal Problems*, 42, 85.
Gardner, R. (1987), *Who Says? Choice and Control in Care*, London, National Children's Bureau.
Gerwirth, A. (1982), *Human Rights: Essays on Justification and Applications*, Chicago, University of Chicago Press.
Glendon, M. (1991), *Rights Talk*, New York, Free Press.
Goldstein, J., Freud, A., Solnit, A. (1979), *Before the Best Interests of the Child*, New York, Free Press.
Gosling, J. and Diarists (1989), *One Day I'll Have a Place of My Own*, London, Central London Social Security Advisors' Forum and Shelter.
Groner, J. (1991), *Hilary's Trial*, New York, Simon & Schuster.
Hafen, B. (1976), 'Children's Liberation and the New Egalitarianism: Some Reservations about Abandoning Children to their "Rights"', *Brigham Young* ULR, 605–58.
Hampton, J. (1984), 'The Moral Education Theory of Punishment', *Philosophy and Public Affairs*, 13 (3), 208–38.
Haworth, L. (1986), *Autonomy*, New Haven, Yale University Press.
Hobbes, T. (1651), *Leviathan*.
Holmes, O. (1897), 'The Path of the Law', *Harvard Law Review*, 10, 457.
Holt, J. (1975), *Escape From Childhood*, Harmondsworth, Penguin Books.
Holtermann, S. (1995), *All Our Futures*, London, Barnardos.
Houlgate, L. (1988), *Family and State, The Philosophy of Family Law*, Totowa, N.J., Rowman & Littlefield.
Hoyles, M. (ed.) (1979), *Changing Childhood*, London, Writers & Readers Publishing Co-operative.
Illich, I. (1973), *Celebration of Awareness*, Harmondsworth, Penguin Books.
James, A. and Prout, A. (1990), *Constructing and Reconstructing Childhood*, Basingstoke, Falmer Press.
Jenks, C. (1996), *Childhood*, London, Routledge.
Kant, I. (1785), in H. Paton, *The Moral Law*, (1948), Hutchinson.
Kaplan, A. (1964), *The Conduct of Inquiry*, San Francisco, Chandler Publishing.
Kellmer-Pringle, M. (1980), *The Needs of Children*, London, Hutchinson.
Killerby, M. (1995), 'The Draft European Convention on the Exercise of Children's Rights, *International Journal of Children's Rights*, 3, 127.
Kleinig, J. (1976), 'Mill, Children and Rights', *Educational Philosophy and Theory*, 8, 14.
Kleinig, J. (1982), *Philosophical Issues in Education*, London, Croom Helm.

Kleinig, J. (1989), 'Persons, Lines and Shadows', *Ethics*, 100, 108.
Koren, M. (1995), 'A Children's Ombudsman in Sweden', *International Journal of Children's Rights,* 3, 101.
La Fontaine, J. (1990), *Child Sexual Abuse*, Oxford, Polity Press
Levy, A. and Kahan, B. (1991), *The Pindown Experience and the Protection of Children*, Stafford, Staffs C.C.
Lomasky, L. (1987), *Persons, Rights and the Moral Community*, New York, Oxford University Press.
Lucy, W. (1990), 'Controversy about Children's Rights', in Freestone, D. (ed.) *Children and the Law: Essays in Honour of Professor H. K. Bevan*, Hull, Hull University Press.
MacCormick, N. (1976), 'Children's Rights: A Test-Case for Theories of Right', *Archiv fur Recht-und Sozialphilosophie* (1976) LXII, 305–16, reprinted in MacCormick, N. (1982), *Legal Right and Social Democracy*, Oxford, Clarendon Press, ch. 8.
MacCormick, N. (1982), *Legal Right and Social Democracy: Essays in Legal and Political Philosophy,* Oxford, Clarendon Press.
MacCormick, N. (1983), 'Dworkin as Pre-Benthamite' in Cohen, M. (ed.), *Ronald Dworkin and Contemporary Jurisprudence.*
Mackie, J. (1984), 'Can There Be a Right-Based Moral Theory?' in Waldron, J. (ed.) *Theories of Rights*, Oxford, University Press.
Margolin, C. (1978), 'Salvation Versus Liberation: The Movement for Children's Rights In a Historical Context', *Social Problems,* 22, 441.
Max, L. (1990), *Children: An Endangered Species?* Auckland, Penguin Books.
Mill, J. S. (1859), *On Liberty*, London, John W. Parker.
Miller, A. (1984), *Thou Shalt Not Be Aware*, New York, Farrar, Straus & Giroux.
Miller, A. (1987), *The Drama of Being a Child*, London, Virago Press.
Mulholland, L. (1990), *Kant's System of Rights,* New York, Columbia University Press.
Narveson, J. (1985), 'Contractarian Rights', in Frey, R. (ed.) *Utility and Rights,* Oxford, Blackwell.
Nelson, S. (1978), *Incest: Fact and Myth*, Edinburgh, Stramullion.
Newell, P. (1989), *Children Are People Too*, London, Bedford Square Press.
Newell, P. (1991), *The UN Convention and Children's Rights in the UK*, London, National Children's Bureau.
Nozick, R. (1974), *Anarchy, State and Utopia*, Oxford, Blackwell.
O'Neill, O. (1988), 'Children's Rights and Children's Lives', *Ethics*, 98, 236.
OPCS (1995), *The Health of Our Children*, Decennial Supplement, London, H.M.S.O.
Oppenheim, C., and Harker, L. (1996), *Poverty: The Facts*, London, Child Poverty Action Group.
Parfit, D. (1984), *Reasons and Persons*, Oxford, Oxford University Press.
Paulsen, M. (1974), 'The Law and Abused Children' in Helfer, R. and Kempe, C. (eds.) *The Battered Child,* Chicago, University of Chicago Press.
Pfuhl, S. (1980), *The Deviance Process*, New York, Van Nostrand.
Pollock, L. (1983), *Forgotten Children*, Cambridge, Cambridge University Press.
Power, S., Whitty, G. and Youndell, D. (1995), *No Place To Learn: Homelessness and Education*, London, Shelter.

Pratt, J. (1989), 'Corporatism: The Third Model of Juvenile Justice,' *British Journal of Criminology,* 29 (3), 236.

Rawls, J. (1972), *A Theory of Justice*, Cambridge, Mass, Harvard University Press.

Rawls, J. (1987), 'On The Idea of an Overlapping Consensus', *Oxford Journal of Legal Studies*, 7, 1.

Richards, D. (1981), 'Rights and Autonomy', *Ethics*, 92, 3.

Rogers, C. and Wrightsman, L. (1978), 'Attitudes Toward Children's Rights: Nurturance or Self-Determination', *Journal of Social Issues,* 34 (2), 59.

Ryan, W. (1976), *Blaming the Victim*, New York, Vintage Books.

Seidler, V. (1986), *Kant, Respect and Injustice,* London, RKP.

Simmonds, N. (1986), *Central Issues in Jurisprudence*, London, Sweet & Maxwell.

Skolnick, J. (1966), *Justice Without Trial*, Chichester, Wiley.

Spitzer, S. (1975), 'Toward a Marxian Theory of Deviance', *Social Problems*, 22, 638.

Sumner, L. (1987), *The Moral Foundation of Rights*, Oxford, Clarendon Press.

Teichman, J. (1982), *Illegitimacy: A Philosophical Examination,* Oxford, Blackwell.

Thompson, B. (1992), 'Africa's Charter on Children's Rights: A Normative Break with Cultural Traditionalism.' *International and Comparative Law Quarterly*, 41, 432.

Tuck, R. (1979), *Natural Rights Theories*, Cambridge, Cambridge University Press.

UNICEF (1991), *The State of the World's Children 1991,* Oxford, Oxford University Press.

United Nations (1989), *Convention on The Rights of the Child*.

Waldron, J. (1987), *Nonsense Upon Stilts*, London, Methuen.

Wasserstrom, R. (1964), 'Rights, Human Rights and Racial Discrimination' *Journal of Philosophy*, 61, 628.

Westen, P. (1990), *Speaking of Equality,* Princeton, Princeton University Press.

White, A. (1984), *Rights*, Oxford, Clarendon Press.

Wikler, D. (1979), 'Paternalism and the Mildly Retarded', *Philosophy and Public Affairs*, 8, 377.

Woodhead, M. (1990), 'Psychology and The Cultural Construction of Children's Needs' in James, A. and Prout, A. (eds.), *Constructing and Reconstructing Childhood,* Basingstoke, Falmer Press.

Woolf, H. (1991), *Prison Disturbances, April 1990*, London, H.M.S.O.

Worsfold, V. (1974), 'A Philosophical Justification for Children's Rights', *Harvard Educational Review,* 44, 142.

Young, R. (1986), *Personal Autonomy: Beyond Negative and Positive Liberty*, London, Croom Helm.

CHAPTER 3

Laws, Conventions and Rights

INTRODUCTION

Thinking about children's rights has come a long way in the past quarter of a century. Hillary Rodham's famous aphorism that children's rights were 'a slogan in search of a definition' (Rodham, 1973) now seems a dated remark as the concept has been debated, analysed and fought over in academic literature and political discussion. Children's rights may not have become the 'primary social value' informing social policy and social planning that Wilkerson looked to twenty years ago (Wilkerson, 1973, p. 305) but the concept is better understood and more widely accepted than was the case when Rodham and Wilkerson were writing. The United Nations Convention in 1989 is likely to be the fulcrum upon which debate about children's rights in the foreseeable future will rest, but it is only a beginning, not even the end of the beginning, and, in truth, as Hawes has remarked, there is no 'obvious end in sight'. (Hawes, 1991, p. 123).

A PRE-HISTORY

But we have come a long way both in our recognition of children's rights and our understanding of childhood (Postman, 1994 and Sommerville, 1990). Early legal statements are conspicuously silent on children's rights: the Ten Commandments, arguably the most influential of all legal codes, contains a clear normative pronouncement on parent-child relations but it is in terms of respect for parents and is silent on the obligation of parents to love and nurture children (Silverman, 1978). Is it then surprising that well in to early modern times children were being prosecuted in England before the ecclesiastical courts for abusing parents, but that prosecutions of parents for beating children appear not to have taken place? (Helmholz, 1993).

One of the earliest recognitions of children's rights is found in the Massachusetts *Body of Liberties* of 1641. Parents are told not to choose their children's mates and not to use unnatural severity against their children (Pleck, 1987). Children, furthermore, are given 'free liberty to complain to the Authorities for redress'. But this is also the law that prescribes the death penalty for children over 16 who disobey parents. There is no evidence that children did successfully litigate against their parents but nor is there any that disobedient children were executed (Hawes, 1991). The document, nevertheless, remains interesting in showing, as it does, that even 350 years ago protection of children went hand in hand with adding the power of the state to parental authority.

The next two centuries can hardly be said to be identified with children's rights. There are concerns to protect children, though these are often clumsy or inchoate. It is pertinent to remark that the documents emanating from the great libertarian revolutions, the American and the French, have nothing specifically to say about children.

The nineteenth century saw the birth of the child-saving movement, the growth of the orphanage, the development of schooling and the construction of separate institutions, including the juvenile court, for delinquent children (Platt, 1969). Child protection legislation also comes about. Yet cruelty remains a social construct and founders of societies to protect children from abuse still vigorously defend corporal chastisement. Thus, one of the founders of the New York SPCC, Henry Bergh, can uphold 'a good wholesome flogging' as appropriate for 'disobedient children'. Children's rights begin to be advocated. Jean Vallès in France, in the aftermath of the Paris Commune (Vallès, 1878) and Kate Douglas Wiggin in the United States are two of the more eloquent expositors of the ideal (Wiggin, 1892). Wiggin's view of childhood, a century ago, is refreshingly modern. Its flavour is well-captured by this:

> As to keeping children too clean for any normal use, I suppose nothing is more disastrous. The divine right to be gloriously dirty a large portion of the time, when dirt is a necessary consequence of direct, useful, friendly contact with all sorts of interesting, helpful things, is too clear to be denied (Wiggin, 1892, p. 11).

She also urged a gentler approach to discipline: 'it seems likely', she wrote, 'that the rod of reason will have to replace the rod of birch' (Wiggin, 1892, p. 19). Janusz Korczak in Poland was expressing similar sentiments (Lifton, 1988). But it was not the voices of Wiggin or Korczak which prevailed.

Some Early History

Korczak himself formulated his ideas during the first world war. *How To Love A Child* (Korczak, 1919) took as one of its main theses the idea that you cannot possibly love a child—your own or another's—until you see him as a separate being with the inalienable right to grow into the person he was meant to be (Veerman, 1992 pp. 93–111). It was more than half a century before others, Farson (1978) and Holt (1975) for example, were to recognize the importance of a child's autonomy.

The first international declaration, the Declaration of Geneva of 1924, was more limited in its aspirations. In its preamble it states that 'mankind owes to the Child the best it has to give'. Its five terse principles emphasize welfare: the requisite means for normal development, food and medicine, relief in times of distress, protection against exploitation and socialization to serve others. The principles, the fifth above all, reflected the aftermath of an imperialist war. One contemporary commentator (Fuller, 1925) compared it with the tendency in Britain to emphasize nationalist and imperialist ideals in education to the detriment of its ideal of world service. According to him, it was from 'the point of view of the world future no less than of the individual the most important and far-reaching of all Principles of the Declaration of Geneva'. (Fuller, 1925, p. 116).

It was another 35 years before children's rights received international recognition again. We get considerable insight into attitudes towards children's rights in the late 1950s (before civil rights issues became rampant) from the discussions which took place at this time. Thus, for example, the French delegate to the Commission on Human Rights in 1959 believed that:

> ...the child was not in a position to exercise his own rights. Adults exercised them for the child.... A child had special legal status resulting from his inability to exercise his rights.

Iraq argued that children's rights posed particular problems for Third World countries which did not have the means, for example, to implement compulsory education. The ideological differences between capitalism and communism were also striking: the communist world saw the primary responsibility for the child as lying with the state; for western delegations this responsibility rested with parents. There were also differences about the treatment of illegitimate children, Israel and Poland wishing to protect them against discrimination, and Italy arguing that it was equally necessary to protect the legitimate family which, the Italian delegate said, constituted 'the foundation of an organized society'. It was Italy also which pressed, ultimately successfully, for the recognition of rights from the time of conception.

What emerged on the 20 November 1959 was the United Nations Declaration of the Rights of The Child. In the end only two countries abstained (Cambodia and South Africa). The ten principles adopted were:

1. Non-discrimination.

2. Special protection and opportunities to develop physically and mentally, morally, spiritually and socially in a healthy and normal manner and in conditions of freedom and dignity. (The principle adds 'In the enactment of laws for this purpose the best interests of the child shall be the paramount consideration'. This is in contrast to the Convention of 1989 where 'a primary consideration' is substituted for 'the paramount consideration').

3. A right to a name and nationality.

4. The right to the benefits of social security; adequate nutrition, housing, recreation and medical services.

5. The right of a special needs child to the treatment, education and care required by his or her particular condition.

6. The need for love and understanding so that the child, wherever possible, is to grow in the care and under the responsibility of his parents and in an atmosphere of affection and of moral and material security. (The principle stresses that payment of state and other assistance toward the maintenance of children of large families is desirable).

7. Entitlement to education, free and compulsory, at least in the elementary stages.

8. To be among the first to receive protection and relief.

9. Protection against all forms of neglect, cruelty and exploitation (including that associated with employment).

10. Protection from practices which may foster racial, religious and any other form of discrimination.

The coverage is broader, though there is distinct overlap with the Geneva Declaration. The emphasis is still firmly on protection and welfare and, what has been called, the 'investment motive' (Meyer, 1973) remains apparent. There is no recognition of a child's autonomy, of the importance of a child's views, nor any appreciation of the concept of empowerment.

The Children's Liberation Movement

1959 is barely a generation ago but, in the period immediately following it, there was a growth in consciousness of the evils of discrimination, first against blacks and other ethnic minority groups and then against women and other disadvantaged groups. The 1970s saw the growth of the child's liberation movement, spearheaded by John Holt (1975) and Richard Farson (1978). The term 'Toward the Liberation of the Child' appeared for the first time as a sub-title of the book *Children's Rights*, published in 1971 (Adams *et al.*, 1971). In this collection Robert Ollendorff argues (and he was probably the first to do so) for the adolescent's right to self-determination (p. 120).

It was self-determination that Farson saw as at the root of all other rights that children were entitled to claim. Responding to the anticipated criticism that such rights might not be 'good' for children, for children's rights hitherto had been geared to furthering 'the good' for children, Farson argued:

> ...asking what is good for children is beside the point. We will grant children rights for the same reason we grant rights to adults, not because we are sure that children will then become better people, but more for ideological reasons, because we believe that expanding freedom as a way of life is worthwhile in itself. And freedom, we have found, is a difficult burden for adults as well as for children' (1978, p. 31).

Farson went on to enumerate nine rights, all derived from the right to self-determination:

1. The right to alternative home environments allowing the child to 'exercise choice in his own living arrangements' (1978, p. 62) (of particular interest now that children 'divorcing' parents has hit the headlines).

2. The right to information that is accessible to adults (for example, children should be allowed to inspect records kept about them).

3. The right to educate oneself (he favoured the abolition of compulsory education). Part of this right is freedom from indoctrination with children choosing their 'belief systems' (1978, p. 110).

4. The right to sexual freedom: pornography would be made available to children as it is to adults and children would be allowed to experiment with their sexuality without fearing punishment.

52 *Chapter 3*

5.   The right to economic power including the right to work, to develop a credit record and to achieve financial independence (1978 p. 154).

6.   The right to political power including the right to vote (see also Franklin, 1986; 1992). Nothing, he suggests, indicates that children will 'vote less responsibly than adults' (1978, p. 182).

7.   The right to responsive design (see also Ward, 1978).

8.   The right to freedom from physical punishment (see also Newell, 1989).

9.   The right to justice (see also Freeman, 1981).

Holt's catalogue is not dissimilar but it includes the right to travel, to drive, to use drugs as well as the rights which Farson enumerates.

It is easy to ridicule Farson, Holt and the liberation school of the 1970s and, indeed, it has been criticized (Hafen, 1976; Freeman, 1983; Purdy, 1992). But it must be remembered that they wrote when child sexual abuse had yet to be discovered and when drugs were less of a social problem than they are to-day (and see Zamora Chavarria, 1992). We would want to protect children from sex and drugs and, indeed, from work and possibly other rights which they would confer on children, but protection was not in their vocabulary. Thus, Holt, writing of drugs, says:

> On the whole I believe that people ought to be able to use the drugs they want. I don't think we should 'protect' children against whatever drugs their elders use, and in a society in which most of their elders do use drugs and many use them excessively and unwisely, I don't see how we can. (1975, pp. 194 & 201).

The Farson-Holt thesis has its limitations and more recent advocacy of children's rights acknowledges the need to protect children (Freeman, 1983; 1992a; and see ch. 2; and see Houlgate, 1980; Eekelaar, 1986; 1992). To some, indeed, it is the duties of parents and others towards children that must be emphasized, rather than children's rights as such (O'Neill, 1988), but this too may be criticized (Campbell, 1992; Freeman, 1992a; and see ch. 2). The importance of the liberation school was in making us address discrimination and recognize the importance of autonomy. To believe in autonomy is to believe that anyone's autonomy is as morally significant as anyone else's.

It is significant that philosophical and legal thought on the requirements to exercise autonomy should have converged. Thus, Haworth (1986) writes of the need for 'critical competence' and Lindley (1986) of capacity for reasoning almost at the same time as Lord Scarman in the *Gillick* decision (1986) is formulating, what has come to be called, '*Gillick*-competence'. There has been a judicial backlash against this since (*Re R*, 1991; *Re W*, 1992; *Re S*, 1994; and see Bainham, 1992; Murphy, 1992; and see ch. 15). The Children Act 1989 nevertheless continues to recognize the right of a child 'of sufficient understanding to make an informed decision' to refuse to submit to a medical or psychiatric examination or other assessment (Freeman, 1998). It has come to be realized that the dichotomy between protecting children and protecting their rights to autonomy is false. Children who are not protected, whose welfare is not advanced, will not be able to exercise self-determination: on the other hand, a failure to recognize the personality of children is likely to result in an undermining of their protection with children reduced to objects of intervention. This is to some extent recognized by the United Nations Convention on the Rights of The Child of 1989.

THE UN CONVENTION ON THE RIGHTS OF THE CHILD

Thirty years separate the UN Declaration and the UN Convention. The thinking of the period in between is reflected in the differences. It was Poland which, in 1978, proposed that there ought to be a Convention—to mark, it said, the International Year of The Child a year later. But Poland would have been satisfied with the Declaration turned into a Convention with the addition of an implementation mechanism (Cohen, 1990; see also Cohen and Naimark, 1990). Early on concern was expressed that the passing of a Convention would undermine the 'moral impact' of the Declaration (Singer, 1986; Weisberg, 1978). The United Kingdom questioned the need for a Convention: in its view those who wanted one had not 'sufficiently demonstrated the advantages' of a Convention. It saw the project as 'premature' (Le Blanc, 1995). These reservations were soon overcome but drafting the Convention proved to be difficult.

The world's first international legal instrument on children's rights was the product of ten years of negotiation among government delegations (though only a small number actively participated), inter-governmental organizations and non-governmental organizations. There were five issue areas where consensus was difficult to achieve (Johnson, 1992): freedom of thought, conscience and religion (where there were Islamic concerns); inter-country adoption (with Latin American countries expressing reservations); the rights of the unborn child (where there were splits on both lines of religion and between more developed and developing countries with policies for curbing over-population); traditional practices (with some African concern on female circumcision); and on the duties of children (favoured by Senegal, and found in the Charter on the Rights and Welfare of the African Child Article 31).

Each of these five areas provided a test case for resolving conflicting cultural and religious perspectives, and in each case a compromise was found. In one case (freedom of religion) the compromise was effected by the adoption of a minimal text, but in the others a minority perspective was incorporated in some way into the final text.

Whether these accommodations are necessarily good for children is contested. To take an example: the Preamble to the Convention states that 'due account' is to be taken of 'the importance of the traditions and cultural values of each people for the protection and harmonious development of the child'. But these 'traditions and cultural values' are not problematized. The practice of female circumcision is a good example (Dorkenoo and Elworthy, 1992; Dorkenoo, 1994; Funder, 1993; and see ch. 7). Medically unnecessary and extremely painful operations are routinely carried out on babies and young girls; in their most severe forms they involve the partial to complete removal of the external female genitalia. The practice impacts on over 100 million women and girls in over 28 countries in Africa and has spread to other countries including the United Kingdom (graphically documented in a BBC 2 Forty Minutes programme 'A Cruel Ritual' broadcast on 21 February 1991). Do these 'traditional values' not undermine the child and, if so, are we to be tolerant of them?

There is thus in the Convention a clear recognition that the child's welfare may well be 'trumped' in certain situations by 'cultural values and traditions'. States are, however, by Article 24(3) to 'take effective and appropriate measures with a view to abolishing traditional practices prejudicial to the health of children', but this is itself qualified by Article 24(4), which provides that states undertake to promote and encourage international cooperation with a view to achieving progressively the full realization of the rights in Article 24. The elimination of harmful traditional practices is seen, then, as the recognition of social or cultural rights, and therefore falls within the realm of progressive obligation (McGoldrick, 1991). Is this acceptable? Surely, practices which are prejudicial to the health of girls and which limit their life choices thereafter should be seen as infringements of a civil right, and therefore be accorded priority.

The Convention is nevertheless important. It is described by Veerman as 'an important and easily understood advocacy tool—one that promotes children's welfare as an issue of justice rather than one of charity' (Veerman, 1992, p. 184). The rights in the Convention may be categorized as:

1. General rights (the right to life, prohibition against torture, freedom of expression, thought and religion, the right to information and to privacy).

2. Rights requiring protective measures (including measures to protect children from economic and sexual exploitation, to prevent drug abuse and other forms of abuse and neglect).

3. Rights concerning the civil status of children (including the right to acquire nationality, the right to preserve one's identity, the right to remain with parents, unless the best interests of the child dictate otherwise, and the right to be reunited with the family).

4. Rights concerning development and welfare, including the child's right to a reasonable standard of living, the right to health and basic services, the right to social security, the right to education and the right to leisure.

5. Rights concerning children in special circumstances or 'in especially difficult circumstances'. These extend to such children as handicapped children, refugee children and orphaned children. Included are special regulations on adoption, the cultural concerns of minority and indigenous children, and rehabilitative care for children suffering from deprivation, as well as a prohibition on the recruitment of soldiers under fifteen years of age.

6. Procedural considerations, particularly the establishment of an International Committee of ten experts to monitor implementation of the Convention (Muntarbhorn, 1992).

The innovative nature of the Convention is brought out well by Philip Veerman (1992, pp. 184–5). He pinpoints first that it says that State agencies will be responsible for the physical, psychological and social reintegration of a child where rights are violated; second that it goes beyond earlier formulations which emphasized the duties of adults and the State to emphasize child participation in decision-making. The Convention is, as he notes, the first explicitly to state that children have a right to 'have a say' in processes affecting their lives. In this way the child is regarded as the 'principal' in the Convention (Pais, 1992). Thirdly, placements in residential care and foster care will now be subject to constant review—a principle very much in line with the new English Children Act (Freeman, 1998). Fourth, the right to identity has never before been formulated in an International Convention (and see Cerda, 1990; and see ch. 10).

Of these innovations Article 12, providing for a child's participation in decisions affecting him or her, is, I believe, the most significant. It is a development from the child liberation philosophy formulated in the 1970s and is in line with the *Gillick* decision and a strand, but only a strand, in the Children Act 1989 (Fox Harding, 1992; Freeman, 1992b). The Article states:

1. States Parties shall assure to the child who is capable of forming his or her own views the right to express those views freely in all matters affecting the child, the views of the child being given due weight in accordance with the age and maturity of the child.

2. For this purpose, the child shall in particular be provided the opportunity to be heard in any judicial and administrative proceedings affecting the child, either directly, or through a representative or an appropriate body, in a manner consistent with the procedural rules of national law.

The right enunciated here is significant not only for what it says, but because it recognizes the child as a full human being, with integrity and personality, and with the ability to participate fully in society. The constituting features of 'freedom of expression', as defined in Article 13 to include 'the right to seek, receive and impart information and ideas of all kinds', and the right in Article 14 to 'freedom of thought, conscience and religion' also look upon children as persons in their own right.

Attention has been focused also on Article 3 which states:

1. In all actions concerning children, whether undertaken by public or private social welfare institutions, courts of law, administrative authorities or legislative bodies, the best interests of the child shall be a primary consideration.

2. States Parties undertake to ensure the child such protection and care as is necessary for his or her well-being, taking into account the rights and duties of his or her parents, legal guardians, or other individuals legally responsible for him or her, and, to this end, shall take all appropriate legislative and administrative measures.

In England in matters of 'upbringing' before the courts the child's welfare is the 'paramount' consideration (it 'determines the course to be followed': *J* v. *C* (1970)). Although the Convention makes the child's best interests only *a* (not *the*) primary consideration, the scope of this directive is considerably wider. The child's best interests are not even a primary consideration in decisions made by this country's education, housing or immigration authorities, an omission perhaps most remarkable in the field of education where a plethora of Acts since 1980 have purported to extend parents' rights in matters relating to schooling whilst ignoring the rights of its primary consumers.

Articles 12 and 3 encapsulate a tension in the whole debate which has been examined here. Article 12 emphasizes the centrality of a child's views (and see Lücker-Babel, 1995), Article 3 the priority to be given to concerns of welfare. The first principle is not overriding (a Polish attempt to make welfare paramount failed), but its imperative and the philosophy of Article 12 can conflict. How, then, will conflicts be resolved? It is a real concern. Those who constructed the Convention themselves paid scant regard to children's views: do we not know that the rights enumerated in the Convention are those that children themselves would have constructed? But Article 12 cannot be underestimated. Children who are capable of forming views must be 'assured' the right to express them on 'all matters affecting' them, and these views must be given 'due weight'. Again this goes beyond the new English Children Act where a child's views and the representation of them is largely confined to the public law arena. A child has a greater 'say' in care than in school or for that matter at home (the Finnish law of 1983 and the new Swedish law make a striking contrast—Savolainen, 1986, and Scotland too has followed the Finnish precedent (see Children (Scotland) Act 1995).

The child's best interests test is well-known. There have been many attempts to 'pour content' into it (Goldstein *et al.*, 1980). It has been criticized for its indeterminacy and for being inevitably value-laden (Mnookin, 1985). But 'the Convention does not seek to provide any definite statement of how a child's interests would be best served in a given situation' (Alston, 1992, p. 8). This is an acknowledgement that the precise implications of the principle will vary over time and from country to country. However, the Committee on the Rights of the Child, established under the Convention, can be expected over time to identify more precise guidelines to give direction to the principle in specific contexts.

THE EUROPEAN CONVENTION ON THE EXERCISE OF CHILDREN'S RIGHTS

The European Convention of 1996 is, as its title conveys, not a further list of children's rights, though it is possible that members of the Council of Europe could have agreed to a more comprehensive agenda than the

United Nations, but a programme for the 'exercise' of children's rights. Its object is:

> in the best interests of children, to promote their rights, to grant them procedural rights and to facilitate the exercise of these rights by ensuring that children are, themselves or through other persons or bodies, informed and allowed to participate in proceedings affecting them before a judicial authority. (Art. 1 (2))

The Convention, like the United Nations Convention, applies to children under 18. Its scope is family proceedings affecting children before a court or administrative authority having equivalent powers. 'Family proceedings' are not defined. They are stated to include 'in particular those involving the exercise of parental responsibilities such as residence and access to children' (Art. 1 (3)). Every State is to specify at least three categories of family cases to which the Convention is to apply. As far as England is concerned major changes will have to take place if proceedings in the private law arena are to be specified (Timms, 1995; Freeman, 1996). Although it is in such proceedings, particularly divorce, that residence and access questions most obviously and commonly arise, English law is better equipped to offer the Convention's procedural rights where questions such as care or adoption arise.

The Convention provides that a child 'considered by internal law as having sufficient understanding' is to be granted and is entitled to request the right to receive all relevant information (presumably also when a court deems it not to be in a child's interest to know certain information), to be consulted and express his or her views, and to be informed of the possible consequences of compliance with these views and the possible consequences of any decision (Art. 3). In addition, the child has the right to apply for a 'Special Representative' where internal law 'precludes the holders of parental responsibilities from representing the child as a result of a conflict of interest with the latter' (Art. 4). The Convention is pro-mediation (see Article 13), but curiously does not extend the procedural rights just listed to this method of dispute resolution. It is thus ironically in line with a trend that sees a growth in children's rights in legal disputes at the same time as we hurtle towards delegalization.

The Convention recognizes the importance of the parental role (see the Preamble) but it does not impose any specific duties, in relation to family proceedings before a judicial authority, on holders of parental responsibilities. This is because it could be difficult for parents to comply with the procedural requirements in certain States, (Killerby, 1995), and additionally there are likely to be conflicts of interest between children and their parents.

It is significant that the Convention doesn't require States to set up a specific body, such as an Ombudsman for children, though such an institution now exists in Norway (see Flekkøy, 1990) and Sweden (Koren, 1995) and may well be adopted by a Labour government in Britain. Instead the emphasis is placed on the functions of national bodies and these may be carried out by a variety of institutions, governmental and non-governmental. The Convention also sets up a Standing Committee (Articles 16–18) to keep under review problems relating to the Convention, especially concerning its interpretation and implementation. This may propose amendments and is also charged with giving advice and assistance to national bodies.

Its is of symbolic importance that the Council of Europe has recognized children and the importance of protecting their rights. But the Convention is a weak document. In particular—and certainly compared with the European Convention on Human Rights—it is toothless. Whether it will have much impact remains to be seen. It is difficult to be optimistic.

CONCLUSION

By contrast, the United Nations Convention is an achievement. But even it is a beginning, no more. We must get 'beyond conventions, towards empowerment' (Freeman, 1992c and see Ch 4). We must re-examine structures, institutions and practices to make children's rights more meaningful. We have ratified the Convention; we have passed a Children Act, though not, it should be noted, a Children's Act (Hough 1995). But children are still passed around 'like packages or pieces of property' (Lady Justice Butler-Sloss in *Re W*, 1997), sexually abused by those 'caring' for them, whisked from their home in 'dawn raids' and held incommunicado. More live in poverty, more are homeless and fewer are entitled to social security than was the case even a decade ago. The Children Act recognizes both sides of the children's rights equation: welfare and self-determination. But is there a serious commitment to either? We have as far to go in the next quarter of a century as we have come in the last if we are truly to take children's rights seriously.

REFERENCES

Adams, P. (1971) *Children's Rights: Toward the Liberation of The Child*. New York: Praeger.

Alston, P. (1992) 'The legal framework of the Convention on the Rights of the Child', *Bulletin of Human Rights*, 91(2), pp. 1–15.

Bainham, A. (1992) 'The judge and the incompetent minor', *Law Quarterly Review*, 108, pp. 194–200.

Campbell, T. (1992) 'The rights of the minor: as person, as child, as juvenile, as future adult' in Alston, P. *et al*., (eds.) *Children, Rights and the Law*. Oxford: Clarendon Press.

Cerda, J. S. (1990) 'The draft Convention on The Rights of the Child: new rights', *Human Rights Quarterly*, 12, pp. 115–119.

Cohen, C. (1990) 'Relationships between the child, the family and the state: the UN Convention on the Rights of the Child' in Bayles, M. and Moffatt, R. *Perspectives on the Family*. Lewiston, N.Y.: Edwin Meller Press.

Cohen, C. and Naimark, H. (1991) 'The United Nations Convention on The Rights of the Child: individual rights concepts and their significance for social scientists', *American Psychologist*, 46(2).

Dorkenoo, E. and Elworthy, S. (1992) *Female Genital Mutilation: Proposals for Change*. London: Minority Rights Group.

Dorkenoo, E. (1994) *Cutting The Rose. Female Genital Mutilation: the Practice and Its Prevention*. London: Minority Rights Publications.

Eekelaar, J. (1986) 'The emergence of children's rights', *Oxford Journal of Legal Studies*, 6, pp. 161–182.

Eekelaar, J. (1992) 'The importance of thinking that children have rights' in Alston, P. *et al*. (eds.) *Children, Rights and the Law*. Oxford: Clarendon Press, pp. 221–235.

Farson, R. (1978) *Birthrights*. Harmondsworth: Penguin.

Fox Harding, L. (1991) 'The Children Act 1989 in context; four perspectives in child care law and policy', *Journal of Social Welfare and Family Law*, pp. 179–94, 285–302.

Franklin, B. (1986) *The Rights of Children*. Oxford: Basil Blackwell.

Freeman, M. (1981) 'The Rights of Children who Do Wrong', *British Journal of Criminology*, 21, 210.

Freeman, M. (1983) *The Rights and Wrongs of Children*. London: Frances Pinter.

Freeman, M. (1992a) 'Taking children's rights more seriously', *International Journal of Law and the Family*, 6, pp. 52–71.

Freeman, M. (1992b) 'In the child's best interests? Reading the Children Act critically', *Current Legal Problems*, 45, pp. 173–212.

Freeman, M. (1992c) 'Beyond conventions—towards empowerment' in Fortuyn, M. D. and de Langen, M. (eds.) *Towards the Realization of Human Rights of Children*. Amsterdam, DCI—Netherlands, pp. 19–39.

Freeman, M. (1998) *Children, Their Families and the Law—Working With The Children Act* (2nd ed.). Basingstoke: Macmillan.

Fuller, E. (1925) 'Great Britain and the Declaration of Geneva V', *The World's Children*. VI(7), p. 116.

Funder, A. (1993) *'De Minimis Non Curat Lex:* The Clitoris, Culture and the Law', *Transnational Law and Contemporary Problems*, 3 pp. 417–67.

Goldstein, J., Freud, A. and Solnit, A. (1980) *Before The Best Interests of Child.* New York: Free Press.

Hafen, B. (1976) 'Children's liberation and the new egalitarianism: some reservations about abandoning youth to their rights', *Brigham Young University Law Review*, pp. 605–58.

Hawes, J. (1991) *The Children's Rights Movement.* Boston: Twayne.

Haworth, L. (1986) *Autonomy.* New Haven: Yale University Press.

Helmholz, R. (1993) 'And were there children's rights in early modern England?' *International Journal of Children's Rights*, 1, pp. 23–32.

Holt, J. (1975) *Escape From Childhood.* Harmondsworth: Penguin.

Hough, J. (1995) 'Why Isn't It The Children's Act?' in Dalrymple, J. and Hough, J. *Having a Voice: An Exploration of Children's Rights and Advocacy.* Birmingham: Venture Press.

Houlgate, L. (1980) *The Child and The State.* Baltimore: Johns Hopkins University Press.

Johnson, D. (1992) 'Cultural and regional pluralism in the drafting of the UN Convention on the rights of the child' in Freeman, M. and Veerman, P. *The Ideologies of Children's Rights.* Dordrecht: Martinus Nijhoff, pp. 95–114.

Killerby, M. (1995) 'The Draft European Convention on the Exercise of Children's Rights', *International Journal of Children's Rights*, 3, pp 127–133.

Korczak, J. (1920) 'How to love a child' in *Selected Works of Janusz Korczak*, Wolins, M. (ed.). Warsaw.

Le Blanc, L. (1995) *The Convention on the Rights of The Child.* Lincoln Nebraska: University of Nebraska Press.

Lifton, B. J. (1988) *The King of Children.* London: Chatto and Windus.

Lindley, R. (1986) *Autonomy.* Basingstoke: Macmillan

Lücker-Babel, M-F. (1995) 'The Right of The Child To Express Views and Be Heard', *Int. Journal of Children's Rights*, 3, pp. 391–404.

McGoldrick, D. (1991) 'The United Nations Convention on the Rights of the Child', *International Journal of Law and the Family*, 5, pp. 132–169.

Meyer, P. B. (1973) 'The exploitation of the American growing class' in Gottlieb, D. (ed.) *Children's Liberation.* Englewood Cliffs, NJ: Prentice Hall.

Mnookin, R. (1985) *In The Interest of Children.* New York: W. H. Freeman.

Muntarbhorn, V. (1992) 'The Convention on the Rights of the Child: reaching the unreached?', *Bulletin of Human Rights*, 91(2), pp. 66–74.

Murphy, J. (1992) 'W(h)ither adolescent autonomy?', *Journal of Social Welfare and Family Law*, pp. 529–544.

Newell, P. (1989) *Children Are People Too.* London: Bedford Square Press.

O'Neill, O. (1988) 'Children's rights and children's lives', *Ethics*, 98, pp. 445–463.

Pais, M. S. (1992) 'The United Nations, Convention on The Rights of The Child', *Bulletin of Human Rights*, 91(2), pp. 75–82.

Platt, A. (1969) *The Child Savers.* Chicago: University of Chicago Press.

Pleck, E. (1987) *Domestic Tyranny.* New York: Oxford University Press.

Postman, N. (1994) *The Disappearance of Childhood.* New York: Vintage Books.

Purdy, L. M. (1992) *In Their Best Interest?—The Case Against Equal rights for Children*. Ithaca, New York: Cornell University Press.

Rodham, H. (1973) 'Children under the law', *Harvard Educational Review*, 43, pp. 487–514.

Savolainen, M. (1986) 'Finland: more rights for children', *Journal of Family Law*, 25(1). pp. 113–126.

Silverman, P. (1978) *Who Speaks for the Child?* Don Mills, Ontario: Musson.

Singer, S. (1986) 'The protection of children during armed conflict situations', *International Review of the Red Cross*, May–June.

Sommerville, C. J. (1990) *The Rise and Fall of Childhood*. New York: Vintage Books.

Timms, J. (1995) *Children's Representation*. London: Sweet and Maxwell.

Vallès, J. (1878) *L'Enfant*. Paris.

Veerman, P. (1992) *The Rights of the Child and the Changing Image of Childhood*. Dordrecht: Martinus Nijhoff.

Ward, C. (1978) *The Child in the City*. New York: Pantheon.

Weisberg, D. K. (1978) 'Evolution of the rights of the child in the western world', *Review of the International Commission of Jurists*, December, pp. 43–51.

Wiggin, K. D. (1892) *Children's Rights*. Boston: Houghton Mifflin.

Wilkerson, A. (1973) *The Rights of Children*. Philadelphia: Temple University Press.

Zamora Chavarria E. M. (1992) 'The rights of the child in democratic societies' in Fortuyn, M. D. and de Langen, M. (eds.) *Towards The Realization of Human Rights of Children*. Amsterdam: DCI—Netherlands, pp. 65–75.

CASES

Gillick v. *West Norfolk and Wisbech A.H.A.* (1986) AC 112.

J v. *C* (1970) AC 668.

Re R (1991) 4 All ER 177.

Re S (1994) 2 FLR 1065.

Re W (a) (1992) 4 All ER 627.

Re W (b) (1992) 2 FLR 461.

CHAPTER 4

Beyond Conventions—Towards Empowerment

Travel it is said, broadens the mind. In my case it certainly broadens the library. Let me share with you the titles of two books I picked up this summer. New Zealand's offering was *Children—Endangered Species?*[1] In California I bought a gripping account of children growing up in the ghetto *There Are No Children Here*.[2] The style of the two books is very different but in their different ways they document the damaged cultural environment, the visible pathologies,[3] in which the lives of children in two of the more advanced nations are spent. A glance at the annual *State of The World's Children*[4] confirms the near universality of the picture and the impression that things are getting worse. If one could indulge in a piece of Rawlsian constructivism[5] and, in the 'original' (or should it be 'pre-original'?) position, choose where one was going to be born—and, just as significantly, to whom—where would one choose? A difficult question, which I won't answer—there are indicia of choice in the *State of The World's Children*. The Netherlands, it should be said with deference to our hosts, would come high in most persons' choices.[6] Of course, it would not have done 50 years ago.

In this week[7] when we remember the Wannsee Conference and speaking to you within gunshot of the house of the most famous child victim of the Holocaust,[8] I dedicate this paper to the memory of the one-and-a-half

---

[1] Lesley Max, *Children—Endangered Species?* Auckland, Penguin, 1990.
[2] Alex Kotlowitz, *There Are No Children Here*, New York, Doubleday, 1991.
[3] R. Heilbronner, 'Lifting The Silent Depression' *New York Review of Books*, XXXVIII (17), 6 (1991).
[4] Published by Oxford University Press, Oxford, annually.
[5] See J. Rawls, *A Theory of Justice*, Cambridge, Mass., Harvard University Press, 1971.
[6] Sixth in the list in *The State of the World's Children 1989*. The U.K. was 15th.
[7] 20 January 1992 was the 50th anniversary.
[8] Anne Frank. Her diary is now published as *De Dagboeken van Anne Frank*, Den Haag, Staatsuitgeverij, 1986 and, in English, as A. Frank, *The Diary of A Young Girl: The Criti-*

million 'children with a star'[9] exterminated as vermin in the pursuit of an ideology with roots firmly embedded within a child-centred Christian culture.[10] And had there been a U.N. Convention in the Rights of the Child?—of course, exactly the same would have happened. For conventions, though important symbols, don't change anything. More, much more, is required if the conditions of children's lives are to improve, if they are to be regarded truly as persons rather than as social problems, burdens or pretty play-things.

THE CONVENTION REVISITED

The U.N. Convention and the World Summit[11] which followed were greeted with such euphoria that it is all too easy to assume that the Convention itself represents the final word on children's rights. In a world in which the child's voice was genuinely heard, the Convention itself might have looked quite different. Article 12 is significant for it requires states to 'assure to the child who is capable of forming his or her own views the right to express those views freely, on all matters affecting the child, the views of the child being given due consideration in accordance with the age and maturity of the child'. Yet, of course, on the major 'matter' of the Convention, there is no evidence that children or children's groups as such participated in drafting or had any real influence in preliminary discussions.[12] Of course, it may be said that codes of women's rights and documents offering equal opportunities for ethnic minorities have, usually, been drawn up respectively by men and by whites. But if two wrongs don't make a right, three certainly don't.

When the Convention is looked at what do we see? Article 3 has been the central focus of attention and with some justification. Let me, therefore, look at this. It states that 'in all actions concerning children, whether

---

cal Edition. New York, Doubleday, 1989. A revised more realistic edition is to be published in 1997.

[9] See D. Dwork, *Children With a Star*, New Haven, Yale University Press, 1991. She points out that in fact a large proportion did not wear the emblem. Apart from those in hiding, children under 6, 10 or 12 depending on the location were not required to wear stars. She also points out that the word 'magen' from which 'star' is derived anyway means 'shield'.

[10] See R. Wistrich, *Anti-Semitism*, London, Methuen, 1991, and R. Hilberg, *The Destruction of The European Jews*, New York, Holmes and Meier, 1985.

[11] See *State of The World's Children* 1991, Oxford Univ. Press, pp. 1–10.

[12] But many non-governmental organizations (NGOs), committed to children's interests, actively participated in the drafting process.

undertaken by public or private social welfare institutions, courts of law, administrative authorities or legislative bodies, the best interests of the child shall be a primary consideration'. I pause to note the conflict between the overtly welfarist stance in this Article and the recognition of autonomy in Article 12, already quoted. But the second paragraph of Article 3 must also be examined. 'States Parties undertake to ensure the child such protection and care as is necessary for his or her well-being, taking into account the rights and duties of his or her parents, legal guardians, or other individuals legally responsible for him or her, and, to this end, shall take all appropriate legislative and administrative measures'.

The context of the Convention, as set out in the Preamble, should also not be overlooked. This acknowledges that 'due account' should be taken of 'the importance of the traditions and cultural values of each people for the protection and harmonious development of the child'. These 'traditions and cultural values' are not problematized. The fact that traditional values have undermined the child is ignored. There is a clear recognition that the child's welfare (*a* primary, but not *the* primary consideration—the difference is crucial and easy to gloss over) may well be 'trumped' in certain situations (but which?) by 'cultural values and traditions'. States are, however, by Article 24(2) to 'take effective and appropriate measures with a view to abolishing traditional practices prejudicial to the health of children', but this in itself is qualified by Article 24(4). This provides that states undertake to promote and encourage international co-operation with a view to achieving progressively the full realization of the rights in Article 24. The elimination of harmful traditional practices, in other words, is seen as the recognition of social or cultural rights, rather than as civil rights, and therefore falls within the realm of progressive obligation.[13] But surely practices which are prejudicial to the health of the child should be a civil right with priority. Article 24(4) also refers to taking particular account of the needs of developing countries. Whilst such traditional practices cannot be seen in terms of 'need', the argument will be couched in terms of the lack of the necessary resources to tackle the question of prevention and protection. There are a number of other references to the culture of the child and to taking account of cultural traditions. There is value in this but also clear dangers. Thus, for example, the assertion by some Islamic states that general or particular international human rights obligations are only to be accepted to the extent that they are consistent with the requirements of the Islamic *Shari'a*—a

---

[13] See, for agreement, D. McGoldrick, 5 *Int. J. of Law and Family* 132, 146 (1991).

specification that has led, under some interpretations of the *Shari'a*, to gross infringements of children's rights.

And yet, although adult values may seem dominant, what has been said so far should be looked at in the context of the rights the Convention protects. The inherent right to life and development. (Art. 6). The right from birth to a name, the right to acquire a nationality and, as far as possible, the right to know and be cared for by his or her parents. (Art. 7). The right to preserve identity. (Art 8).[14] The right of the child not to be separated from his or her parents against their will, except when competent authorities subject to judicial review determine, in accordance with applicable law and procedures, that such separation is necessary for the best interests of the child. (Art. 9). The child is to be given an opportunity to participate in separation proceedings and make his or her views known. (Art. 9)(2). But why is there no right to representation? In England the recent Children Act[15] has strengthened the child's representation by an independent social worker (a guardian *ad litem*) and a lawyer where separation is related to abuse or neglect (in the public law arena, in other words), but not, ironically, in the 'private' realm of marital breakdown, where the protection afforded the child is less than it was previously.[16]

To continue with the rights in the Convention, it goes on to enumerate further the right to express views and for these to be accorded due weight (again, it may be noted, without the right to separate representation) (Art. 12); the rights to freedom of expression, freedom of thought, conscience and religion (Arts. 13 and 14) but states are to respect the rights and duties of parents or legal guardians 'to provide direction to the child in the exercise of his or her right…in a manner consistent with the evolving capacities of the child' (Art. 14)[17]; the rights of the child to freedom of association and to freedom of peaceful assembly (Art. 15) and the right to privacy. (Art. 16). Article 24 recognizes the right of the child to enjoy the highest attainable standard of health and to facilities for the treatment of illness and rehabilita-

---

[14] Inspired by the 'enforced or involuntary disappearance' of children in Argentina since the 1960s.

[15] Passed in 1989, it came into operation in October 14 1991. See section 41. See also the discussion in M. Freeman, *Children, Their Families and The New Law*, Basingstoke, Macmillan, 1997.

[16] Hannah Arendt noted that private and deprivation had the same etymological root (*The Human Condition*, Chicago, University of Chicago Press, 1958 pp 58–67), an appropriate observation in this context. See, further, J. Roche, 'Once A Parent Always A Parent?', *Journal of Social Welfare and Family Law*, 345, 1991 and M. Freeman, 'In The Child's Best Interests?', *Current Legal Problems*, 173, 1992, (and ch. 14).

[17] Including on matters of religion.

tion of health, though not as such the right to food (though malnutrition is to be combated). Children in institutional care have the right to care, protection and treatment of physical and mental health and 'periodic review'. There is, surprisingly in a Convention on the Rights of the Child, no reference to the issue of the consent of the child.[18] The Convention also recognizes the right to benefit from social security and to an adequate standard of living. (Arts. 26 and 27). Art. 28 recognizes the right to education and school discipline is to be administered in a manner consistent with the child's human dignity and in conformity with the Convention. (Art. 28(2). Those who have opposed compulsory education[19] should be re-assured by the way the Convention, in Article 29, states the objectives of education. But when the meaning of this is teased out there are strong real conflicts. Thus, education is to be directed to the development of both cultural identity and values and national values as well as of civilizations different from the particular child's. This is easier said than done, particularly in today's multi-cultural societies.[20] This provision should be looked at in conjunction with that which protects the rights of minority[21] children and children of indigenous origin.[22]

The Convention also recognizes the right to rest and leisure (in Article 31). More significantly, it asserts protection against economic exploitation, (Art. 32) narcotics, (Art. 33) sexual exploitation, (Art. 34), trafficking, (Art. 35) torture and capital punishment. (Art. 37) Children are to be protected against participation in armed conflict, but in reality only those under 15 are covered (Art. 38)—an appalling concession to the norms of so-called international humanitarian law.[23] Many 15-year-olds, it has to be said, and children much younger would wish to fight for their country or their God.[24] But is this right ('the right to die for one's country') one which ought to be rec-

---

[18] See, further, P. Alderson, *Childright*, 73, 7 (1991).

[19] See, for example, M. Duane in (ed.) P. Adams, *Children's Rights*, London, Panther, 1972; J. Kozol, *Death At Any Early Age*, New York, Houghton, Mifflin, 1967.

[20] Some of the problems of which are discussed in S. Poulter, *English Law and Ethnic Minority Customs*, London, Butterworths, 1986.

[21] But 'minority' is not further explained. The Canadian Indian *Lovelace* case. U.N. Doc A/36/40 166 (and see A. Bayefsky (1982) 20 *Canadian YIL* 244).

[22] And see the recent New Zealand legislation, Children, Young Persons and Their Families Act 1989.

[23] And see D. Johnson in M. Freeman and P. Veerman. *The Ideologies of Children's Rights*, Nijhoff, 1992.

[24] See C. P. Cohen (1989) 28 *International Legal Materials*, 1448 at 1451; also Elahi (1988) 19 *Columbia Human Rights Law Rev.* 259.

ognized or is it one so 'irrational' that we ought to dismiss it.[25] Of course, we tolerate mistakes in adults. We cannot take rights seriously unless we accept that someone may have the right to do something that is wrong for him or her to do.[26] Is it possible, then, to justify other standards for children? Elsewhere I have argued that it is.[27] I have defended a limited view of paternalism ('liberal paternalism'). This confines irrationality to actions which could lead to a major, irreversible impairment of interests, a destruction of future life choices. Fighting in armed conflict, even if motivated by a belief that fallen heroes (or heroines) go straight to 'Paradise', seems as good a paradigm example of this as any. There is, finally, 'the right of every child alleged as, accused of, or recognized as having infringed the penal law to be treated in a manner consistent with the promotion of the child's sense of dignity and work'. (Art. 40). A minimum age is envisaged but not universally specified.

This list, whatever its imperfections, has to be accepted as an impressive manifesto on behalf of children. With the qualifications indicated, they are certainly claims, which, given the capacity and opportunity, we would expect children to make on their own behalf. They protect children: they also protect their rights.[28] Thus, the right to 'know' parents in Article 7 and the right to 'preserve his or her identity' can be seen as human rights which transcend basic rights of welfare. Similarly, recognition of freedom of expression and freedom of thought, conscience and religion anticipate a rationally autonomous adulthood.

And Article 5 is crucial to the future of children's rights. It recognizes the need for children's rights to be promoted but, curiously, it places the burden on, in most cases, parents.[29] And States Parties are to 'respect' this role. The assumption is that adults, in particular parents, will promote the rights of children. They are expected to give 'direction and guidance' and this must be aimed towards the 'exercise' of the rights and not their undermining. Article 14 is similarly constructed. But it will not escape attention that those so charged may well have an interest in ensuring that the child does not exercise the rights the Convention accords him or her. The concept 'evolving

---

[25] See M. Freeman, *The Rights and Wrongs of Children*, London, Frances Pinter, 1983, p. 55.
[26] See R. Dworkin, *Taking Rights Seriously*, London, Duckworth, 1978, p. 188–189.
[27] 'Taking Children's Rights More Seriously', *International Journal of Law and The Family*, 6, 52, (1992), and ch. 2.
[28] R. Farson, *Birthrights*, Harmondsworth, Penguin, 1978, p. 9.
[29] And see B. Walsh, 'The UN Convention and the Rights of the Child—A British View' *International Journal of Law and The Family*, 5, 170 (1991).

capacities' is particularly fraught with difficulty. The problem is faced by all legal systems. The English response in the *Gillick* decision in 1985[30] was to accept the child as a decision-making person when he or she had such maturity and understanding. But according to whom? It would seem that the English solution was 'whoever otherwise would be the decision-maker'. And so, in *Gillick* itself, that determination would fall upon the doctor to whom the girl wanting the 'pill' had presented herself. And it could equally well be the school or the housing authority and, in cases of conflict, the court. Whether the child has capacity depends on adult judgment—a view endorsed by the Convention.

This leads to the question of enforcement. The Convention makes provision for the establishment of a Committee on the Rights of the Child. (Art. 43). Members serve in their personal capacity, as independent experts (though no particular expertise in a child-related discipline is required). The first ten elected to serve come from an assortment of countries not especially noted for their recognition of children's rights or, for that matter, rights, but they serve, as indicated, as individuals and not representatives.

The principal function of the new Committee is to operate the system of periodic reporting provided for in the Convention (Articles 44–45). States undertake to submit to the Committee reports on the 'measures they have adopted which give effect to the rights recognized...and on the progress made on the enjoyment of those rights'. The initial report is to be submitted within 2 years of the entry into force of the Convention for the State concerned. Subsequent reports have to be submitted every five years. What turns up on the second anniversary on the 2nd September this year should provide interesting reading. The reports submitted are to indicate 'factors and difficulties', if any, affecting the 'degree of fulfilment' of the Convention obligations. They should also contain sufficient information to provide the Committee with a comprehensive understanding of the implementation of the Convention in that country. States are to make their reports widely available to the public. It will be interesting to see how this is interpreted and how responsive States are to criticisms of implementation. Every two years the Committee is to submit 'reports on its activities' to the General Assembly, through the Economic and Social Council. In addition, Specialised Agencies, UNICEF and other U.N. organs are entitled to be represented at the consideration of the implementation of the Convention provisions which fall within their mandate. They may be invited to submit reports on the implementation of the Convention in the areas within the scope of their

---

[30] [1986] A.C. 112, on which see A. Bainham, 'The Balance of Power in Family Decisions', *Cambridge Law Journal*, 161 (1986).

activities. The Committee 'may' invite Specialised Agencies, UNICEF and 'other competent bodies' as it may consider appropriate to provide expert assistance in the implementation of the Convention in areas within the scope of their respective mandates. 'Other competent bodies' includes a large number of non-governmental organizations concerned with various aspects of children' rights (there were 30 involved in an informal association during the drafting of the Convention). The Committee must, if it considers it appropriate, transmit to the Agencies, UNICEF and the competent bodies any reports from states parties that 'contain a request, or indicate a need, for technical advice or assistance, along with the Committee's observations and suggestions' on these matters. The Committee may recommend to the General Assembly that it requests the Secretary-General of the UN to undertake studies on specific issues relating to children.

And when there are failings? The Committee may make 'suggestions and general recommendations' based on information received. These are to be sent to the state party concerned and reported to the General Assembly, together with any comments from the state party. The phrase 'suggestions and general recommendations' has not been used before in international documents. The International Covenant on Civil and Political Rights used the expression 'general comments'(Article 40), the meaning of which has never been satisfactorily resolved.[31] The practice has been that the 'general comments' adopted by the Human Rights Committee have concerned the general implementation of specific articles of the Covenant. They have not been addressed to problems in specific states or attempted to assess the implementation of the Covenant in a specific state. It may be that the position under the Convention will be different. Article 45(d) implies that the comments deal with the implementation of the Convention in the 'State Party concerned'. But we still need to know the scope of 'suggestions and general comments'.

There is no provision for inter-state complaints or individual complaints. The only implementation mechanism is therefore the reporting procedure. Whether this is successful is dependent on the quality of reports submitted by states, the range and quality of outside information submitted and the ability of the Committee (their critical acumen, their willingness to grapple with the issues, their initiatives on constructive dialogue, what they make of 'suggestions and general comments'). Without being unduly pessimistic, this enforcement procedure looks to be weak. It is not even clear whether the

---

[31] See D. McGoldrick, *The Human Rights Committee: its Role in The Development of The International Covenant on Civil and Political Rights*, Oxford, Oxford University Press, 1991, paras. 3.29–3.38.

General Assembly will discuss the 'suggestions and general recommendations' of the Committee.

How frank will States Parties' reports be? The British government believes that domestic legislation which came into operation last October (the Children Act 1989) meets in all or part (which phrase is not further explained) 13 out of the 40 main articles. That is its interpretation but not the opinion of experts in the United Kingdom.[32] The U.K. ratified the Convention, belatedly in December 1991, but with major reservations (immigration, employment of under-18s, the use of adult jails for young offenders) but many believe ratification to be a token gesture.[33] Little is being done to stem the rise of (let alone eradicate) poverty and deprivation amongst the young. Can we expect the U.K. report to talk to these issues? What account is the Brazilian report going to give of the extermination of street children (about one a day in Rio de Janeiro alone currently)?[34] Perhaps now the Russian report will speak to psychiatric abuse—a recent report[35] has shown 'orphan' and 'oligophrenia' are almost the same word—but would it have done until very recently? And what of the countries which have not, and probably will not, ratify the Convention, the most egregious example of which is the U.S.A.

I would like to see more intensive policing of the Convention. If the fulcrum of enforcement is to be the Committee, let it have more powers. It ought to be a Permanent Bureau. Expertise in child-related disciplines ought to be a pre-requisite . It ought to be pro-active, with the ability to conduct strategic investigations and garner evidence. It ought to have access to children and young people. But I would go further and allow for inter-state complaints and for complaints by individuals who consider themselves aggrieved by shortcomings in the laws or practices of their own country. The model of the European Convention on Human Rights is instructive. Why not a system whereby aggrieved children can complain and seek redress when their State, though a party to the Convention, violates rights contained within it?

The Convention constitutes the end of the beginning, but we are very far from the beginning of the end of our quest to see children treated as persons accorded equal respect and concern.

---

[32] As reported in *Community Care*, 896/7 2–9 January 1992, p. 5.
[33] For example, P. Newell, *The UN Convention and Children's Rights in the UK*, London, National Children's Bureau, 1991.
[34] See *The Independent*, 30 November 1991 and *Childright* 71, 11, 1990.
[35] See Report from Christian Solidarity International, Leigh-on-Sea, Essex, 1991.

Towards Empowerment

We can improve the structure of the Convention by giving it more 'teeth'; we can add to the rights contained within it, for example by diluting the emphasis on adult values; we can make the rights more specific—an example might be restating Article 19 so that a child was given the right not to be hit as in the Nordic countries and Austria. All such measures would be valuable. But we have to consider also the limits of this approach. I do not, as some do,[36] reject the rights approach. Rights are 'valuable commodities',[37] but that does not mean they are things or possessions. They refer to doing more than having. They refer to social relationships that enable or constrain action. Rights are relationships: they are institutionally defined rules specifying what people can do in relation to one another. A child's life is not necessarily improved by giving him or her more 'rights'.

The Convention presupposes an agenda of liberal legalism and provides according to this agenda abstract legal mandates. Formal legal guarantees of the sort that the Convention envisages States Parties adopting have value, but as a catalyst rather than as a source of change. Surely we can learn from the experiences of other marginalized 'social groups'—women, for example. In how many countries with equal pay legislation is there equal pay?[38] How well have those countries with legislation outlawing sex discrimination coped with pregnancy?[39] Nor should we overlook the importance of interpretation and experiences of interpretation in other areas. Again, using the perspective of women as a model, look at the way the Constitution of the U.S.A. has been interpreted: there is a right to bear arms (Amendment 2), but not, if poor, to obtain an abortion,[40] a right to sell 'artistically redeeming' pornographic magazines,[41] but no right to equal educational expenditures.[42]

---

[36] See F. Olsen (1992) 6 *Int. J. of Law and the Family* 192.

[37] R. Wasserstrom's expression: see *Journal of Philosophy*, 61, 628 (1964). See also L. Lomasky, *Persons, Rights and The Moral Community*, New York, Oxford University Press, 1987.

[38] Certainly not in the United Kingdom, where some still on average earn two-thirds of the average male wage.

[39] See D. Rhode, *Justice and Gender*, Cambridge, Mass., Harvard University Press, 1989.

[40] *Harris* v. *McCrae* 448 US 297 (1980).

[41] *Miller* v. *California* 413 US 15 (1973).

[42] *San Antonio Independent School District* v. *Rodriguez* 411 U.S. 1 (1973).

Nor should it be overlooked that the Convention, in laying down rights for children, has to a large extent[43] attempted to extend access rather than to alter the basic fabric of the existing institutions.

Furthermore, the Convention has done little to reduce the equation that being dependent (as to a greater or lesser extent all children must be) means being deprived of basic rights. Dependency implies a sufficient justification to suspend basic rights to privacy, respect and individual choice. Being dependent implies being legitimately subject to the often arbitrary and invasive authority of social service providers and other public and private administrators, who enforce rules with which the dependent must comply, and otherwise exercise power over the conditions of their lives. In meeting the needs of the dependent, often with the aid of social scientific disciplines,[44] welfare agencies also construct those needs themselves. Medical and social service professionals know what is good for those they serve, and those who are dependent do not have the right to claim to know what is good for them.[45]

Dependency should not be a reason to be deprived of choice and respect. An important contribution of feminist moral theory has been to question the firmly embedded assumption that moral agency and citizenship rights require a person to be independent, totally autonomous. Feminists, such as Carol Gilligan in *In A Different Voice* and Marilyn Friedman,[46] have questioned this deeply held assumption. It is, they argue, derived from a specifically male experience of social relations which values competition and solitary achievement. It is inappropriately individualistic. Dependence is a basic human condition.[47] We have all been dependent and many of us have passed through phases of dependency or will do so. The Convention, using largely an autonomy model, would as much as possible give children the opportu-

---

[43] I think the Article on the content of educational instruction (Art. 29) cannot be so construed.

[44] A. Wolfe, *Whose Keeper?—Social Science and Moral Obligation*, Berkeley, Calif., University of California Press, 1989.

[45] N. Fraser, 'Women, Welfare and the Politics of Need Interpretation', *Hypatia: A Journal of Feminist Philosophy* 2 103–22 (1987); A. Ferguson, 'On Conceiving Motherhood and Sexuality: A Feminist Materialist Approach' in (ed.) J. Trebilcot, *Mothering: Essays In Feminist Theory*, Totowa, J. J. Rowman and Allanheld.

[46] 'Care and Context In Moral Reasoning' in (ed.) C. Harding, *Moral Dilemmas: Philosophical and Psychological Issues In The Development of Moral Reasoning*, Chicago, Precedent, 1985.

[47] *Cf.* N. Hartsock, *Money, Sex and Power*, New York, Longman, 1983, ch. 10.

nity to be independent. But it is also possible, as feminism argues,[48] to accord respect and participation in decision-making to those who are dependent. The new English Children Act, in emphasizing 'partnership' and recognizing the value of partnership with children, takes account of this. And if practice falls in with the blueprint it will be a real achievement. But we must look beyond the specific to the more general. And this is where ombudswork comes in.

It is a loose, mongrel term. The flyer for this conference admitted the term was 'undefined'. It is clear though, that its concern is with the politics of empowerment. It embraces the variety of activities and functions. The emphasis, says the flyer, is on 'creating possibilities for children to realize their human rights as human beings'. A vision is projected of children as subjects of the law.

I argued earlier in this paper that rights were not possessions so much as relationships. What of power? It has been common to talk of this in terms of distribution.[49] But conceptualizing powers in distributive terms means conceiving power as something to be possessed in greater or lesser amounts. But power too is a relation rather than a thing.[50] The exercise of power often depends on the possession of certain resources—money, knowledge,[51] military equipment—but it is wrong to confuse the resources with the power itself. The power consists in a relationship between the person who exercises it and others through whom he or she communicates intentions and meets with their acquiescence. Further, a distributive understanding of power as a possession of particular individuals or groups over-simplifies by ignoring the supporting and mediating function of third parties.[52] Judges are powerful but their power depends on the practices of others (police, prison warders, lawyers, executioners etc.). As far as children are concerned school teachers are powerful but their power also is interlocked with that of others (parents, social workers, the media and other ideological forces). A distributive understanding of power misses the structural phenomena of domination. By domination is meant the structural or systemic phenomena which ex-

---

[48] V. Held, 'A Non Contractual Society' in (eds.) M. Hanen and K. Nielsen, *Science, Morality and Feminist Theory*, Calgary, University of Calgary Press, 1987.

[49] See, for example, W. Connolly, *The Terms of Political Discourse*, Oxford, Martin Robertson, 1983.

[50] See P. Bachrach and M. Baratz 'Two Faces of Power' in (eds.), R. Bell, D. Edwards and H. Wagner, *Political Power*, New York, Free Press, 1969.

[51] See M. Foucault, *Power/Knowledge*; Brighton, Harvester Press, 1980.

[52] T. E. Wartenburg, *The Forms of Power: An Essay in Social Ontology*, Philadelphia, Temple University Press, 1989.

clude people from participating in determining their actions or the conditions of their action. Domination has to be understood as structural because the constraints that people experience are usually the intended (sometimes the unintended) product of the actions of a network of many people, as in the examples just given. The structured operation of domination whose resources the powerful draw upon must be understood as a process. Foucault's elegant grasp of this is worth reproducing:

> What, by contrast, should also be kept in mind is that power, if we do not take too distant a view of it, is not that which makes the difference between those who exclusively possess and retain it, and those who do not have it and submit to it. Power must be analysed as something that circulates, or rather something which only functions in the form of a chain. It is never localised here or there, never in anybody's hands, never appreciated as a commodity or piece of wealth. Power is employed and exercised through a net-like organisation. And not only do individuals circulate between its threads; they are always in the position of simultaneously undergoing and exercising their power'.[53]

The empowerment of children is not then a question, or simply a question, of redistribution of power. Putting children on to decision-making committees—school boards or community homes—only scratches the surface and does little to undermine entrenched processes of domination. More is clearly required—ultimately a re-thinking of the culture of childhood. This has happened before: childhood is not a decontextualized construct.[54] Concepts of childhood have undergone sea changes in early modern times[55] and then again with the emergence of industrial capitalism.[56] What contribution can ombudswork make to this cultural evolution?

This question can be answered on a number of levels. It can seek to discover the social and historical causes of oppression. The answers to this will sometimes be culture and economy-related (for example, child prostitution in Thailand or the Philippines), but not always so. It can foster the establishment of child-oriented institutional structures within countries. Institutions which will probe and question both existing and mooted laws

---

[53] *Op. cit.*, note 51, p. 67.
[54] See A. James and A. Prout, *Constructing and Reconstructing Childhood*, Basingstoke, Falmer Press, 1990.
[55] See P. Ariès, *Centuries of Childhood*, London, Jonathan Cape, 1964; S. Shahar, *Childhood In The Middle Ages*, London, Routledge, 1990.
[56] H. Cunningham, *The Children of The Poor*, Oxford, Blackwell, 1991; V. A. Zelizer, *Pricing The Priceless Child*, New York, Free Press, 1985.

and practices, which will examine critically the impact of structures and designs on the everyday lives of children and not just those institutions targeted at children (schools, youth courts, neglect and abuse procedures) but also those which hitherto have paid scant regard to the interests of children (shops, the city,[57] the environment generally). On a third level, ombudswork can concentrate on child advocacy at grass-roots level—the representation of the child in trouble, the lawbreaker, the abused child, the child in conflict with his or her parents. The three levels are inter-related.

The first is the most theoretical, but it is also the most difficult work to sustain. It requires the collective enterprise of historians, sociologists, lawyers, educationalists, psychologists, anthropologists, theologians and other disciplines. It involves research into the past and a critical probing of existing attitudes which seek their intellectual strength in historical practices. The history of childhood, a nightmare from which we are only now beginning to awake, was, until recently, a gap in our cultural knowledge. We need revisionist history to challenge the often superficial images of childhood that appear in official versions of the truth. This first level of ombudswork is a subsidiary concern of this conference and yet its importance cannot be underestimated. From an understanding of the cultural foundations of childhood will come the ammunition to destroy the faces of oppression, and out of the rubble a reconstruction of childhood with the child de-reified and accorded the concern and respect owing to him or her as a person and as a participant in social processes. For anyone concerned with the degradation and pollution of children that we call child abuse, this should strike a chord. For, surely we now recognize that the roots of child abuse lie not in parental psycho-pathology or in socio-environmental stress (though their influences cannot be discounted), but in a sick culture which denigrates and depersonalizes, which reduces children to property, to sexual objects so that they become the legitimate victims of both adult violence and lust.[58]

The first level of ombudswork is important for three reasons. It will give us an understanding of how childhood has been constructed and reconstructed and in so doing may, as just indicated, throw light on major wrongs from which children suffer (and not just abuse and neglect, the examples just given, but attitudes to their wrongdoing, methods of social control of them and even questions such as abortion). Secondly, it will assist the tasks of those who undertake ombudswork on the other two levels. Thirdly, and in

---

[57] Colin Ward, *The Child In The City*, New York, Pantheon, 1978.
[58] S. Nelson, *Incest: Fact and Myth*, Edinburgh, Stramullion Press. Particularly valuable in the context of Ombudswork is M. Bray, *Poppies On The Rubbish Heap*, Edinburgh, Canongate Press, 1991.

combination with the other two levels of ombudswork, it will work towards a day when its work will no longer be necessary. This day is far in the future and none of us will ever see it. It will work towards a time when with a new cultural revolution childhood is so constructed that the problems for which ombudswork is developing will no longer exist.

The second level of ombudswork concerns the establishment and development of child-oriented institutional structures. A number have been mooted and some, like the ombudsperson itself in Norway,[59] New Zealand[60] and Costa Rica are in operation. It by no means follows that the same model is appropriate for all countries. Different political structures and different states of development may require different responses.

A Minister for Children has often been postulated. One such suggestion was formulated by Brian Jackson in 1976.[61] Only New Zealand and Norway have introduced a ministry as such with responsibilities specifically for children. A categorical answer to whether a Minister for Children would be a good idea is not really possible. Much clearly depends on the structure of government in the country—if, on nothing else, the relationship between the government and the governed. To argue that a Ministry for Children would be of no more than symbolic significance is to say nothing in countries where departmental responsibility is itself no more than a veneer or smokescreen. But even in those countries where there is some devolution of decision-making, would a Ministry for Children really empower children? In Britain it is feared that the Minister would necessarily be committed to Government policy. S/he might be as much concerned with excusing decisions as with making them. In reality all ministers should be prepared to see the impact on governmental decisions on children and to represent children's interests.

It is because this is over-idealistic that I favour, and proposed in 1987, the child impact statement.[62] This idea has now been taken up by Peter Newell and Martin Rosenbaum.[63] It is important that all those who formulate policy should be compelled to consider the impact their policies have on children. I use the word 'policy', rather than 'law', deliberately. It is wider and embraces a congeries of activities which affect our lives, intentionally or unin-

---

[59] See M. G. Flekkøy, *A Voice For Children*, London, Jessica Kingsley, 1991; G. Melton (1991) 23 J. Int. L. Case Western Reserve.

[60] See G. Maxwell, I. Hassall and J. Robertson, *Toward A Child and Family Policy for New Zealand*, Wellington, Office of the Commissioner for Children, 1991.

[61] *New Society.*

[62] *Children and Society*, 1, 299 (1977–8).

[63] *Taking Children Seriously*, London, Calouste Gulbenkian Foundation, 1991.

tentionally. All too rarely is consideration given to what policies formulated at the level of government, bureaucracy or local state level do to children. This is all the more the case where the immediate focus of the policy is not children. But even in children's legislation the unintended or indirect effects of changes are not given the critical attention they demand. But where the policy is not 'headlined' children, immigration policy or housing policy for example, the impact on the lives of children is all too readily glossed over. Even where the effect on children could so easily be predicted, South Carolina's policy of incarcerating drug-addicted pregnant women is a good contemporary illustration,[64] the impact that this is likely to have is not seriously thought through by those responsible for developing the policy.

It is equally important that the actual effects of policies in action should be regularly monitored. And it is not just legislation which needs to be so examined. The policies and practices of local state institutions, education authorities, housing departments, social services committees which directly penetrate the lives of children should also be rigorously scrutinized. So should the activities of the courts (and not just juvenile or youth courts) and the police (the impact of policing on ethnic minority youth has given concern in a number of countries).

But who should be undertaking this work? I have long favoured an institution along ombudsman lines—it matters not what it is called. Målfrid Flekkøy's account, *A Voice For Children*,[65] puts the case eloquently and I would not wish to add to it. The concept is spreading, though as yet only to countries with relatively small populations. The case for, what they call, a Children's Rights Commissioner has now been put in the United Kingdom by Peter Newell and Martin Rosenbaum in a pamphlet entitled *Taking Children Seriously*.[66] The purpose of the Commissioner (I still prefer the term 'ombudsperson', because of its associations in the public mind) would be to influence policy-makers and practitioners to take greater account of children's rights and interests, to promote compliance with the minimum standards set by the U.N. Convention and to seek to ensure that children have effective means of redress when their rights are disregarded. The Commissioner would highlight failures to respect rights and interests, conduct formal investigations, analyse and comment upon proposed government policies (the child impact statement in particular is stressed), to conduct and commission research linked to policy development, and monitor the use by

---

[64] See Glink (1991) *Univ. of Illinois L.R.* 533; Lewin, *New York Times*, 5 February 1990 A.14.
[65] See, in particular, ch. 5 ('Lessons To Be Shared').
[66] See also their article in *Childright*, 78, 7 (1991).

children of complaints procedures. It is not envisaged that the Cc would deal with individual complaints. This may be wise, in... would require a vast bureaucracy, or a filtering process such as exists with the ombudsman in the U.K. with complaints to him coming through an M.P. But I would hope that the Office would develop strategies to consider embedded injustices reflected in group complaints.

The third level of ombudswork is child advocacy at grass-roots level. There are different forms of advocacy, legal advocacy, legislative advocacy, administrative advocacy.[67] But, as Knitzer[68] has argued, the underlying assumptions of advocacy programmes are the same:

(i) Advocacy assumes people (in this case children) have, or ought to have, basic rights.

(ii) Advocacy assumes rights are enforceable by statutory, administrative or judicial procedures.

(iii) Advocacy efforts are focused on institutional failures that produce or aggravate individual problems.

(iv) Advocacy is inherently political.

(v) Advocacy is most effective when it is focused on specific issues.

(vi) Advocacy is different from the provision of direct services.

As such advocacy activities embrace all three levels of ombudswork. I wish to concentrate briefly on child advocacy in the context of courts. Again it cannot be stressed too greatly that any model of this has to be related to the legal culture of the society: what kind of process it uses (adversarial or inquisitorial for example), what values underline it (how independent of state structures are the courts?), the presence or absence of a basic law and so on. Nevertheless, we may draw out some general considerations.

It is surprising how little attention has been given to what is entailed by the representation of children in courts. Yet the concept of representation in the political arena is well-trodden.[69] As in the political context, we may ask—what is the function of representation? Is it to represent the child's best interests (his or her welfare) or to advocate his or her wishes, to assist the furtherance of the child's autonomy? In a sense the dualism fits neatly

---

[67] See, further, G. Melton, *Child Advocacy*, New York, Plenum Press, 1983.
[68] 'Child Advocacy: A perspective', *Amer. J. of Orthopsychiatry* 46, 200, 1976.
[69] For example, Hannah Arendt, *Representation*.

into the debate about children's rights itself. Is this concerned with protecting children (with their 'salvation') or with protecting their rights (with their 'liberation', with autonomy)? An understanding of function and role is crucial in determining who the advocate should be. If the 'mandate' view is adopted (that is the representative should carry out the wishes of the child) the legal profession would seem to be the best qualified. If, on the other hand, the 'independence' view is adjudged most appropriate, social workers may be thought the ideal choices. A categorical answer is difficult to elicit: there are so many variables (the age of the child; the type of evidence being adduced; the orientation to be adopted by the representative (should it be legalistic, social work, educational?)

The question has also been asked as to whether there is 'anything unique'[70] about the role of lawyering for the child. Three Canadian researchers[71] have identified three models. The adversary role is traditionally combative—it envisages a lawyer using skills within the framework of a trial governed by strict rules of law and procedure to convince a court that the cause argued for has merit and should prevail. The *amicus curiae* model is, to quote Bernard Dickens,[72] 'comparably legalistic but neutral as to outcome'. It envisages assistance to the court to resolve a conflict by presenting another perspective from the strictly partisan cases presented by the opposing parties. The social work model is intended to help the child 'by proposals, concession and collaboration to put him or her into the most satisfactory condition that can be achieved'. But should lawyers adopt the roles of other professionals? And should their roles be conceived differently when they are representing children as opposed to adults? There seems to be an assumption that they should, but this, I would suggest, is yet another instance of the way we project our reluctance to see children as participants in processes which affect them.

The conflict is well illustrated by the dilemmas faced by the lawyer who is asked to advocate a course of action by a child when those presenting the welfare case for that child would wish a different view to be presented. In England this is graphically portrayed in sex abuse cases, in particular where an adolescent girl is represented by a solicitor and a guardian *ad litem*, the latter an independent social worker. What the guardian *ad litem* deems to be in the girl's best interests may not cohere with the arguments she wishes her advocate to present. The problem is rendered the more complex by the fa-

---

[70] See Note, 'Lawyering for the Child', *Yale Law Journal*, 87, 1126.
[71] Dootjes, Erickson and Fox, *Canadian J. of Criminal Corrections*, 14, 132 (1972).
[72] See (eds.) M. Baxter and M. Eberts, *The Child and The Courts*, 1978 at p. 280.

mous *Gillick* ruling and the so-called *Gillick* competency test it has spawned. Is she of sufficient understanding and maturity to make the decision for herself? And, in the context of the example I have given, do intellectual maturity and emotional maturity necessarily coincide? The problem of the 'sexually traumatized' raises the issue of representation and of what is to be represented in acute form.[73]

There are, then, three levels of ombudswork, all important. The significance of the first can all too easily be underestimated. The importance of the second is undeniable. The third is very valuable for the individual child, but of limited value to children as a whole. The system emerges intact and oppression is but little undermined.

THE VOTE?

A paper on empowerment which says nothing on extending the vote to children may be thought peculiarly defective. One which considers it, only to reject it may be considered self-defeating. The arguments for extending the suffrage to children are difficult to counter. Indeed, some of those postulated against voting rights for children could be used equally to disenfranchise many adults.[74] In the past I have cautioned against seeing 'votes for children' as a panacea.[75] It is not so much that I am opposed to the principle as that I believe we could all too readily deceive ourselves that suffrage rights amounted to empowerment. In doing so the other strategies depicted here might be given less attention, and some might fall by the wayside. Nevertheless, I believe further extensions of the suffrage are inevitable and to be welcomed and I would like to think that those countries which lowered the age of voting to 18 in the 1970s gave consideration to a further lowering to 16.[76]

But this in itself would not guarantee empowerment. Women have had the vote for more than half a century in Britain. There has even been a government headed by a woman Prime Minister. But it has to be accepted that democracy is, as yet, far from 'engendered'.[77] Children need, as

---

[73] And now complicated by the Court of Appeal's ruling in *Re R* [1991] 4 All E.R. 177 that appears to suggest that a *Gillick*-competent girl can say 'yes' to medical treatment, but her decision to say 'no' can be gainsaid by a parent or wardship court. See ch. 15.

[74] G. Scarre, *Philosophy*, 55, 117 (1980).

[75] In *The Rights and Wrongs of Children*, 1983, p. 2.

[76] Brazil has done so (*Childright*, 46, 3, 1988). On the views of MPs in the UK see *Childright*, 46, 13, 1988.

[77] See A. Phillips, *Engendering Democracy*, Oxford, Polity Press, 1991.

women have and continue to need, advancement as a group, and giving more of them the vote is unlikely to achieve this.

Conclusion

Hitherto, the concentration has been on encoding rights. What we must now set our minds to is finding ways of giving children a voice. Only with empowerment will come true recognition of children as persons entitled to equal concern and respect.

CHAPTER 5

The Limits of Children's Rights

There can be no doubt that children are amongst the most vulnerable and powerless members of our societies to-day. In the past thirty years, but not before, we have been reminded of this each time a dramatic incident of child abuse is brought to public attention. In Britain, if not elsewhere, the sad face or logo of Maria Colwell,[1] a victim at the hands of her step-father, still haunts the consciousness of society. It is perhaps fitting that the vulnerability of children should be associated with parental violence (and, now of course, sexual abuse) because for so long the argument prevailed that parents were the guardians of their children's welfare making the need for and development of children's rights otiose. It would not render children's rights advocacy redundant even were it true (as, of course, it is for most children most of the time) for the love, nurture, care and protection afforded children would still be that which particular parents deemed appropriate. Children are in this sense at their parents' 'mercy' and, as Joel Feinberg put it,[2] 'no amount of love and compassion' is an adequate substitute for the ability to demand what is ours by right.

THE IMPORTANCE OF RIGHTS

Rights are important—few would now deny this. They have been called 'valuable commodities',[3] important moral coinage. In Bandman's[4] words, they 'enable us to stand with dignity, if necessary to demand what is our due without having to grovel, plead or beg'. If we have rights we are enti-

---

[1] J. Howells, *Remember Maria*, Butterworths (1974).
[2] 'Duties, Rights and Claims', *American Philosophy Quarterly* 3, 137 (1966).
[3] Per R. Wasserstrom, 'Rights, Human Rights and Racial Discrimination', *Journal of Philosophy* 61, 628 (1964). See also A. Buchanan, 'What's So Special About Rights?' *Social Philosophy and Policy* 2(1), 61 (1984).
[4] 'Do Children Have Any Natural Rights?' *Proceedings of the 29th Annual Meeting of Philosophy of Education Society* (1973), p. 234 at p. 236.

tled to respect and dignity: no amount of benevolence or compassion can be an adequate substitute.

The children's rights movement, in some shape or form, has been with us for a century or more. An article with the title 'The Rights of Children' appeared as early as June 1852.[5] In France Jean Vallès attempted to establish a league for the protection of the rights of children in the aftermath of the Paris Commune.[6] This was also the period of the child-saving movement and thus of the development of juvenile justice, as well as of the establishment of compulsory education. But, at this stage, it is the 'investment motive'[7] which is critical to the thinking behind children's rights: society's concern for the child is seen very much in terms of the child's usefulness to society. Children are objects of intervention rather than legal subjects. Talk of children's rights has been couched predominantly in child-saving language, in terms of salvation.[8] Its essential concern has been with protecting children, individual children, rather than with upholding the rights of children in general. And, although the distinction between two approaches to children's rights, between the 'nurturance' and 'self-determination'[9] orientation, has now been widely recognized, it is still the former that largely characterizes public debate and social policy.

It is in part because of this that concern for children is still often firmly rooted in the individual child rather than children in general. With advocacy of children's rights it is not a question of protecting a particular child against an abusive or uncaring adult. The children's rights movement has now moved on to a plane where what is in issue is institutional discrimination, not a shortfall in parental or other adult behaviour.

THE IMPORTANCE OF CHILDREN'S RIGHTS

There are still those who argue that, however important rights are, it is not necessary to recognize as such children's rights. Where such arguments are put, they tend to employ one of two myths.

---

[5] By, improbably, one Slogvolk (see *Knickerbocker*, No. 36 (1852), p. 439).
[6] On which see T. Zeldin, *France 1848–1945*, Oxford University Press (1973).
[7] Per P. B. Mayer, 'The Exploitation of the American Growing Class', in D. Gottlieb (ed.), *Children's Liberation*, Prentice Hall (1973), p. 51.
[8] See C. R. Margolin, 'Salvation versus Liberation: The Movement for Children's Rights in a Historical Context', *Social Problems*, 22, 441 (1978).
[9] See C. M. Rogers and L. S. Wrightsman, 'Attitudes Toward Children's Rights: Nurturance or Self-Determination', *Journal of Social Issues* 34 (2), 59 (1978).

One, to which brief reference has already been made, idealizes adult-child relations: it emphasizes that adults (and parents in particular) have the best interests of children at heart. Those who argue in this way tend, like Goldstein, Freud and Solnit[10] or indeed the British government which was recently responsible for major children's legislation,[11] to adopt a *laisser-faire* attitude towards the family.[12] Thus, the only right for children which Goldstein *et al.* would appear to accept is the child's right to autonomous parents.[13] A policy of minimum coercive intervention by the state accords, they maintain, with their 'firm belief as citizens in individual freedom and human dignity'.[14] But *whose* freedom and *what* dignity does this uphold? It certainly would not appear to be those of the child. The English Children Act of 1989 very much reflects this philosophy.[15] It is somewhat unfortunate that in an age when so much abuse is being uncovered that governments and writers should cling to the 'cereal packet' image of the family.

The second myth can be captured more succinctly. It sees childhood as a golden age, as the best years of our life. Childhood is synonymous with innocence. It is a time when we are spared the rigours of adult life; it is a time of freedom, of joy, of play. The argument runs that, just as we avoid the responsibilities and adversities of adult life in childhood, so there should be no necessity to think in terms of children's rights. Whether or not the premise underlying this is correct or not (and I think the carefree nature of a child's life can be exaggerated), it represents an ideal state of affairs, and one which ill-reflects the lives of many of to-day's children and adolescents.

There are countries which to-day are systematically exterminating children as if they were vermin (Brazil and Guatemala are two well-documented examples).[16] Poverty, disease, exploitation are rife in every

---

[10] *Before The Best Interests of The Child*, Free Press, New York (1979).

[11] Children Act 1989. Similar ideology is found in the recent New Zealand Children, Young Persons and their Families Act 1989.

[12] To some associated with "privatization". See, for example, A. Bainham, 'The Privatisation of the Public Interest in Children', *M.L.R.* 53, 206 (1990) and M. Freeman 'In the Child's Best Interest?' (1992) *C.L.P.* 173, and *post*, ch. 14.

[13] *Op. cit.*, note 10, p. 18.

[14] *Ibid.*, p. 12.

[15] And see A. Bainham, *Children, Parents and The State*, London, Sweet & Maxwell (1988). See also L. Fox Harding, *Perspectives in Child Care Policy*, Harlow, Longman (1991).

[16] See A. Vittachi, *Stolen Childhood*, Oxford, Polity Press (1989). According to a recent report a child a day is "exterminated" in the streets of Rio de Janeiro (*The Times*, No-

part of the globe: the briefest of glances at the annual *State of the World's Children* publication soon reveals that.[17]

Even in the developed world the lives of children are fraught with deprivation. Thus, the latest data to 'emerge' from Britain reveals that, in a decade in which awareness of children's rights has heightened, the number of children living in poverty has more than trebled. In an authoritative report[18] (written by Jonathan Bradshaw for the National Children's Bureau) the conclusion is drawn that during the 1980s 'children have borne the brunt of the changes that have occurred in the economic conditions, demographic structure and social policies of the United Kingdom'.[19] More than three and a half million children in Britain (that is 33 per cent of the total number) live in poverty with 6 per cent of all children living below the poverty line (that is 830,000 children). For contrast the percentage of those in 1979[20] living in poverty was 10 per cent.

The case posited to attack those who espouse children's rights does not, therefore, command respect. Rights are important because possession of them is part of what is necessary to constitute personality. Those who lack rights are like slaves, means to others' ends, and never their own sovereigns.[21] It is surely significant that when we wish to deny rights to those who have attained chronological adulthood we label them (blacks in South Africa, the mentally retarded) children. To be a child, one does not have to be young. Foucault's aphorism[22] that 'madness is childhood' rings very true. Childhood is, of course, a social construct, a man-made phenomenon: those in authority determine who is a child.[23] That they have not done so with any consistency or, it would seem, coherent thought cannot detain us here.

To say that rights are important, and important also for children, is not to gainsay the crucial part which other morally significant values, such as love, friendship and compassion, have and play in life's relationships.

---

vember 30, 1991). Even in New Zealand children have been described as an "endangered species". See L. Max, *Children—Endangered Species*, Penguin, Auckland (1990).

[17] Published by Oxford University Press on behalf of UNICEF.

[18] *Child Poverty and Deprivation in the UK*, National Children's Bureau, London (1990).

[19] *Ibid.*, p. 51.

[20] The year when the Conservative Government came to power.

[21] See I. Kant in translation by H. Paton, *The Moral Law*, Hutchinson, London (1948) (originally published in 1785).

[22] *Madness and Civilisation*, Tavistock, London (1967), p. 252.

[23] See A. James and A. Prout, *Constructing and Reconstructing Childhood*, Falmer Press, Basingstoke (1990).

John Kleinig[24] is surely correct to argue that 'a morality which has as its motivation merely the giving of what is due...is seriously defective'. But, short of a cultural revolution beyond our wildest dreams, rights will remain important.

And, it will remain important to recognize children's rights. As Howard Cohen put it,[25] when he explained the importance of associating the children's rights movement with other rights' movements (women, civil rights *etc.*), '"rights" is a militant concept to the extent that it is used as part of the ideology in a campaign for social change'. It is generally agreed that denial of rights is a bad thing, so that something should be done about it. 'Rights' enables one to talk in terms of 'entitlements'.

RIGHTS AND DIGNITY

Ronald Dworkin[26] has not given any thought to children's rights but his thesis can be generalized. It is his thesis that if persons have moral rights to something, they are to be accorded these rights even if a utilitarian calculation shows that utility would be maximized by denying it to them. He invokes Rawls's *A Theory of Justice*[27] to illuminate the moral foundations of the rights thesis. Rawls proposes a methodology of reflective equilibrium whereby we try to fashion formulations of moral principles to the coat of moral judgement until we no longer feel inclined to change our judgments to fit the theory or our theory to fit the judgments. The ideal is a perfect fit. The mechanism for this reflective equilibrium is the social contract model: it conceives of persons in the 'original position' behind a 'veil of ignorance' (and thus ignorant of their identity, interests and entitlements) choosing the structure of the society in which they will live. Dworkin believes that these individuals 'have a responsibility to fit the particular judgments on which they act into a coherent program of action'.[28] He sees this as analogous to the way lawyers construct principles from precedent. Thus interpreted, he believes the contractual mechanism can be dropped: it is nothing more than a moral metaphor. Instead, he be-

---

[24] 'Mill, Children and Rights', *Educational Philosophy and Theory* 8, 14 (1976).
[25] *Equal Rights for Children*, Littlefield, Totowa, New Jersey (1980), p. 45.
[26] See, in particular, *Taking Rights Seriously*, Duckworth, London (1978).
[27] Published by Harvard University Press, Cambridge Massachusetts in 1972. Rawls has refined his theory since. For a review of later developments see R. Arneson 'Symposium on Rawlsian Theory of Justice', *Ethics* 99, 695 (1989).
[28] *Op. cit.*, note 26, p. 160.

lieves we can, and should, focus on the idea that all other principles derive from the principle of equal concern and respect for each person.[29]

For Dworkin, anyone who proposes to 'take rights seriously' must accept the ideas of human dignity and political equality. He argues in favour of a fundamental right to equal concern and respect, and against any general right to liberty. The advantage of his so doing, as acknowledged by Mackie,[30] is that the right to equal concern and respect is a final and not merely 'a *prima facie* right' in the sense that one person's possession or enjoyment of it does not conflict with another's. Dworkin puts this forward as a 'postulate of political morality',[31] a fundamental political right: governments must treat citizens with equal concern and respect.

RIGHTS—FROM WHERE?

It may be thought that, however persuasive, this argument does not take us far enough. The question still not answered is where rights come from?[32] Why do we 'have' the rights we do? In posing this question, I am asking why we have the 'moral' rights we have (and assuming that we have some), and not posing the same question about legal rights. It is obvious why we have legal rights: on *one* level the answer is that they are set out in laws (the right to consult a lawyer when in police custody[33] or the right, if adopted, to see one's original birth certificate);[34] on *another*, we have them because historical struggles to acquire them have been successful (for example the right to vote or to strike). But it is less clear why we have the moral rights we do. What 'is' there when there 'are' rights? There must be, Narveson argues, 'certain features or properties of those who "have" them such that we have *good reason to acknowledge* the obligation to refrain from interfering with, or possibly to sometimes help other bear-

---

[29] This is developed in *op. cit.*, note 26, chs. 7, 9, 11–13. It is noteworthy that in Janusz Korczak's Declaration of Children's Rights the "right to respect" was placed only after "the right to love". On the reverse (more common) see A. Miller, *The Drama of Being a Child*, London, Virago (1988), ch. 3.

[30] 'Can There Be a Rights-Based Moral Theory?' in J. Waldron (ed.), *Theories of Rights*, Oxford, Oxford University Press (1964), p. 168.

[31] *Op. cit.* note 26, p. 272.

[32] See L. W. Sumner, *The Moral Foundation of Rights*, Oxford, Clarendon Press (1987).

[33] In England See Police and Criminal Evidence Act 1984, s. 58.

[34] In England, see Adoption Act 1976, s. 51. But it is not an absolute right (see *R* v. *Registrar General ex parte Smith* (1991) 1 FLR 255.

ers to do the things they are said to have the right to do, or have those things they are said to have a right to have'.[35]

All then hinges on 'good reason', on moral argument. It is interesting, if surprising, that Robert Nozick,[36] an arch-apostle of rights, should do no more than assert peremptorily that 'individuals have rights'. A common justifying principle is sought in relating rights to interests.[37] Thus, Feinberg writes[38] that 'the sort of beings who can have rights are precisely those who have (or can have) interests.' Though superficially attractive this argument ultimately fails. More than the existence of an interest is required to establish a right. Conversely, so may less for if rights only exist when interests are expressed, we would have to deny rights to the comatose,[39] the mentally handicapped[40] and to babies (as well, of course, to trees,[41] rocks and animals[42] but then those who do this conflate our moral responsibilities to lesser beings, and to the environment into rights-type language with unfortunate consequences).

Another argument often put forward is purely formal. It is that all persons ought to be treated alike unless there is good reason for treating them differently.[43] Dworkin accepts this: he sees the right to treatment as an equal as the morally fundamental idea. It is that which requires that each person be accorded the same degree of concern and respect as every other person. The problem with this argument lies in deciding what constitutes a 'good reason' for treating persons differently. Gender and colour are now almost universally accepted as indefensible distinctions, but age, of course, continues to ground (at both ends, be it noted) legitimate discrimination in the opinions of many. The principle looks egalitarian but it can backfire and become an argument used to undermine egalitarianism.

---

[35] 'Contractarian Rights' in R. G. Frey (ed.), *Utility and Rights*, Oxford, Blackwell (1984). p. 161 at 164.
[36] *Anarchy, State and Utopia*, Blackwell, Oxford (1974).
[37] See for example, H. J. McCloskey, 'Rights', *Philosophical Quarterly* 15, 115 (1965).
[38] 'The Nature and Value of Rights', *Journal of Value Enquiry* 4, 243 (1970).
[39] See H. Rolston, 'The Irreversibly Comatose: Respect for the Sub-Human in Human Life', *Journal of Medicine and Philosophy* 7, 337 (1982).
[40] See M. D. A. Freeman, 'Sterilising the Mentally Handicapped', *post*, ch. 16.
[41] See C. Stone, *Should Trees Have Standing*, Los Altos, California, William Kaufmann (1974).
[42] See T. Regan, *The Case for Animal Rights*, Berkeley, University of California Press (1983). And using Rawls, D. Van De Veer 'Of Beasts, Persons and the Original Position', *The Monist* 62, 368 (1979).
[43] See P. Westen, *Speaking of Equality*, Princeton University Press, Princeton, New Jersey (1990).

Dworkin himself, attempts to identify the existence of a moral right against the state when for 'some' reason the state would 'do wrong' to treat a person in a certain way, 'even though it would be in the general interest to do so'.[44] But, since what it is 'wrong' for the state to do is what the state has a duty not to do, Dworkin appears to be defining rights in terms of duties. It is 'wrong' for the state to act in a particular way when the individual has a 'right' on which state action of a particular sort would illegitimately trample. The circularity of the argument will be readily apparent.

The Dworkinian thesis then takes us so far—but not, it seems, far enough. Equality by itself cannot explain what Dworkin is trying to explain, namely that rights as such 'trump'[45] countervailing utilitarian considerations. Something more is needed: the concept of autonomy may supply this. A plausible theory of rights may take account not just of equality but of the normative value of autonomy, the idea that persons as such have a set of capacities that enables them to make independent decisions regarding appropriate life choices. The deep structure of the rights thesis is equality and autonomy. Kant expressed this by asserting that persons are equal and autonomous in the kingdom of ends. It is the normative value of equality and autonomy that lies at the root of the Rawlsian contractarian conception. To see people as both equal and autonomous is to repudiate the moral claim of those who would allow utilitarian calculations of the greatest happiness of the greatest number to prevail over the range of significant life choices which the rights thesis facilitates and enhances.

Utilitarianism, by contrast, insists that the pattern of individual life choices be overridden if others are thus made better off. To treat persons as utilitarianism requires is to focus almost obsessively on aggregated pleasure as the only ethically significant goal. But this is to ignore the crucial fact that persons experience pleasure, and that pleasure has human and moral significance only in the context of the life that a person chooses to lead. It is the rights thesis that protects the integrity of that person in leading his or her life.

One of Dworkin's insights was to link Rawlsian contractarian theory to the language of rights. One of his failings was not to appreciate that both notions at the root of Kantian moral theory (equality and autonomy) were equally morally significant. When we take both equality and autonomy seriously we are back at the contractarian thinking to be found in Kant and

---

[44] *Op. cit.*, note 26, p. 139.
[45] *Ibid.*, p. 178.

centrally in Rawls's morality. The reason is that equality is best expressed as an original position of equal beings, and that autonomy cannot be expressed better than as the choice of those equal beings under a 'veil of ignorance'.

CHILDREN AND DOUBLE STANDARDS

But what is the relevance of this to children? For, so the argument may be proffered, children are different. They (or at least some of them) have lesser abilities and capacities, are more vulnerable, need nurturance and protection. This, it may be thought, justifies the upholding of the double standard which is deeply embedded in our social practices and well-established in our laws, with one set of rights for adults (providing them with opportunities to exercise their powers) and another for children (providing them with protection and at the same time keeping them under adult control).

A double standard can be considered unjust where the distinction upon which it relies is not relevant: thus, for example, the colour of a person's skin is not a distinguishing mark to justify giving persons of one colour the right to vote and denying this right to persons of another (as institutionalized by the system of *apartheid* in South Africa or, indirectly, through the use of differential literacy tests in the United States before the 1964 Civil Rights Act). Is age then a relevant or a suspect point of distinction? Part of the problem lies in the fact that if we are going to give adults rights and deny them to children we must have a precise place at which to draw the line between the two (or at least that is received wisdom). Most developed countries currently draw the line at 18[46] (though it was common, previously, to set the line at 21 (for no other sound reason than that 21 was the age at which medieval England deemed a man strong enough to bear full armour and fight as a knight). But no one can seriously believe there is a real distinction (in powers, competence etc.) between someone of 18 years and a day and someone of 17 years and 364 days.[47] The drawing of the line is arbitrary. The law abhors uncertainty and has a tendency accordingly to think in dichotomies[48] (guilty/not guilty, though the Scots with a greater penchant for indeterminacy retain a 'not proven'

---

[46] Though this does not preclude conferring legal capacities to do specific things (make contracts, get married are examples) at earlier ages and 21 was the age of majority for homosexual activity until 1994.

[47] *Cf.* H. Cohen, *op. cit.*, note 25, p. 49.

[48] See V. Aubert, *In Search of The Law*, Oxford, Martin Robertson (1983), p. 93.

verdict; liable/not liable; male/female—most legal systems are ill at ease with transsexualism).[49] Similarly, the law categorizes persons into adults with full capacity and minors with little or none.

But the arguments adduced to deny children and adolescents rights can equally well be produced to deny those of 'mature' years those very same rights. Take, for example, the right to vote. In England, and in most developed countries with sufficient political stability to allow political choice, the right to vote is exercisable at the age of eighteen. However, many 16-year-olds, and doubtless many children of a younger age, are politically aware and are capable of making an informed political choice. We do not give them the vote because there is a widely-held belief that children in general are incompetent to exercise the responsibilities and discharge the obligations associated with full citizenship. But, if competence is the test, a by-no-means insignificant proportion of children must be granted full political status and a larger number of adults would have to be disenfranchised. Apart from incompetence, the other argument adduced is the child's lack of experience and understanding. It suggests, or at least implies, that these are gained during the traditional period of childhood. This argument typically adduces the fact (if fact it be) that children lack foresight, that given the capacity to make decisions they will make disastrous ones. But is this not the case with adults too? Look at the governments voted in by adults in Britain, the United States, Israel in recent years! If experience and/or understanding is the criterion, many children would have the vote and many adults would not.

A further argument would justify denying children the franchise in terms of a belief that the decisions of children are not based on rational considerations. Rationality can be judged from a number of perspectives, but it seems common that those who attack children's rights do so from utilitarian considerations. Thus, Scarre[50] (justifying paternalism and not specifically the withholding of democratic rights) argues for intervention in an individual's affairs 'when there is reason to believe his decisions are not based on rational considerations, and that they are likely to result in a diminution of his stock of existing good, or underachievement of his possible stock of good'. To Scarre 'rational actions are those which are directed to maximizing the expected utility of the agent'. 'In addition', he says, 'actions backed by rational decisions typically manifest themselves as elements of a systematic approach adopted by the agent for maximising

---

[49] See I. Kennedy, *Treat Me Right*, Oxford University Press (1983), p. 93.
[50] See 'Children and Paternalism', *Philosophy* 55 (1980), 117.

his good'. Scarre's concept of rationality is unduly confined but leaving that aside, can it really be said that adults' actions are always motivated by rational considerations? Indeed, it would not be difficult to find examples of decisions motivated by rational considerations which did not maximize the agent's utility, nor were expected to do so.

It is relatively easy to demolish the arguments adduced to support the double standard employed in our treatment of adults and children. It is also not difficult to show that children to-day occupy a different status from that of the young in earlier centuries and in different cultures: the line between adulthood and minority was not drawn as clearly by earlier generations.[51] Thus children in past ages participated in what we designate as adult activities (work, sex, leisure) in ways that would shock to-day. What conclusions should we draw from this? If moral argument and history appear to be on the side of the enfranchisers and liberators, are we to admit that we are wrong? Should we abandon the distinction between children and adults, even if this means, as Hafen put it, 'abandoning children to their rights'?[52]

LIBERATING CHILDREN

Few, it would seem, would go quite this far. Even the most extreme proponents of children's liberation would preserve some protective legislation, though wisely they would look at all claims to protect children with scepticism.[53] But the conclusion is nevertheless drawn by some that, if children worked in earlier societies then the sort of restrictions we find on child labour in developed societies should be removed. Thus Martin Hoyles[54] in *Changing Childhood* can write of the 'crucial separation which modern children *suffer* (my emphasis) is the separation from work'. He can write this from the perspective of England (incidentally in 1979, IYC, in a book welcomed by the U. K. Association for the International Year of the Child). In England to-day, if anything, far too many children are *forced*

---

[51] See P. Ariès, *Centuries of Childhood*, J. Cape, London (1962). But *cf.* L. Pollock, *Forgotten Children*, Cambridge University Press, Cambridge (1983).

[52] 'Puberty, Privacy and Protection: the Risks of Children's Rights', *American Bar Association Journal* 63, 1383 (1977).

[53] An excellent new history is H. Cunningham, *The Children of The Poor*, Oxford, Blackwell (1991).

[54] Writers and Readers Publishing Co-operative, London (1979), p. 5.

to work,⁵⁵ allegedly part-time and often in conditions of exploitation—and they are lucky compared with children in much of the third world.⁵⁶ Certainly, when children had the 'right' to work (when 'Victorian values'⁵⁷ so beloved of Thatcher and her cronies prevailed) they suffered. Leading liberationists, like Farson⁵⁸ and Holt,⁵⁹ would give children the right to work: in Farson's view it is part of the 'a right to economic power'.⁶⁰

But they would give the child the right to do, in general, what any adult may legally do. Thus Holt writes:⁶¹ '*In important matters, nobody can know better than the child himself*'. So central is this to his thought that he italicizes the sentence to emphasize its significance. But he recognizes that young children are egocentric: they are 'animals and sensualists; to them what feels good *is* good. They are self-absorbed and selfish.... They are barbarians, primitives'.⁶² Farson's manifesto is strikingly similar and so are his arguments. Thus, overriding all 'birthrights', he argues, is the right of self-determination. Children should have the right to decide 'the matters which affect them most directly'.⁶³ That these arguments are heard less volubly to-day attests to the experiences of the last decade when manifold forms of child exploitation, not least sex abuse, have captured the public imagination.

On the other hand, it must be asked how many of the structures, institutions and practices created, particularly during the twentieth-century and often under the influence of the child-saving or protectionist ideology, to 'protect' children actually achieve this goal.⁶⁴ Has this really been achieved, for example, by the juvenile court,⁶⁵ whatever its good inten-

---

[55] See C. Pond and A. Searle, *The Hidden Army: Children at Work in the 1990s*, London, Low Pay Unit (1991).

[56] The Anti Slavery Society publishes a continuing series on child labour.

[57] The expression was first used by R. Boyson in *Down With The Poor* (1971). Mrs Thatcher first used it in a speech reported in *The Daily Telegraph*, 16 April 1983.

[58] *Birthrights*, Penguin, Harmondsworth (1978).

[59] *Escape from Childhood,* Penguin, Harmondsworth (1975).

[60] *Op. cit.*, note 58, p. 154.

[61] *Op. cit.*, note 59, pp. 175–176.

[62] *Ibid.*, p. 114.

[63] *Op. cit.*, note 58, p. 12.

[64] See L. Taylor, R. Lacey and D. Bracken, *In Whose Best Interests?*, London, Cobden Trust and Mind (1979).

[65] See, for example, H. Parker *et al.*, *Receiving Juvenile Justice*, Oxford, Blackwell (1982). The juvenile court was renamed the 'youth court' in England in 1992.

tions? Or by the institutions[66] to which children in need of protection are sent? Or by the whole panoply of powers developed to protect children from abuse and neglect? Do systems of mandatory reporting, such as operate in the United States[67] and now elsewhere including parts of Europe,[68] or child 'protection registers' protect children or do they serve rather to ease adult conscience and offer insurance policies to social workers and others involved in the control of the problem?[69] The examples could be multiplied. But the essential failing of these systems as of others is our failure (that is the failure of all of us, and not just professionals) to recognize the moral integrity of children and treat them as persons entitled to equal concern and respect. Thus, for example, few countries only (the Nordic ones and Austria)[70] have now accepted that it is morally wrong to hit children—legislation which is likely to have a greater impact upon the conquest of child abuse than any system of reporting, registers or care legislation.[71]

THE LIMITS OF AUTONOMY

In looking for a children's rights programme we must thus recognize the limits of protection: we must also note the dangers inherent in the liberationist prospectus. Too often writers on children's rights (like lawyers) have dichotomized: there is either salvation or liberation, either nurturance or self-determination—in Farson's pithy phrase[72] the one protects children, the other their rights. To take children's rights seriously requires us to take seriously both protection of children and recognition of their autonomy.

---

[66] See the official account of 'pin-down': A. Levy and B. Kahan. *The Pindown Experience and the Protection of Children.* Stafford, Staffordshire CC (1991).

[67] In the US it is reckoned that, despite the law, only a third of all instances of child abuse are reported. (K. Burgdorf, *Recognition and Reporting of Child Maltreatment*, Rockville, Md, Westat (1980).

[68] See J. Christopherson, 'European Child-Abuse Management Systems' in O. Stevenson (ed.), *Child Abuse*, Brighton, Wheatsheaf (1989), p. 74. Also see further K. Jones in J. Hutton *et al.* (eds.) *Dependency To Enterprise*, London RKP (1991) at p. 34.

[69] See A. Solnit 'Child Abuse: The Problem' in J. Eekelaar and S. Katz (eds.) *Family Violence*, Toronto, Butterworths (1978), p. 143.

[70] See the discussion in P. Newell, *Children are People Too*, London, Bedford Square Press (1990). And also now Cyprus.

[71] See M. Freeman, *The Rights and Wrongs of Children*, London, Frances Pinter (1983), pp. 111–114.

[72] *Op. cit.*, note 58, p. 9.

The view I put forward is premised on the need to respect individual autonomy and to treat persons as equals. It is not dependent on actual autonomy but on the capacity for it. For an understanding I turn again to Rawls's theory of justice.[73] It is, as I have indicated,[74] the normative value of equality and autonomy which form the substructure of the Rawlsian conception of the social contract. The principles of justice which Rawls believes we would choose in 'original position' are equal liberty and opportunity, and an arrangement of social and economic inequalities so that they are both to the greatest benefit of the least advantaged and attached to offices and positions open to all under conditions of fair equality and opportunity.[75]

The principles confine paternalism[76] (the philosophy at the root of salvation or protection) without totally eliminating it. Parties to a hypothetical social contract would know that some human beings are less capable than others; they would know about variations in intelligence and strength, and they would know of the very limited capacities of small children and the rather fuller, if incomplete, capacities of adolescents. They would take account of the insights from cognitive psychology, which suggests that children even as young as 12 (and certainly children of 14) are as capable of making decisions about their lives as adults are for them.[77] They would also bear in mind how the actions of those with limited capacities might thwart their autonomy in a future time when their capacities were no longer as limited.

These considerations would lead to an acceptance of interventions in people's lives to protect them against irrational actions. But what is to be regarded as 'irrational' must be strictly confined. Subjective values of the would-be protector must not intrude. Irrationality must be defined in terms of a neutral theory capable of accommodating pluralistic visions of the 'good'. Further, we should only be prepared to dismiss an action as irrational when it is manifestly so, 'severe and systematic', as David Richards

---

[73] This was set out in *A Theory of Justice*, Cambridge, Mass., Harvard University Press (1971). It has since gone through refinement and reformation. This article from the 1971 statement, though draws in later developments.

[74] *Ante*, p. 90.

[75] In later Rawlsian writing parties in the hypothetical deliberations of the original position are now identified as giving priority to their Kantian interests in the development and exercise of their moral powers of rational autonomy and fair dealing.

[76] See J. Feinberg, 'Legal Paternalism', *Canadian Journal of Philosophy* 1, 105 (1971).

[77] See W. Damon, *The Social World of The Child*, San Francisco, Jossey Bass (1977); J. J. Conger, *Adolescence and Youth: Psychological Development in a Changing World*, New York, Harper and Row (1973).

puts it,[78] and when taking the action will lead to major irreversible impairment of interests. We must tolerate mistakes, for, as Dworkin rightly observes,[79] 'someone may have the right to do something that it is wrong for him to do'. We cannot treat persons as equals without also respecting their capacity to take risks and make mistakes. We would not be taking rights seriously if we only respected autonomy when we considered the agent was doing the right thing. But we also do not recognize a child's integrity if we allowed him to take an action (such as using hard drugs or refusing to attend school) which would seriously impair the attainment of full personality and development subsequently. The test of 'irrationality' must also be confined so that it justifies intervention only to the extent necessary to obviate the immediate harm, or to develop the capacities of rational choice by which the individual may have a reasonable chance of avoiding such harms.

The question we should ask ourselves is: what sort of action or conduct would we wish, as children, to be shielded against on the assumption that we would want to mature to a rationally autonomous adulthood and be capable of deciding on our own system of ends as free and rational beings? We would, I believe, choose principles that would enable children to mature to independent adulthood. One definition of irrationality would be such as to preclude action and conduct which would frustrate such a goal. Within the constraints of such a definition we would defend a version of paternalism. This version is not paternalism in its classical sense for within those perimeters there would be little room for children's rights at all. Furthermore, it has to be stressed that this version of paternalism is a two-edged sword in that, since the goal is rational independence, those who exercise constraints must do so in such a way as to enable children to develop their capacities.

All paternalistic restrictions require moral justification. In many cases it is not difficult to adduce sufficient convincing reasoned argument. Thus, it is not difficult to present the case for protecting children against actions which may lead to their death or serious physical injury or mental disability. Nineteenth century legislation making it illegal for children to go down coal mines or be employed as chimney sweeps or undertake arduous work in factories (if paternalistic—for there were undoubtedly other sources also at play) can thus be defended without much trouble. So, I think, can laws designed to protect children from sexual exploitation and

---

[78] 'The Individual, The Family and The Constitution', *New York University Law Review* 55, 1 at p. 18 (1980). See also his 'Rights and Autonomy', *Ethics* 92, 13 (1981).

[79] *Op. cit.*, note 26, pp. 188–189.

harassment. There are clear dangers that the suggestions of Holt, Farson and others that a child's right to self-determination includes the right to a sexual relationship with whomsoever he or she pleases could become a paedophile's charter.[80] On the other hand 'ages of consent', whether pitched at an age like 16 (as in England) or 12 (as in Dutch legislation) are meaningless: the crucial factor is the presence or absence of exploitation, so that age *difference* may be of greater significance than the age of the child. A system of compulsory education (and, concomitantly, restrictions on employment) can also be defended, contrary to the arguments of some liberationists, though, it should be stressed, by 'education' is not necessarily meant education as conventionally defined. This has often been too narrow and not directed towards the development of capacities required for autonomous self-determination.

What should legitimize all these interferences with autonomy is, what has been called,[81] 'future-oriented consent'. The question is: can the restrictions be justified in terms that the child would eventually come to appreciate? Looking back, would the child appreciate and accept the reason for the restriction imposed upon him or her, given what he or she now knows as a rationally autonomous adult?

The dichotomy drawn is thus to some extent a false divide. Dichotomies and other classifications should not divert us away from the fact that true protection of children does protect their rights. It is not a question of whether child-savers or liberationists are right, for they are both correct in pointing out part of what needs recognizing, and both wrong in failing to see the claims of the other side. To take children's rights seriously requires us to take seriously nurturance *and* self-determination, demands of us that we adopt policies, practices and laws which both protect children and their rights. Hence the *via media* I propose.[82]

Thus far this paper has looked at the limits to children's rights as these are expressed in the two paradigmatic orientations of protection and self-determination. But the limits to children's rights can be viewed from a quite different perspective as well.

---

[80] See T. O'Carroll, *Paedophilia: The Radical Case*, Boston, Alyson Publishers (1980). *Cf.* J. Ennew, *The Sexual Exploitation of Children*, Oxford, Polity Press (1986).

[81] By G. Dworkin 'Paternalism' in R. Wasserstrom (ed.), *Morality and the Law*, Belmont, California, Wadsworth (1972), p. 77.

[82] And see M. D. A. Freeman, *The Rights and Wrongs of Children*, London, Frances Pinter (1983).

PUTTING RIGHTS INTO PRACTICE: SURMOUNTING LIMITS

First, crucial though it is to see children's rights recognized, we must be careful not to mistake the words for the deeds. The passing of laws is only a beginning: it is a signal that must be taken up by society's institutions. That both national laws (albeit patchily) and international conventions recognize the language of rights and concepts inherent in them like dignity as applied to children is important. The case that children have rights has to a large extent been won: the burden now shifts to monitoring how well governments honour the pledges in their national laws and carry out their international obligations.

Take national laws. What impact has the recognition that juveniles deserve 'due process' had on juvenile court practices.[83] The *Gillick* ruling[84] in England that once a child had sufficient intelligence, maturity and understanding and could weigh up the 'pros and cons' of a decision-making process (in this case about contraception, but the ruling may be generalized), she was in a position to make the decision herself. This ruling has influenced, though not consistently, the most recent children's legislation in England (the Children Act 1989),[85] but the extent to which it has influenced practice is debatable. In England too the courts have established that access (visitation, contact) is now a child's right,[86] but contact is still forced upon children in unfavourable circumstances, in ways which suggest the honouring of the right in the breach rather than the observance.[87] We have to guard against mere tokenism. We must be wary for it is easy to take the words for the act and think that because the words have been enacted the condition of children's lives has changed.

The same point can be made of the United Nations Convention. It is an important achievement, particularly given the cultural diversity and widely different legal systems and traditions of the States represented in the General Assembly of the United Nations. But enacting the Convention is one thing: implementing it in the different countries of the world another. There are clearly difficulties. It is doubtful whether poorer countries can by themselves afford the Convention. They have larger populations and

---

[83] In the light of which see G. B. Melton, 'Taking *Gault* Seriously: Toward a New Juvenile Court', *Nebraska Law Review 68*, 146 (1989).

[84] *Gillick* v. *West Norfolk and Wisbech Area Health Authority* [1986] A.C. 112. But see the back-tracking in *Re R* [1991] All E.R. 177.

[85] See, for example, sections 1, 43, 44.

[86] See *M* v. *M* [1973] 2 All E.R. 81 and sections 8 and 34 of the Children Act 1989.

[87] There are numerous examples of this until very recently.

smaller incomes and a higher percentage of their populations tend to be children. And, though it tends to be assumed that the developed world should have no difficulty in complying, that cannot be taken for granted.

The United Kingdom for one will not find it easy to convince its critics, both within and without, that it can comply with a number of the most basic of the protections set out in the Convention. For example, Articles 26 (on social security), 27 (on a standard of living adequate for the child's physical, mental, spiritual, moral and social development) and, in some parts of the country, 28 (on the right to education—there are parts of London, for example, within a couple of kilometres of the Bank of England and the Stock Exchange, where primary education is often not available). Indeed, doubt has been cast upon whether the U.K. collects statistics in sufficient detail to demonstrate whether it can meet the rights or not.[88] But, statistics or not, there is little doubt that it does not comply with Article 10 which commits States to deal with applications by a child or his/her parents to enter or leave for the purpose of family reunification 'in a positive, humane and expeditious manner'. The administration of the immigration laws falls far short of this ideal.[89] Indeed, there were hints that Article 10 might prove the stumbling-block to the UK ratifying the Convention. This obstacle was overcome by entering a reservation, but this has not had much impact on poverty, social security standards and education. And, if the U.K. cannot overcome these problems, what of the poorer nations?

There is a danger, of course, that the Convention may become nothing more than a way of keeping the developed world up to scratch. Much of the world has as much chance of implementing the Convention as sending its citizens to the moon. Unfortunately, most countries would also rather do the latter. Of course, one of the reasons why it is important that we have an international Convention is that the world as a community, having shown a commitment to the rights of children, should now take on international responsibility to ensure that all countries are able to carry out their obligations to children. But international social justice is a pious aspiration and is likely to remain such.

Legislation, national and international, is important as a symbol. This can neither be gainsaid nor underestimated. But the true recognition of children's rights requires implementation in practice. Un-implemented,

---

[88] By Jonathan Bradshaw, *Op. Cit.*, note 18, pp. 3–4, 14–15, 52.
[89] See, further, D. McGoldrick, 'The United Nations Convention on the Rights of the Child,' *International Journal of Law and the Family* 5, 132 (1991); B. Walsh, 'The United Nations Convention on the Rights of the Child: A British View', *International Journal of Law and the Family* 5, 170 (1991).

partially implemented or badly implemented laws (and this applies equally to international legislation) may actually do children more harm than good.

Secondly, the passing of laws can have unfortunate side-effects and unintended consequences. Prohibition in the U.S.A. was not intended to promote the interests of the Mafia. Laws which restrict abortions are not intended, via the crime tariff, to promote the back street abortion. Rights can too easily backfire. Reform movements intended to enhance children's rights and the concomitant development of professional structures to implement such reforms often generate their own sets of problems and these can, not unnaturally, have deleterious effects on children's rights.

The reforms of one era are apt to become the problems of the next. Many examples could be given: the invention of the IQ test,[90] development of the juvenile court,[91] the practice of cautioning juveniles and thus diverting them from formal processes. Looked at in this way, can we be sure that an injection of rights into the juvenile court system (more 'due process') would not at the same time lead to an increase in more informal 'justice without trial',[92] or that more rights for children in the divorce process would not be used as a stick to control their mothers?[93] This is not to advocate caution in furthering children's rights, but care in so doing, and to recommend adequate surveillance of the institutional practices of those to whom the task of operationalizing children's rights is entrusted. And it may be doubted whether the structure to be established to oversee children's rights within the Convention is adequate within these terms.

Thirdly, rights without services are meaningless. As Monrad Paulsen wrote,[94] in relation to laws regarding the reporting of child abuse, 'no law can be better than its implementations, and implementation can be no better than resources permit'. In many, indeed most, countries children get far too little of the cake that is handed around. In the U.S.A. the phrase the

---

[90] See, S. Rose, L. J. Kamin and R. C. Lewontin, *Not in Our Genes*, Harmondsworth, Penguin (1984), ch. 5, where the purposes of Binet in 1905 are described as 'entirely benign' (p. 84).

[91] Described as the best plan 'for the conservation of human life and happiness ever conceived by civilized man' (C. W. Hoffman in J. Adams (ed.), *The Child, The Clinic and The Court*, New York, New Republic (1927), p. 266).

[92] J. Skolnick, *Justice Without Trial*, Wiley, Chichester (1966).

[93] Note the emphasis is on the 'primary caretaker' and its impact on women. See M. Fineman, 'The Politics of Custody and Gender' in C. Smart and S. Sevenhuijsen, *Child Custody and the Politics of Gender*, London, Routledge (1989).

[94] 'The Law and Abused Children' in R. Helfer and C. Kempe, *The Battered Child*, University of Chicago Press, Chicago (1974).

'feminization of poverty'[95] has been coined and popularized: families headed by women are said to constitute the 'new poor'. The point can be generalized. There is little point creating an improved legal framework, recognizing the existence of children's rights and even heightening rights-consciousness, unless resource allocation is addressed and redressed. Ultimately, the question of rights for children dissolves into questions of distributive justice.[96]

IMPLEMENTING RIGHTS

Where next? The recognition of children's rights, particularly on the international level, is a major advance. But, as just indicated, rights need implementation. The states, the institutions, must adapt their practices to fit in with the new ideology. On the level of national systems, we need to develop institutions like the Norwegian children's ombudsman[97] to make an ongoing assessment of the impact of policies and practices on children. Independent organizations with power and a commitment to promote the interests of children are vital if noble ideals are not to perish on the altar of political expediency. Within institutions themselves such as welfare agencies, the development of monitoring and complaints agencies[98] and advocacy services along the lines of the 'children's rights officer' pioneered in England by Dr Mike Lindsay in Leicestershire is to be commended.[99]

On the international level, it may be doubted whether the Convention pays enough attention to these problems. The implementation of the Convention is to be governed (as is so much national legislation) by the principle of the 'best interests of the child' (Article 3), though this is not further explained and is, of course, a rather indeterminate notion.[100] A ten-

---

[95] By Diana Pearce, 'Welfare Is Not *For* Women: Why The War on Poverty Cannot Conquer the Feminization of Poverty' in L. Gordon (ed.), *Women, The State and Welfare*. University of Wisconsin Press (1990), p. 265.

[96] See D. Wikler, 'Paternalism and the Mildly Retarded', *Philosophy and Public Affairs* 8, 377 (1979).

[97] See M. G. Flekkøy. *A Voice For Children*, London, Jessica Kingsley (1991).

[98] In England, this process has received an impetus from the Children Act 1989 (s. 26(3)) but see M. Lindsay 'Complaints Procedures and Their Limitations', (1991) *J. S. W. F. L.*, 432.

[99] See M. Lindsay, 'The Rights of The Child', *Panel News* (IRCHIN) 9, 10 (1989).

[100] And see R. Mnookin, 'Child-Custody Adjudications: Judicial Functions in the Face of Indeterminacy', *Law and Contemporary Problems* 39(30, 226 (1975).

member committee supervises the implementation of the Convention by States which are parties to it. This committee consists of 'experts of high moral standing and recognized competence in the field': they serve in their personal capacity. (Article 43). State Parties are required to submit written reports to the Committee 'on the measures they have adopted which give effect to the rights recognised herein, and on the progress made on the enjoyment of those rights' (Article 44). It is to be assumed, in line with practice elsewhere, that these reports will be discussed by the General Assembly, though, surprisingly, the Convention is silent as to this. The emphasis in the Convention is on assisting State Parties to meet their obligations rather than on penalizing non-compliance. Specific provisions (in Article 45) permit reference of requests for technical assistance directly to UNICEF and specialized agencies. These agencies and bodies are, unusually, given a role in the Committee's monitoring process.

These measures create an innovative structure of enforcement but, I fear, an incomplete one. If the concept of an Ombudsman for children can be operationalized in a national context even in a supposedly third world country like Costa Rica, why not in an international one too?[101] If systems for reviewing child complaints can be advocated within domestic orders, why not a system whereby aggrieved children can complain and seek redress when their State, though a party to the Convention, violates rights contained within it?[102] Perhaps these concepts are too ambitious for a nascent development like international children's rights. But these are directions in which we must ultimately look.

---

[101] See Flekkøy, *op. cit.*, note 97, p. 197–199.
[102] As under the European Convention on Human Rights.

Conclusion

Children's rights, in a famous aphorism, was once described as a 'slogan in search of a definition'.[103] It has got well beyond that stage now but it has a lot further to go if children's lives are to be measurably improved. It is often said that you can judge a society by its concern and treatment of its less privileged citizens. The same must now be said about the world community.

---

[103] By H. Rodham, 'Children Under the Law', *Harvard Educational Review* 43, 487 (1973).

CHAPTER 6

English Law and the United Nations Convention on the Rights of the Child

When Lloyd de Mause referred to childhood as a "nightmare"[1] he wrote in very general terms, but many would claim that childhood as experienced by English children has come close to this description. Of course, things have changed since the graphic portrayals in Victorian novels such as *Jane Eyre, David Copperfield, The Water Babies* and *The Way of All Flesh*,[2] but these changes in child-rearing and in attitudes have been recent and are, perhaps, not all that profound. It is with this historical understanding in mind that I come to appraise the question of children's rights in England.

There are references to the importance of children's rights in English case law[3] from the 1970s onwards. The United Kingdom, it is true, has ratified the U.N. Convention,[4] albeit belatedly, although its support for the Convention was half-hearted, with a number of reservations being entered.[5] An aura of complacency greeted its ratification—the government minister in charge, Virginia Bottomley, saying publicly on several occasions that "of course" English law went further than the Convention. She was referring principally to the Children Act of 1989,[6] which has been hailed as each previous Children Act as a "children's charter".[7] As we shall see, there are features of the Act which highlight a child's autonomy, but other values dominate the Act and, it may be thought, trump children's

---

[1] *The History of Childhood* (London: Souvenir Press, 1976), p. 1.
[2] See P. Coveney, *The Image of Childhood* (Harmondsworth: Penguin, 1967).
[3] For example, *M* v. *M* [1973] 2 All E.R. 81, the first decision to hold that access to a parent is a child's right. On 'access' ('contact') as a child's right see further ch. 8.
[4] See B. Walsh (1991) 5 *International Journal of Law and Family* 170.
[5] Notably on immigration and citizenship.
[6] On which see M. D. A. Freeman, *Children, Their Families and The Law* (Basingstoke: Macmillan, 1992). A new edition is to be published in 1998.
[7] This was particularly so as regards the Children Act 1975.

rights.[8] The judiciary has continued to assert, as did one of its number, Lady Justice Butler-Sloss in the *Cleveland* report, that children are "persons and not objects of concern".[9] Yet this principle has not been upheld consistently, even by judges, like Butler-Sloss, who proclaim it most vociferously.[10]

This chapter examines some of the key provisions in the Convention and appraises English law and practice in the light of them. In taking this approach, my intention is not to endorse the Convention as the final word on children's rights. There are provisions in it, often reflections of international compromise,[11] which could be re-drafted to show distinct improvements. But that is not the goal of this chapter. It is to show ways in which English law can be improved in the light of, what is currently, world consensus on the status of children. The UN Committee on the Rights of The Child has already castigated the British government for failing children in nearly every aspect of their lives.[12] It voiced serious concern about the number of children living in poverty, as well as about social welfare cuts. The Committee is alarmed at the number of children begging and sleeping on the streets: accounts of 'street children' usually concentrate on the 'developing world'.[13] The report does have positive things to say: it welcomes the Children Act of 1989 and initiatives on bullying in schools, cot deaths and the sexual abuse of children. But it expresses concern on 16 different issues, ranging from treatment of children as young as ten under Northern Ireland's emergency powers legislation to the extent of child poverty and the plight of child refugees (the latter problem since aggravated by new legislation on asylum seekers[14]). It is critical of the law which allows children to be hit[15] and of the plans to set up detention centres for offenders aged 12 to 14.[16] It calls for the age of criminal responsibility to be raised. It wants children to have greater

---

[8] See L. Fox Harding (1991) *Journal of Social Welfare and Family Law* 179, 285. *Cf.* ch. 14.

[9] Report of *Inquiry into Child Abuse in Cleveland* Cm. 412 (H.M.S.O.1988).

[10] For example in *Re B* [1992] 2 FLR 1, 5.

[11] See D. Johnson in M. Freeman and P. Veerman, *The Ideologies of Children's Rights* (Dordrecht: Martinus Nijhoff, 1992), p. 95.

[12] United Nations, *Concluding Observations of The Committee on the Rights of The Child: United Kingdom of Great Britain and Northern Ireland*, CRC/C/15 Add. 34 (1995).

[13] See Judith Ennew, *Outside Childhood: Street Children's Rights* in Bob Franklin (ed.), *The Handbook of Children's Rights* (London: Routledge, 1995), p. 201.

[14] See The Immigration and Asylum Act 1996.

[15] In particular Children and Young Person Act 1933 s. 1 (7).

[16] See, further, on this ch. 12.

rights in the education system.[17] The government's response to this criticism—'Britain can hold its head up high on child welfare, and every parent knows that'[18] is hardly likely to convince.

The chapter does not purport to be exhaustive of the issues raised. Each article of the Convention could occupy a paper itself. All that is attempted here is to highlight problems, to point to shortcomings and to suggest improvements and modifications in English law and practice.

THE BEST INTERESTS OF THE CHILD

Article 3 of the Convention is, together with Article 12, arguably the most important provision in the Convention. It provides in sub-paragraph 1:

> In all actions concerning children, whether undertaken by public or private social welfare institutions, courts of law, administrative authorities or legislative bodies, the best interests of the child shall be a primary consideration.

It will be observed that the Convention says that the children's best interests are "a primary consideration", not *the* primary consideration or *the paramount* consideration. It is regrettable that the Convention does not set a *standard* as high as that found in English law.[19] Where the child's interests are paramount, they "determine" the course to be followed.[20] But, on the other hand, the *scope* of the provision far exceeds the range of decisions within the remit of English law set out in the Children Act 1989.

English law applies the paramountcy principle only to courts and not even to all court decisions. In adoption the child's welfare is only the "first consideration,"[21] though this is in line with the U.N. standard. In divorce proceedings, the child's welfare is not considered at all, though it is the "first consideration" (again congruent with the U.N. standard) when

---

[17] It talks of children being consulted over the running of their school.

[18] *Per* John Bowis, the health minister responsible for children, quoted in *The Guardian*, January 28, 1995. See also Virginia Bottomley, 'Safe in Our Hands', *The Guardian*, 28 December, 1994 (criticized in an editorial 'Facts of Family Life' the same day). Also valuable is Gerison Lansdown, 'Minor Offences', *The Guardian*, 18 January, 1995, which anticipates the Committee's criticisms. The government's own report is also instructive: see *The U.K.'s First Report to the U.N. Committee on the Rights of the Child* (London: H.M.S.O. 1994).

[19] See Children Act 1989 s.1 (1).

[20] *J* v. *C* [1970] AC 668, 710 *per* Lord MacDermott.

[21] Adoption Act 1976 s. 6.

matters of money and property are considered[22]—at least that is the theory, for the Child Support Act of 1991 has clearly prioritized the rights of taxpayers over the interests of children.[23] In situations where one parent is trying to oust the other form the family home, because of violence or other molestation, the child's welfare is merely one consideration.[24] The Court of Appeal was quick to point out that the Children Act had not changed the law on this.[25] Even in wardship, where the "golden thread" is that the child's welfare comes "first, last and all the time,"[26] the courts have found questions relating to children which are not governed by the paramountcy rule.[27] The paramountcy principle does not govern applications for secure accommodation either.[28] Nor, pursuant to s. 17(1) of the Children Act, are local authorities obliged to treat the welfare of individual children as their paramount consideration.[29] It has also been held on several occasions[30] that the child's welfare is not paramount when determining whether to restrict a publication that might be harmful to a child. Where, so it has been held, the allegedly harmful publication does not relate to the care and upbringing of children over whose welfare the court is exercising a supervisory role, then not only is the child's welfare not paramount, but it is not relevant at all.[31] And, where the parent is also a child, it may well be, following a House of Lords' ruling,[32] that the child parent's welfare will not be considered paramount.[33]

Outside "courts of law", as narrowly construed, there are a vast range of tribunals dealing with matters affecting children which are in no way bound by the "best interests" principle. The *Bulger* case[34] has reminded us that

---

[22] Matrimonial Causes Act 1973 s.25 (1) (added by amending legislation in 1984).
[23] Though based on a report called *Children Come First*, Cm. 1264 (1990).
[24] Matrimonial Homes Act 1967 s.1 (3).
[25] *Gibson* v. *Austin* [1992] 2 FLR 349. See also *Pearson* v. *Franklin* [1994] 1 FLR 246.
[26] Per Dunn J. in *Re D* [1977] Fam. 158.
[27] See *e.g. Re C* [1991] 2 FLR 168.
[28] Under s. 25 of the Children Act 1989: see *Re M* [1995] 1 FLR 418.
[29] In deciding what level of services to provide for children is needed.
[30] *Re H-S* [1994] 2 All ER 390; *Re R* [1994] Fam. 254.
[31] *R* v. *Central Independent Television plc* [1994] Fam. 254.
[32] *Birmingham City Council* v. *H* [1994] 2 AC 212.
[33] The question whether an application by a parent who is a child for contact with her own child could be a question with respect of the 'upbringing' of the child or whether that question related only to the child's position as a parent and not to his 'upbringing' was left open by the Lords (see *op. cit.*, note 32, p. 223).
[34] On which see G. Sireny, *The Independent on Sunday*, 13 and 20 February 1994. This is now an appendix to her *The Case of Mary Bell* (London: Pimlico, 1995). See also ch. 12.

criminal courts are not so constrained: in what sense can the trial processes, which were in no way adapted to the needs of 11-year-olds—and, indeed, the sentence in that case—be said to be impressed by the best interests of the two boys involved? In most European countries, Thompson and Venables, who were aged ten at the time of their crime, could not have stood trial: indeed even in England had they committed the murder of James Bulger six months earlier they would have been presumed conclusively to lack the capacity for criminal activity.[35] Yet the Home Secretary, bowing to public pressure, purported by executive act to increase their sentences. It is to the credit of the courts that his actions were roundly condemned.[36]

So far as tribunals are concerned, the list is endless, and only a few will be picked out for comment. Tribunals hearing nationality and immigration appeals are not bound by any best interests principle. Tribunals in the education system, hearing appeals on such matters as school choice, school exclusions and special educational needs are not so bound. Nor are social security tribunals, though these may hear appeals from young people of 16 and 17 who are denied benefits.

Outside the courts, the absence of the "best interests" principle in any number of areas calls out for examination. Perhaps most glaring of all is the way successive Education Acts have shamefacedly refused to acknowledge children's rights in the area of education. The messages conveyed by recent education legislation are very clear: education is to be centrally directed and market-driven and the consumers of education are parents, not children.[37] Our schools are depressing places for those sympathetic to the rights of young people. Schools have been said to operate in ways that 'express contempt for the values of a free society'.[38] Pupils excluded from school are denied the right even to 'make representations' to the body deciding whether or not they may be readmitted to school. Until 1986 there was a trend toward increased student involvement in decision-making processes at school,[39] but the Education Act of that year put an end to this by excluding anyone under

---

[35] Ten being the age of criminal responsibility.

[36] *R* v. *Home Secretary ex p. Venables, ex p. Thompson* [1997] 1 All ER 327.

[37] See, further, Tony Jeffs, 'Children's Educational Rights to a new ERA' in (ed.) Bob Franklin, *The Handbook of Children's Rights* (London: Routledge, 1995), p. 25 and Michael Freeman, 'Children's Education: A Test Case For Best Interests and Autonomy' in (eds.) Ron Davie and David Galloway, *Listening To Children in Education* (London: David Fulton, 1996), p. 29.

[38] See K. Strike, *Learning and Liberty* (Oxford: Martin Robertson, 1982), p. 147.

[39] See C. Cullingford, *Children and Society: Children's Attitude To Power and Politics* (London: Cassell, 1992).

18 from membership of governing bodies.[40] Government education policy with its emphasis on centralization severely constrains the scope for any extension of children's rights within education.[41] The goal is now 'a mass, standardized product'.[42] The national curriculum curtails choice. As Clanchy, a member of the National Curriculum Council explained, this narrowing down is 'no accident'.[43] 'The right of children to a broad-based, intellectually stimulating education has been sacrificed on the high altar of competition.'[44] And conflict, disenchantment, indifference and absenteeism readily follow.

Similarly, housing legislation contains no "best interests" principle: the placement of a child in "bed and breakfast" accommodation thus cannot be challenged by reference to any principle such as that in the Children Act (or U.N. Convention). This leaves unanswered the question whether a judicial review examining such a decision would be governed by the paramountcy principle. It is an interesting argument, but not, it is thought, one likely to succeed. Nor does the planning system identify children's interests.

Even social services departments' obligations do not necessarily extend to giving first consideration to children's interests. The Children Act requires them to "safeguard and promote the welfare of children within their area who are in need".[45] But "in need" can be, and in practice is, interpreted restrictively.[46] There is a thin line between setting priorities and re-interpreting legislation. The latter is unlawful, but a successful challenge to it would be difficult to mount.

The Children Act requirements have gone a long way towards ensuring that institutions dealing with children act in their best interests. There are duties on community homes, voluntary homes, private children's homes, boarding independent schools[47] (though the duties as regards these have already been diluted). But these duties—to safeguard and promote the child's

---

[40] See s. 15 (14).
[41] See, further, S. Ranson, *Local Democracy for The Learning Society* (London: National Commission for Education, 1992).
[42] Per J.H. Best, 'Perspectives on the Deregulation of Schooling in America', *British Journal of Educational Studies* 41 (2), 122, (1993).
[43] 'Tense but not the point', *Times Educational Supplement*, 5 March 1993.
[44] Per Jeffs, *op. cit.*, note 37, p. 29.
[45] Section 17.
[46] See S. Barber, *Community Care*, 840, 23 (1990), and, in the context of housing, L. Clements, *Community Care*, 28 July–3 August 1994, p. 20.
[47] See sections 61, 64, 67, 86, 87.

welfare—do not apply to maintained schools or to non-maintained special schools.

Further, there is no best interests principle either in the health service[48] or in the penal system, either in primary legislation or in rules applying to penal institutions for young people.

THE CHILD'S RIGHTS OF PARTICIPATION

Article 12 of the Convention requires State Parties to:

> assure to the child who is capable of forming his or her own views the right to express those views freely in all matters affecting the child, the views of the child being given due weight in accordance with the age and maturity of the child.

For this purpose, the child is to be given "the opportunity to be heard in any judicial and administrative proceedings affecting the child".

In formulating this right the Convention goes well beyond earlier international documents.[49] It is the first explicitly to state that children have a right to have a say in processes affecting their lives. Marta Pais has argued that this converts the child into a "principal" in the Convention, and that this is an act of enormous symbolic importance.[50] Article 12 can be seen as a development from the child liberation philosophy of the 1970s,[51] and it is in line with the *Gillick* decision in the House of Lords in 1985.[52] In Lord Scarman's words "parental right yields to the child's right to make his own decisions when he reaches a sufficient understanding and intelligence to be capable of making up his own mind on the matter requiring decision".[53]

The initial impression is thus that English law complies with Article 12. There is much in the Children Act to reinforce this perception. A child, ad-

---

[48] See Zarrina Kurtz, 'Do Children's Rights To Health Care in the U.K. Ensure Their Best Interests?', *Journal of the Royal College of Physicians* 29, 508 (1995).

[49] Where the emphasis was on rights as protection or the furtherance of welfare. But Article 12 does not say that a child has the right to be listened to. See K. Kufeldt (1993) *International Journal of Children's Rights* 1, 155.

[50] *Bulletin of Human Rights* 91.2, p. 75, 76.

[51] See in particular R. Farson, *Birthrights* (Harmondsworth: Penguin, 1978) and J. Holt, *Escape from Childhood* (Harmondsworth: Penguin, 1975).

[52] [1986] AC 112. In Scotland this ruling now has statutory force: see Age of Legal Capacity (Scotland) Act 1991.

[53] *Ibid.*, p. 189.

mittedly after leave (perhaps an unnecessary and unjustifiable filter), can seek a residence or contact order.[54] Courts making decisions about a child's upbringing, albeit in a limited range of circumstances, are required to have regard to the "ascertainable wishes and feelings of the child concerned" in the light of that child's age and understanding.[55] Local authorities, before making any decision as regards a child whom they are looking after or are proposing look after, are required to ascertain the wishes and feelings of the child, so far as this is reasonably practicable.[56] There is a range of provisions in the Children Act allowing a child of sufficient understanding to make an informed decision the right to refuse to submit to a medical or psychiatric examination or other assessment in the context of a child assessment order, emergency protection or similar protective measure.[57]

It is, however, worth examining this example, itself a logical progression from the *Gillick* ruling, to see how the judges have interpreted it. When we do, we come up against interpretational backlash, as judges confront what they see as the reality of the problem. A result of these cases is that the *Gillick* principle does not it seems confer upon a competent child a power of veto over treatment, but merely allows him (or her) to give valid consent to such treatment. A girl of 17, if competent within the terms of the *Gillick* test, can thus consent to an abortion, but should she refuse to consent her pregnancy can nevertheless be terminated.[58] The *consent* of a *Gillick*-competent child cannot be overridden by those with parental responsibility, except by the court, but the Court of Appeal ruled in *Re W*, a case of a 16-year-old anorexic girl who tried to starve herself that *refusal* to accept treatment by such a child can be overridden by someone who has parental responsibility. The Master of the Rolls, Lord Donaldson, did, however, concede that "such a refusal is a very important consideration in making clinical judgments and for the parents and the court in deciding whether themselves to give consent".[59] Lowe and Juss have said that "in this way…the court fuses the principle of child autonomy with the practice of intervention".[60] This may be so.

---

[54] When the Family Law Act 1996 comes into operation, also a non-molestation order and an exclusion order.

[55] Section 1 (3) (a).

[56] Section 22 (4).

[57] In section 43 (8), 44 (7), 38 (6) and Sch. 3, para. 4.

[58] *Re R* [1991] 4 All ER 177; *Re W* [1992] 4 All ER 627. These cases are discussed in more detail in ch. 15.

[59] Though the judges denied that in practice this could happen, because doctors would not allow it to happen.

[60] *Op. cit.*, note 33, pp. 639–640.

But what does it leave to child autonomy? It is hardly surprising that in *South Glamorgan C.C.* v. *W and B*[61] a first instance judge should hold that despite the statutory right of veto in s.38(6) of the Children Act (and, presumably, also that conferred by sections 43(8), referred to above, s.44(7) and Schedule 3, paragraph 4), the court could exercise its inherent jurisdiction[62] to override the child's refusal.

These cases show a judiciary unable to digest the implications of the Children Act—and, it should be added, the U.N. Convention. And it leaves the law in a mess. Major questions are raised, not least what children can do if they believe that they are unfairly deemed to be incompetent. That they can seek a specific issue order from a court is hardly a satisfactory answer, but it is the last resort.

The Children Act is quite positive on Article 12, but not consistently so. It offers considerable scope for the representation of a child's wishes and feelings in the public welfare area.[63] But when it comes to private law disputes such as divorce, it is difficult to see where, if at all, the wishes and feelings of the child have up until now been considered or represented. The child is not independently represented: the emphasis on the guardian *ad litem* in public law has been quietly overlooked in such private law disputes.[64] It seems to be forgotten that the child may need independent representation as much when his or her parents are at war as when there is some conflict between them and the local authority, for example when abuse or neglect is alleged. There has, hitherto, been no voice for the child in divorce.[65] In relation to divorce, the Children Act is parent-centred, not child-centred, legislation. Whether this would improve under the new law of divorce, likely to come into operation in 1999, we must wait and see. The potential is there: whether the resources will be made available is less certain.[66]

But then it might be asked why children should be able to express their views at the juncture of a divorce when the law provides no mechanism for them to have a say at home. In English law, as in virtually every other legal system, parents do not have to ascertain or have regard to their children's

---

[61] (1993) 56 *Modern Law Review*, 865, 870.
[62] [1993] 1 FLR 574.
[63] See section 41.
[64] See J. Roche (1991) *Journal of Social Welfare and Family Law* 345. More generally see *The Future of Children* vol. 4 (1) (1994).
[65] The fear that this would be even less if the proposals on divorce procedure in *Looking To The Future* (H.M.S.O., 1993) were implemented has proved unfounded: indeed, the Family Law Act 1996 strengthens the status of children.
[66] *Looking To The Future* is an adult-orientated paper.

114 *Chapter 6*

wishes before making decisions, even major ones, which affect the child. In Finland the Child Custody and Right of Access Act of 1983 states that before a parent who has custody

> makes a decision on a matter relating to the person of the child, he or she shall, where possible, discuss the matter with the child taking into account the child's age and maturity and the nature of the matter. In making the decision the custodian shall give due consideration to the child's feelings, opinions and wishes.[67]

And this has provided the model for a similar provision in Scotland.[68]

The Scottish Law Commission found it attractive because it thought there was value in such a provision "even if it was vague and unenforceable", believing that it could have an "influence upon behaviour".[69] There is considerable force in this argument. If parents were expected to take their children's opinions and wishes seriously, it is likely that they would demand similar attention to the rights of children to participate by given by public authorities. And this, despite the Children Act, certainly does not happen at present.

A clear example of this failing is the field of education. There is a certain irony in this one of the aims of education is to enhance the capacity for decision-making and yet in crucial areas participation in major decisions is removed from those most affected by those decisions. Article 12(2) provides that children should be given an opportunity to be heard in judicial and administrative proceedings affecting them, but such provision is egregiously absent from school exclusion procedures, in the procedures for choosing a school and in school choice appeals and in all the discussion over such matters as the school curriculum. English education law bears little resemblance to the participatory model spelled out in Article 12, but when attempts were made during the passage of the Education Act 1993 to incorporate a right of the child to be heard in line with this Article, the Government Minister in charge came close to calling the idea 'dotty' and condemned it as 'politically correct'. The irony in this is that the 1993 Education Act is the first major children's legislation passed since the United Kingdom ratified the Convention, yet the Government scorned an obvious opportunity presented to bring the law in line with international obligations.

---

[67] See M. Savolainen (1986) 25 *Journal of Family Law* 113, 117.
[68] See Children (Scotland) Act 1995 s. 6.
[69] Scottish Law Commission Discussion Paper, *Parental Responsibilities and Rights* (H.M.S.O. 1990), para. 2.1 *et seq.*; 2.60 *et seq.*

ABUSE AND NEGLECT

Article 19 requires State Parties to:

> take all appropriate legislative, administrative, social and educational measures to protect the child from all forms of physical or mental violence, injury or abuse, neglect or negligent treatment, maltreatment or exploitation including sexual abuse....

English law, both criminal and civil, clearly targets abuse and neglect.[70] Parents who abuse or neglect children may be prosecuted[71] and protective measures including emergency protection orders and child assessment orders,[72] and care orders and supervision orders are available.[73] The linchpin of the protective system is "significant harm".[74] A care order (or a supervision order) may be made if a child is suffering significant harm or is likely to suffer significant harm if no order is made, and this is attributable to the quality of parental care not being what a reasonable parent could give or the child being beyond parental control. The Children Act extended the ambit of care to include suspicion that a child is at risk.[75]

There have been other statutory changes recently which have made it easier for children's accounts of abuse, in particular of sexual abuse, to be brought before a criminal court.[76] American research findings[77] indicate that the introduction of these innovatory techniques to assist the abused child to give evidence are not working successfully—prosecutors for example being reluctant to use them for fear that juries will believe they have a weak case. There is no replicating evidence in England, but a suspicion that similar patterns of under-use would be found here too. The lesson is clear: changing laws (in this case procedures) changes nothing un-

---

[70] Children Act 1989 s. 31 (2).

[71] Under the Children and Young Persons Act 1933, s. 1.

[72] Children Act 1989 s. 44.

[73] Children Act 1989 s.33, 35.

[74] On which see M. Adcock, R. White and A. Hollows, *Significant Harm* (Croydon: Significant Publications, 1991). I discuss the concept in (ed.) D. Freestone, *Children and The Law* (Hull: Hull University Press, 1990), p. 130, and in (ed.) A. Levy, *Refocus on Child Abuse* (London: Hawksmere, 1994), p. 17.

[75] *Cf. Essex C.C. v. TLR.* [1978] 9 Fam. Law 15.

[76] Criminal Justice Acts 1988 and 1991. See also the *Memorandum of Good Practice* (H.M.S.O., 1992).

[77] E. Gray, *Unequal Justice* (Macmillan, 1993). On the need for a 'support person' for child witnesses in criminal proceedings see J. Morgan and J. Williams (1993) 23 *British Journal of Social Work* 113.

less you also convert those who are to operate the new laws or administer the processes to their value. It has also become more difficult to prove abuse in the civil courts as the courts, in a well-meaning effort to protect innocent parents, have increased the standard of proof.[78]

But laws also achieve little without the injection of resources: one of the lessons of the English struggle to conquer child abuse is of the failure to address the resources question. Social services departments are consistently reporting that they have children on child protection registers with no social worker allocated to them.[79] Reports of inquiries into child deaths have constantly reiterated the need for greater resources to target families at risk.

Article 19, though, goes beyond abuse in its narrow and accepted sense. It pledges states to protect children not just from abuse but from "all forms of physical...violence". English law, however, permits parents to use "reasonable chastisement".[80] The provision in the Children and Young Persons Act 1933, which makes cruelty an offence specifically excludes physical punishment.[81] The Newson studies point to its prevalence in England and to the fact that the use of an implement or its threat remains common.[82] Five European countries have prohibited all physical punishment of children (Sweden in 1979; Finland in 1984; Norway in 1987; Austria in 1989 and Cyprus in 1994).[83] A recommendation of the Council of Europe Committee of Ministers in 1985 urged Member States (the United Kingdom is one) to "review their legislation on the power to punish children in order to limit or indeed prohibit corporal punishment, even if violation of such a prohibition does not entail a criminal penalty".[84] And yet in England one of the controversies of 1993–1994 concerned the 'right' of a child-minder to smack children with prominent Government ministers supporting her liberty to do so.[85]

---

[78] *Re M* [1994] 1 FLR 59; *Re P* [1994] 2 FLR 751.

[79] In relation to which see C. Jones and T. Novak (1993) 23 *British Journal of Social Work* 195 and M. Walton (1993) 23 *British Journal of Social Work* 139.

[80] See P. Newell in (ed.) A. Levy, *Refocus on Child Abuse* (London: Hawksmere, 1994), p. 93.

[81] See Children and Young Persons Act 1933 s. 1 (7).

[82] For example, Four Years Old in an Urban Community (London: Allen and Unwin, 1968). See also their The Extent of Parental Physical Punishment in the UK (1986) (91 per cent of boys, 59 per cent of girls hit with an implement by the age of 7).

[83] Germany is committed to this reform too and it is possible that Switzerland, Poland and Canada will follow the Nordic lead.

[84] Recommendation 85 (40) para. 12 (26 March 1985).

[85] On the litigation see *L.B. Sutton v. Davis* [1994] 1 FLR 737. See *The Guardian*, 28 September 1994; *The Times*, 3 December 1994 on the Governmental support for smacking and the new guidelines.

The Children Act, while it continued the progress to outlaw corporal punishment outside the home, though it seems without extending the ban to child-minders, did not take up the issue of physical chastisement by parents. And yet nothing is a clearer statement of the position that children occupy in society, a clearer badge of childhood than the fact that children alone of all people in society can be hit with impunity. There is probably no more significant step that could be taken to advance both the status and protection of children than to outlaw the practice of physical punishment. Much child abuse is, we know, punishment which has gone awfully wrong.

England thus continues to allow moderate and reasonable physical chastisement but Sweden in its Parent and Guardianship Code outlaws not just the hitting of children but "other humiliating treatment" as well.[86] Is it too much to hope that England will follow the lead of Sweden and the other European countries that have declared the hitting of children to be unacceptable? For how much longer will what has been called 'the English vice'[87] continue? When will the British legislature bow to the inevitable and accept that the legitimization of violence against children is unacceptable in civilized society?

FREEDOM OF EXPRESSION

The Convention says the child shall have the right to "freedom of expression" (Article 13). This right is to include "freedom to seek, receive and impart information and ideas of all kinds...either orally, in writing or in print, in the form of art, or through any other media of the child's choice". The only restrictions (Art. 13(2)) are to protect the rights and reputations of others (the law of defamation, for example) and to protect national security and public order as well as public health and morals. The Convention states that the child's right to freedom of expression *includes* the forms of expression listed, but it is therefore not exhaustive of them. The "freedom to hold opinions" and to receive and impart information and ideas without interference by public authority"[88] in the European Convention on Human Rights is thus arguably also embraced within Article 13.

There are a number of ways in which English law fails to sustain this freedom. Governmental intrusions on school curricula, limiting teaching

---

[86] See P. Newell, Children Are People Too (Bedford Square Press, 1989) pp. 70–86 on Sweden and its legislation.
[87] See I. Gibson, *The English Vice* (London: Duckworth, 1978).
[88] See Article 10.

about homosexuality,[89] forbidding "the pursuit of partisan political activities by pupils" and the "promotion of partisan political views" in the teaching of any subject in the school,[90] restricting sex education[91] are all potentially breaches of Article 13.

The insistence by schools on the wearing of school uniforms may also be considered to be a breach of Article 13. English courts have upheld head teachers' insistence on the wearing of uniforms, in one case agreeing with a head who sent home a girl who wore trousers (she had had rheumatic fever, but no doctor's letter was offered in support of her mother's decision to send her to school so dressed).[92] The European Commission in the *Stevens* case in 1986 rejected a mother's application alleging that the rules on school uniform breached her and her son's rights under the European Convention. But it admitted that "the right to freedom of expression may include the right of a person to express his ideas through the way he dresses".[93] The Commission did not think it had been established on the facts that the child had been prevented from expressing a particular "opinion or idea by means of...clothing". What then of a child refused permission to wear a CND badge, an earring signifying homosexuality or a *kippah* proclaiming a commitment to Judaism? The American Supreme Court upheld school students' rights to wear black arm bands to protest the Vietnam war. "It can hardly be argued", it pronounced, "that either students or teachers lose their constitutional rights to freedom of speech or expression at the schoolhouse gate."[94] English schools regularly breach both the letter and spirit of this and hitherto have got away with it. But there is a strong arguable case that the Convention would find many of their practices unacceptable. Further, it is difficult to see how they could be justified by Article 13(2) of the U.N. Convention.

---

[89] Local Government Act 1988 s. 28 (homosexuality is defined as a 'pretended family relationship'). See further D. T. Evans, Sexual Citizenship (Routledge, 1993) ch. 5 and C. Lind, '"Pretended Families" and the Local State in Britain and the U.S.A.', (1996) 10 *International Journal of Law, Policy and the Family* 134. It is possible that Thatcher herself was behind 'Clause 28' (see N. De Jongh, *The Guardian*, 8 April 1988).

[90] And see G. Haydon (1993) 1 *International Journal of Children's Rights* 213 (child's right to an open future).

[91] Sex education is now compulsory in maintained secondary schools (Education Act 1993 s. 241). But teaching about HIV, AIDS and STDs have been removed from the National Curriculum. On the dangers of withdrawal from classes see A. Weyman in Concern No. 86, p. 3 (1993).

[92] *Spiers* v. *Warrington Corporation* [1954] 1 QB 61.

[93] *Stevens* v. *United Kingdom* [1986] 5 EHHR 137.

[94] *Tinker* v. *Des Moines School District* 393 U.S. 503 (1969).

FREEDOM OF THOUGHT, CONSCIENCE AND RELIGION

The Convention requires State Parties to respect the right of the child to freedom of thought, conscience and religion.[95] Freedom to manifest religion may be subjected only to such limitations "necessary to protect public safety, order, health or morals or the protection of the rights and freedoms of others". The European Convention on Human Rights lays down a similar right, though it does so in stronger terms emphasizing the right to change religion and to "manifest" religion in worship, teaching, practice and observance".[96]

Nowhere does English law articulate similar norms. To conform with the U.N. Convention there ought to be statutory confirmation of the rights set out in the Convention. Schools which deny Muslim children the opportunity to pray on Fridays or insist upon Jewish children attending schools on Saturday clearly breach the U.N. Convention. English education law which gives parents a right to withdraw their children from religious worship and instruction in schools and even allows them to request special lessons in a particular religion also breaches the Convention because it does not give children similar rights.[97] The continuing reluctance of British governments to approve funding for voluntary-aided Muslim schools—while allowing this for Church of England, Catholic and Jewish schools—is a breach of both the "religion" article and of Article 2.[98] The imposition by the Education Reform Act of 1988 of collective worship 'of a broadly based Christian character' may result in breaches of Article 29 for it can hardly be said to inculcate respect for the child's cultural identity and values, where the child comes from a minority group.[99]

Arguments by some,[100] allegedly in the cause of children's rights, to ban circumcision of male babies clearly also fly in the face of the freedom of religion article. The British government has resisted the weak arguments proffered to outlaw the practice—as indeed has every other government today. It has been banned in such 'rights-conscious' countries as the Soviet Union and Nazi Germany. Is further comment necessary?

---

[95] In Article 14.
[96] See Article 9 (1).
[97] It also breaches the discrimination Article (see Art. 2) because substitute lessons (in the child's religion) must be paid for.
[98] Prohibiting discrimination. It is thought that such status is more likely to be granted since the Education Reform Act 1993, though as yet no evidence of any change.
[99] Minority Rights Group, *Education Rights and Minorities* (London: MRG, 1994).
[100] Particularly Alice Miller, Peter Newell and Penelope Leach (see *post*, note 110).

Children in care may not be brought up "in any religious persuasion other than that in which [they] would have been brought up if the order had not been made."[101] On one level this is right, but what of the child who does not wish to be brought up in care in the religion of his (or her) family, perhaps associating it with the abuse to which s/he has been subjected? Or the child who does not wish to be brought up in any religion? In theory, the *Gillick* case should cater for such children, provided, of course, they are deemed to have sufficient understanding of the issues and sufficient maturity and intelligence to have thought rationally about them. And, certainly, regulations under the Children Act[102] should satisfy this requirement, but in practice the Christian ethos of many child-care organizations may not make this particularly easy.

It may be noted also that wards of court are, at least in theory, also denied freedom of religion, since the court has the power to direct this.[103] In practice, it is doubtful whether the problem exists. Nevertheless, it ought to be made clear by statute that the powers of the wardship court, in effect the inherent jurisdiction of the High Court,[104] cannot be used in derogation from the principle set out in the U.N. Convention on the Rights of the Child.

FREEDOM OF ASSOCIATION

The Convention recognizes the right of the child to freedom of association and to freedom of peaceful assembly, subject only to restrictions necessary in a "democratic society in the interests of national security or public safety, public order, the protection of public health or morals or the protection of the rights and freedoms of others".[105]

The refusal of schools to allow union activity or, for example, CND meetings or anti-apartheid meetings or meetings to celebrate a particular national day of an ethnic group within a school breaches this article. We have had an Education Act almost annually in recent years. Is it too much to hope that the next one will encode some basic rights for school children? Similar problems arise in the context of local authority care: it is known that the National Association of Young People in Care (NAYPIC)

---

[101] Section 33 (6) (a).

[102] Children's Homes Regulations 1991, r. 11. See also *The Children Act Guidance*, vol. 4 paras. 1. 121–1. 124.

[103] It can take a decision on any matter of significance relating to the child.

[104] There is no real distinction between wardship and inherent jurisdiction now.

[105] Article 15 (2).

English Law and the U.N. Convention on the Rights of the Child 121

has had difficulty organizing some areas. Again it has to be stressed that local authorities which obstruct such activity are in breach of the U.N. Convention.

It is doubtful whether British Public Order Legislation, in particular the restrictive Public Order Act of 1986 and the Criminal Justice and Public Order Act of 1994, satisfies the Convention. The offence of "disorderly conduct" in the 1986 Act is wider than the exceptions allowed in this Article. Certainly, the police could interpret it, and have done, to restrict gatherings by young people. The new powers in the 1994 Act, for example, in relation to 'raves',[106] and the new offences of aggravated trespass and trespassory assembly, confine assembly to the young even further.

THE PROTECTION OF PRIVACY

Article 16 states:

> No child shall be subjected to arbitrary or unlawful interference with his or her privacy, family, home or correspondence, nor to unlawful attacks on his or her honour and reputation.

To a large extent a child's privacy is controlled by parents or other caretakers and to a large extent also the privacy that parents can offer is related to their income and other resources. The poor have never had much privacy: their lives have always been more public than that of more affluent people. The privacy provision cannot, therefore, be entirely disentangled from another Article in the Convention which proclaims the right of every child to an adequate standard of living.[107] Children condemned to live in bed and breakfast accommodation, perhaps because local authority housing is sold to potential Tory voters as in the City of Westminster,[108] have neither an adequate standard of living, nor any degree of privacy. It may be added that they are hardly likely to have the opportunities for play and recreational activities set out in the Convention[109] or, indeed, to find the right to education,[110] guaranteed by the Convention, of much import.

A child's privacy is interfered with in a number of ways. Within the home this may be difficult to provide for, but in institutions, where there is

---

[106] See Sections 63–67.
[107] Article 27.
[108] As in the City of Westminster (so revealed in January 1994).
[109] Article 31.
[110] Article 28 (on the goals of education see Article 29).

widespread abuse of privacy, English law has done far too little to protect the freedom guaranteed by Article 16. Even where attempts have been made, for example, by Regulation under the Children Act,[111] there is growing evidence that these attempts are frustrated in practice. The right to private correspondence is not protected in all institutions which house children and young persons. In some residential institutions children cannot even use toilets in complete privacy. There may be communal bathing facilities only. There are institutions in which the periods of young women are monitored by staff. In some children's homes, notably but not exclusively secure accommodation, closed circuit video cameras and two-way mirrors are used to observe children. This may be done without their knowledge, let alone their consent.

There are many other ways in which a child's privacy is invaded and to which all too little attention has been given. For example, the growing practice of advertising children for adoption with exposure of biographical details and the use of a photograph is a clear breach of this Article of the Convention. Whether it should be stopped is another matter. If adoption or another form of permanent placement is in the best interests of the child concerned, it may be thought unduly legalistic to insist upon this "lesser" right and therefore sacrifice a "greater" one. The Convention does after all, in Article 21, mandate those countries which permit adoption to "ensure that the best interests of the child shall be the paramount consideration" (a provision which, as we shall see, English law does not currently comply with). At the very least it must be hoped that the current "advertising" practice would be subjected to sustained scrutiny and reasoned debate.

ADOPTION

As already indicated, English law falls short of its Convention obligations in relation to Article 21, the adoption article.

First, the "best interests" of the child is only the "first consideration" in adoption proceedings in England.[112] The Convention requires them to be the "paramount" consideration. "First" suggests, as is indeed the case, that there are other considerations, such as the rights of biological parents: "paramount" suggests, by contrast, that the best interests of the child should be determinative. If the report of the Inter-Departmental Review on Adoption is implemented, English law will be brought into line with the

---

[111] See, in general, *The Children Act Guidance* vol. 4, part 1.
[112] Adoption Act 1976, s. 6.

Convention.[113] Plans to do this may stumble as the 'Right' resists, what it considers to be, politically correct aspects of proposed adoption reforms.

Secondly, the Convention requires that the "persons concerned (should) have given their informed consent to the adoption on the basis of such counselling as may be necessary" (Article 21(a)). In England, counselling is not always available and, where given, often is offered after the adoption has taken place. Furthermore, English law (unlike that in Scotland[114]) has never required the consent of the person most concerned, namely the child. Again, the recent Adoption Review will, if and when implemented, remedy, at least to some extent, this defect. But it proposes the age of 12 as the appropriate one.[115] This is unduly cautious: a child can clearly express a desire for or against a particular adoption at a much earlier age than this. I would advocate fixing the age no higher than 7. A transplant to a new family is too important a step to contemplate against the wishes of a child able to express wishes and feelings about its desirability.

Thirdly, there is the issue of inter-country adoption. This was one of the more controversial areas covered by the Convention, with some countries, notably Venezuela, being understandably unhappy with the whole concept.[116] It needs to be said that if other provisions in the Convention were universally fulfilled (adequate standard of living,[117] adequate health care for mothers and children[118] being the most obvious examples), there would be little need for inter-country adoption. But in the foreseeable future and particularly in the light of the upheavals in Eastern Europe in the late 80s and 90s, there will be a felt necessity to rescue children from orphanages and bring them to more prosperous and stable countries like the United Kingdom. In the light of this it may be said that English law is insufficient to assist the process of inter-country adoption. The *Luff* decision, in particular, showed an insensitivity to the needs of Romanian orphans.[119] But where inter-country adoption is allowed, it is clear that English law and practice falls short of the Convention obligation to ensure that the safeguards and stan-

---

[113] *Review of Adoption Law: Report To Ministers of Interdepartmental Working Group* (Dept. of Health, 1992), para. 7 (1).

[114] Children (Scotland) Act 1995 s. 156.

[115] *Op. cit.*, note 87, para. 9.5.

[116] For a rather different perspective see E. Bartholet, *Family Bonds* (New York: Houghton Mifflin, 1993).

[117] Article 27.

[118] Article 24 (2).

[119] [1992] 1 FLR 59. On the new Convention see N. Cantwell (1993) 10 *International Journal of Children's Rights Monitor* 22.

dards are "equivalent" to those existing in the case of national adoption. With the implementation of the Hague Convention on the Protection of Children and co-operation in respect of inter-country adoption of May 1993 this should change. But we must wait and see.

HEALTH AND HEALTH SERVICES

The Convention states that:

> States Parties recognise the right of the child to the enjoyment of the highest attainable standard of health and to facilities for the treatment of illness and rehabilitation of health.[120]

States are to "strive to ensure that no child is deprived of his or her right of access to such health care services". The United Kingdom sets no standards as such for children's health services. There is no sense that the allocation of resources within the National Health Service reflects the needs of children. There are known to be wide regional variations in provisions too. Further, poverty is strongly associated with increased risk to child health,[121] so that full implementation of this Article requires sustained measures to eradicate child poverty. But this has increased steeply in the eighteen years of the Conservative administration: in 1979 one in ten children was living in a low-income family—today poverty hits one in three.[122] But part of the problem is that the health of children, indeed, the population generally, is the responsibility of unelected health authorities. Their power to purchase services is now shared with fund-holding GPs. As the number of such general practitioners and the type of health care they may purchase increases, the balance of purchasing power is shifting away from the health authority. But there is no way of knowing whether GPs have the same values regarding health as health authorities or whether either of them shares the values of "the public". A recent study by Bowling,[123] however, indicated that doctors gave much greater priority to reducing mental

---

[120] Article 24 (1).

[121] *DHSS, Inequalities In Health* (the Black Report) (DHSS 1980); G. Davey Smith *et al.* (1990) *British Medical Journal* 301, 373.

[122] See C. Woodroffe and M. Glickman, *Children and Society* (1993) 7 (1), 49, and Department of Social Security, *Households Below Average Income: A Statistical Analysis 1979–1991/2* (H.M.S.O. 1994). And these figures do not take account of hidden poverty experienced by children (and their mothers) when income is not shared fairly within the family.

[123] *Local Voices in Purchasing Health Care: An Exploratory Exercise in Public Consultation in Priority Setting* (Bartholomew's Hospital Medical College, 1992).

illness than was given by the public. Do they target child health as the public would wish them to do? We have no way of knowing.

In particular the Article requires a number of measures. It requires measures to be taken to diminish infant and child mortality.[124] This has declined, but the decline has slowed,[125] is slower than many comparable countries, and is high in comparison with, for example, France, Italy and Sweden.[126] The U.K. has the highest post-neonatal mortality rate of seven European countries, as reported in a 1990 study.[127] It also requires an emphasis on primary health care. There is concern that recent changes in the delivery of health services may work to the detriment of this, particularly as regards children.

It further requires measures to tackle the "dangers and risks of environmental pollution".[128] There is evidence of an association between respiratory illnesses in children and the amount of pollution in the areas where they live.[129] More could be done to cut air pollution. Much more could be done to tackle smoking now that the evidence of the effects of environmental tobacco smoke is incontestable.[130] Smoking could be banned in public places. Cigarette advertising could be stopped, including sponsorship of sporting and other events. Taxation on tobacco products could be vastly increased. More could be done to discourage smoking by children. The right to a smoke-free environment must "trump"[131] the so-called freedom of smokers to destroy themselves and others. Questions must also be raised about nuclear installations in the growing light of clear association between them and childhood leukaemia.[132]

---

[124] Article 24 (2) (a).

[125] World Health Organisation Regional Office for Europe, *Health For All Indicators*, Eurostat/PC (WHO, 1992).

[126] See Woodroffe and Glickman, *op. cit.*, note 122, p. 50.

[127] Article 24 (2) (a).

[128] World Health Organization Regional Office for Europe, *Health For All Indicators*, Eurostat/PC (WHO, 1992).

[129] See U.S. Environment Protection Agency, *Respiratory Health Effects of Passive Smoking* (Washington: U.S. Environmental Protection Agency, 1992).

[130] Children's Legal Centre, 'Children and the Environment', *Childright*, no. 59. p. 9.

[131] The expression is Ronald Dworkin's: see *Taking Rights Seriously*, Duckworth, 1978.

[132] V. Beral, 'Leukaemia and Nuclear Installations: Occupational Exposure of Fathers To Radiation May Be The Explanation', *British Medical Journal*, 300 (6722), p. 411. See also Health and Safety Executive, *Investigation of Leukaemia in the Children of Male Workers at Sellafield* (London: H.M.S.O. 1993).

An EEC Directive of 1980[133] was supposed to be implemented by 1982: Britain was not fully in compliance with this in the early 1990s—there were promises of full compliance by 1993—but it is doubtful whether in the north of England in particular the air is still satisfactory.[134]

The Article also requires appropriate pre- and post-natal health care of mothers. There are regional variations here as well as class differences and little doubt that more could be done. Health education is also inadequate. It is not, however, in the National Curriculum.[135]

Article 24 also contains one of the most controversial provisions in the Convention. In paragraph 3, States Parties are required to take "all effective and appropriate measures with a view to abolishing traditional practices prejudicial to the health of children". There is legislation prohibiting female circumcision:[136] and this was the main target of the provision. It cannot, however, be said that the legislation is working very effectively. There have been no prosecutions in England. France takes a more heavy-handed approach to the problem and parents have been imprisoned there for performing such acts on their daughters. Education may be thought to be a better approach, but there is little evidence of any such campaign among the communities concerned in England.

There is no evidence that male circumcision, properly carried out, is prejudicial to the health of male babies. To associate this with female genital mutilation is simplistic, though a number of children's rights advocates including Alice Miller, Penelope Leach and Peter Newell, continue to do so.[137]

Other traditional practices have been targeted at various times: for example, the Yoruba practice of making excisions in the faces of male children was the subject of a well-publicized prosecution in 1974,[138] though there can be little doubt that the practice continues. Ear and nose piercing arguably also falls within the purview of this Article but, in a world where children are victimized in so many more harmful ways, it hardly warrants attention.

---

[133] Directive on Radiation Safety Standards, 80/836 O.J.L. 256, 17 September 1980.

[134] See European Community Directive 80/779/EEC (1980).

[135] This is set out in the Education Report Act 1988 s. 3.

[136] Prohibition of Female Circumcision Act 1985. Guidance was issued under the Children Act in 1991 to alert social workers to the problem. (Dept. of Health, *Children Act Guidance* vol. 8, para. 1.7.16). But see L. Eaton, *Community Care*, 21–27 July 1994, p. 16.

[137] See A. Miller, *Banished Knowledge* (Virago, 1990), pp. 135–140; P. Leach, *Children First* (London: Michael Joseph, 1994) p. 204; P. Newell, *The UN Convention and the Rights of the Child in the U.K.* (London: N.C.B. 1991).

[138] *R v. Adesanya*, The Times, 17 and 17 July 1974.

A Concluding Comment

This survey has shown that complacency about children's rights in England is totally misplaced. It has directed attention to some of the areas where legislative change is required, where practice needs to be better monitored, where greater thought has to be given to protecting the interests and furthering the rights of children.

Progress towards these ends needs a structure. The development of this will require positive action.

First, the U.N. Convention should be incorporated into English law:[139] breach of a provision of the Convention should be an infringement of English law with all the implications that this would have.

Secondly, the concept of a child impact statement should be introduced.[140] All legislation, including subsidiary and local, should be accompanied by an assessment of its effect on children. This should apply also to health plans, education innovations (the National Curriculum for example) and other policy changes. Only as a result of a sustained critique was any attempt made to do this in the Family Law Act 1996.

Thirdly, England should follow the example of Norway[141] and other countries[142] which have introduced the concept of an *ombudsman* for children.[143] Such an office would be information-gathering, complaint-receiving and litigation-initiating. It would also monitor United Kingdom compliance

---

[139] Spain and Sri Lanka have done this.

[140] I first developed this in 1987 at the Brian Jackson Memorial Lecture entitled 'Taking Children's Rights More Seriously': see (1988) 1 *Children and Society* 299, 316–317. See more fully M. Rosenbaum and P. Newell, *Taking Children Seriously* (London: Calouste Gulbenkian 1991).

[141] On which see M. G. Flekkøy, *A Voice for Children* (London: Jessica Kingsley, 1991).

[142] Costa Rica, New Zealand and Sweden.

[143] The Labour Party has pledged to do so.

with the Convention and publicize areas where law and practice fall short of the ideals and norms in the Convention.

The structure sketched here would give some teeth to the Convention in England. The Convention can only be seen as a beginning, but it will not have an impact on the lives of children until the obligations it lays down are taken seriously by legislatures, governments and all others concerned with the daily lives of children, in reality by all adults.

CHAPTER 7

Children's Rights and Cultural Pluralism

In 1968 a man went to a doctor in South London for medical treatment of a venereal disease. He introduced his young wife to the doctor and let it be known that he had already taken her to a clinic to be fitted with a contraceptive appliance. The doctor was concerned and reported the matter to the police who brought a complaint to the juvenile court that she was in need of care because she was being exposed to moral danger.[1] The couple were Nigerian Muslims[2]: he was in his mid-twenties and she was at most 13, but may have been as young as 11. They had married in northern Nigeria shortly before coming to England. The court made a 'fit person order'[3] under the Children and Young Persons Act 1963 and the girl was admitted to the care of a local authority. The reasons which prompted the court to conclude that she was in moral danger are encapsulated in the following statement:

> Here is a girl, aged 13, or possibly less, unable to speak English, living in London with a man twice her age to whom she has been married by Muslim law. He admits having had sexual intercourse with her at a time when according to the medical evidence the development of puberty had almost certainly not begun.... He further admits that since the marriage...he has had sexual relations with a prostitute in Nigeria from whom he has contracted venereal disease. In our opinion a continuance of such an association, notwithstanding the marriage, would be repugnant to any decent-minded English man or woman. Our decision reflects that repugnance.[4]

This decision was reversed on appeal by the Divisional Court. The Lord Chief Justice, Lord Parker, conceded that it was possible to hold that a

---

[1] *Alhaji Mohamed v. Knott* [1969] 1 Q.B.1.
[2] They were domiciled in Nigeria.
[3] Fit person orders were replaced by care orders in 1969.
[4] *Op. cit.*, note 1, p. 15.

validly married wife was in moral danger, but he refused to accept that the girl in this case was. He said:

> I would never dream of suggesting that a decision by this bench of justices, with this very experienced chairman, could ever be termed perverse: but having read that, I am convinced that they have misdirected themselves. When they say that "a continuance of such an association notwithstanding the marriage would be repugnant to any decent-minded English man or woman", they are I think, and can only be, considering the view of an English man or woman in relation to an English girl and our Western way of life. I cannot myself think that decent-minded Englishmen or women, realising the way of life in which this girl was brought up, and this man for that matter, would inevitably say that this is repugnant. It is certainly natural for a girl to marry at that age. They develop sooner, and there is nothing abhorrent in their way of life for a girl of 13 to marry a man of 25.... Granted that this man may be said to be a bad lot, that he has done things in the past which perhaps nobody would approve of, it does not follow from that that this girl, happily married to this man, is under any moral danger by associating and living with him. For my part, as it seems to me, it could only be said that she was in moral danger if one was considering somebody brought up and living in our way of life and to hold that she is in moral danger in the circumstances of this case can only be arrived at, as it seems to me, by ignoring the way of life in which she was brought up, and her husband was brought up.[5]

The Divisional Court held that the marriage was entitled to recognition by the English courts. It followed from this that the husband was not committing the offence of unlawful sexual intercourse[6]—unlawful meant outside marriage.[7] Nor was she in moral danger.

The case, understandably, provoked considerable controversy. The *Daily Express* was outraged. So was Baroness Summerskill who initiated a debate in the House of Lords.[8] The decision was branded as racist, a failure by white institutions to protect a vulnerable black child. Olive Stone thought the case 'disturbing'[9] and Ruth Deech believed its 'practical con-

---

[5] *Ibid.*, pp. 15–16.
[6] Sexual Offences Act 1956 s. 6(1) (intercourse with a girl under 16).
[7] *Cf. R v. Chapman* [1959] 1 QB 100 (on the interpretation of s. 19(1) of the 1956 Act).
[8] *Hansard* H.L. vol. 290, cols. 1321–1323.
[9] *Family Law*, 1977, p. 40.

sequences would be disastrous'.¹⁰ It led Ian Karsten to call for a minimum age to be prescribed for recognition purposes.¹¹ But other commentators welcomed the decision. It showed a willingness to embrace the customs and culture of another society.¹² What was 'moral danger' was being tested by the morality of the culture to which the couple belonged. The decision was seen to be consonant with an acceptance of moral pluralism.¹³

Whichever stance one adopted, the case had troubling features. An analysis of Lord Parker's judgment reveals prejudices and misconceptions galore, not least a concern that his understanding of Islamic culture in Northern Nigeria may not have been very deep, assumptions and biases filling in gaps in his knowledge base. It is not clear what evidence, if any, was given to either court about the life realities of Muslim Nigeria.

About the same time as *Mohamed* v. *Knott* was going through the courts, the question arose in a different context in *R* v. *Derrivierre*.¹⁴ A West Indian father was charged with an assault upon his 12-year-old son occasioning him actual bodily harm. The boy had been disobedient and the father punished him by punching him a number of times in the face. English law provides a defence to the crime of wilfully assaulting a child¹⁵ if the purpose is chastisement and the punishment is moderate and reasonable.¹⁶ The father was given a six months term of imprisonment for what the Deputy Chairman of the Inner London Quarter Sessions described as a 'brutal attack'. On an appeal against sentence the Criminal Division of the Court of Appeal upheld the decision and set out the broad principle involved:

> Standards of parental correction are different in the West Indies from those which are acceptable in this country; and the Court fully accepts that immigrants coming to this country may find initially that our ideas are different from those upon which they have been brought up in regard to the methods and manner in which children are to be disciplined. There can be no doubt that once in this country, this country's

---

[10] 'Immigrants and Family Law' (1973) 123 NLJ 110,111.

[11] 'Child Marriages' (1969) 32 MLR 212, 215–216.

[12] Brenda Hoggett, *Parents and Children*, Sweet & Maxwell, 1977, p. 110.

[13] M. D. A. Freeman, *The Legal Structure*, Longmans, 1974, p. 48.

[14] (1969) 53 Cr. App. Rep. 637.

[15] See Children and Young Persons Act 1933 s.1(7).

[16] As to which see Cockburn C. J. in *R* v. *Hopley* (1860)2 F & F 202. See further P. Newell, *Children Are People Too*, Bedford Square Press, 1989. On the religious roots see P. Greven, *Spare the Child*, Vintage Books, 1992. Echoes of this can be detected in M. Straus, *Beating The Devil Out of Them: Corporal Punishment in the American Family*, Lexington Books, 1994.

laws must apply; and there can be no doubt that, according to the law of this country, the chastisement given to this boy was excessive and the assault complained of was proved. Nevertheless had this been a first offence, and had there been some real reason for thinking that the appellant either did not understand what the standards in this country were or was having difficulty in adjusting himself, the Court would no doubt have taken that into account and given it such consideration as it could.[17]

In fact Derrivierre had a previous conviction for assaulting his daughter only a year before and thus had already received a fair warning of the unacceptable nature of this type of behaviour in England. But the case does show a willingness by English courts to take supposedly different standards of another culture into account in sentencing.[18] More recently, in a child care case,[19] the practices of a mother who was by origin Vietnamese were judged against the 'reasonable objective standards of the culture in which the children have hitherto been brought up',[20] though the judge was careful to add, 'so long as these do not conflict with our minimal acceptable standards of child care in England'.[21] But, of course, the judge heard no evidence of what the 'reasonable objective standards' of rural Vietnam were, though he was convinced that the mother's disciplinary measures were unacceptable in that culture too. Neither *Derrivierre* nor *Re H* (the Vietnamese case) provoked the interest or the controversy which *Mohamed* v. *Knott* fuelled. But that is hardly surprising, given our ambivalence to questions of the physical chastisement of children.[22]

These extended case studies are but two examples of the problem posed when legislation comes up against the practices of another culture.[23]

---

[17] *Op. cit.*, note 14 pp. 638–639.

[18] On which matter see S. M. Poulter, *English Law and Ethnic Minority Customs*, Butterworths, 1986, pp. 271–274.

[19] *Re H* [1987] 2 FLR 12.

[20] *Ibid.*, p. 17.

[21] *Idem*.

[22] This came to the fore yet again in Britain in 1994 over the question of the moral propriety and legality of a childminder smacking a child in her care. See *London Borough of Sutton* v. *Davis* [1994] 1 FLR 737. It has now been 'resolved' by Government Guidance permitting a childminder to smack, but only where a parent gives consent (*The Times*, 3 December 1994).

[23] On scarification see *R* v. *Adesanya*, *The Times*, 16 and 17 July 1974 (and S. Poulter, 'Foreign Customs and The English Criminal Law' (1975) 24 ICLQ 136); on West African fostering practices see *Re O* (1973) 3 Fam. Law 40, *Re E O* (1973) 3 Fam. Law 48 and *Re*

It is a problem well known to drafters of international conventions and the two examples drawn from England could be added to by reference to confrontations in other countries. But the temptation to document such examples will be resisted and I will focus on two international conventions instead.

Seventy-eight years ago the International Labour Organisation adopted a convention fixing the minimum age for admission of children to industrial employment.[24] Article 2 of this states:

> Children under the age of fourteen years shall not be employed or work in any public or private industrial undertaking, or in any branch thereof, other than an undertaking in which only members of the same family are employed.

For most Western States the age of 14 was accepted. But the Commission on Children's Employment, responsible for preparing the Labour Conference, met strong objection from countries in Asia where child labour under the age of 14 was—indeed still is—widespread and where the financial resources for implementing rapid change did not exist. 'Should modifications of the Convention be allowed in the case of those countries with special climatic and industrial conditions?', asked Sir Malcolm Delevinge of the United Kingdom.[25] A trades unionist from Britain, Margaret Bondfield, was in no doubt that such exceptions were unacceptable but a compromise at her initiative was effected. Speaking of what became Article 6 of the Convention, she said:

> With regard to one of the main objections, namely the nature of the Indian industries. We have carefully drafted this amendment to exclude all those industries that could be considered purely native industries or that are small industries. It is especially drafted to refer only to those industries which are being modelled on Western ideas, which are to some extent under control of factory legislation and which are mainly supervised by Western people.[26]

A (1978) 8 Fam. Law 247. Also interesting is *Re H* [1978] Fam. 65 (returning a battered Pakistani child of 4 to her parents who were returning to Pakistan).

[24] See Philip Veerman, *The Rights of The Child and The Changing Image of Childhood*, Martinus Nijhoff, 1992 ch. XIII.

[25] League of Nations, *International Labour Conference*, First Annual Meeting, *International Labour Conference*, First Annual Meeting, p. 96.

[26] *Idem.*

And so Article 6 declares boldly that Article 2 'shall not apply to India' and then sets a lower age (twelve) below which children are not to be employed in factories 'working with power and employing more than ten persons' or in mines, transport or the docks. India continued to raise reservations, in particular relating to the 'difficulties which local customs would place in the way of organising adequate primary education'.[27] In the event India did not ratify this Convention though it did ratify (in 1921) another ILO Convention adopted in 1919 on the prohibition of nightwork.[28] The 1919 Convention on minimum age has been replaced by one adopted in 1973.[29] This states that every State Party is to undertake progressively to raise the minimum age for admission to employment or work 'to a level consistent with the fullest physical and mental development of young persons'.[30] Developing countries are, nevertheless, still allowed to specify a minimum age for employment at 14 years.[31] The U.N. Convention on the Rights of the Child recognizes the right of the child to be protected from economic exploitation and from performing hazardous work or work likely to interfere with education[32] but no minimum age is specified.

But it is another Article of the U.N. Convention to which attention must now turn. Article 24, dealing with health and health services, confronts the issue of cultural difference in paragraph 3. This states:

> State Parties shall take all effective and appropriate measures with a view to abolishing traditional practices prejudicial to the health of children.

There are many traditional practices which may harm children but no one is in any doubt that one practice in particular is targeted by this provision

---

[27] International Labour Review vol. III, nos. 1–2, July–August 1921, p. 16.

[28] Convention 6 (it is reproduced in Veerman, *op. cit.*, note 24, p. 420). India did originally ask for preferential treatment on this Convention too: so did Japan and Belgium (whose request to except the glass industry was rejected by the Conference).

[29] ILO Convention No. 138 (reproduced in Veerman, *op. cit.*, note 24, p. 484).

[30] Article 1.

[31] Article 2(4). They must state a reason or alternatively agree to renounce 'the right to avail itself of the provisions in question as from a stated date' (Article 2(5)). India by the Child Labour (Prohibition and Regulation) Act 1986 has prohibited those under 14 working in certain hazardous employments and regulated their working conditions in certain other employments.

[32] Article 32. States Parties must provide a minimum age for employment and provide for penalties or other sanctions to ensure effective enforcement. (Art. 32 (2) (a) and (c)). On India see Myron Weiner, *The Child and the State in India*, Oxford University Press, 1991.

viz. female circumcision.[33] This is prevalent in wide areas of the world[34]: takes a number of forms[35] and infibulation—genital mutilation of the grossest kind—is particularly common in the Sudan, Somalia, Ethiopia and Mali. At least three Western countries have legislated against it,[36] including the United Kingdom in 1986,[37] and France has prosecuted and imprisoned parents involved in it. Nevertheless, in formulating Article 24, paragraph 3 caution had to be taken. Senegal, for example, warned that a more direct condemnation would force the practice underground.[38]

Four examples have now been used: child marriages, child labour, female circumcision and corporal chastisement practices. Of female child circumcision more will be said. But at this stage attention must turn to the concept of cultural pluralism and its justification. And pluralism must be distinguished from two other political ethical theories, relativism and monism (or universalism).

---

[33] Delegates of Canada, the United Kingdom and the U.S.A. were in favour of formulations of the Article that would have referred specifically to female circumcision. See D. Johnson 'Cultural and Regional Pluralism in the Drafting of the UN Convention on the Rights of The Child' in M. Freeman and P. Veerman, *The Ideologies of Children's Rights*, Martinus Nijhoff, 1992, p. 95, 109–110.

[34] See Alison Slack (1988) 10 Human Rights Quarterly 437. See also Stephen James (1994) 8 Bioethics 1.

[35] See Efua Dorkenoo and Scilla Elworthy, *Female Genital Mutilation: Proposals for Change* (Minority Rights, 1992).

[36] The United Kingdom has the Prohibition of Female Circumcision Act 1986. There is also legislation in the United States (The Female Genital Mutilation Act of 1993, H.R. 3247). This is discussed in *Berkeley Women's Law Journal*, 9, 206 (1994).

In France there is no specific law but the violence involved in circumcision brings the activity within a more general proscription. The recent *Gréon* case in France, which led to a one year suspended sentence, promoted an outcry (see *The Guardian,* 17 September 1994).

[37] For the view of social workers towards it see Lynn Eaton, 'A Fine Line', *Community Care*, 21–27 July 1994, p. 16. See also Bryan Hartley (1994) *Archives of Diseases of Childhood*.

[38] And pointed to son preference as another harmful traditional practice.

Cultural Pluralism

The fact of cultural pluralism was known as early as the Greek historian, Herodotus,[39] and it is traced through Montaigne,[40] Vico,[41] Hume[42] and Montesquieu[43] who perhaps was the first to try to explain cultural difference). But it is to twentieth-century anthropology that we must look for articulation of the concept.[44]

Pluralism is a theory about the sources of value (as are relativism and monism).[45] Pluralists believe that there are many reasonable conceptions of a good life and many reasonable values upon which the realization of good lives depend. There are conflicts among reasonable conceptions of a good life as well as among reasonable values. Political ethics needs to cope with these conflicts, to attempt to surmount difficulties caused by the incompatibility and incommensurability of values whose realization is thought to be essential. Where values are incompatible—for example a belief in equality of the sexes and a belief that men are superior—the realization of one value must exclude the other. Values are incommensurable where there is no measuring rod by which they can be compared.

Incommensurable values need not necessarily be incompatible, and where they are not they can co-exist. If values were only incommensurable the problem would not be too great—a vision which allowed for and required discrete but compatible conceptions of the good life is not beyond the scope of imagination. It is the incompatibility of values that constitutes the stumbling-block.

---

[39] See his *Persian Wars* ('if one were to offer men to choose out of all the customs in the world such as seemed to them the best, they would examine the whole number, and end by preferring their own') (Book 3, ch. 38).

[40] See C. Geertz, 'Anti Anti-Relativism', *American Anthropologist* 86, 263 at 264.

[41] *The New Science* (1744).

[42] See, in particular, his *A Dialogue* in *Enquiries concerning Human Understanding and concerning the Principles of Morals* (ed.) L. A. Selby-Bigge revised by P. H. Nidditch, Clarendon Press, 1975, p. 324.

[43] *The Spirit of The Laws* (1748).

[44] In particular to Franz Boas (see *e.g.* 'The Mind of Primitive Man', *Journal of American Folklore* 14, 1 (1901)), Ruth Benedict, *Patterns of Culture*, Houghton Mifflin, 1934 and Melville Herskovits, *Cultural Relativism: Perspectives in Cultural Pluralism*, Random House, 1972.

[45] And see Charles Larmore, 'Pluralism and Reasonable Disagreement', *Social Philosophy and Policy* 11(1), 61, 64 (1994).

Pluralists accept that conflicts among values can be resolved by appealing to some reasonable ranking of the values in question. They acknowledge that a plurality of reasonable rankings also exists.

Monism

Monism or universalism,[46] by contrast, is committed to there being an overriding value or set of values and, if the latter, a ranking scheme on the basis of which values can be compared in a way that all reasonable people would find acceptable. Pluralists object to monism because they cannot accept the idea that there is an overriding value, that there is some consideration which always takes precedence over all other considerations. Monism also overlooks those cases of moral conflict where no standard can legitimately claim a monopoly of the truth (the issue of abortion[47] is the best example of this). Where pluralists and monists agree is in accepting the need for a reasonable method of resolving conflict.

Relativism

Pluralists also reject relativism. Pluralism may have emerged out of relativism and the two are often confused.[48] Pluralists and relativists agree that there are no overriding values, that all values are conditional, that there is a plurality of incompatible and incommensurable values. They agree on the need for conflict resolution. But relativists go beyond pluralism and think that all values are conventional. Relativism emerged in reaction to cultural evolutionism, which was European and often racist.[49] As Hatch puts it: 'It goes without saying that people who were thought to be the least cultured were also thought to be the least intelligent and the darkest in pigmentation'.[50] When cultural relativism emerged in the first third of this century it was seen as a challenge to racist, Eurocentric notions of

---

[46] There are different models of monism, ranging from the Platonic 'Idea of The Good' (see his *Republic*, 504–509) and to different versions of utilitarianism, using in its simplest model a felicific calculus (see Jeremy Bentham, *Introduction to the Principles of Morals and Legislation*).

[47] And see Ronald Dworkin, *Life's Dominion*, Harvard University Press, 1993.

[48] Joseph Raz claims not to know what cultural pluralism is (see 'Moral Change and Social Relativism', *Social Philosophy and Policy* 11(1), 139 (1994)).

[49] G. W. Stocking Jr., *Race, Culture and Evolution*, Free Press, 1968.

[50] E. Hatch, *Culture and Morality: The Relativity of Values in Anthropology*, Columbia University Press, 1983, p. 26.

progress.[51] Cultural relativism like pluralism is a theory about the way evaluations or judgments are made. But to the relativist, 'evaluations are relative to the cultural background out of which they arise'.[52] So to Ruth Benedict, one of the founders of relativism, tolerance is a key element of cultural relativism[53]; and to Herskovits it is necessary to recognize the 'dignity inherent in every body of custom'.[54] The philosopher Charles Taylor talks of the presumption of the equal worth of cultures.[55]

The attractions of relativism are difficult to ignore. It is rooted in egalitarianism, in liberalism, in modernism. It belongs perhaps to a disenchanted vision of the world.[56] It is anti-assimilationist, it is anti-imperialist, it is hostile to ethnocentrism.[57] It is sympathetic to, and would wish to protect, the traditions and rights of indigenous peoples.[58] It has the value also in a sort of Millian way,[59] of enhancing the prospects of achieving moral knowledge, though this presupposes the possibility of real communication across cultures and this is not always possible.[60]

Relativists regard all values as the products of the customs, practices and beliefs which have as a matter of fact developed within a particular tradition. They deny that any value has any authority, epistemological or moral, outside of this cultural context. They deny that conflict between values belonging to different traditions can be settled in any reasonable way, because, so they argue, what is reasonable is itself a product of particular cultures. And so they demand of us that we ask not whether social practices like child marriage or female circumcision, or for that matter purdah, suttee or polygamy, are justified by the moral considerations that we find cogent, but rather

---

[51] Alison Dundes Renteln, *International Human Rights: Universalism Versus Relativism*, Sage, 1990.

[52] *Per* Melville Herskovits, *op. cit.*, note 44, p. 14.

[53] *Op. cit.*, note 44, p. 37. See also Hatch, *op. cit.*, note 50, pp. 99–100.

[54] *Man and His Works*, Alfred A. Knopf, 1947, p. 76.

[55] *Multiculturalism and "The Politics of Recognition"*, Princeton University Press, 1992, p. 72.

[56] Charles Larmore so characterizes it (*op. cit.*, note 45, p. 71).

[57] See Abdullahi, A. An-Na'im, 'Religious Minorities Under Islamic Law and The Limits of Cultural Relativism', *Human Rights Quarterly*, 9, 1 (1987).

[58] See Will Kymlicka, *Liberalism, Community and Culture*, Oxford University Press 1989. See also Alan Gewirth, 'Is Cultural Pluralism Relevant To Moral Knowledge?', *Social Philosophy and Policy* 11(1), 22, 35 (1994).

[59] See J. S. Mill, *On Liberty* (1859).

[60] But see Chandran Kukarhas, 'Explaining Moral Variety', *Social Philosophy and Policy* 11(1), 1, 18 (1994).

whether they are sanctioned by the relevant social understandings of the cultures within which they are practised.

But, if that means that a culture can only be judged by endogenous value judgments, and that moral principles which derive from outside that culture have no validity, morality has become a slave to custom,[61] the 'ought' has relinquished any transcendental power that it may have had to critique the 'is'. However, if, as Amy Gutmann has argued persuasively in a recent article, 'cultural relativists agree that there can be standards for judging justice that are independent of social consensus, then they give up the distinctive premise of cultural relativism'[62]. I would argue that they must. The argument for any practice must be more than that the practice exists. A culture which permits child marriage or female circumcision must be able to support these practices by a stronger argument, or series of arguments, than that there is— if, indeed, this is the case—social consensus. An examination of the social understandings within the culture may reveal that there is no social understanding at all or that there are conflicting understandings, misunderstandings or inconsistencies. Often, it will reveal that the so-called dominant understanding is in reality the understanding of the dominant.[63] Many cultural practices when critically examined turn on the interpretation of a male élite, with a consensus having been engineered to cloak the interests of a section of the society.[64]

Both monists and pluralists disagree. Monists because they believe that a practice can be judged by an overriding value: pluralists because they claim that there are values independent of the context of the culture in question to which we can reasonably appeal in settling conflicts. There is surely no dispute that there are certain needs which do not vary either temporally—they are historically constant—or culturally—they are the requirement of people everywhere. This does not mean that there are not differences in the ways in which these needs are met. There is a need for food: not a need for meat and two vegetables.[65] There is a need for shelter but it does not have to be a

---

[61] J. S. Mill wrote of the 'despotism of custom'.

[62] 'The Challenge of Multiculturalism in Political Ethics', *Philosophy and Public Affairs*, 22, 171, 177 (1993).

[63] *Ibid.*, p. 176.

[64] Stephen A. James argues persuasively that this is the case with female circumcision in African societies. See 'Reconciling International Human Rights and Cultural Relativism: The Case of Female Circumcision', *Bioethics,* 8, 1, (1994).

[65] And the need is for food as nutrition. Food may have secondary purposes such as the fulfilment of religious obligations. This is not addressed by Michael Walzer in *Spheres of Justice*, Basic Books, 1983, p. 8 ('If the religious uses of bread were to conflict with its nutritional uses...it is by no means clear which should be primary'). Only a relativist could

semi-detached house. Nor are these needs only physiological. There are psychological needs too: for comfort, affection, companionship. There are social needs: for order, security, dignity, respect, privacy. There are minimum requirements of human welfare. They must be met whatever the conception of what constitutes a good life and regardless of what other values are upheld in any particular culture.[66]

It is easy to distinguish this model of pluralism from one of relativism. Relativists do not acknowledge these primary values and therefore fail to see that there are standards independent of a particular culture by which it can be judged. It is less easy to distinguish it from monism, but it is a different claim for primary values may conflict with each other, in which case it may become necessary to put the conflict into its cultural context to determine which, if either, should prevail. The contribution that the achievement of the particular value makes to the life of the individual concerned may also be significant: which of two values, for example, enhances the goal of his or her 'good life'.

RESPONDING TO THE CASE STUDIES—RELATIVISM

We may return now to the examples used at the beginning of this essay: child marriages, corporal punishment practices, child labour and female circumcision. The relativist would situate each of the case studies into its cultural context and would, I would argue, be impotent to offer any real critique. It is surely one of the limitations of a belief in cultural relativism that it can lead us to conclude that 'anything goes'. A consequence of this is that we lack the ammunition to protect the individual against the group. The challenge of rights is easily snuffed out. We are forced to condone practices which we find repressive or intolerable because we are told that is only our opinion and had our enculturation been into the culture we are now criticizing our opinion would be different. The relativist has little to offer the child either by way of protection or empowerment, any more I suggest than it could have offered Jews living in Nazi Germany or blacks in South Africa under apartheid.[67]

---

    say this: it is crystal clear that the religious use of bread is of secondary importance to its use as nutrition. Nutrition is a basic, primary value: religion (*cf.* John Finnis, *Natural Law and Natural Rights*, Clarendon Press, 1980, p. 89) is not.

[66] And see John Kekes, 'Pluralism and The Value of Life', *Social Philosophy and Policy*, 11(1), 44, 49 (1994).

[67] Renteln, *op. cit.*, note 51, believes that relativism is 'out of favor' mainly because of this supposed impotence (p. 67). J. Cook described relativism as 'nihilistic': see 'Cultural

THE MONIST RESPONSE

The monist response is more positive. It points to there being an evaluative consideration, an overriding value, which trumps all other considerations. It may take the form of a categorical imperative,[68] a harm principle[69] or a principle of generic consistency[70] or many other forms.

The epistemic relevance of these may be questioned. Certainly, a relativist might observe the use here of conceptions of reason and rationality firmly rooted within Western Enlightenment culture; there are other conceptions of 'reason' to which other cultures appeal including myth, religious faith, intuition and tradition. Why, it may be asked, should alien reasoning processes be admitted when cultural practices external to the culture are ruled irrelevant? This is not unreminiscent of the debates about the relevance of human rights language to non-Western traditions.[71] And there are parallel debates about the meaning of childhood in different cultures and political economies.[72]

The response of the monist to our four examples would depend upon the overriding value or values chosen. Abstracting values from international human rights norms[73] would lead to condemnation of female child circumcision,[74] would result in castigation of countries which permitted child labour

---

Relativism as an Ethnocentric Notion' in (eds.) R. Beehler and A. R. Drengson, *The Philosophy of Society*, Methuen, 1978, p. 289.

[68] As with Immanuel Kant.

[69] As with John Stuart Mill (and see, *op. cit.*, note 59).

[70] As with Alan Gewirth, *Reason and Morality*, University of Chicago Press, 1978. See also 'The Epistemology of Human Rights', *Social Philosophy and Policy*, 1(2), 1 (1984), and, briefly, *op. cit.*, note 58. Deryck Beyleveld, *The Dialectical Necessity of Morality: An Analysis and Defence of Alan Gewrith's Argument To The Principle of Generic Consistency*, University of Chicago Press, 1991 a sustained defence.

[71] See *e.g.* Josiah A. M. Cobbah, 'African Values and the Human Rights Debate: An African Perspective', *Human Rights Quarterly*, 9, 309 (1987); Donna E. Arzt, 'The Application of International Human Rights Law in Islamic States', *Human Rights Quarterly* 12, 202 (1990); Ann Mayer, *Islam and Human Rights Tradition and Politics*, Westview Press, 1992.

[72] See Philippe Ariès, *Centuries of Childhood: A Social History of The Family*, Jonathan Cape, 1962; Barbara A. Hanawalt, *Growing Up In Medieval London: The Experience of Childhood In History*, Oxford University Press, 1993; Rex and Wendy Stainton Rogers, *Stories of Childhood: Shifting Agendas of Child Concern*, Harvester Wheatsheaf, 1992.

[73] See John O'Manique, 'Universal and Inalienable Rights: A Search for Foundations', *Human Rights Quarterly*, 12, 465 (1990).

[74] Using the Universal Declaration of Human Rights, Article 25 (and 15). And see further James, *op. cit.*, note 64, pp. 12–22.

and would give no unequivocal answers on the other two matters. The U.N. Convention on the Rights of the Child has nothing to say on marriages of the very young and whether it allows corporal punishment at all depends upon how Article 19 is interpreted.[75]

THE PLURALIST APPROACH

To the pluralist the practices found in the case studies at the beginning of this essay have to be looked at both in terms of primary values and the cultural context in which the individuals concerned lived. If one takes preservation of physical integrity to be a primary value then even situating this within relevant cultural contexts leads to a condemnation of child female circumcision. Apart from ritualistic circumcision, where the clitoris is merely nicked and there is little mutilation or long-term damage, the term 'female circumcision' is a euphemism which has only the remotest similarity with male circumcision in terms of its physical effects. The practice has been described by Alison Slack as follows:

> The practice can be broken down into four basic forms that vary in degrees of severity. The first, and least severe form, is…ritualistic circumcision…. The second form is simply called circumcision or 'sunna' by the Muslims. This involves the removal of the clitoral prepuce—the outer layer of the skin over the clitoris, sometimes called the 'hood'; the gland and body of the clitoris remain intact. Occasionally, the tip of the clitoris itself is removed. Sunna has been equated with male circumcision, because the clitoris itself is generally not damaged.
>
> A third, and more harsh form of the practice, is called excision or clitoridectomy. This is the most common form and involves the removal of the gland of the clitoris—usually the entire clitoris—and often parts of the labia minora as well.
>
> Finally, the most severe form of the practice is infibulation…, where virtually all of the external female genitalia are removed—removing the entire clitoris and labia minora—and, in addition, much or most the labia majora is cut or scraped away. The remaining raw edges of the labia majora are then sewn together with acacia tree thorns, and held in place with catgut or sewing thread. The entire area is closed up by this process leaving only a tiny opening, roughly the size of a matchstick, to allow for

---

[75] But a case can be put that it would proscribe it, as Sweden, amongst other countries, has done.

the passing of urine and menstrual fluid. The girl's legs are then tied together—ankles, knees and thighs—and she is immobilized for an extended period varying from fifteen to forty days, while the wound heals.[76]

Often one of the harsher forms of the practice occurs, even though a milder type was intended because the girls struggle due to the blunt instruments used and the lack of anaesthesia. The instruments used range from kitchen knives, old razor blades, broken glass and sharp stones to scalpels: the wounds are frequently treated with animal dung and mud to stop the bleeding. The practice occurs most often on young girls between the ages of three and eight. It is primarily found in areas where there is considerable poverty, where hunger, insanitary conditions and illiteracy are rife, and where there is little in the way of health care facilities. It is also pertinent to note that the economic and social status of women characteristically is low where female child circumcision is prevalent.

The practices are supported by a number of arguments. The control of female sexuality is the central justification.[77] It prevents wantonness and preserves the virginity of a future bride.[78] Where infibulation has taken place, the girl has to be 're-opened' surgically so that her husband may have sexual intercourse with her, reassured that he is the first to have done this. The preservation of virginity is essential for determining a woman's social position in these societies and in some areas the value of a prospective bride is based on the size of the infibulated opening.[79] There is a belief also that female circumcision is a religious imperative[80]: thus the belief is widely held among Muslims that the practice is scripturally mandated by the Koran.[81] Although the practice is often supported by Muslim leaders, there is no mention of either excision or infibulation in the Koran. Female circumcision is supported by these leaders as being a positive 'sunna', or

---

[76] 'Female Circumcision: A Critical Appraisal', *Human Rights Quarterly*, 10, 437, 441–442 (1988). See also Efua Dorkenoo and Scilla Elworthy, *op. cit.*, note 35; K. Brennan, 'The Influence of Cultural Relativism on International Human Rights Law: Female Circumcision as a Case Study', *Law and Inequality* VIII, 367 (1989); K. Boulware-Miller, 'Female Circumcision: Challenges To The Practice as a Human Rights Violation', *Harvard Women's Law Journal*, 8, 155 (1985).

[77] Lawrence P. Cutner, 'Female Genital Mutilation', *Obstetrical and Gynecological Survey*, 40(7), 438 (1985).

[78] See Slack, *op. cit.*, note 76, p. 445.

[79] *Ibid.*, p. 446.

[80] The practice does not exist in the teachings of any formal religion. Slack, *op. cit.*, note 76, p. 446 notes it is practised amongst Jews in Africa, but this is not correct. The Falashas in Ethiopia may have practised circumcision.

[81] See Asma A. El Dareer, *Woman, Why Do You Weep?*, Zed Press, 1982, p. 71.

tradition, one that serves to attenuate sexual desire in women.[82] Muslim men in Africa hold uncircumcised women in contempt. One of the worst insults in Muslim Africa is to be called 'Son of an uncircumcised mother'.[83]

Justification of the practice also finds support in a number of myths including the belief that the clitoris represents the male sexual organ and, if not cut, will grow to the size of a penis,[84] that females are sterile until excised, the operation being thought to increase fertility, that the operation is a biologically cleansing process that improves the hygienic and/or aesthetic condition of female genitalia.[85] There is also the argument that the adherence to the tradition of female circumcision amounts to a right to cultural self-determination and that the pursuit of this right brings psychological benefits to women. Research in Sudan, Egypt and Nigeria suggests that the importance of tradition[86] is the most significant of justificatory arguments for the practice, and that the support amongst women for the tradition is hardly less than that by men.[87]

These justifications can be examined utilizing the cultural pluralist framework that I have offered. That there is a violation of physical integrity, at least in the case of clitoridectomy and infibulation, is incontestable. To the monist or universalist that is the end of the question. But the cultural pluralist must go on to ask how important a value physical integrity is to women in Sudan or Somalia, particularly when its preservation may lead to their being social outcasts. If an analogy may be given, it is clear that life is a primary

---

[82] Directing it, so it is said, to 'the desirable moderation' *per* Marie Bassili Assaad, 'Female Circumcision in Egypt: Social Implications, Current Research, and Prospects for Change', *Studies In Family Planning,* 11(1), 5 (1980). Hanny Lightfoot-Klein nevertheless found that sexual desire and pleasure were experienced by the majority of women subjected to the most extreme form of circumcision, in spite of their being culturally bound to hide these experiences. ('The Sexual Experience and Marital Adjustment of Genitally Circumcised and Infibulated Females In the Sudan', *Journal of Sex Research,* 26, 375 (1989). See also her *Prisoners of Ritual, An Odyssey Into Female Genital Mutilation In Africa,* Haworth Press, 1989.

[83] Raqiya Haji Dualeh Abdalla, *Sisters In Affiliation: Circumcision and Infibulation of Women in Africa,* Lawrence Hill, 1982, p. 84.

[84] Nayra Atiya, *Khul-Khaal: Five Egyptian Women Tell Their Stories,* Syracuse University Press, 1982, p. 11.

[85] Note, 'Female Circumcision', *The Lancet,* 12 March 1983, p. 569.

[86] Robert A. Myers *et al.,* 'Circumcision: Its Nature and Practice Among Some Ethnic Groups in Southern Nigeria', *Social Science and Medicine,* 21, 584 (1985); El Dareer, *op. cit.,* note 81, p. 141 *et seq.;* Atiyo, *op. cit.,* note 84, p. 11.

[87] El Dareer interviewed over 4,500 adults in Sudan: 82.6 per cent of women approved of circumcision regardless of the type and 87.7 per cent of men approved the practice.

value, but we can all think of circumstances, being in a persistent vegetative state for example, when we would not wish to continue to live. A PVS condition may constitute life but hardly a 'good life'.

What this overlooks is the age of those who undergo female circumcision. They are for the large part very young children in no position to give informed consent. And yet the operations carried out upon them may severely and irreversibly affect their future sexual experience. It may lead to their having difficulty with childbirth. There is an increased risk of sterility. Many are afraid of sex or can experience little enjoyment from sexual relationships. These are potential harms and years in the future. There are immediate harms too: severe pain, shock, infection, scarring, bleeding, even death.[88] According to a UNESCO report, emotional reactions 'may present themselves as chronic irritability, anxiety, depressive episodes, conversion reactions or frank psychosis'.[89] Circumcision is thus within the understanding of the cultures which legitimate the practice dysfunctional. Even so were it practised on adult women with their full and informed consents, we might be inhibited from attacking it (though whether the House of Lords, the final court of appeal in the United Kingdom, would find similar hesitation in the light of its condemnation in *Brown's* case[90] of sado-masochism may be doubted). We allow breast implants and even gender reassignments,[91] and both are carried out on the national health. Were girls purportedly to consent to circumcision we might still employ, what I have defended elsewhere, as 'liberal paternalism', to protect them from the consequences of actions that will prevent them subsequently enjoying rationally autonomous adulthood.[92] But here we have a situation where many of the girls concerned cannot consent, but it seems that looking at their circumcision as adult women would have done so. There are real dilemmas here which cannot be avoided them by resorting to relativism, for then there would be no debate, or by seeking the refuge of monism, for this would impose a decontextualized overriding value. It would be comforting to rest in the moral certitudes of monism but this study has shown the fragility of the moral determinacy for which it stands.

---

[88] Slack, *op. cit.*, note 76, discusses these at pp. 450–455; Dorkenoo and Elworthy, *op. cit.*, note 35, do so at pp. 8–10.

[89] *Draft Report of the Working Group on Traditional Practice Affecting The Health of Women and Children*. U.N. Doc. E/CN.4/H.C.42/1985, 12 September 1985, p. 13.

[90] [1993] 2 All E.R. 75.

[91] Though we do not grant much in the way of rights to transsexuals: see *Corbett v. Corbett* [1971] P. 83, and *Rees v. U.K.* (1986) 9 EHRR 56.

[92] *The Rights and Wrongs of Children*, Frances Pinter, 1983, pp. 54–60.

How is then the cultural pluralist to respond? The answer lies in subjecting the practice to an internal critique, in deconstructing the arguments that are used to support it. The arguments in the case of female circumcision are, it will be recalled, four-fold. It is claimed as a control on female sexuality. Whilst there can be little doubt that it reduces sensitivity and responses to stimulation', it offers no guarantee that a woman has not had sexual experiences and, indeed, even infibulation is no guarantee: an unmarried woman can have sexual intercourse and then be re-infibulated immediately before her marriage to disguise this fact from her husband.

It is supposedly based on religion, but there is no evidence for this and at least a suspicion that it is an elitist religious fraud perpetrated by a clerical oligarchy on vulnerable women.

It rests also upon sexual myths and these—such as that the clitoris is a masculine feature and will grow to the size of a penis—need to be shown for what they are. If features of the other sex need to be removed is there any move in any of these societies to excise male nipples?

And, as for the supposed benefits, it has already been shown that, to the contrary, there are physical and psychological harms which surely outweigh any social or cultural benefits.

It would be easier to empathize with the arguments put if there were not in addition a suspicion that the cultural values upheld by the practices depicted here were not the values of a section of the society rather than the whole of it. Of what value are the norms of a community when they are directed at a group at best devalued but more likely excluded from it? It is concerns such as these which lead me to ask whether in a clash between the value of physical integrity and the value of cultural identity, the latter can possibly prevail.[93]

It also leads me to conclude—though it has not been necessary to discuss the question in this paper—that, using similar reasoning processes, it would not be difficult to show that in a similar clash over male circumcision it would be the latter value, namely cultural (or religious) identity that would prevail.

On the other case studies set out at the beginning of this paper, much briefer answers must be given. The cultural pluralist is likely to come to the same conclusion on child marriages as the Divisional Court did in *Mohamed*

---

[93] Attacks on the practice of male circumcision have been launched by eminent thinkers like Alice Miller. There is also an organization called NOHARMM in the United States (National Organization to Halt The Abuse and Routine Mutilation of Males). See also Denise Winn, 'A Campaign to Save The Foreskin', *The Independent*, 20 April 1993.

v. *Knott*. But s/he would need a deeper understanding of the cultural context than it would seem the English courts had.

The cultural pluralist's response to child labour in the developing world would require greater tolerance of the problems attendant on poverty, a greater understanding of the global economy and a more sophisticated approach to the relationship between child labour and education questions than is often found, but a conclusion not dissimilar from that in the U.N. Convention is likely to result from these deliberations.[94] On punishment practices s/he could be more categorical: there can be no reason for tolerating excessive punishment in the name of cultural difference; there is no cultural tradition or identity at stake. Of course, it would be so much easier if we knew what such punishment was different from.

A Concluding Comment

I have set out in this paper three approaches that may be adopted towards cultural conflict and children's rights. I reject cultural relativism because it renounces normative judgment. The moral determinacy of monism offers blanket solutions but fails to address cultural difference. Cultural pluralism, a via media perhaps between two extremes, situates values within cultural context and offers dialogue and change. Nothing can provide solutions to the difficult cases thrown up by the ways different societies treat children, but cultural pluralism does, I believe, offer a challenge. It is one that those concerned with children, their welfare and their rights, must take up.

---

[94] *Cf.* Myron Weiner, *The Child and the State in India: Child Labor and Education Policy in Comparative Perspective.* Oxford University Press, 1991 with Olga Nieuwenhuys, *Children's Lifeworlds: Gender, Welfare and Labour in The Developing World*, Routledge, 1994. See also her review of his book in *Int. Journal of Children's Rights* 2, 205 (1994) and his article in *Int. Journal of Children's Rights* 2, 121 (1994).

CHAPTER 8

Contact with Absent Parents: An Emergent Child Right

INTRODUCTION: THE UNITED NATIONS CONVENTION

The United Nations Convention on the Rights of the Child states in Article 9 (3) that:

> States Parties shall respect the right of the child who is separated from one or both parents to maintain personal relations and direct contact with both parents on a regular basis, except if it is contrary to the child's best interests.

The African Charter (*The Charter on the Rights and Welfare of the African Child*) encapsulates in Article 19 (2) the same principle in more or less identical language, but omits the exception designed in the United Nations Convention to prioritize the child's welfare over his or her self-determination. The Convention and the Charter date respectively from 1989 and 1990, and are the first recognitions in international documents of a child's right to access or contact (as it is now called in English legislation[1]) or, to use American terminology, visitation rights.

EARLIER BILLS OF RIGHTS

In the 1960s the first attempts to formulate contact as a child's right are found in declarations emanating from Family Courts in the U.S.A.[2] The Family Court Judges of Milwaukee in 1966 assembled a *Bill of Rights of Children in Divorce Actions* which included: 'The right to know the non-custodian parent and to have the benefit of such parent's love and guid-

---

[1] Children Act 1989, s.8.
[2] These are reproduced by Philip E. Veerman, *The Rights of The Child And The Changing Image of Childhood* (Dordrecht: Martinus Nijhoff, 1992), p. 468 and 469.

ance through adequate visitation' (Article 4).³ *The Children's Bill of Rights* of the Dane County Family Court Counseling Services in Madison at roughly the same time recognized both 'the right to a continuing relationship with both parents', and the 'right to be able to experience regular and consistent contact with both parents and to know the reason for cancellation of time or change of plans' (Articles 1 and 9).

ACCESS AS A PARENT'S RIGHT

The novelty of looking at contact as a child's right becomes apparent when the case law of only a generation ago is examined. Thus, in England, in 1962, the Court of Appeal had no difficulty reversing a first instance judge who had denied an adulterous mother, who had left her husband and two young children, access to them. He admitted this was a 'very strong thing to do'.⁴ But the Court of Appeal saw it differently. As Wilmer L.J. said: 'Here the wife is asking for no more than periodical access to her own children. In the ordinary way that would be no more than the basic right of the parent'.⁵

In 1974 the Superior Court of New Jersey had no doubt that a father had visitation rights, and its concern was as to whether his homosexuality should require these to be restricted.⁶ This decision is contemporaneous with the publication of the highly influential *Beyond The Best Interests of The Child*. Goldstein, Freud and Solnit saw the question not in terms of any legally enforceable right of the non-custodial parent, but then neither did their formulation amount to seeing it as a child's right. They argued that 'the custodial parent should have the right to decide whether it is desirable for the child to have such rights'.⁷ The language seemingly implies we are talking of a child's right, but in reality what was being advocated was a shift of right from one parent to the other, and at the same time an abdication of state responsibility for the question.

---

[3] See Robert W. Hansen, 'The Role and Rights of Children in Divorce Actions' in *Journal of Family Law*, 6, 1–14 (1966).

[4] *S v. S* [1962] 1 WLR 445, 447.

[5] *S v. S* [1962] 2 All ER 1, 3–4.

[6] *In The Matter of J, S and C* 324 A. 2d 90 (1974).

[7] J. Goldstein, A. Freud, A. Solnit, *Beyond The Best Interests of The Child* (New York: Free Press, 1973), p. 38. But see now E. E. Maccoby and R. H. Mnookin, *Dividing The Child* (Cambridge, Mass: Harvard University Press, 1992), p. 285–288.

Contact as a Child's Right: England

By the 1970s the courts in England and Australia were beginning to conceive of, what is now called, contact as a child's right. In England, in 1973, the courts made their first ruling to this effect.[8] But when the language of the court is carefully examined, the dichotomy between the two views is seen to be blurred. Thus, Wrangham J. says,

> the companionship of a parent is in any ordinary circumstances of such immense value to the child that there is a basic right in him to such companionship. I for my part would prefer to call it a basic right in the child rather than a basic right in the parent. That only means this, that no court should deprive a child of access to either parent unless it is wholly satisfied that it is in the interests of the child that access should cease....[9]

Latey J. states that the right of the parent to access means 'not that a parent has any proprietorial right to access but that, save in exceptional circumstances, to deprive a parent of access is to deprive a child of an important contribution to his emotional and material growing up in the long term'.[10] The importance of the ruling lay in its emphasis on the value of contact for the child, rather than the importance of not denying the parent contact with the child. The dictum in *M* v. *M* that access is a child's right has been approved very many times.[11] In *Re H*,[12] the Court of Appeal ordered the resumption of contact after a three years' break, with the 'wisdom' of Latey J's remarks being 'fully' endorsed by Balcombe L.J.[13] In *Re R*[14] Butler-Sloss L.J. stated that the principle had been repeatedly stated by the appellate courts, was endorsed in the Children Act and underlined in the UN Convention.

---

[8] *M* v. *M* [1973] 2 All ER 81.
[9] *Ibid.*, p. 85.
[10] *Ibid.*, p. 88.
[11] See *S* v. *O* [1982] F.L.R 15; *A* v. *C* [1985] F.L.R 445; *Re D* [1987] 2 F.L.R 365; *Re KD* [1988] 2 F.L.R 139; *Re W* [1989] 1 F.L.R 163; *F* v. *Metropolitan Borough of Wirral District Council and Another* [1991] 2 F.L.R 114; *Re H* [1992] 1 F.L.R 148; *Re S* [1992] 2 F.L.R 313.
[12] [1992] 1 F.L.R 148.
[13] *Ibid.*, p. 151.
[14] [1993] 2 F.L.R 762.

CONTACT AS A CHILD'S RIGHT: AUSTRALIA

In Australia the lead was taken by the federal legislature. The Family Law Act 1975 section 43 (c) pointed the way with its reference to the need to protect the rights of children. In 1976, in *Mazur* v. *Mazur*,[15] Wood J. said of this that it was a statutory provision "possibly unique to Australia.... One sees with regret so many statutes designed to promote the welfare of children which proceed on a very paternalistic basis with little thought having been given to the fact that those rights are to be protected. It is very salutary indeed to find such an expression in the Family Law Act 1975 and to note that the protection of rights is allied with the obligation upon the court to promote the children's welfare. This would seem to me to suggest that when the welfare of the child is being taken into account, the child's rights must certainly not be overruled."

The same judge extended the principles stated in *Mazur* v. *Mazur* in *In the Marriage of Parsons and Puncheon*.[16] In this case the child was unwilling to submit to access by his father. Indeed, when the father attempted to achieve contact, the effects on the child were traumatic. Wood J. observed that, under section 64 (1) (a) of the 1975 Act, he was to regard the welfare of the child as the paramount consideration and he would not be protecting the rights of this child if he was to grant access in a situation where past experience indicated that the child would be subject to distress and emotional upheaval. He continued: "His rights demand that the court do not do this to him, and to my mind, it goes without saying that to make such an order could not be said to be promoting his welfare, nor could it be said to be regarding his welfare as the paramount consideration. It would, in fact, be putting the father's commendable and honest aspirations in advance of the welfare of the child, and no matter how much sympathy I feel for the father in this unfortunate case, that is not a course which I am able to take."

CONTACT AS A CHILD'S RIGHT: CANADA

Similarly, in Canada, there has been a shift in thinking. Cases as late as 1985[17] suggest an entitlement in the non-custodial parent in the absence of

---

[15] [1976] F.L.C. 75, 625, 75, 629.
[16] [1978] F.L.C. 77, 533.
[17] *AW* v. *CP* [1985] 67 N.S.R. 294.

clear danger to the child.¹⁸ The Canadian courts seem unwilling to grant a non-custodial parent contact in the absence of benefit accruing to the child from such a relationship.¹⁹ In *Michael v. Hanley*,²⁰ for example, it was held that the 'parental right' to contact is not absolute, to be denied only when danger to the child is perceived, but is to be granted only after assessing the presumed benefits to the child of their being contact.

RIGHTS: WELFARE AND AUTONOMY

There is thus a growing acceptance that contact is a child's right rather than a claim inhering in the non-custodial parent. But what does this mean? What kind of right are we talking about? It will have been noted how difficult the courts in formulating the right have found it to reconcile rights language with what they consider to be in a child's best interests. Are we, therefore, talking of a claim-right that can be enforced? And, if so, how significant is the child's age and competence? How is the right related to the child's welfare and how related to the exercise by him or her of self-determination? Does the child's right to contact mean that he or she can say 'no' to access as well as 'yes'.

These questions bring us back to the U.N. Convention and to a conflict in its provisions. The Convention is the first explicitly to state that children have a right to 'have a say' in processes affecting their lives. In this way, says Pais, the child is regarded as a 'principal' in the Convention.²¹ The provision in question (Article 12) is the most innovative in the Convention, and arguably, the most significant.²² It is a development from the child liberation philosophy which emerged in the 1970s with writers like Richard Farson and John Holt,²³ and is congruent also with the House of Lords decision in *Gillick v. West Norfolk and Wisbech Health Authority.*²⁴ The Article states:

---

[18] See also *Boileau v. Boileau* [1979] 13 R.F.L. 275; *Re Stroud and Stroud* [1974] 4 O.R. (2d) 567.

[19] See *Wiess v. Kopel* [1980] 18 R.F.L. (2d) 289.

[20] (1988) 12 R.F.L. (3d) 372.

[21] M. S. Pais, 'The United Nations Convention on the Rights of The Child', *Bulletin of Human Rights*, 91/2, 75–82, (1992).

[22] See P. Veerman, *The Rights of The Child and The Changing Image of Childhood* (Dordrecht: Martinus Nijhoff 1992), pp. 184–185.

[23] See *Birthrights* (Harmondsworth: Penguin, 1978) and *Escape From Childhood* (Harmondsworth: Penguin, 1975).

[24] [1986] A.C. 112. The backlash against these decisions in *Re R* [1991] 4 All E.R. 177

1. States Parties shall assure to the child who is capable of forming his or her own views the right to express those views freely in all matters affecting the child, the views of the child being given due weight in accordance with the age and maturity of the child.

2. For this purpose, the child shall in particular be provided the opportunity to be heard in any judicial and administrative proceedings affecting the child, either directly, or through a representative or an appropriate body, in a manner consistent with the procedural rules of national law.

But, equally important is Article 3 of the Convention. This requires the best interest of the child to be 'a primary consideration' in all actions concerning children 'whether undertaken by public or private social welfare institutions, courts of law, administrative authorities or legislative bodies'. Best interests are only a primary consideration: they are not, as in England[25] and elsewhere,[26] the paramount consideration. A Polish attempt[27] to make welfare 'paramount' failed. There is nevertheless a tension between this provision, where priority is accorded to concerns of welfare and Article 12, where the emphasis is firmly on the centrality of the child's views.

The Convention, as Philip Alston acknowledges, 'does not seek to provide any definite statement of how a child's interests would be best served in a given situation'.[28] But what are the courts to do where their conception of what is a child's best interests collides with the expression of a child's views? The problem is not unique to the questions of contact: it arises in many other areas, acutely for example, where an adolescent's view of sexual abuse differs strongly from professional assessments. Nevertheless, in the context of contact it offers a real dilemma.

---

and *Re W* [1992] 4 All E.R. 627 is discussed by M. Freeman, 'Removing Rights from Adolescents', *Adoption and Fostering*, 17 (1), 14–21 (1993), and in ch. 15. See also *South Glamorgan County Council* v. *W and B* [1993] 1 F.L.R. 574.

[25] Children Act 1989 s. 1; *J* v. *C* [1970] A.C. 68; *Re KD* [1988] A.C. 806. For the problem that arises where parent and child are both children see *Birmingham City Council* v. *H*, [1994] 2 A.C. 212.

[26] In Australia, *In The Marriage of Kress* [1976] F.L.C. 75, 593; *D* v. *S* [1983] F.L.C. 78, 322.

[27] See S. Detrick, *The United Nations Convention on The Rights of The Child: A Guide To The 'Travaux Préparatoires'* (Dordrecht: Martinus Nijhoff, 1992), p. 132.

[28] 'The Legal Framework of The Convention On The Rights of The Child', *Bulletin of Human Rights*, 91/2, p. 1–15 (1992).

It is one with which the English Court of Appeal has recently had to grapple. In *Re S*,[29] an 11-year-old boy had lived with his mother since his parents had separated 8 years previously. The father now sought a residence order.[30] The boy, S, said he wished to live with his father. The Official Solicitor was appointed as his guardian *ad litem* and recommended, with the support of a child psychiatrist, that S should continue to live with his mother and have less contact with his father. S applied for the Official Solicitor to be removed as his GAL.

He argued that his parents were not entitled to be heard on that application. The judge ruled against S on both issues. There was concern in his mind that S's wishes were influenced by his father. The Court of Appeal said that the relevant rules[31] did not confer any right on the parents to be heard on S's application, but a judge always had a discretion to hear any party in the interests of justice. Its view was that a judicious balance had to be struck between the principle of treating children as people in their own right,[32] and the need to protect children's interests. On the evidence before him the judge had to assess the understanding of the individual child in the context of the proceedings in which he or she wished to participate.

The appellate court thought the judge was right to believe that S lacked sufficient understanding to participate as a party in proceedings which were emotionally complex and highly fraught. The case, it said, cried out for an objective experienced judgment which the Official Solicitor was well-fitted to supply. Finding that S lacked sufficient understanding is, of course, a convenient way of disposing of an intractable problem. Had S been older and able to provide the reasoning expected of a 'competent' child,[33] the court would have had to have grasped the nettle. In recent cases concerning medical treatment,[34] they have not found this easy. But the consequences of contact, even where these are deemed to be against a

---

[29] [1993] 2 F.L.R. 437.
[30] Under Children Act 1989 s.8.
[31] Family Proceedings Rules 1991 r.9. 2A.
[32] Rather than as 'packages or pieces of property' *per* Butler-Sloss L.J. in *Re W* [1992] 2 F.L.R. 461. See also *Re S* [1992] 2 F.L.R. 313, 321.
[33] As to which see P. King and I. Young, 'The Child as Client', *Childright*, 95, 15–17 (1993) or, more fully, P. King and I. Young, *The Child as Client* (Bristol: Family Law, 1993).
[34] See *Re R* [1991] 4 All E.R. 177, *Re W* [1992] 4 All E.R. 627 and *Re K, W and H* [1993] 1 F.L.R. 240. And see ch. 15.

child's best interests, are not, or are not usually, as irrevocably deleterious as the failure to administer medical treatment.

How then do the courts tackle access where the child wants it and it is thought to be against his best interests, or the child is unwilling and the court deems a continuing relationship with an absent parent to be welfare enhancing? The latter problem has arisen in England a number of, times. The former has hitherto been submerged because of the child's inability to ask for contact. But this has changed with the Children Act and instances of it could well arise.

THE RECALCITRANT CHILD

The problem of the recalcitrant child has been well considered in a number of cases, and in the United States has recently caused enormous controversy. The English courts have taken the view that contact should be refused if the child's opposition to it is so marked that to allow it would harm him or her.[35] They have affirmed this even where the opposition is the result of indoctrination by the parent having care and control of the child.[36] A recent instance is *Re N*,[37] 'a case where...the child had been worked upon by the mother to the point that [he] himself had developed so powerful an opposition to seeing his father again that he would suffer serious emotional upset if he was forced to see him against his will'.[38] The child in this case was only five-and-a-half. In *Re S*,[39] by contrast, where children of 13 and 11 had expressed the wish not to see their father in any circumstances, the Court of Appeal, though stressing once again that 'access is the access of the child, not the access of the parent',[40] refused to terminate contact once and for all. Acting on the 'general principle', 'not to be lost sight of', that relationship between children and the non-

---

[35] *B v. B* [1971] 3 All E.R. 682; *M (P) v. M (C)* [1971] 115 Sol. Jo. 444; *Churchard v. Churchard* [1984] F.L.R. 635; *Re M* [1995] 1 F.L.R. 274. See also *Sheppard v. Miller* [1982] 3 F.L.R. 124 (where there was no evidence of harm).

[36] *B v. B* [1971] 3 All E.R. 682 (Edmund Davies L.J. said it was 'the duty of parents, whatever their personal differences may be, to seek to inculcate in the child a proper attitude of respect for the other parent' (p. 688)); *Williams v. Williams* [1985] F.L.R. 509.

[37] [1992] 1 F.L.R. 134.

[38] *Ibid.*, p. 138 per Ward J.

[39] [1992] 2 F.L.R. 313.

[40] *Ibid.*, p. 319 *per* Butler-Sloss L.J. Later in her judgment she says: 'It is the children we are thinking about and their right to have a part of their father' (p. 321).

custodial parent is beneficial to the children', and given that the children had 'several years of minority left in which they have the possibility of valuable future contact with their father',[41] it was ordered that active steps should be taken to promote future access. It is difficult to understand this decision, the more so since the judge constantly articulates children's rights sentiments. Thus, she insists that "nobody should dictate to children of this age, because one is dealing with their emotions, their lives and they are not packages to be moved around. They are people entitled to be treated with respect'.[42] The father is a religious bigot whose idea of a treat for the children was a pilgrimage and yet the judge hoped the children would be able to separate the two issues, 'their religion' and 'their thoughts about their father".[43]

Re S is in many ways a surprising decision. The cases establish all sorts of reasons for refusing a non-custodial parent contact and these include where this will seriously affect the child's health[44] or would otherwise be harmful to him or her (the usually-cited authority for this being a case[45] rather like Re S where harmful religious indoctrination was the cause). Re S, however, pales into insignificance when set against the recent American case In The Marriage of Marshall and Nussbaum.[46] Two girls, aged 12 and 8, refused to visit their father in breach of a court ordered agreement between the parents. The judge held both children to be in civil contempt: he 'grounded' the 8-year-old (she was not allowed to leave the mother's home, watch television or have friends visit her) and placed the 12-year-old in a juvenile detention facility. Because the case was a contempt hearing, not a custody dispute, best interests was not in issue—the judge appeared to be uninterested in evidence that the 12-year-old on previous visits had been kept up to 4 a.m. for 'father-daughter' sessions and had been taken on bird-shooting expeditions which caused her trauma—and the custody agreement was treated like a contract for the exchange of property. That the Illinois Court of Appeals has recently reversed the sanctions on the girls should not surprise: it could hardly do otherwise.[47]

---

[41] Ibid.
[42] Ibid., p. 321.
[43] Ibid., p. 320.
[44] Geapin v. Geapin [1974] 4 Fam. Law 188 (the child was asthmatic).
[45] Wright v. Wright [1980] 2 F.L.R. 276.
[46] 663 N.E. 2d 1113.
[47] 663 N.E. 2d 1122.

But it accepted that a less restrictive alternative punishment had to be found. The judge was not criticized: the children were.

THE RECALCITRANT PARENT

So far as is known there is no reported pre-Children Act case in England in which a parent's refusal to have contact with his or her child has been in issue. Nor is it easy to see how one can have arisen. Nor have I been able to trace one in any Commonwealth or common law jurisdiction. The Children Act allows a child to apply for leave to seek a contact order.[48] Leave may be granted if the court is satisfied that he or she has sufficient understanding to make the proposed application.[49] The first attempt to use this mechanism arose in the *Lucas* case.[50]

A boy of 15 sought to force his mother to spend more time with him. The case was only reported as a decision by a county court judge sitting in Southampton to transfer the matter to a High Court judge. The task of the High Court was then to apply the paramountcy principle in section 1 (1) of the 1989 Act and the welfare checklist in the same Act, including the 'ascertainable wishes and feelings of the child'[51] in the light of his age and understanding. It would be odd not to listen to a 15-year-old and Matthew Lucas's wishes were both ascertainable and clear. Unfortunately, at least for those of us with an interest in legal precedents, the case seems to have been settled, with what result we cannot tell. Questions nevertheless remain.

Can a parent be forced to see a child? Can it be in a child's best interests to see a parent who does not want to see him? If courts are reluctant to make children see parents, should they also not be slow to order a parent to see a child? If contact is a child's right, perhaps this case is the ultimate challenge, and therefore no surprise that, when the Bible wished to instruct us about wisdom, it chose a custody dispute![52]

---

[48] Children Act 1989 s. 10 (2) (b).
[49] Children Act 1989 s. 10 (8).
[50] *The Times*, 16 April 1993. *The Guardian* in a leading article 'The Voice of The Children' is in no doubt that the courts should resist this application (21 April, 1993, p. 23).
[51] Children Act 1989 s. 1 (3).
[52] Jon Elster, 'Solomonic Judgments: Against the Best Interest of the Child', *University of Chicago Law Review*, 54, 1 (1987).

CONTACT AFTER SEXUAL ABUSE

Returning to the problem of when contact with a child will be refused a parent, it is instructive to concentrate on one problem area, sexual abuse, using this as a case study. Child abuse is only now coming to be taken seriously,[53] the child's voice to be heard.[54] At the same time concern has been expressed at the incidence of abuse allegations to counter an ex-husband's or (partner's) demands for contact.[55] The most protracted custody litigation ever in the U.S.A., and arguably anywhere, hinged on abuse allegations.[56] The abuse of a child on an access visit to an estranged or divorced father may, Jean La Fontaine argues, 'be the result of his feelings about the separation and his (ex-)wife, or a demonstration that this is still "his child".'[57] But the most comprehensive piece of research on allegations of sexual abuse in the context of custody and access disputes has found no evidence that they are more likely to be found false in this than in any other context.[58]

We know very little about the subject. For example, where child abuse takes place on access visits is this a continuation of abuse that took place during the marriage/relationship or does it start upon separation or divorce? A small study based at the University of Michigan found that of 69 validated cases of sexual abuse by non-custodial fathers in only 7 was there evidence that the abuse started before the marital demise.[59] But in

---

[53] The Violence Against Children Study Group, *Taking Child Abuse Seriously* (London: Unwin, Hyman, 1990).

[54] Madge Bray, *Sexual Abuse: The Child's Voice* (Edinburgh: Canongate Press, 1991).

[55] See Blodgett, 'Spouses Use Allegations To Up The Ante in Divorce Case', *American Bar Association Journal* 1 May, 1987, p. 26.

[56] Morgan v. Foretich 846 F. 2d 941; 546 A. 2d 407. And see Jonathan Groner, *Hilary's Trial* (New York: Simon and Schuster, 1991).

[57] *Child Sexual Abuse* (Cambridge: Polity Press, 1990), p. 143. See also Beatrix Campbell, *Unofficial Secrets* (London: Virago, 1988), p. 171–175.

[58] N. Thoennes and P. G. Tjaden, 'The Extent, Nature and Validity of Sexual Abuse Allegations in Custody/Visitation Disputes,' *Child Abuse and Neglect*, 14, 151–163 (1990). Many allegations remain unsubstantiated, but this does not mean they are false (though some may be). Carol-Ann Hooper, *Mothers Surviving Child Sexual Abuse* (London: Routledge, 1992) refers to the suggestion that allegations are false as a 'new myth' (p. 18). See, further, D. L. Corwin *et al*, 'Child Sexual Abuse and Custody Disputes', *Journal of Interpersonal Violence*, 2 (1), 91–105 (1987) and L. Berliner, 'Interviewing Families' in K. Murray and D. Gough (eds.), *Intervening in Child Sexual Abuse* (Edinburgh: Scottish Academic Press, 1991).

[59] Kathleen Coulborn Faller, 'Sexual Abuse by Paternal Caretakers: A Comparison of

two-thirds of the cases there were signs of the offender's sexual attraction to the children during the marriage. An unsupervised access visit enhances the opportunity. 'The absence of rules about household functioning may encourage the offender to violate other rules, for example, the incest taboo'.[60] One further finding of some interest is that non-custodial fathers were also significantly more likely to abuse boys sexually[61]—an index, according to Faller, of 'their repressed and disorganised state at the time of divorce'.[62] But mistakes are made, as the recent English case of *KS* v. *GS* illustrates.[63] When a 3-year-old girl returned from an access visit in a disturbed state, the mother jumped to the conclusion that some sort of inappropriate sexual play had taken place between father and daughter. In fact she was reacting to news that her grandfather had died. But in the meantime social services had rushed to the conclusion not just that access should be suspended but terminated, without any endeavour to ascertain the father's point of view.

There are a number of reported cases in England.[64] One of the matters to which a court is directed by the checklist in determining disputed applications for a contact order is any harm which the child has suffered or is at risk of suffering. The harm does not have to be significant.[65] All the cases turn on their own facts but 'the principle is clearly established that cases of sexual abuse which show a danger of the repetition of that conduct if access is afforded to a parent, or indeed which show continuing or recent disturbance, may warrant...a total withdrawal of access'.[66] Where there has been serious sexual abuse, there would be no question of a father's rights—only one whether the children would benefit from seeing their father.[67] But English courts have been prepared to allow contact, even where

---

Abusers Who Are Biological Fathers in Intact Families, Stepfathers and Non-custodial Fathers' in Anne L. Horton, Barry L. Johnson, Lyan M. Roundy and Doran Williams (eds.) *The Incest Perpetrator* (Newbury Park, Calif: Sage, 1990), p. 65–73 (see p. 68–69).

[60] *Idem.*

[61] 28 per cent were male (5 per cent only in intact marriages).

[62] *Op. cit.*, note 57, p. 70.

[63] [1992] 2 F.L.R. 361.

[64] *Re R* [1988] 1 F.L.R. 206; *S* v. *S* [1988] F.L.R. 213; *C* v. *C* [1988] 1 F.L.R. 462; *H* v. *H* [1989] 1 F.L.R. 212; *Re H* [1989] 2 F.L.R. 174; *L* v. *L* [1985] 2 F.L.R. 16. See also the early surrogacy case reported in 1985 as *A* v. *C* [1985] F.L.R. 445 (but decided in 1978).

[65] *Cf.* Children Act 1989 s. 31 (2).

[66] *Re H* [1989] 2 F.L.R. 174, 184–5.

[67] *H* v. *H* [1989] 1 F.L.R. 212.

there has been sexual abuse. This is hardly surprising given their willingness in certain circumstances to allow a child to live with his or her abuser.[68] Thus, in *C* v. *C*,[69] where there had been vulgar and inappropriate horseplay, said to fall short of sexual abuse, access to a loving and intelligent father, who was now aware of the risks attendant upon his behaviour, was allowed. And, in *L* v. *L*,[70] where there was a close bond between father and daughter and where she loved and enjoyed seeing him (he was '*the father-figure in her life*'[71]), where she benefited from the access and was socially well-adjusted and showed no disturbance after the abuse, access with a supervision order was upheld by the Court of Appeal. If contact is to be seen as a child's right, then it is difficult to fault this decision. The child concerned was only 5 years old but she had expressed her feelings as forcibly as she could (though it is interesting that she had insisted upon wearing trousers for an access visit) and the use of a supervision order and assistance of sensible grandparents seemed to offer her sufficient protection.

In many abuse cases only one of the children will have been abused. This poses a particular problem: can contact be granted to the non-abused children and denied the abused child? In *Corkett* v. *Corkett*[72] (not a case where sexual abuse was involved), the Court of Appeal said that the question of access should be considered independently as regards each child. It was clear that the girls, aged 14 and 12, did not want access but there remained a boy of 7—and the possibility of access to him was left to be investigated. His views were not known and probably had not been sought. But then this is a case where access is seen implicitly as a father's right. In *S* v. *S*,[73] by contrast, where there had been serious sexual abuse of a stepdaughter of 7, who suffered significant disturbance as a result, the Court of Appeal ruled that all three children must be treated as a unit (there were also girls of 5 and 4). Access was denied to all three. A first instance decision to allow access to the younger children on an experimental basis for a limited period was overturned. Fox, L.J. reasoned thus: 'If this order is given effect to, how will these three children be brought up as a single unit? It is very likely to create many tensions and there will be a lack of

---

[68] *Re B* [1990] 2 F.L.R. 317.
[69] [1988] 1 F.L.R. 462.
[70] [1989] 2 F.L.R. 16.
[71] *Ibid.*, p. 20 *per* Sir Stephen Brown P.
[72] [1985] F.L.R. 708.
[73] [1988] 1 F.L.R. 213.

162 *Chapter 8*

balance in this family, which will be exacerbated by the circumstances of the access.... The access is not likely to be productive of any results of value to them'.[74] This may well be the correct decision on its facts (the younger girls barely recognized their father), but if contact is to be seen as a child's right, each child should be considered individually.

CONTACT AND SUPPORT

The major problem in the area of contact has long been the recalcitrant custodial parent. Courts have long struggled to find ways of enforcing access.[75] With concerns also about the enforcement of support obligations, the question of relating the two has been constantly raised, not least by non-custodial fathers angry at a legal system which expects them to fulfil the financial burdens of parenthood without, necessarily, allowing them to enjoy its benefits.

Kitch[76] recently allied herself with the lobby that would condition child support payments on access.[77] There are many problems with making this link. Children subject to conditioning orders may be financially disadvantaged. More families will become dependant on the welfare system.

And, most significantly, such a proposal would reinforce the law's gender bias. As Czapanskiy put it in an excellent article:[78]

> The central metaphor is that contact with a child is a commodity to be brought and sold. But unlike normal commodity contracts, the buyer and seller are not equals. Here, only the buyer has legal control. If he elects to purchase contact with the child by paying support, he has the right to do so; the seller cannot refuse to sell. If the buyer elects not to pick up his purchase, the seller cannot require him to do so. Since

---

[74] *Ibid.*, p. 217. *Corkett* v. *Corkett* is not referred to and I suppose *S* v. *S* could be regarded as *per incuriam* but Bevan, *Child Law* (London: Butterworths, 1989, para. 3.84) sensibly prefers to distinguish the two cases on the grounds of the conduct (the sexual abuse) of the father and the fact that all the children were girls in the later case.

[75] See *V-P* v. *V-P* [1978] 1 F.L.R. 336; *Churchard* v. *Churchard* [1984] F.L.R. 635. A rare example of imprisonment as a sanction is *C* v. *C* [1990] 1 F.L.R. 462.

[76] 'Conditioning Child Support Payments on Visitation Access: A Proposal;' *International Journal of Law and The Family*, 5, 318–350 (1991). And see *Anderson* v. *Anderson* 291 NW 508 [1940].

[77] Comment, 'Child Support v. Rights to Visitation: Equity, Economics and The Rights of The Child', *Stetson Law Review*, 16, 139 (1986).

[78] 'Child Support and Visitation: Rethinking The Connections', *Rutgers Law Journal*, 20, 619 (1989).

nearly all residential parents are women and non-residential parents are men, the buyers are nearly always fathers.[79]

She is surely right to observe that under conditioning rules:

> the father's desire for contact with this children is give a preference over the mother's need for regular financial support for the children. Further, she is subject to indefinite and restrictive standards about facilitating the father's access to the child, while he is subject to no standards about what he must do.[80]

For anyone concerned with children's rights conditioning proposals which commodify[81] children cannot pass muster. The development of such a package would turn the clock both generally and more specifically in relation to contact: a trend in favour of regarding contact as a child's right would become a marketable good of the non-custodial parent.

---

[79] *Ibid.*, p. 650.
[80] *Ibid.*, p. 646.
[81] See the similar attack mounted on the institution of surrogacy by M. Radin, *Harvard Law Review*, 100, 1849, at p. 1926.

CHAPTER 9

Do Children Have the Right Not to Be Born?

If the title tantalizes, it is meant to. Even those who accept that children have rights, and most now do,[1] may find the paradox puzzling. The designation of those not yet born as 'children' may be thought to embody a particular value position with which some may be uncomfortable. It is not intended to discomfort in this way. This is not an examination of the morality of abortion.[2] Why I call the as yet unborn 'children' will become apparent in the course of this paper, and it will have implications for abortion[3] though again I emphasize that is not my concern.

THE RIGHT TO BE A PARENT

The right to be a parent, to marry and found a family, as it is formulated in international documents,[4] is commonly asserted. Thus, we can expect the Labour party to be attacked if it persists with its intention of removing NHS funding from IVF treatment.[5] Of responsible parenthood we hear rather less.[6] One of the rights I believe children have—and this is seldom

---

[1] But see Laura M. Purdy, *In Their Best Interest?* (Ithaca: Cornell University Press, 1992). More conventionally see David Archard, *Children: Rights and Childhood* (London: Routledge, 1993).

[2] A thoughtful article on the intractable conflict involved here is Amy Gutmann and Dennis Thompson, 'Moral Conflict and Political Consensus', 101 Ethics 64 (1990).

[3] In particular raising the question of whether there are circumstances in which it is morally right to terminate a pregnancy.

[4] For example, the European Convention on Human Rights, Article 12 ('Men and women of marriageable age have the right to marry and to found a family according to the national laws governing the exercise of this right'). See also Cyril Hegnauer, 'Human Rights and Artificial Procreation by Donor' in (eds.) John Eekelaar and Petar Šarčević, *Parenthood in Modern Society* (Dordrecht: Nijhoff, 1993, p. 207).

[5] *The Independent*, 18 April 1995.

[6] But see Robert Bellah *et al*, *The Good Society* (Berkeley: University of California Press, 1991). See also Patricia Hewitt and Penelope Leach, *Social Justice, Children and Families*

invoked—is the right to responsible parents. But that is not, at least directly, my concern here. But responsibility, the moral correlative of rights, is in issue and must be addressed. Without in any way wishing to gainsay the right to have children, the question must be raised as to whether there are any circumstances in which it would be wrong to bring a child into existence. Are there circumstances in which life would be 'demonstrably so awful' (the test posited in the first English defective neonate case in 1981[7]) that it would be unfair to subject a child to it, circumstances such that never to have been born would have been preferable to being born with particular disabilities? And if such circumstances exist, do potential parents have the duty not to procreate? It has taken a long time for us to conceptualize the parent-child relationship in terms of parental responsibility rather than as a bundle of parental rights.[8] It will be part of the argument of this paper that our moral reasoning could usefully employ the concept of parental responsibility[9] in this context too.

PARENTAL AUTONOMY AND ITS LIMITATIONS

John Stuart Mill, writing in *On Liberty* many years before many of the problems I am addressing could have been anticipated, was aware of the problem. He wrote:

> It still remains unrecognised, that to bring a child into existence without a fair prospect of being able, not only to provide food for its body, but instruction and training for its mind, is a moral crime, both against the unfortunate offspring and against society.[10]

But, as Mill recognized for this 'crime' there was a relatively easy remedy:[11] 'if the parent does not fulfil this obligation, the State ought to see it fulfilled, at the charge, as far as possible, of the parent'.[12]

(London: IPPR, 1993) and Report of the Commission on Social Justice, *Social Justice* (London: Vintage, 1994, pp. 320–322).

[7] *Re B* [1981] 1 WLR 1421.

[8] The change can be traced back to a Justice report, *Parental Rights and Duties and Custody Suits* (London: Justice, 1975). I was a member of the Committee.

[9] As now found in the Children Act 1989 sections 2 and 3.

[10] *On Liberty* in *Utilitarianism* (ed. by Mary Warnock) (London: Fontana, 1972, p. 239).

[11] But not a remedy which commended itself to too many in 1859 when *On Liberty* was published.

[12] *Op. cit.*, note 10, p. 239.

FEINBERG AND BIRTHRIGHTS

For Mill this constituted a limitation to autonomy. It was not so much an application of his famous principle of 'harm to others',[13] as an additional justification for interfering with an individual's freedom. But the contemporary philosopher Joel Feinberg, in the first of four volumes exploring the moral limits of the criminal law, which he entitles *Harm To Others*,[14] does examine the question under scrutiny using the concept of harm. He concludes, for reasons which will be discussed shortly, that biological parents 'do not harm' a child even if the child comes into existence in a state that makes a 'life worth living' impossible.[15] But it is still possible, he argues, to talk of a right not to be born. This refers to 'the plausible moral requirement' that:

> No child be brought into the world unless certain very minimal conditions of well-being are assured, and certain basic "future interests" are protected in advance, at least in the sense that the possibility of his fulfilling those interests is kept open. When a child is brought into existence even though these requirements have not been observed, he has been wronged thereby....[16]

Feinberg's concern is with 'birthrights'.[17] So, if the conditions to enable him to fulfil his most basic interests are destroyed before he is born 'and we permit him nevertheless to be born, we become a party to the violation of his rights'.[18] Feinberg concedes that not all interests should qualify for prenatal legal protection,[19] only the very basic ones whose satisfaction is indispensable. But Feinberg's list of these is compendious and difficult to take seriously. Harris called it 'astonishing'.[20]

> ...severe mental retardation, congenital syphilis, blindness, deafness, advanced heroin addiction, permanent paralysis or incontinence, guar-

---

[13] *Ibid.*, p. 135.
[14] (New York: Oxford University Press, 1984).
[15] *Ibid.*, p. 102.
[16] *Ibid.*, p. 101.
[17] Used in a different sense from that made famous in one of the early child liberation books (see Richard Farson, *Birthrights*, Harmondsworth: Penguin, 1978). But more germane is Robert Lee and Derek Morgan, *Birthrights: Law and Ethics at the Beginning of Life* (London: Routledge, 1989).
[18] *Op. cit.*, note 14, p. 99.
[19] *Idem.*
[20] *Wonderwoman and Superman* (Oxford: Oxford University Press, 1992), p. 91.

anteed malnutrition, and economic deprivation so far below a reasonable minimum as to be inescapably degrading and sordid....²¹

Feinberg clearly cannot intend this catalogue to be cumulative—it would be unimaginably cruel to be dealt all these blows. But if one examines each of these 'ills' individually, the implications would be, for example, that the very poor should never procreate, and nor should the congenitally blind or congenitally deaf because of the likelihood that offspring would also suffer from these disabilities. Children born in such circumstances would be 'harmed'—it is a disadvantage to be born deaf or to very poor parents—but would they be 'wronged' (remembering this is Feinberg's test)? There are blind and deaf and even extremely poor people who lead happy and fulfilling lives and their children may do so too.²²

In a more recent article,²³ Feinberg has concluded that it is possible to harm someone by being responsible for his being brought into existence. He says his inability to see this in *Harm To Others* resulted from his failure to clarify what it means to say that someone has been made 'worse off'. But this can mean more than one thing. It could be interpreted to mean 'worse off than he was *before* the wrongdoer acted' (Feinberg designates this 'the worsening condition').²⁴ But no one can be worse off than he was before he existed—it would be absurd to compare the individual before he existed with the individual after he existed. In some cases, however, the individual who has been harmed is not worse off than he was but worse off than he would have been, had the wrongdoer not acted as he did. This expresses, what Feinberg has called, a 'counterfactual' condition.²⁵ The counterfactual claim amounts to saying that the individual would be better off not coming into existence, or 'better off unborn'.

Better Off Unborn

But what is meant by saying that someone is 'better off unborn'? It may help, as Steinbock suggests in *Life Before Birth*, to consider first what is

---

²¹ *Op. cit.*, note 14, p. 99.

²² It is always difficult to use actual examples and rather boring to cite Beethoven. It is also embarrassing to think that on all the tests cited in this paper Stephen Hawkins, acknowledged to be one of the most brilliant men of this generation, would not have been born.

²³ 'Wrongful Life and the Counterfactual Element in Harming', *Social Philosophy and Policy*, 4(1), 145 (1986). (This is reprinted in *Freedom and Fulfilment* (Princeton: Princeton University Press, 1992, p. 3).

²⁴ *Ibid.*, p. 149.

²⁵ *Ibid.*, p. 150.

meant by 'better off dead'. This phrase, she suggests, means that 'life is so terrible that it is no longer a benefit or a good to the one who lives'.[26] In the case of a competent adult, the criterion by which to judge whether a person is better off dead is ordinarily whether the person himself considers life not worth living. But this is not a test that can be applied to infants. It is not just that they cannot express their preferences: they lack the intellectual equipment to have preferences. They cannot understand the choice between a severely handicapped existence and no existence at all. Therefore, it does not make any sense to ask what the infants would want, if they could only tell us. As Buchanan and Brock demonstrate clearly,[27] the test of 'substituted judgment' is not applicable in the case of never-competent individuals.

It now becomes possible to project this analysis onto the state of being better off not existing or 'better off unborn'. The unborn cannot be consulted about whether they wish to be born, nor can an infant be asked whether his present existence is preferable to not having been born. It would be possible to raise a presumption in favour of life, any life. But there are surely lives that are demonstrably so awful that no one could possibly wish it on a child. These cases are rare. More common are those where the child is severely handicapped. Robertson[28] considers the case of profoundly retarded, non-ambulatory, blind and deaf infant who will spend his time in a state institution and he comments:

> One who has never known the pleasures of mental operation, ambulation and social interaction surely does not suffer from the loss as much as one who has. While one who has known these capacities may prefer death to a life without them, we have no assurance that the handicapped person, with no point of comparison, would agree. Life and Life alone, whatever its limitations, might be of sufficient worth to him.[29]

A life that a normal individual might find intolerable might not be so awful for an infant who has experienced nothing else.

It is difficult, therefore, to make a choice based on the infant's particular interests. But it is possible to offer the judgment of a 'proxy chooser'.

---

[26] (New York, Oxford University Press, 1992), p. 120.
[27] *Deciding For Others* (Cambridge: Cambridge University Press, 1989).
[28] 'Involuntary Euthanasia of Defective Newborns: A Legal Analysis', *Stanford Law Review*, 27, 213 (1974).
[29] *Ibid.*, p. 254.

Rather like a guardian *ad litem*, this person would act as an advocate of the child's best interests. The proxy chooser cannot express the child's own preferences, but neither should he allow his values to obtrude. Feinberg puts it thus:[30]

> [The infant] may not yet have any values, goals, ideals or aspirations, the stuff of which interests are made. But the proxy chooser is not therefore required to substitute his own, ascribing them hypothetically to the infant. Rather, he exercises his judgment that *whatever* interests the impaired party might have, or come to have, they would already be doomed to defeat by his present incurable condition. Thus, it would be irrational—contrary to what reason decrees—for a representative and protector of those interests to prefer the continuance of that condition to nonexistence. The proxy might also express the retroactive preference, on the incompetent's behalf, not to have been born at all.

Note there are two important features of the proxy's choice. The choice of non-existence must be required by reason, not just in accordance with it. 'A preference for non-existence over continued existence with a cut finger is clearly contrary to reason; a preference for non-existence to inescapable hideous torture might be required by reason.'[31]

Feinberg offers us a thought experiment in which we are given the opportunity after death to be reincarnated, 'but only as a Tay-Sachs baby with a painful life expectancy of four years to be followed by permanent extinction or [we] can opt for permanent extinction to begin immediately'.[32] Feinberg is of the opinion that we would have to be 'crazy'[33] to select the first option and that if required to make the choice for a loved one we would also opt for immediate non-existence. Secondly, non-existence is rationally preferable only if all interests, present and future, are 'doomed to defeat'.[34] Such a test works optimally where there is chronic pain combined with such severe mental retardation that the child will not be able to develop any compensating interests. It is instructive to examine and compare the facts of the two well-known English cases.

---

[30] *Op. cit.*, note 23, p. 164.
[31] *Ibid.*, p. 165.
[32] *Ibid.*, p. 164.
[33] *Idem.*
[34] *Idem.*

Better Off Dead

The first, alluded to already, is that of 'Baby Alexandra' (*Re B*).[35] She was born a Down's Syndrome baby with an intestinal blockage. The Court of Appeal sanctioned surgery, which was thought to give her a life expectancy of 20 to 30 years (the normal life span of someone with Down's). The test applied was whether it could be said that Alexandra's life was demonstrably going to be so awful that she should be condemned to die, or whether it was so imponderable that she should be allowed to live.[36] This conclusion appears to be right and certainly as an application of the 'doomed to defeat' test would fall clearly into the category where reason would prefer existence to non-existence. But the case also throws light on the problem of proxy choice. The decision in *Re B* was only taken by a court because parents, the most obvious proxy choosers, preferred their daughter to die. This was a preference they later came to regret and they successfully requested the return of Alexandra to their custody when she was ten months old.[37] This illustrates both the difficulties of proxy choice and perhaps also the dangers of leaving such decisions with parents. As such the case is an interesting test for the Goldstein, Freud and Solnit parental autonomy thesis.[38]

The second case is *Re J*.[39] J was a baby born prematurely at 27 weeks gestation. At birth he weighed 1.1 Kg: he was not breathing, was placed on a ventilator and given antibiotics on a drip to avoid infection. When taken off the ventilator at three to four months he suffered repetitive fits and cessations of breathing requiring resuscitation by ventilation. The prognosis was severe brain damage arising from prematurity. The most optimistic neonatologist thought that there would be serious spastic quadriplegia. It was likely that J would never be able to sit up or hold his head upright; he would probably be blind and deaf, and would be most unlikely to develop even the most limited intellectual abilities. On the other hand, there was evidence that he would be able to feel pain to the same extent as a normal baby. Life expectancy at its highest was late teens, and probably

---

[35] [1981] 1 WLR 1421.
[36] *Ibid.*, p. 1424.
[37] This was reported in *The Observer*, 5 December 1982.
[38] *Before The Best Interests of The Child* (New York: Free Press, 1979). In *The Rights and Wrongs of Children* (London: Frances Pinter, 1983), I have criticized their thesis (see ch. 7): I show in particular the problems inherent in applying it to a case like *Re B* (see pp. 259–63).
[39] [1990] 3 All E.R. 930.

would be considerably shorter. To the question what should be done if J suffered a further collapse, the first instance judge directed there should be no further ventilation, but the Court of Appeal held that a medical course of action could be approved which would fail to prevent death. There was, it held, no absolute rule that life-prolonging treatment should never be withheld except in the case of a terminally ill child. Nor, it said, was the 'demonstrably so awful' test, propounded in *Re B*,[40] to be treated as a quasi-statutory yardstick. While there was a strong presumption in favour of life, regard had to be had to the quality of life, and to any additional suffering that might be caused by the life-saving treatment itself. In assessing the quality of life if treatment were given, the court thought the correct approach was to assess whether such a life judged from the child's viewpoint would be intolerable to him. J's case does surely come within Feinberg's 'doomed to defeat' category as Baby Alexandra's does not. But relatively few impaired new-borns will be like J and many more will have similar conditions and prognoses to Baby Alexandra. This demonstrates the limits of Feinberg's test. Applied in the context of examining the right not to be born it would suggest that this right only exists, if at all, where the child when born would exist only at the very margins of life.[41] And it would, of course, narrow the category of cases in which there could be said to be a right not to be born to a small proportion of those in Feinberg's original list. It may be observed also, before we leave *Re J*, that the court applied the 'substituted judgment test', which, as already indicated, is difficult to sustain where the patient has never been competent. The court appeared to recognize this problem for it purported to apply the welfare principle but did so in such a way as to appear to equate the best interests of the child with a hypothetical projection of what that child would have wished if he had been fully competent.[42]

A RIGHT NOT TO BE BORN?

It is easier to examine the dilemma of those 'better off unborn' from the perspective of the disabled new-born. But we must now take the problem back in time—how far is a matter of considerable controversy[43]—and ask

---

[40] *Op. cit.*, note 35, p. 1421.
[41] And see Celia Wells '"Otherwise Kill Me": Marginal Children and Ethics at the Edges of Existence' in Lee and Morgan, *Op. cit.*, note 17, p. 195.
[42] And see Celia Wells, Peter Alldridge and Derek Morgan, 'An Unsuitable Case for Treatment' (1990) 140 *New Law Journal* 1544.
[43] See John Harris, *op. cit.*, note 20, ch. 3.

the question at the kernel of this paper whether it is morally right to bring into existence certain children or in certain circumstances to allow procreated but as yet unborn children to continue to exist. So much attention has focused on the morality of abortion (when women could be allowed to terminate their pregnancies[44]) that our attention has been deflected from the equally interesting question—and one which in time may become more significant[45]—as to when it would be morally wrong not to abort. Is a woman who as a result of an amniocentesis test finds her foetus has spina bifida acting ethically in continuing with her pregnancy? Or should she terminate her pregnancy and try again for a healthy baby? And, if she is warned that she is always likely to give birth to a baby with a major disorder such as spina bifida, should she avoid conception?[46]

The problem, initially conceptualized as one of problematic children, is beginning to bifurcate into two. As Harris puts it: 'The first involves an examination of potential children for their adequacy as children; and the second involves examining potential parents for their adequacy as parents.... One dimension of the problem involves asking whether we might do wrong by bringing particular children into existence because of problems relating to...the constitution of those children, in virtue of which we might expect them to have less than adequate or satisfactory lives. The second concerns the question of whether we might do wrong by permitting children to be brought into existence who will suffer from less than adequate parenting'.[47] The latter question is the subject of an important new book *Who's Fit To Be A Parent?* by Mukti Jain Campion.[48] I will address this issue only briefly—and in passing. It is at the root of another right that needs exploration—the right to responsible parents. It is to the former question that I now turn and concentrate my attention. Different issues are involved in the two questions but we will see that the concept of parental responsibility ultimately unites them.

The complexity of the first question and the dilemma of understanding what is meant by acting in a parentally responsible manner is well brought

---

[44] For example, Rosalind Hursthouse, *Beginning Lives* (Oxford: Basil Blackwell and Open University, 1987).

[45] See Janet Hadley's comment in 'God's Bullies: Attacks on Abortion', *Feminist Review*, number 48, 94, 108–109.

[46] If we believe in the right to have a family, should she be rewarded for acting ethically by being admitted to a form of IVF treatment which will avoid the problem?

[47] *Op. cit.*, note 20, p. 50.

[48] (London: Routledge, 1995). I describe the book as important though I have considerable reservations both about its content and style.

174 *Chapter 9*

out in two contrasting examples that Derek Parfit gives.[49] He invites us to consider the dilemmas of two women:

> The first is one month pregnant and is told by her doctor that, unless she takes a simple treatment, the child she is carrying will develop a certain handicap.... Life with this handicap would probably be worth living, but less so than normal life. It would obviously be wrong for the mother not to take the treatment, for this will handicap her child....[50]
>
> ...There is a second woman, who is about to stop taking contraceptive pills so that she can have another child. She is told that she has a temporary condition such that any child she conceives now will have the same handicap; but that if she waits three months she will then conceive a normal child. And it seems (at least to me) clear that this would be just as wrong as it would be for the first woman to deliberately handicap her child.

The first case is relatively uncontentious. It could be rendered more complicated if the simple treatment would harm the pregnant woman or if, as with AZT for those with HIV infection, undergoing the treatment now to help the unborn child would preclude subsequent treatment to assist herself.[51] But the norm of parental responsibility would dictate that she should put her child first and undergo the treatment now for the child's sake. I am reminded of the way the courts have come to import welfare into adoption decisions. Lord Hailsham in *Re W*[52] said that 'although welfare *per se* is not the test, the fact that a reasonable parent does pay regard to the welfare of his[53] child must enter into the question of reasonableness as a relevant factor'.[54] Just as the objectively reasonable mother would put her child before herself in deciding whether or not to agree to adoption, so, it may be argued, would she in Parfit's first example.

---

[49] 'Rights Interests and Possible People' in S. Gorovitz (ed.), *Moral Problems In Medicine* (Englewood Cliffs, N.J.: Prentice Hall, 1976). p. 76.

[50] But what if the 'treatment' alters the genetic composition of the child, changing its identity into that of a different person?

[51] On this see the research reported in *The Lancet* in 1995. Of Interest also is R. Alto Charo, 'Protecting Us to Death: Women, Pregnancy and Clinical Research Trials' 38 *St Louis University Law Journal* 135 (1993).

[52] [1971] A.C. 682.

[53] It is characteristic of Lord Hailsham to use the male pronoun even when the vast majority of cases (including the instant one) involved mothers.

[54] *Op. cit.*, note 52, p. 699.

The second case, however, is far from straightforward as Parfit himself acknowledges. When he discusses in *Reasons and Persons* attempts to persuade a 14-year-old girl to delay having a child he notes that we might say to her: 'You should think not only of yourself, but also of your child. It will be worse for him if you have him now'.[55] As he shows, the weak link in this claim is the phrase 'worse for him', for clearly if she has a child later it will not be the same child. If the woman takes the advice she deprives a potential person, albeit one with a handicap, of the chance of having a life. It is his/her only chance. S/he may be glad to have the opportunity. Locke,[56] using a similar example[57] to Parfit's second case, invokes, what he calls the 'the Possible Persons Principle', that is, 'the principle that in judging the rightness or wrongness of an action or decision we need to take account not merely of those who actually do, or will, exist, but also of those who would have existed if there had been a different action or decision'.[58] But acceptance of this principle would have enormous repercussions, not least for abortion. If, therefore, the second case can be explained by a more limited (or at any rate different) principle, it would be better to invoke this.

In seeking this it is well to remember Richard Brandt's observation that *'no person is frustrated or made unhappy or miserable by not coming to exist'*.[59] Appeal to the concept of deprivation may assist us to understand the difference between being born with a handicap and not being conceived. As Steinbock pithily puts it: 'the point of morality is to make people...happy, not to make more happy people'.[60] We may thus be able to conclude that the woman in Parfit's second example also does the right thing if she postpones conception and avoids having a handicapped child. But suppose that the second woman is told that any child she bears, now or in the future, will be handicapped, should she avoid conception? Unlike the woman in the second case, she will be depriving herself of the interest of being a mother (though

---

[55] *Reasons and Persons* (Oxford: Oxford University Press, 1984), pp. 358–359.
[56] 'The Parfit Population Problem', 62 *Philosophy* 131 (1987).
[57] The 'fated child' who will inevitably die of a heart attack at 25.
[58] *Op. cit.*, note 56, p. 138.
[59] 'The Morality of Abortion' in Robert L. Perkins (ed.), *Abortion: Pro and Con* (Cambridge, Mass: Schenkman Publishing Co, 1974), p. 163. See also Mary Ann Warren, 'Do Potential People Have Moral Rights?' in R.I. Sikora and Brian Barry (eds.), *Obligations To Future Generations* (Philadelphia: Temple University Press, 1978, p. 25) and Matthew Hanser, 'Harming Future People', 19 *Philosophy and Public Affairs* 47 (1990).
[60] *Op. cit.*, note 26, p. 74.

the value of this interest may be diminished in the circumstances), but again it cannot be said that she is depriving anyone else of life.[61]

WRONGFUL LIFE ACTIONS

But if failing to have a child is not wrong, having a child may, in certain circumstances, be wrong. Indeed, the belief that a child may be wronged by being brought into existence in certain circumstances has given rise to so-called 'wrongful life' actions.[62] The first was *Zepeda* v. *Zepeda* in 1963.[63] In this case a healthy infant plaintiff claimed that his father had injured him by causing him to be born illegitimately. The Illinois appellate court declined to permit recovery, fearing the floodgates would be opened to all manner of wrongful life suits brought by parties born under adverse conditions. It is a comment upon our times that a generation on from *Zepeda* and *Williams* it is dubious whether illegitimate (or non-marital) birth would even be considered adverse.[64] The American courts have since distinguished between being born under adverse conditions and being born with a severe handicap or fatal disease. A clear statement of this distinction is found in the judgment of Justice Jefferson in *Curlender* v. *Bio-Science Laboratories*, a case where a child was born, suffering from Tay-Sachs disease:

> A cause of action based upon impairment of status—illegitimacy contrasted with legitimacy—should not be recognizable at law because a necessary element for the establishment of any cause of action in tort is missing, *injury* and damages consequential to that injury. A child born with severe impairment, however, presents an entirely different situation because the necessary element of *injury* is present.[65]

But what constitutes an injury? Is to be born underweight because of the mother's smoking whilst pregnant? Is to be born with a low IQ? Is to be

---

[61] On the difficult philosophical issues involved here see John Harris, *op. cit.*, note 20, pp. 66–68.
[62] An early and formative discussion of which is G. Tedeschi, 'On Tort Liability for "Wrongful Life"', 1 *Israel Law Review* 513 (1966).
[63] 190 N.E. 2d 849 (1963). See also *Williams* v. *State of New York* 223 N.E. 2d 343 (1966).
[64] Illegitimate births now constitute a third of live births, about a 400 per cent increase since the days of *Zepeda*.
[65] 106 Cal. App. (3d) 811, 165 Cal. Repts. 477 (1980).

born into 'a polluted world infested with war and insecurity'?[66] Or in 1945 rather than 1955?[67] And, as the ability to manipulate genetic material develops,[68] will it be an injury to be born X rather than Y, a boy rather than a girl, gay rather than heterosexual,[69] with criminal propensities rather than integrity,[70] with a defect uncorrected that could have been corrected?

The courts have not been receptive to wrongful life claims, though they have succeeded in a number of American states (California,[71] New Jersey,[72] Washington[73]) as well as in Israel.[74] The English courts have rejected the concept. In *McKay* v. *Essex Area Health Authority*,[75] the Court of Appeal expressed the view that 'the difference between existence and non-existence was incapable of measurement by a court'.[76] Ackner L.J. said that he could not accept that: 'the common law duty of care to a person can involve, without specific legislation to achieve this end, the legal obli-

---

[66] David Heyd, *Genethics* (Berkeley: University of California Press), p. 34.

[67] Heyd's example (*idem*). But, of course, both 10 years later would be a different person.

[68] In particular germ-line gene therapy. On this see Harris, *op. cit.*, note 20, ch. 8. It is condemned by David Suzuki and Peter Enudson, *Genethics* (London: Unwin, Hymen, 1989). See also the article by Andrea Bonnicksen, 'National and International Approaches To Human Germ-Line Gene Therapy', 13(1) *Politics and the Life Sciences* 39 (1994) and the *Symposium* that this stimulated in volume 13(2) of the same journal. Robert Winston's view that the threat is 'exaggerated' is found in the Symposium at p. 237. In relation to identity the controversial article by Noam J. Zohar 'Prospects for "Genetic Therapy"—Can A Person Benefit From Being Altered?', 5 *Bioethics* 275 (1991) may be consulted. It has provoked a debate which continues: see, as examples, Nicholas Agar, 'Designing Babies: Morally Permissible Ways To Modify The Human Genome', 9 *Bioethics* 1 (1995) and Ingmar Persson, 'Genetic Therapy, Identity and Person-Regarding Reasons', 9 *Bioethics* 16 (1995). I doubt whether Ruth Chadwick's concern that someone 'who discovers that her parents had an extra gene or genes added...may suffer from...an identity crisis' (see *Ethics, Reproduction and Genetic Control* (London: Routledge, 1987, p. 126) should cause real concern.

[69] See D. H. Hamer *et al.*, 'A Linkage Between DNA markers on the X Chromosome and male Sexual Orientation', *Science* 262, 578 (1993). And see Steve Jones, *The Language of the Genes* (London: Flamingo Press, 1994, pp. 239–241.

[70] This has been highlighted in the *Mobley* case in Georgia in 1995. On the CIBA conference held in London in February 1995 see *The Guardian*: 14 February 1995.

[71] *Curlender* v. *Bio-Science Laboratories* 106 Cal. App (3d) 811, 165 Cal. 477 (1980).

[72] *Berman* v. *Allen* 404 A 2d 8.

[73] *Harbeson* v. *Parke-Davis Inc* 656 P. 2d 483 (1983).

[74] *Zeitsov* v. *Katz* (1986) 40 (ii) P.D. 85. It is discussed in David Heyd, 'Are "Wrongful Life" Claims Philosophically Valid?' 21 *Israel L. Rev.* 574 (1986).

[75] [1982] 2 All E.R. 7711.

[76] *Ibid.*, p. 790.

gation to that person, whether or not *in utero*, to terminate his existence'.[77] Such a proposition he thought, ran wholly contrary to the concept of the sanctity of human life. In New York 'the fundamental right of a child to be born as a whole, functioning human being' was briefly maintained,[78] but that state's Court of Appeals soon and forthrightly denied that there was any such right.[79] The Congenital Injuries Act of 1976 now prevents such actions and Missouri also has enacted legislation banning lawsuits based on wrongful life,[80] and others have passed laws limiting recovery of compensation.[81]

It is not surprising that the courts should have had problems with the notion of wrongful life. That one should have thought it involved a retreat 'into the meditation on the mysteries of life',[82] or that another should have thought the issues involved were 'more properly left to the philosophers and theologians'.[83] Their concerns are concrete, with establishing legal liability and calculating loss for the purposes of compensation. Mine in this paper are more abstract. It may be that if one can sustain a reasoned argument for a moral right not, in certain circumstances, to be born, that this will provide the foundation for a legal action in tort (or, though less attention has been given to this, for a criminal prosecution[84]). My concern, though, is with moral entitlement and the moral duties of potential parents. Accordingly, I turn now to parental responsibility.

PARENTAL RESPONSIBILITY

Philosophical discussion of procreation has tended to concentrate on the rights of parents or potential parents (in the case of abortion on the rights of women[85]). Perhaps this is not surprising: after all, until very recently,

---

[77] *Ibid.*, p. 787.

[78] *Parker* v. *Chessin* (1922) 400 N.Y.S. 2d 110 (an infant born with polycystic kidney disease).

[79] *Becker* v. *Schwartz* (1978) 413 N.Y.S. 2d 895.

[80] 130 R.S.Mo (1989).

[81] California (see Cal. Civ. Code 43.6 (1991), Minnesota (see Minn. Stat. 145.424 (1990)), Indiana (see Ind. Code Ann 34-1-1-11 (1990), South Dakota (see S.D. Codified Laws 21-55-11-4) (1991)) and Utah (the first to do so: see Utah Code 78-11-(23-25)(1983)).

[82] In *Curlender* v. *Bio-Science Laboratories*.

[83] In *Zeitsov* v. *Katz, op. cit.*, note 74.

[84] Though this would involve overturning the Congenital Disabilities (Civil Liability) Act of 1976.

[85] The strand in feminist philosophy which emphasizes the ethics of care (see Carol Gilligan,

we tended to think in terms of parental rights rather than parental obligations.[86] The furore over the Child Support Act 1991 is a latter-day manifestation of this.[87] Discussion has focused on the right to have children, often in the context of population control.[88] In an article entitled 'Is There A Natural Right To Have Children?',[89] Floyd and Pomerantz, who deny that there is such a right, briefly address the interrelationship between such a (putative) right and the right not to be born, but their concern is with the right to have children, not with the right not to be born. They do, however, observe that it is wrong for us to conceive a child that we know will 'lead a short but miserable life...because [the child] has a right not to be born which outweighs our right to be parents'.[90] But they do not develop this or indicate why this should be so. Harris's essay, 'The Right To Found a Family',[91] much of it subsequently incorporated into *Wonderwoman and Superman*,[92] does address the problem and reaches the conclusion that the 'desire' to found a family is 'constrained only by consideration for the fate of the children who will constitute that family'. Note, despite the title of his essay, the weaker concept of 'desire'[93] has been substituted for 'right', and it is 'consideration'[94] for children, rather than the stronger 'responsibility' that acts as a constraint. He does, however, state that where children are or will be severely handicapped, there 'may be an obligation not to bring them into or allow them to continue in a world where the existence will be genuinely terrible'.[95] The reason for this obligation is not developed. One of the few essays which does emphasize pa-

---

In *A Different Voice* (Cambridge, Mass: Harvard University Press, 1982) has been strangely muted on parental responsibility issues.

[86] At least until the *Gillick* case (see [1986] A.C. 112.

[87] See Mavis Maclean and John Eekelaar, 'Child Support: The British Solution', (1993) 7 *Int. J. Law and Family* 285.

[88] As to which see Michael D. Bayles (ed.), *Ethics and Population* (Cambridge, Mass: Schenkman, 1976).

[89] From (ed.) John Arthur, *Morality and Moral Controversies* (Englewood Cliffs, New Jersey: Prentice Hall, 1981), p. 131.

[90] *Ibid.*, p. 136.

[91] See (ed.) Geoffrey Scarre, *Children, Parents and Politics* (Cambridge: Cambridge University Press, 1989), p. 133.

[92] *Op. cit.*, note 20, ch. 4.

[93] *Op. cit.*, note 91, p. 151.

[94] *Ibid.*, p. 152.

[95] *Idem.*

rental duties, Onora O'Neill's 'Children's Rights and Children's Lives',[96] does not address the decision to have children at all.

But we do now regard parental responsibility as integral to an understanding of adult (especially parent) -child relations.[97] Does it, therefore, cast any light on the constraints, if any, on having children? I believe it does. I also believe that the limitation imposed upon the exercise of parental autonomy by the Act[98] which constitutes parental responsibility, the so-called minimum threshold condition of 'significant harm',[99] may offer some clues as to what may be expected of those endowed with parental responsibility.

What does a principle of parental responsibility entail? It offers a normative standard by which to judge the decisions and actions of parents or those who wish to become parents.[100] What it will look like will depend upon how it is justified. Eekelaar,[101] writing of parents' moral obligation to care for their children, convincingly shows that contractarian theories, motivated at least in part by self-interest, cannot really account for the obligation to care. He found the true basis for those moral obligations in Finnis's theory of human flourishing.[102] Eekelaar's arguments have equal force in our context.

To exercise parental responsibility is to put the interests and welfare of children or future children above one's own needs, desires or well-being. Welfare is, it must be accepted, an indeterminate and value-laden concept and the problems inherent in this cannot be ignored.[103] But there is an irreducible minimum content to a child's well-being, and these must be satisfied by anyone carrying out the role of, or purporting to become, a parent. The principle of parental responsibility requires that individuals should desist from having children unless certain minimum conditions can be satisfied. Responsible parents want their children to have good and fulfilling lives. They are prepared to forgo pleasures and make sacrifices to ensure their

---

[96] 98 *Ethics* 445 (1988).

[97] See, for example, the Children Act 1989 and the Child Support Act 1991.

[98] That is the Children Act 1989 (see sections 2 and 3).

[99] See Children Act 1989 s. 31(2).

[100] See John Eekelaar, 'Parental Responsibility: State of Nature or Nature of the State?' (1991) *Journal of Social Welfare and Family Law* 37.

[101] 'Are Parents Morally Obliged to Care for Their Children?' 11 *Oxford Journal of Legal Studies* 340 (1991).

[102] See John Finnis, *Natural Law and Natural Rights* (Oxford: Clarendon Press, 1980), pp. 80–99.

[103] As shown most convincingly by Robert Mnookin, 'Child-Custody Adjudication: Judicial Functions in the Face of Indeterminacy', 39(3) *Law And Contemporary Problems* 226 (1975).

children are able to flourish. Despite the rhetoric of the Children Act, the principle here enunciated sits uncomfortably with the individualism and greed of the 1980s and 1990s. Is it any wonder that, as Etzioni puts it, society[104] places more value on 'Armani suits, winter skiing and summer houses than on education'?[105]

What is the significance of this principle of parental responsibility as far as prospective parents are concerned? It means that the very young should not become parents (Derek Parfit's 14-year-old mother example[106] immediately springs to mind). It means that the old should also forgo the pleasures of child-bearing and rearing. I rarely agree with Virginia Bottomley but she was surely right to condemn the birth of twins to a 59-year-old woman on Christmas Day 1993.[107] It means that pregnant women should not smoke or drink excessively and that drug addicts[108] and women who are HIV-infected[109] should not have children. Since we are talking of responsibility these are decisions that must be taken by parents. The state, insofar as it has a role in this at all, can only encourage and educate: there is no question of particular people not being allowed to have children or being punished for so doing.

Even so, some of these examples will be unpopular and condemnations suggesting that it encourages the policing of pregnancy will be heard. Yet we are in no doubt that child abuse is unacceptable. Why, therefore, should we be unprepared to condemn the use of noxious substances by pregnant woman or the willingness of women with HIV to pass on their illness to their children? On what test does not this behaviour also constitute child abuse?[110]

---

[104] The existence of which was denied by Margaret Thatcher.

[105] *The Spirit of Community* (New York: Simon and Schuster, 1993), p. 66.

[106] *Op. cit.*, note 55.

[107] See *The Independent*, 28 December 1993. It would be equally wrong for a man of that age to father a child, though, I concede, this is not uncommon.

[108] This raises the spectre of the well-known English case of *D* v. *Berkshire C.C.* [1987] 1 All E.R. 20, where the child was, controversially, removed from the parents at birth. An interesting United States comparison is *Reyes* v. *Superior Court* 75 Cal. App. 3d 214 (1977). Steinbock, *op. cit.*, note 26, discusses maternal-fetal conflict in ch. 4.

[109] Fetal harm is not the sole preserve of expectant mothers. See Joseph Losco and Mark Shublak, 'Paternal-Fetal Conflict: An Examination of Paternal Responsibility to the Fetus', 13(1) *Politics and The Life Sciences* 63 (1994) (and see the *Symposium* in 13(2)).

[110] There is a lot of discussion of this in American legal literature. Examples are Note, 'Maternal Rights and Fetal Wrongs: The Case Against The Criminalization of Fetal Abuse', 101 *Harvard Law Review* (1988); John E. B. Myers, 'Abuse and Neglect of The Unborn: Can The State Intervene?' 23 *Duquesne Law Review* 76 (1984) and Stacey L. Arthur, 'The

I am not arguing for criminal sanctions nor necessarily for the removal of the child.[111] Nor am I urging that there is any moral obligation, as part of parental responsibility, to abort a child (though there may be cases where the child's life will be so unmitigatedly bad that a termination will be thought an appropriate exercise of parental responsibility). What I argue is that, for example, a woman who is HIV-infected has a moral obligation not to conceive a child. It is true that there is a good chance that she will not pass the virus on to her baby (the risk of actual perinatal HIV infection is between 20 and 30 per cent).[112] It is also true that the severity of the disease varies widely: at its worst, the most severely afflicted children present with adult-style opportunistic infections in the first year of life and die a painful death a month or two after diagnosis. But others develop milder manifestations, are diagnosed later and live longer. According to Arras only a small percentage (10 to 20 per cent) of those born HIV-infected fit 'the worst-case scenario', and others live longer, 'perhaps to the age of ten or beyond'. And he comments: 'The longer these children live with a tolerable quality of life, the more their lives will be worth living. A child who lives at home, goes to school, and attends summer camp does not fall into the same category as a Tay-Sachs baby.'[113] It is, of course, also true (indeed trite) that other inherited traits can be passed on to children by parents. Yet it remains the fact that, to use Children Act concepts, a child born to an HIV-infected mother (and probably a similarly-afflicted father) is likely to suffer significant harm. Even if the infection is not passed on, the child is likely to be orphaned when very young.[114] Deliberately to conceive a child with the knowledge that you are HIV-infected is, I conclude, morally wrong. It is in the interest of such potential children not to be born. Whether this right should be upheld by requiring an abortion where an HIV-infected woman does conceive, deliberately or not, is more difficult. Clearly the law does (and should) permit abortion in these circumstances.[115] The case for counselling such a woman to undergo a termination of pregnancy is strong. But would we say she has a

---

Norplant Prescription: Birth Control, Woman Control or Crime Control?' (1992) 40 *UCLA Law Rev.* 1.

[111] By emergency protection order.

[112] John D. Arras, 'AIDS and Reproductive Decisions: Having Children In Fear and Trembling', 68 *The Milbank Quarterly* 353, 355 (1990).

[113] *Ibid.*, p. 365.

[114] Nor can the quality of parenting be all that it should be given the health of the parent (most probably parents).

[115] Under the latest legislation, the Human Fertilisation and Embryology Act 1990 until full term (see s. 37).

moral obligation not to go through with her pregnancy? Would she be acting in a morally reprehensible way if she took the risk that her child would not inherit her infection and carried him/her to term? It may be thought to be an act of parental responsibility to have an abortion rather than possibly condemning the child to a short, bleak and, in our society, stigmatized life.

There are worse fates than to be born with HIV-infection but comparisons—with Tay Sachs or Huntington's Chorea for example—are invidious.[116] They are all diseases which it would be unfair and wrong to inflict upon a child, such that it may be argued that it would be wrong to bring a child into the world so inflicted. It could be said, using Feinberg's revamped test, that such children are 'doomed to defeat',[117] in the long-term if not immediately. But a comparison with the facts in *Re J*[118] puts these problem cases into perspective. Feinberg's test will give to too few the right not to be born.[119] It will deny that right to many whose lives will be truly awful: as just two examples neither the HIV sufferer and the person who will between 35 and 50 succumb to Huntington's disease fits Feinberg's criterion. And the test by focusing on bad lives deflects attention from the very people who take the initial decisions—the parents.

To view the problem through the lens of parental responsibility is to focus on the decision-making process. It is to recognize the commitment involved in bringing a child into the world. It is to acknowledge that having children is an exercise of autonomous will and is (or certainly should be) a commitment to love, nurture and care. It is to accept that parents should want the best for their children. To exercise parental responsibility—I use the concept normatively rather than descriptively—is to plan parenthood sensibly and with the empathy for the needs of the child. It is not an exercise of parental responsibility to bring a child into the world who will suffer pain and agony and die a miserable death. It is not an exercise of parental responsibility to bring a child into the world when that child will be cruelly deprived of all or most of the basic goods of human flourishing.[120]

---

[116] On Huntington's Chorea see Laura Purdy, 'Genetic Diseases: Can Having Children Be Immoral?' in (ed.) John Arras and Nancy K. Rhoden, *Ethical Issues In Modern Medicine* (Mountain View, Calif.: Mayfield Publishing Company, 1989) (3rd ed.), p. 311.

[117] See *ante*, 168.

[118] [1990] 3 All E.R. 930.

[119] *Ante*, 167.

[120] The decision to have a child always involves risk, which may be greater or lesser, depending upon known circumstances. For a discussion of this, albeit in a different context, see Carl F. Cranor, 'Some Moral Issues In Risk Assessment', 101 *Ethics* 123 (1990).

In putting this emphasis on parents (and potential parents) I am not dissenting from the view I have previously expressed[121] that the decision as to whether a defective new-born child should live cannot be left to the parents. Thus, for example, the Court of Appeal in 'Baby Alexandra'[122] was right to judge the propriety of an operation in terms of the child's, rather than the parents', interests. But there is a difference between condemning an infant to die and taking the calculated decision not to bring a life—likely to be blighted—into existence.

In focusing on parental responsibility I am also redefining the question as posed. If 'children' have, as I believe, the right not to be born this can only be because their 'parents' have duties not to procreate. And it is better in this context[123] to focus upon obligations, on agents rather than recipients. The right not to be born begins to look more like another right, briefly referred to at the outset of this paper, namely the right to responsible parents.[124] In this paper it has been possible only to sketch the contours of this new, inchoate and, as yet, ill-defined right. Its meaning, content and significance will have to await another occasion.

---

[121] In *The Rights and Wrongs of Children, op. cit.*, note 38, pp. 259–263.

[122] *Op. cit.*, note 7.

[123] Though not, I think, elsewhere in children's rights issues. Here I differ from Onora O'Neill (see *op. cit.*, note 96). I have criticized her views in 'Taking Children's Rights More Seriously', 6 *International Journal of Law and The Family* 52, 56–59 (1992). See also Tom Campbell in the same issue (at pp. 12–16).

[124] Everything I say applies with equal force to fathers. And on the equal obligations of both parents see Virginia Held, 'The Equal Obligations of Mothers and Fathers' in (eds.) Onora O'Neill and William Ruddick, *Having Children* (New York: Oxford University Press, 1979, p. 227).

CHAPTER 10

The Rights of the Artificially Procreated Child

The modern movement of children's rights is barely a generation old,[1] but it has veritable antiquity besides the fledgling 'reproduction revolution'.[2] The technology of inner space, the bio-technological revolution, is less than two decades old but it has fired the public imagination in a way matched only perhaps in recent years by the quest to discover outer space. Meanwhile, the celebration of children's rights has reached a crescendo with international recognition,[3] even a symbolic children's summit.[4] But, as yet, there has been little attempt to match the emergent recognition of children's rights to the responsibilities incumbent on parents and society in general and science in particular to the children produced by our new knowledge, as well as to the concept of childhood itself. The gap becomes all the more striking when the relative silence is contrasted with the cacophony of sound and fury produced by feminists on the woman question and reproductive technology.[5] Though some attention has been given to the 'commodity'[6] produced by the 'mother machine',[7] it palls in signifi-

---

[1] See M. D. A. Freeman, *The Rights and Wrongs of Children* (London: Frances Pinter, 1983) for the development of children's rights. The earliest modern book is Paul Adams *et al*, *Children's Rights* (London: Panther, 1972).

[2] The term is that of Peter Singer and Deanne Wells (see *The Reproduction Revolution*, Oxford: OUP 1984).

[3] A good account of which is Geraldine van Bueren, *The International Law on the Rights of the Child* (Dordrecht: Martinus Nijhoff, 1995).

[4] In 1990. The declaration can be found in *The State of the World's Children 1991* (Oxford: OUP for UNICEF, 1991, pp. 53–57).

[5] For example, Helen B. Holmes and Laura M. Purdy, *Feminist Perspectives in Medical Ethics* (Bloomington: Indiana University Press, 1992); Patricia Spallone, *Beyond Conception* (Basingstoke: Macmillan, 1989); Susan Sherwin, *No Longer Patient* (Philadelphia: Temple University Press, 1992); Robyn Rowland, *Living Laboratories* (London: Lime Tree Press, 1992).

[6] See the debate between Sara Ann Ketchum and H. M. Malm in (eds.), Holmes and Purdy, *op. cit.*, note 5, p. 284 and 295.

[7] The term is Gena Corea's: see *The Mother Machine* (London: Women's Press, 1988).

cance besides that accorded the impact of the new technology on women. This is not to underestimate or undervalue the feminist literature, though it can skew the debate, as it has done with the issue of the propriety of abortion.[8]

But that which has been neglected must now be addressed. This paper is directed towards this task.

After a brief introduction to children's rights and to assisted reproduction, children's rights in the context of assisted reproduction is addressed. The emphasis is on the right to identity, an interest long neglected and constantly denied. Issues of parentage and legitimacy are then discussed. These are issues closely related to the identity question but nevertheless deserving of separate treatment, particularly given the complexity of concepts and confusion of ideologies now found in English law in relation to it. I have discussed elsewhere the problem of so-called 'wrongful life', albeit not in the context of the children of the reproduction revolution. The question is, however, germane to the rather broader concern that assisted reproduction has had a deleterious impact on children as a class. Whether this has led to children being 'made to order', whether they have been turned into 'commodities' is an important question, and no one concerned with the advancement of the status of the child or with children's rights can ignore these issues. This article accordingly closes with a short coda exploring the impact on artificial reproduction on the personality and integrity of the child. But the problem merits a paper in itself and a more detailed treatment of it must thus be reserved for another occasion.

CHILDREN'S RIGHTS

Children's rights have come a long way since Hillary Rodham described them as a 'slogan in search of a definition'.[9] They have been given sustained academic attention.[10] The efforts of the international community

---

[8] See Ronald Dworkin, *Life's Dominion* (London: Harper Collins, 1993) especially at pp. 50–60.

[9] 'Children Under the Law' 43 *Harvard Educational Review* 487 (1973). See returned to the subject in 1979: See 'Children's Rights: A Legal Perspective' in (eds.) Patricia A. Vardin and Ilene N. Brody, *Children's Rights: Contemporary Perspectives* (New York: Teacher's College Press, 1979), p. 21). It is doubtless galling to her as 'First Lady' that the U.S. has still not ratified the U.N. Convention.

[10] Two of the more recent books are Laura M. Purdy, *In Their Best Interest?* (Ithaca: Cornell University Press, 1992) and David Archard, *Children—Rights and Childhood* (London: Routledge, 1993).

have produced an international convention; new institutional structures, notably the concept of a children's ombudsperson, have been established, though not in Britain.[11] In the United States and England children's rights have received clear if cautious judicial recognition.[12] In England there has been some limited legislative endorsement.[13] Five European countries[14] have accepted that a child should be immune from physical chastisement, particularly significant given that exposure to physical assault as a means of punishment has long been a badge of social inferiority. It has come to be accepted that, as Franklin puts it,[15] children 'form a large, long-suffering and oppressed grouping in society' with a forgotten and excluded status. We have begun to 'take children's rights seriously',[16] to accept that the young are to be objects of 'equal concern and respect'. It is wise not to exaggerate the significance of all of this. Rights without services are of limited value, and services in the absence of adequate resources and funding are seldom a reality. Whilst the world was debating children's rights in New York, children were being exterminated as vermin in Brazil and Guatemala, dying of starvation in Ethiopia and Sudan, being neglected in orphanages in Romania, gassed in Iraq and getting poorer in Britain. In May 1989 UNICEF noted that:

> ...new and subtler forms of deprivation may have been caused by the profound changes occurring over the last forty years in labour markets, in environmental conditions, in family structure, in internal and international migration, in the organisation of society and in other aspects of life.[17]

---

[11] See Målfrid Grude Flekkøy, *A Voice for Children* (London: Jessica Kingsley, 1991).

[12] On the U.S. see S. Gluck Mezey, 'Constitutional Adjudication of Children's Rights Claims in the United States Supreme Court 1953–1992', 27 *Family Law Quarterly* 307 (1993). In England an early example is *M* v. *M* [1973] 2 All E.R. 81.

[13] In the Children Act 1989. See C. Lyon and N. Parton, 'Children's Rights and the Children Act 1989' in (ed.) Bob Franklin, *The Handbook of Children's Rights* (London: Routledge, 1995, p. 40).

[14] Sweden, Norway, Finland, Austria and Cyprus. Though it is often said Denmark has done this too, this is not correct. See Linda Nielsen and Lis Frost in (ed.) Michael Freeman, *Children's Rights—A Comparative Perspective* (Aldershot: Dartmouth, 1996, p. 65, 79–80).

[15] See *The Rights of Children* (Oxford: Blackwell, 1986, p. 1).

[16] See M. D. A. Freeman, 'Taking Children's Rights More Seriously', [1992] 6 *Int. J. Law and Family* 52. And see ch. 2.

[17] *The State of the World's Children* 1991 (Oxford: Oxford University Press for UNICEF, 1991), p. 9.

Nevertheless, rights are important. They are 'valuable commodities',[18] important moral coinage. In the words of Bandman, they 'enable us to stand with dignity, if necessary to demand what is our due without having to grovel, plead or beg'.[19] Children's rights have often been characterized in terms of protecting the individual child, rather than in terms of liberating children as such, or even protecting their rights as a group. It is in part because of this that concern for children is still often rooted in the individual child, rather than children in general. But when the debate moves to how best to advocate children's rights, to further the cause of children, it is not a question of protecting a particular child against an abusive or uncaring adult, so much as establishing structures to protect children's rights, preserving their integrity, recognizing their personality.

To say that rights are important, and important also for children (both symbolically and instrumentally) is not to ignore the significance of other moral values, love, friendship, compassion and so on. As Kleinig wrote,[20] 'a morality which has as its motivation merely the giving of what is due...is seriously defective'. But, short of a cultural revolution way beyond our wildest dreams, rights will remain important. And, it will remain important to recognize children's rights. As Howard Cohen put it when he explained the importance of associating the children's rights movement with other rights' movements, '"rights" is a militant concept to the extent that it is used as part of the ideology in a campaign for social change'.[21]

RIGHTS AND INTERESTS

There is little point talking rights-based language or arguing for normative recognition using the concept of rights until the 'good' embodied in the putative right has been identified. As Neil MacCormick explains, these are:

> common features shared by all that we call "rights": normative orders can afford to individuals security in the enjoyment of what are normally goods for individuals; that someone has a right implies (a) that x or freedom or discretion in relation to x is a good, and (b) is true if in

---

[18] See Richard Wasserstrom, 'Rights, Human Rights and Racial Discrimination', 61 *Journal of Philosophy* 628, 629 (1964). Joel Feinberg uses very similar language.

[19] 'Do Children Have Any Natural Rights?', *Proceedings of the 29th Annual Meeting of Philosophy of Education Society*, p. 234, 236 (1973).

[20] 'Mill, Children and Rights', 8 *Educational Philosophy and Theory* 14 (1976).

[21] *Equal Rights for Children* (Totowa, N.J.: Littlefield Adams, 1980, p. 17).

one mode or another the individual fulfils the conditions for having some appropriate from of normative security over x or freedom or discretion in relation to x.[22]

At the root of rights are interests:[23] it is those who fail to recognize this, in particular those who espouse the will theory of rights such as Herbert Hart, who find talk about children's rights 'idle'. Rights ground requirements for action in the interest of other persons. And, although an individual may have rights which it is against his interest to have (for example a right to citizenship of a country about to conscript him to fight in an unjust war), it is as well to try to identify the interests to be protected by conferring on the artificially-procreated rights to know their parentage and other rights consonant on this.

As Katherine O'Donovan[24] has also observed, the interest involved may amount to one or more of the following concerns:

1. A desire to know one's origins. Interest in *identity* without which one is 'deracinated'.

2. A wish to know *medical history* so as to avoid the possibility of marriage within the prohibited degrees of consanguinity with the problems attendant upon this.

3. The benefit of being qualified to take property in the event of the death of a social parent. This is a *material* interest.

Of the three it is the first which has tended to assume the greatest importance in the growing literature,[25] and there is increasing evidence that it is this interest which is of greatest concern to those who have been artificially procreated.[26] The third consideration can, anyway, readily be discounted in those legal systems which have by now assimilated the rights of the illegitimately born to those of children born within marriage. Eng-

---

[22] 'Rights, Claims and Remedies', 1 *Law and Philosophy* 337, 346 [1982].

[23] See Neil MacCormick, *Legal Right and Social Democracy* (Oxford: Clarendon Press, 1982).

[24] 'A Right To Know One's Parentage?' 2 *International Journal of Law and the Family* 27, 29 (1988).

[25] For anthropological insight see Marilyn Strathern, 'Displacing Knowledge: Technology and its Consequences for Kinship', in (ed.) Ian Robinson, *Life and Death Under High Technology Medicine* (Manchester: Manchester University Press, 1994, p. 65)

[26] A graphic illustration of his, albeit in the context of adoption, is *Re B* [1995] 1 F.L.R. 1 (an Arab brought up to believe he was Jewish by orthodox Jewish adopters attempting, and failing, to have the adoption overturned when aged 35).

land and Wales eventually achieved this with the Family Law Reform Act of 1987, though disparities still remain notably in rights of citizenship.[27]

As far as the second consideration is concerned, this has played a major part in the thinking of policy-makers in Britain. It is the interest emphasized in the Warnock Report of 1984.[28] It is also to some extent recognized in the Human Fertilisation and Embryology Act of 1990, which only allows an underage person to require the requisite authority to supply information when he or she is about to marry and wishes to discover whether or not there is a blood relationship with the projected spouse.[29]

It is surprising that this concern should have taken such a prominent position in official thinking about the reproduction revolution. The real chances (despite some evidence of like being attached to like) of persons who are related wishing to marry must be infinitesimal, and the feared horrible consequence of their mating could come about just as easily as a result of a sexual relationship short of marriage (where there is no duty to release information). It is surprising because it is not the concern recognized in the analogous situation of adoption. English law (the Children Act of 1975) gives the adopted child, when 18, a right to access to the original birth certificate.[30] In fact this does not amount to very much and the adopted person who really wishes to discover his genetic history will require persistence and tenacity as well as skills of detection. Whatever little right is given, it is clear that the rationale of opening up access to the original birth certificate is predicated on interest in identity and not medical history. Adoption had moved from an institution based on secrecy to one of emergent openness and the 1975 Act recognized this.[31] One prominent proponent in the House of Commons (Leo Abse MP) asserted that there was 'a basic human right that every child should know his origins'.[32] John Triseliotis, whose research had been influential on those who argued

---

[27] See British Nationality Act 1981 s. 50 (9): even an unmarried father with parental responsibility cannot bestow British citizenship on his child.

[28] See Mary Warnock, *A Matter of Life* (Oxford: Blackwell, 1985), para. 4.13.

[29] See s. 31 (6).

[30] See s. 26 (see now Adoption Act 1976 s. 50). The courts have said the right is not an absolute one (*R* v. *Registrar-General ex parte Smith* [1991] 2 Q.B. 393.)

[31] But a remarkable, if imperceptible, shift has occurred and the emphasis is now as much on the birth parent being able to trace the child given up.

[32] *Hansard*, H.C. vol. 983, col. 1862.

for the legislation, wrote subsequently of the idea behind the provision that 'no person should be cut off from his origins'.[33]

It is an intriguing, and unanswered, question as to why with adoption the interest upheld by a policy of relative openness has been the desire to avoid 'genealogical bewilderment',[34] whereas with the artificially-procreated child it has been a desire to avoid genetic disaster. Could it be that the child reproduced artificially owes his birth to medical intervention, whereas the child transplanted to an adoptive family has been the subject only (I use that word deliberately) of social work intervention? Certainly, doctors carry more weight than social workers. But, just as significantly, they also have an interest to protect and were it to happen that inter-marriage and in-breeding resulted from infertility services the *cause célèbre* that would result could lead to blame being attributed to them.

Whatever the reason it is the medical consideration which has been uppermost in the deliberations of policy-makers in Britain. But this is hardly conclusive. The status of the interest was barely debated by the Warnock committee or in Parliament. If the question is: should the artificially-procreated child have the right to know his/her parentage, the moral argument and the grounds upon which it is based can still be constructed and, if need be, the arguments adduced by Warnock and others supplanted.

ADOPTION AND ARTIFICIAL REPRODUCTION

Are, therefore, the arguments used in the context of adoption, where identity clearly was the issue, persuasive? Or is the example of adoption not a true analogy at all but rather a false trail? There are important voices, including Katherine O'Donovan,[35] urging that we should not be misled by the example of adoption.

O'Donovan has argued that the need to know genetic ancestry is socially induced, as well as relatively recent in origin. It is her view that our emphasis should be on changing the attitudes which have become entrenched to the importance of the blood relationship, rather than undermining the protection of anonymity which gamete donors in Britain have

---

[33] 'Obtaining Birth Certificates' in Philip Bean (ed.) *Adoption: Essays in Social Policy, Law and Sociology* (London: Tavistock 1984) p. 38.

[34] See H. Sants, 'Genealogical Bewilderment in Children with Substitute Parents', 37 *British Journal of Medical Psychology* 133 (1964).

[35] *Op. cit.* note 24. See also 'What shall We Tell The Children? Reflections on Children's Perspectives and the Reproduction Revolution' in (ed.) Robert Lee and Derek Morgan, *Birthrights* (London: Routledge, 1989) p. 96.

even after the implementation of the Human Fertilisation and Embryology Act 1990. She questions also the idea that adopted persons are searching for their true identity. She may well be correct that there is no convincing empirical evidence to support the view that the adopted have an obsession with their identity or a desire to seek out their biological parents.

As I will indicate later in this paper, I have some sympathy' with O'Donovan's view that changing social attitudes to artificial reproduction may ultimately prove beneficial to children as a whole (and not just those so produced). But to argue that the need to know is socially induced is to say very little. So is the desire for children. So are, it may be argued, the needs of the infertile for children. And, it may be added, their need for secrecy can also be seen as socially constructed. But then so can a considerable amount of medical treatment. Doctors treat 'pain' but they do not treat all pain: what our societies regard as pain to take to a doctor is to a large extent also socially constructed.

Despite the caution urged by O'Donovan, comparisons and, indeed, contrasts with adoption remain worth making.

What are the similarities?

1. Both create families: one provides children with parents, whilst the other provides adults with children. Adoption today may not be an infertility service but in the past it has served this function. Artificial reproduction is clearly an infertility service.

2. In both, families are created in response to a need (that previously identified), though the symmetry of need in adoption is not met in the case of artificial reproduction, where the child is only born to satisfy a need. This may make artificial reproduction closer to the creation of families in the 'normal' case than adoption.

3. Both involve professional intervention: in the one case social work procedures as well as legal and administrative processes: in the other the intervention of a specialized medical profession, save where *in vitro* fertilization is not required. With artificial reproduction the skills involved may be more specialized, but the subsequent processes are less complex.

4. As Erica Haimes describes it, both types of families have 'a constructed nature',[36] one result of which is that they can be seen as dif-

---

[36] '"Secrecy": What can Artificial Reproduction learn from Adoption?' 2 *International Journal of Law and the Family* 46, 47 (1988).

ferent, even as abnormal or deviant. From this it is but one step to studying them as 'social problems'.

5. And this leads also to another similarity. Given their difference, their marginality, questions arise as to how to tackle this difference. 'Normal' families are left alone with decisions as to what to tell children. Whether they reveal their child's genealogy is up to them. But in the case of both adoption and artificial reproduction the state has a say in what information is to be revealed to the child about his/her origins. Where a regulated body keeps that information, as is the case in Britain with the Authority established by the 1990 Act, that which is vouchsafed may even be standardized.

6. In both there is a plurality of interests to consider. This may be clearer with the 'adoption triangle', though it can be illustrated no better than in the sort of 'tug-of-love' cases that we have come to associate with dysfunctional surrogacy arrangements.[37] But decisions on what to tell the child must inevitably impact on genetic parents and potential donors.

7. In listing similarities one more should be noted. In England, at least but not exclusively, both the institution of adoption and the development of medical and non-medical methods of assisted reproduction have ante-dated any attempt to impose legal, administrative or structural controls on them. De facto adoption took place long before the legal system recognized adoption (belatedly in 1926).[38] The regulation of artificial reproduction has been more speedy but cultural lag[39] has been experienced once again.

This large number of similarities must not deceive us into believing that the problems are identical. They are not. Clear differences between adoption and artificial reproduction can also be identified, though with increasing legislation and regulation of the latter some of these differences become less pronounced.

---

[37] The most famous instance of which is in *The Matter of Baby M* 537 A 2nd 1227 (1988), on which see Mary Beth Whitehead *A Mother's Story* (London: Arrow Books, 1990).

[38] See *Humphreys* v. *Polak* [1901] Note Jack Goody's remark that there is no entry for adoption in the whole thirteen volumes of Holdsworth's *History of English Law (The Development of the Family and Marriage in Europe* : Cambridge: CUP 1973, p. 73).

[39] See W. G. Ogburn, *Social Change with Respect to Culture and Original Nature* (New York: Vintage Books, 1950).

1. In the case of adoption, a child exists. He/she may be a small baby (decreasingly so)[40] or a child with a real life history. In the case of artificial reproduction a child is created to satisfy the needs of the infertile.

2. Since with adoption there is a pre-existing child there is also documentation, for example birth records, agency reports, possibly letters requesting that the child be adopted. In this sense there is more data to reveal, or keep secret. Fewer records will exist for the deliberately-created child. This raises acutely questions of secrecy and openness.

3. It was suggested above that both institutions are unusual or deviant. It should by now be clear that artificial reproduction is the more deviant situation. It is hardly surprising, therefore, that there is even less consensus on how to respond to it.

4. In adoption usually neither adoptive parent is biologically related to the child[41]: in cases of surrogacy, egg and semen donation, one of the social parents is also the genetic parent. On the one hand this may create less of a problem (the child is half the product of the family): on the other, it may create additional problems for the family so created. The imbalance is not dissimilar from that which occurs where adoption is by a step-parent.[42]

5. As indicated above, different professions are involved. There can be no disputing the fact that the medical profession has more power and greater authority, than the social work profession. Therefore, as Haimes also notes, 'whatever is decided by the medical profession as being appropriate to their procedures carries much more weight than that of social workers in adoption.'[43] This cannot but have an impact on such questions as secrecy and openness.

---

[40] The number of babies adopted has declined from 23 per cent of children adopted in 1977 to 12 per cent in 1991. (*Judicial Statistics 1993*, Table 5.6) See also Department of Health, *Adoption: The Future* (London: H.M.S.O. 1993), Cm 2288, ch. 3.

[41] Though in the past it was not uncommon for an unmarried mother to adopt her own child to obliterate the 'legal' stigma of illegitimacy. Today, adoption by parent and step-parent is common (and see note 42).

[42] Which is increasingly the case. In 1993, 47.4 per cent of adoptions were of this type and this is despite legislation trying to discourage step-parent adoptions. It has now been proposed that step-parents should be permitted to adopt without the biological parent having to do so as well (see Department of Health, *op. cit.*, note 40, para. 5.22).

[43] *Op. cit.*, note 36, p. 48.

ARTIFICIAL REPRODUCTION

No-one knows how many children are born each year as a result of assisted reproduction. A commonly quoted estimate is 1,500 though this is bound to underestimate the number of 'unofficial' donor inseminations. In 1993 over 9,000 couples were treated at infertility centres in the United Kingdom.[44] More couples are now treated than adopt. There are still five times as many adoptions as children born as a result of assisted reproductive methods, but we can expect the number of children conceived through gamete donation to overtake the number of adoption orders early in the next century.

Because assisted reproduction is a service for the infertile, it is upon their interests and those of the service providers that attention has concentrated. In one sense this is not surprising: in the early days of adoption this was so as well. But in another it should alarm us. Given the attention we now give to the paramountcy of a child's welfare and to the importance of the wishes and feelings of children in so many matters, though ironically not in adoption,[45] it is of concern that the interests of children should count for so little where decisions about artificial reproduction are being taken. The role of responsible parenthood, so little explored elsewhere,[46] is deftly ignored. Whether children have a right not to be born— the subject of increasing interest where disability is an issue[47]—has raised rarely a ripple of interest in this context, and then only because, within surrogacy at least, an effect has been to commodify children[48] which is the very negation of seeing them as rights-bearing persons. That, as O'Donovan observes, 'there is, as yet, no language available for explaining to a child that egg, sperm or embryo donation form part of its inheritance'[49] is indicative of this failure to make children principals in the processes rather than goals.

The reproduction revolution is associated, and rightly, with the development of *in vitro* fertilization in the 1970s. But artificial procreation has a much longer history. Artificial insemination by a donor (AID as it was

---

[44] See Human Fertilisation and Embryology Authority.
[45] *Cf.* Children Act 1989 s. 1(1) with Adoption Act 1976 s. 6 ('first consideration').
[46] But see Andrea L. Bonnicksen, *In Vitro Fertilisation* (New York: Columbia University Press, 1989), ch. 4.
[47] And see my 'Do Children Have the Right Not To Be Born?' (and ch. 9).
[48] As to which see *post*, 211.
[49] See 'What Shall We Tell the Children?...', *op. cit.*, note 35, p. 96.

called, DI as it is now known, allegedly to prevent confusion in the popular consciousness with AIDS) has been practised throughout the twentieth century.[50] Most of the literature, including an excellent *Symposium* in *Politics and The Life Sciences*,[51] concentrates upon donor insemination. The problems of this, and the lessons learnt in tackling it, are, I argue, sufficiently close to those attendant upon other assisted reproductive techniques for the subject, at least insofar as it impacts upon children, to be treated as a whole. The rights of children, whether the result of donor insemination, ovum donation or surrogacy, and no matter what the process involved (IVF,[52] GIFT,[53] ZIFT[54] etc.) should be similarly constructed. Whether they should be similar to those conferred upon adopted children is a different question and one which will be addressed.

IDENTITY

There can be few more basic rights than a right to one's identity. This is recognized by totalitarian régimes which have undermined opposition by removing children and having them brought up by lackeys of the régime itself. Argentina is only the most recent example of this practice.[55] But it was the Argentinean experience which led the drafters of the United Nations Convention on the Rights of the Child to include the right to identity within its provisions.[56] It is the first human rights treaty expressly to recognize a right to identity. The Convention also stipulates a right to know parents, though this is hedged with the qualification 'as far as possible'.[57]

---

[50] Though it did not attract a lot of attention until after the Second World War. Archbishop Fisher's commission recommended in 1948 that it be criminalized (*Report of Commission Appointed by his Grace the Archbishop of Canterbury*, 1948).

[51] *Politics and the Life Sciences* 12(2), 155–203 (August 1993).

[52] *In vitro* fertilization, in which a woman's egg is fertilized by mixing with sperm outside the body in a petri dish.

[53] Gamete intra-fallopian transfer, where sperm and eggs are inserted directly into the fallopian tubes, with fertilization occurring *in vivo*.

[54] Zygote intra-fallopian transfer, where eggs fertilized *in vitro* are transferred to the fallopian tubes at the zygote (*i.e.* pronuclear) stage.

[55] According to Amnesty International over 200 children (and this is likely to be an under-estimate) between 1975 and 1983 were given to childless military or police couples who raised them as their own.

[56] See J. S. Cerda, 'The Draft Convention on the Rights of the Child: New Rights' (1990) 12 *Human Rights Quarterly* 115.

[57] See G. A. Stewart, 'Interpreting The Child's Right to Identity in the UN Convention on the Rights of the Child', (1992) 26 *Family Law Quarterly* 221 (1992). See further

The Convention does not address these questions with the artificially-procreated child in mind, nor are such children anywhere the focus of the Convention. Nevertheless, the recognition of these two rights is important.

English law did not examine these questions at all in the context of assisted reproduction[58] until the Human Fertilisation and Embryology Act 1990. This provides for the Human Fertilisation and Embryology Authority to keep a register of information relating to the provision of treatment services, the keeping or use of the gametes of any identifiable individual or of an embryo taken from any identifiable woman 'or if it shows that any identifiable individual was, or may have been, born in consequence of treatment services'.[59] A person may ask the Authority for information but only upon attaining the age of eighteen[60]—the clearest of ripostes to children's rights—and then only such information as the Authority is required by regulations to give,[61] and after the applicant has been given a 'suitable' opportunity for 'proper' counselling.[62] No regulations have been made: so any children conceived using donated material will not be able to obtain any information about their genetic background. Regulations can be expected to follow the Warnock committee recommendation[63] that there should be access to basic information about the donor's 'ethnic origin and genetic health', but not to provide identifying information. This is in striking contrast to the position of adopted children who, when adult, have a legal right to discover their natural parents.

The HFEA Code of Practice requires that treatment centres, which offer treatment involving the use of donated gametes should take into account, amongst other factors 'a child's potential need to know about his or her origins.'[64] A 'potential need' is not, of course, a right. The epithet 'potential' in itself suggests the need to know is only a remote contin-

---

Douglas Hodgson, 'The International Legal Protection of the Child's Right To A Legal Identity and the Problem of Statelessness', (1993) 7 *International Journal of Law and the Family* 255.

[58] Though it did in the context of adoption, beginning with the Children Act 1975 s.26. See John Triseliotis, 'Obtaining Birth Certificates' in (ed.) Philip Bean, *Adoption: Essays in Social Policy, Law and Sociology* (London: Tavistock, 1984 p. 38).

[59] Section 31(3)(a).

[60] See s. 31(3).

[61] See s. 31(4)(a).

[62] See s. 31(3)(b).

[63] See Mary Warnock, *A Matter of Life* (the 'Warnock Report') (Oxford: Blackwell, 1985, para. 4.21).

[64] Para. 3.12.

gency and not one of overwhelming importance. The way the Code deals with the counselling of adults who wish to become recipients of gamete donation also shows thin understanding of rights issues. Thus, clients are to be invited to consider 'the advantages and disadvantages of openness about the procedure'[65] and 'their perceptions of the needs of the child throughout his or her childhood and adolescence.'[66] The Code gives little positive guidance and relies on the judgment of professionals, who may well have interests other than the children to protect. Whether the legislation or the Code complies with the United Nations Convention may be doubted.

There is another provision in the Act to which attention should also be given. An applicant, even one of 16,[67] may require the Authority to disclose if he or she is genetically related to a person whom they propose to marry.[68] The provision is defective because only on the application of both intending marriage partners would the Authority be able to disclose whether there is genetic relationship.[69] Note, only for marriage, and therefore to protect against the very remote possibility of in-breeding, is an application by a child actually allowed.

Whether there should be a right, whether openness is the value to be upheld, remains contentious. In Sweden, where artificially-procreated children are allowed access to the name of their genetic parent when 'sufficiently mature',[70] the number of available donors declined,[71] but it is rising again. It apparently also had the effect of changing the profile of donors: where once semen donors had, as in Britain still, been students, now they were mainly older men.[72] Germany has also abolished the sperm do-

---

[65] Para. 6.10.

[66] Para. 6.12.

[67] 16 is the minimum age for marriage. But it is possible that someone domiciled abroad could seek the information at an even earlier age (cf. the facts of *Mohamed v. Knott* [1969] Q.B.1).

[68] See s. 31(6), (7).

[69] Derek Morgan and Robert G. Lee, *Blackstone's Guide to the Human Fertilisation and Embryology Act 1990* (London: Blackstone, 1991) also note this (see p. 166).

[70] No. 1139 (1984) Art. 4 following SOU 1983:42 (*Children Conceived by Artificial Insemination*, pp. 9–16).

[71] See K. W. Back and R. Snowdon, 'The Anonymity of the Gamete Donor'. 9 *Journal of Psychosomatic Obstetrics and Gynaecology* 191 (1988).

[72] *Ibid.*

nor's anonymity[73] and so have Austria and Switzerland.[74] The Swiss change resulted from a referendum: amongst the substantive rules to be enacted is one which guarantees 'a person's access to the data concerning his ancestry'.[75] This includes the identity of one's biological parents.[76] There is, however, said to be reluctance on the part of medical professionals to adapt their practices to the new constitutional provision.

The arguments for secrecy rarely invoke the interests of the child. As Snowden concedes, 'no one [has] ever set out to explain...why...secrecy [is] the best course of action'.[77] There was, he says, an 'unspoken assumption that being open about the subject would be harmful, whether to those taking part and/or to the child'.[78] I will examine presently whether disclosure may harm participants in the process, and whether this is important. But, as far as the children are concerned, I would endorse John Eekelaar's comment that the view that information about one's origins should be withheld from children because it is in their best interest to do this is 'a stark form of welfarism which could be used to justify many forms of state manipulation deemed to be of benefit to citizens'. Surely he is right to pose the question: 'Would anyone choose to live his or her entire life on the basis that he or she had been deliberately deceived about their genetic origin?'[79]

This is not the line taken by the leading researchers in this country, Susan Golombok and her colleagues at the Clinical and Health Psychology

---

[73] See NJW 1989; Fam. RZ 1989, 255, discussed by Rainer Frank, 'Federal Republic of Germany: New Problems, New Solutions', 29 *Journal of Family Law* 371, 375–376 (1990–1991).

[74] On Austria see Derek Morgan and Erwin Bernat, 'The Reproductive Waltz: The Austrian Medically Assisted Procreation Act, 1992' [1992] *Journal of Social Welfare and Family Law* 420. On Switzerland see Olivier Guillod, 'Everybody Has The Right To Know His Origins!', 33 *Journal of Family Law* (1995). For a comparison of Germany, Austria and Switzerland see E. Bernat, 'Between Rationality and Metaphysics: The Legal Regulation of Assisted Reproduction', 12 *International Journal of Medicine and Law* 493 (1993).

[75] The referendum was in 1987. The new law dates from 1992. See Art. 24 novies al. 2 lit. g.

[76] As shown by the Parliamentary debates: *Bulletin Officiel des Délibérations des Chambres Fédérales, Conseil des Etats* 1990, p. 477 *et seq.*; *Conseil National* 1991 p 556 *et seq.*, 622.

[77] 'Sharing Information About DI in the UK', 12 (2) *Politics and the Life Sciences* 194 (1993).

[78] *Idem.*

[79] 'Families and Children' in C. McCrudden and Chambers (eds.), *Individual Rights and the Law in Britain* (Oxford: 1994).

Research Centre in the City University. They conclude from the practice of DI parents not to tell their children about their origins and from clinical practice that is biased towards secrecy that 'it is insufficient to consider only the welfare of the child: a satisfactory outcome for the child is dependent upon its parents, and thus the welfare of the entire family should be the primary concern'.[80] But it is difficult to see why telling would detrimentally affect family welfare, particularly given this group's other recent research finding that 'the quality of parenting in families with a child conceived by assisted conception is superior to that shown by families with a naturally conceived child'. They found that families constructed by assisted reproduction obtained 'significantly higher scores on measures of mother's warmth to the child, mother's emotional involvement with the child, mother-child interaction, and father-child interaction.[81] Of course, such parents tend to be older and the child is often an only and 'extremely wanted'[82] child. But why should such 'good' parents want to deprive their child of knowledge of its genealogy? Are parents who hide a child's origins neglectful of their parental responsibility? And, if so, does this cast a shadow on the quality of their parenting? In both studies the children were under eight. We can but speculate as to whether outcomes will look as good as the children progress through adolescence and what impact, if any, the policy of not telling will have as and when the families negotiate crises. It is also puzzling how the rationalization that explanations are difficult should be so convincing when these difficulties have been surmounted with the equally complex concepts involved in adoption.[83]

Those who argue for secrecy, in effect denying children access to their own personal map, are wont to argue that secrecy protects the interests of children. Thus, it is said by Snowden and Mitchell[84] that there is a genuine fear among DI practitioners that to reveal the truth to a donor child would

---

[80] Rachel Cook, Susan Golombok, Alison Bish and Clare Murray, 'Keeping Secrets: A Study of Parental Attitudes Toward Talking about Donor Insemination', *American Journal of Orthopsychiatry* 65, 549 (1995).

[81] Susan Golombok, Rachel Cook, Alison Bish and Clare Murray, 'Families Created by the New Reproductive Technologies: Quality of Parenting and social and Emotional Development of the Children', 64 *Child Development* 285, 295 (1995).

[82] *Ibid.*, p. 297.

[83] Books are now being produced. Daniels and Taylor, *op. cit.* note, quote one produced by the NSW Infertility Social Workers Group in 1988 entitled *How I Began; The Story of Donor Insemination*. I understand the DI Network in Sheffield has produced a similar booklet.

[84] *The Artificial Family: A Consideration of Artificial Insemination by Donor* (London: Allen and Unwin, 1981).

create insurmountable social and psychological problems for the child, as well as for his or her family. But, as Daniels and Taylor argue in the most cogent presentation of the case for openness: 'although it is the children that secrecy is supposed to protect, it may be the adult parties (the couple, the donor, and even the medical professionals) who become most vulnerable if their involvement in donor insemination is made public. It is often their position (either personal or professional) which is threatened by the move towards more openness in DI.'[85]

There are, of course, other interests involved: the couple themselves (particularly, where DI is involved, the infertile husband[86]); the donor (though concerns about paternity suits, maintenance liability and inheritance claims have now dissipated[87]); the medical profession (though its concerns are surely exaggerated[88]); and, what has been called, the 'ideal of the family'.[89] Jiri Haderka, for example, arguing in favour of the very secretive practices in operation in Czechoslovakia, sees the claim to allow a child knowledge of his/her genetic origins as 'an unthinkable intrusion into the privacy of family life'.[90] But, in other areas where a child's interests conflict with those of others, we treat the child's interests as paramount.[91] So why not in this context too? Surely, Snowden and Mitchell are right to argue that 'if we really believe that it is the child who is our primary concern, then the whole issue of keeping that child in ignorance of his or her true origins and of setting up procedures to ensure that such ig-

---

[85] *Op. cit.* note 51, p. 157.

[86] R. Snowden, G. D. Mitchell and E. M. Snowden, *Artificial Reproduction: A Social Investigation* (London: Allen and Unwin, 1983); J. N. Lacker and S. Borg, 'Secrecy and the New Reproductive Technologies' in (eds.) L. M. Whiteford and M. L. Poland, *New Approaches to Human Reproduction: Social and Ethical Dimensions* (Boulder: Westview Press, 1989).

[87] See W. W. Beck, 'Two Hundred Years of Artificial Insemination' 41 *Fertility and Sterility*, 193 (1984): D N Joyce, 'The Implications of Greater Openness Concerning AID' in *AID and After* (London: BAAF, 1984 p. 59).

[88] G. Annas, 'Fathers Anonymous: Beyond the Best Interests of the Sperm Donor', 14 *Family Law Quarterly* 1 (1980).

[89] H. D. Kirk, *Adoptive Kinship* (Toronto: Butterworths, 1981) (said as regards adoption, where the 'domestic sovereignty' of the adoptive family now lacks the security it may have had in 1981).

[90] 'Artificial Reproduction in Czechoslovak Law with Special Reference to Other European Socialist Countries', [1987] *International Journal of Law and the Family* 72, at p. 85.

[91] See *J* v. *C* [1970] A.C. 668; *Re W* [1993] 2 FLR 625.

norance is maintained needs to be examined very carefully'.[92] Why should we protect the donor at the child's expense?[93] Is it yet just another example of a silencing of the child's voice? In the conflicts that exist, are the interests of children receiving the least attention because there is a tendency to infantilize them and not see them as people who will become adults?[94] Mary Warnock herself, writing three years after the report that bears her name, observed:

> The child is being used as a means to the parents' ends, namely to have, or seem to have, a 'normal' family; and I do not think that using one person as a means to another's ends can ever be right, unless the person has consented to be so used. As the AID children grow towards adulthood...they are more and more being made an object of contempt.... I could not bear to associate with a grown-up child of my own from whom I had hidden the secret of his or her birth. I cannot argue that children who are told their origins...are necessarily happier, or better off in any way that can be estimated. But I do believe that if they are not told, they are being wrongly treated.[95]

At the root of this 'wrongful treatment' is, I believe, deception. Children have the right not to be deceived. Lies can, as Sissela Bok has shown, be justifiable in certain circumstances.[96] But, as she also notes:

> Those who learn that they have been lied to in an important matter—say, the identity of their parents, the affection of their spouse, or the integrity of their government—are resentful, disappointed and suspicious. They feel wronged; they are wary of new overtures.[97]

It may be, as she also acknowledges, that children are deceived 'with the fewest qualms'.[98]

---

[92] *Op. cit.*, note 51.

[93] See also Erica Haimes, 'Recreating the Family? Policy Considerations Relating To The "New" Reproductive Technologies' in (eds.) Maureen McNeil, Ian Varcoe, Steven Yearley, *The New Reproductive Technologies* (Basingstoke: Macmillan, 1990) p. 154, 160.

[94] See Robyn Rowland, 'Social and Psychological Consequences of Secrecy in Artificial Insemination by Donor' in *Adoption and AID: Access to Information?* (Melbourne; Monash University Centre for Bioethics, 1984).

[95] 'The Good of the Child', *Bioethics* 141, 151 (1987).

[96] *Lying: Moral Advice in Public and Private Life* (New York: Rainbow House, 1978) ch. 3.

[97] *Ibid.*, p. 21.

[98] *Ibid.*, p. 217.

Adoption research indicates that feelings of genealogical insecurity can arise in children who do not know who one or both of their biological parents are. Sants argues that 'a genealogically bewildered child is one who either has no knowledge of his natural parents or only uncertain knowledge of them. The ensuing state of confusion and uncertainty fundamentally undermines his security and this affects his mental health.'[99] It may well be that these traumas will be greater where relationships are unsatisfactory,[100] but we nevertheless accept the right of adopted children to seek their genealogical origins. There is less research as yet on children born as a result of assisted procreation. But Geithner[101] and Baran and Pannor,[102] who have studied DI adults' points of view, have reached broadly the same conclusions as those who have researched the adopted: namely, that such people have a need to be told. Alexina McWhinnie reports likewise as regards two DI adults with whom she has been able to speak. Both, she says, are 'adamant that they should have been told and that this should have been done in an appropriate way'.[103]

Comparisons and contrasts with adoption were made earlier in this article. O'Donovan's advice that we should be cautious about drawing too many parallels was also noted. But we should not ignore the lessons from adoption. The institution has been under scrutiny in the past few years and stands perhaps at the threshold of a new era.[104] If this is to be one of increasingly greater openness, one where the needs and rights of the child are central, if our focus in adoption is to be on the child as client, if we are to continue to integrate adoption within child welfare services, are there not here lessons and possible directions for assisted reproduction? Can we continue to promote assisted reproduction as a private matter?[105] Is it right for us to prioritize the interests of others over those of the child? Can we

---

[99] 'Genealogical Bewilderment in Children with Substitute Parents', 37 *British Journal of Medical Psychology* 133 (1964).

[100] J. Triseliotis *In Search of Origins: The Experience of Adopted People* (London: RKP, 1973); M. Humphreys and H. Humphreys, 'A fresh look at genealogical bewilderment' 59 *British Journal of Medical Psychology* 133 (1986).

[101] 'The Secret of Artificial Insemination by Donor: The Offspring's Experience', Smith College, Northampton, Mass, 1988 (unpublished paper).

[102] *Lethal Secrets* (New York: Warner Books, 1989).

[103] 'Creating Children—The Medical and Social Dilemma of Assisted Reproduction' 16(1) *Adoption and Fostering: The Future* 29, 37 (1992).

[104] See Department of Health, *Adoption: The Future* (London: H.M.S.O. 1993, Cm. 2288).

[105] The case against so conceptualizing it is strongly urged by Robert H. Blank, *Regulating Reproduction* (New York: Columbia University Press, 1990).

justify offering children a lifetime of deceit? Identity as what we know and what we feel is an organizing framework for holding together our past and our present and it provides some anticipated shape to future life. It is an inner personal landscape, a 'feeling of being at home in one's own body'.[106] Is it morally right to deny this well-being to children? It is no response to say that ignorance is bliss for in too many cases a chance remark, the sort one later regrets, will reveal enough to sow seeds of inquisitiveness into many of those who owe their existence to a third party.

If children who are born as a result of assisted conception are entitled to know about their biological origins—and this is a moral right in the 'ideal' sense that it ought to be a positive institutional right[107]—then it follows that there is a duty inhering in their parents[108] not to deceive them about their true origins. And this duty extends to others including those providing treatment services. Such clinics, indeed HFEA itself, have the capacity to lead public opinion: where, as in Australia and New Zealand, openness is widely encouraged, the level of support for breaking down the barriers of secrecy reflects this.[109] Thus Rowland found that 60 per cent of semen donors would not mind meeting the child at age eighteen[110] and Daniels that 68 per cent of donors were happy for identifying information to be given to DI offspring after the age of eighteen to enable them to trace the donor. 77 per cent of his respondents thought that children had a right to non-identifying information about the donor and 73 per cent said that they would still be prepared to donate if their DI offspring could trace them later on.[111] In the most recent study, Purdie *et al.* found that 68 per cent of donors were agreeable to their identity being made available when offspring reached maturity.[112]

I argue, therefore, that the right to identity is a right not to be deceived about his true origins. The Warnock recommendation, which would give

---

[106] *Per* E. H. Erikson, 'The Problem of Ego Identity' 4 *Journal of American Psychological Association* 56, 74 (1956).

[107] See Joel Feinberg, *Social Philosophy* (N. J. Englewood Cliffs: Prentice Hall, 1973) p. 84 (and see M. D. A. Freeman, *The Rights and Wrongs of Children* (London: Francis Pinter, 1983, pp. 34–35).

[108] I refer here to *social* parents, one of whom will also be a biological parent.

[109] See Daniels and Taylor, *op. cit.*, note 51 pp. 162–163.

[110] 'Attitudes and Opinions of Donors on an Artificial Insemination by Donor (AID) Programme', 2 *Clinical Reproduction and Fertility* 249 (1983).

[111] 'Semen Donors: Their Motivations and Attitudes To Their Offspring', 7 *Journal of Reproductive and Infant Psychology* 21 (1989).

[112] 'Identifiable Semen Donors: Attitudes of Donors and Recipient Couples', 105 *New Zealand Medical Journal* 27 (1992).

access to knowledge about ethnic origin and genetic health,[113] offers far too little. The analogies with adoption are more powerful than the differences and it is this model to which we should be looking. The opportunity should also be taken to reconsider the limitations on access to information in adoption to those of 18 and over. A cautious reform could reduce this to 16[114]: a bolder approach would tie the ability to seek identifying information to the possession of sufficient knowledge and understanding. In Austria, identifying information can be sought at the age of 14. Competence, '*Gillick*-competence' as it is usually called,[115] it must be stressed requires not just 'book knowledge'. Those who parrot Lord Scarman's words that a competent child is one who 'achieves a sufficient understanding and intelligence to enable him or her to understand fully[116] what is proposed' tend not to note that he goes on to add and has 'sufficient discretion to enable him or her to make a wise choice in his or her own interests'.[117] In overlooking the latter we discount personal experiential knowledge. This is more readily available, more valuable and more likely to be found in the concerned and inquisitive adolescent. To implement these proposals requires new structures: birth certificates, for example, should note that the birth resulted from semen, ovum or embryo donation;[118] and new registers will have to be established. There will need to be more counsellors and better counselling services and greater integration (a new 'working together'[119]) between treatment services and social services. All these proposals prioritize the artificially-procreated child's interests above those of other interest groups. They recognize that we should regard the issues involved as related to children's welfare and their rights and that there is a necessity to place the subject firmly within child law. Only then will we come to realize that, thus far, we have treated these children with less than the concern or respect that they deserve.

---

[113] *Op. cit.*, note 28, para. 4.21.

[114] The age at which consent to medical treatment may be given (see Family Law Reform Act 1969 s.8).

[115] See *Gillick* v. *West Norfolk and Wisbech A.H.A.* [1986] A C 112.

[116] The significance of this word is rarely considered: very few adults would be "Gillick competent" if this really were required.

[117] *Op. cit.*, note 115, p. 189.

[118] It is already possible to do this (certainly in the case of DI) but it is doubtful whether more than a very small minority take advantage of the facility. An attempt to ensure that the birth certificate of a child born as a result of treatment services should have this fact endorsed failed in the House of Commons.

[119] See *Working Together* (London: H.M.S.O., 1991)

Parenting and Legitimacy

The other rights to which artificially-procreated children may be entitled can be considered more cursorily. Those relating to status and parentage are closely intertwined with the identity issue. They are addressed in the Human Fertilisation and Embryology Act 1990 but so unsatisfactorily that the law and its implications are too complex for many to understand.

The Act provides (s.27) that a woman who has carried a child as a result of the placing in her of an embryo or sperm and eggs (GIFT or ZIFT procedures) is the mother of that child whatever its genetic makeup. But, whether this gestational mother also becomes the social mother will depend upon whether the genetic mother, and her husband, apply for a parental order under section 30 of the same Act.[120] Section 30 is designed to save surrogacy arrangements.[121] Who becomes the child's legal parents thus depends upon the fertility and married status of the adults involved: if the gestational mother is infertile she will be the mother; if she is the surrogate for an infertile woman that woman will become the legal mother upon the granting of a parental order, provided she is married to the commissioning father. If they are not married, the gestational mother remains the legal mother even if she hands the child over to the genetic mother, who will, of course, also become the social mother. The genetic/social mother could seek an adoption order, but not together with the genetic/social father.[122] Elsewhere, the Act (s.13(5)) provides, in one of the most extraordinarily-worded provisions in all legislation, that 'a woman shall not be provided with treatment services unless account has been taken of the welfare of any child who may be born as a result of the treatment (including the need of that child for a father)'.[123] This is not a special provision for parthenogenesis:[124] all children have fathers! It is rather a mandate to uphold basic values by insisting that a woman seeking treatment should have a man, though perhaps curiously it does not insist she be

---

[120] This came into operation on 1 November 1994. The provision was introduced to tackle the problems in the so-called 'Cumbria' case of *Re W* [1991] 1 FLR 385.

[121] Upon which English Law adopts an ambivalent position (see Surrogacy Arrangements Act 1985 and Human Fertilisation And Embryology Act 1990 s. 36).

[122] For a couple to adopt they must be married to each other.

[123] On this see Gillian Douglas, 'Assisted Reproduction and The Welfare of the Child', (1993) 46 *Current Legal Problems*, 37.

[124] The reproductive process whereby a gamete develops into a new individual without fertilization. And see *op. cit.*, note 28, para. 12.10.

married to him.¹²⁵ It is noteworthy that an application for parental order is a 'family proceeding',¹²⁶ as defined by the Children Act, so that other s.8 orders could be made instead: but it is not governed by any paramountcy principle¹²⁷ (nor is the child's welfare even a 'first consideration'¹²⁸) and courts are not constrained not to make orders unless doing so would be better for the child.¹²⁹ The welfare checklist is also irrelevant.¹³⁰

The Warnock report also wished to discourage the use by a widow of her dead husband's semen for AIH.¹³¹ But the interest it wished to uphold was not any that a child might have in being fatherless—after all it is this potential child's only chance of life—but the interest of those who administer estates in finality. It accordingly recommended¹³² that such children should not be able to inherit from their fathers. This recommendation has not, as yet, been implemented, but like those which have it places adult interests, in the case property interests, above those of children.

Section 28 defines 'father' for the purposes of the 1990 Act. The law has always guarded carefully the concept of paternity but never has it created the extraordinary mess that is s.28.

Section 28(2) provides that, where a woman is married, if she becomes pregnant following embryo transfer, GIFT or ZIFT or DI, her husband is to be treated as the father of any child who results from such treatment. But, if he can show that he did not consent to the treatment service, he is not to be treated as the father under s.28(2), though he will remain the presumed father by virtue of s.28(5) (preserving the common law presumption of paternity). It may be supposed that a husband who did consent but changed his mind in the nine months between treatment and birth will also be the presumed father, if not treated as the father under s.28(5).

Section 28(3) provides that if no man is treated as the father of the child by virtue of s.28(2), in effect because the woman is unmarried, the man with whom the woman seeks infertility treatment and who is not the sperm donor is to be treated as the father of the child, subject to the pre-

---

[125] The Code of Practice does not make the welfare of a resulting child a paramount consideration (*op. cit.*, note 65, para. 10) but says treatment should be refused if it would not be in the interests of any resulting child (para. 16).
[126] See s. 8(4).
[127] See s. 1(1).
[128] Adoption Act 1976 s. 6.
[129] Children Act 1989 s. 1(5).
[130] Children Act 1989 s. 1(3).
[131] See M. Warnock, *A Matter of Life* (Oxford: Blackwell, 1985) p. 55.
[132] *Ibid.*, para. 10.9.

sumptions in s.28(5). If the woman is married, but not to the man with whom she is seeking treatment services, her husband will be treated as, or presumed to be, the father, unless he can defeat both the statutory provision and the common law presumption. When Harold Laski made his famous comment, that it was an 'exercise in logic, not life',[133] he was referring to Kelsen's normative jurisprudence, but he was not to encounter this Act. And yet it gets worse. Where a man is by virtue of s.28(2) or (3) treated as a child's father, s.28(4) provides that no other man is to be so regarded. Section 28(6), which is intended to protect a donor whose sperm is used with his consent to establish a pregnancy to which a married woman's husband has not consented, provides that the donor is not to be treated as the father of the child. But, if the mother's husband is not the father and the donor is not the father, who is? The answer is no one: in law the child has no father. Furthermore, if the sperm is used without the donor's consent, he may not be protected by s.28(6)(a) and so may be treated as the child's father without his consent. He may, for example, have agreed to donate sperm for research purposes, but not treatment services.

The Act succeeds in creating a second category of the legally fatherless by the way it tackles posthumous births. Section 28(6)(b) provides that where the sperm of a man, or any embryo the creation of which was brought about with his sperm, was used after his death, he is not to be treated as the father of the child. This means that the child, produced using frozen sperm left by a soldier who falls in battle after expressly consenting to his wife's using it after his death, does not have a legal father, and is also illegitimate, since the marriage ended on the soldier's death, unless the widow remarried, in which case the new husband is treated as the child's father under s.28(2). The goal, as Warnock made clear,[134] is to discourage posthumous pregnancies. This is a goal for which there may be some support: is it parentally responsible to bring a child into the world in these circumstances? But is it right to punish children to discourage their mothers? This dilemma is found elsewhere, for example in the Child Support Act,[135] with a similar resolution. But these are not policies designed to put the interest of children into the forefront.

The law is no more satisfactory as regards the paternity and legitimacy of children born as a result of post-mortem inseminations. No presumption of legitimacy can apply because the marriage ended on death. But there is

---

[133] *Grammar of Politics* (4th ed.), p. vi.

[134] *Op. cit.*, note 131, paras. 4.4 and 10.9

[135] Nor is this a problem alleviated by the reform of this legislation in 1995.

an argument[136] that a statutory provision dealing with void marriages may by analogy assist here too.[137] A child of a void marriage is legitimate if at the time of insemination resulting in his or her birth, or at the time of the child's conception, or at the time of the celebration of the marriage if later, both or either of the parties reasonably believed that the marriage was valid (the so-called 'putative marriage'). If for the purposes of conception *in vitro*, conception takes place when the ovum is fertilized, and not when the resulting embryo or zygote is replaced in the uterus, then if either of the parties believed the marriage was valid, a child born years later from a frozen embryo, even after the man's death, would be legitimate. This would seem to place such a child in a better position than one whose parents were married—a truly absurd conclusion. Can this be the result of rational law-making? Or is it rather a game played with concepts with little anticipation of the consequences?

This analysis has laid bare the confusion and incoherence of the present law. It has also uncovered the values secreted within it. The law is adult-orientated, not child-centred. It is concerned with protecting property rights, with stability and orderly succession. Nor are the interests it upholds necessarily congruent with those it supports elsewhere. The emphasis on parental responsibility in the Children Act and in child support legislation is conspicuously absent. Thus, where there is both a biological and a social father (or step-father), as is often the case after divorce, the law preserves the responsibilities of the biological father, at the same time upholding his rights, in the name of the 'best interests of the child'.[138] But contrast this with DI, where there is also a biological and a social father, and we find the law following public opinion and investing rights of paternity in the social father.

THE REPRODUCTIVE REVOLUTION: CHILDREN AS COMMODITIES

The children's rights movement has been concerned to establish that children are persons rather than property. In this it has had considerable success. We do think of children differently today from only a generation ago. The famous blood-tie adoption case, we need to remind ourselves, was

---

[136] *Op. cit.*, note 69, p. 158.
[137] See Legitimacy Act 1976 s. 1(1) (originally Legitimacy Act 1959 s. 2).
[138] See further C. Barton and G. Douglas, *Law and Parenthood* (London, Butterworths, 1995).

decided less than thirty years ago.[139] But does the reproduction revolution have the capacity to turn the clock back? To borrow from the language of wrongful life litigation, are children as a whole being wronged by being made the objects of assisted reproduction? Are these merely alarmist concerns, invocations of the slippery slope?[140] Or are these real worries? Should we, particularly those of us concerned with children's rights, sound the trumpet of alarm?

The concern has been voiced particularly with reference to surrogacy arrangements. This is where the concern should be focused, for only here does anything resembling a commercial market operate.[141] But if the concern is real with surrogacy, can we be confident that the fall-out will not be felt, ultimately, with other forms of assisted procreation? Or is this, again, merely to capitulate to doubtful and unprovable slippery slopes?

It must be a potential consequence of the emergence of surrogacy, or it would be if surrogacy became at all common, that children may come to be seen as commodities. Even if surrogacy were confined to its altruistic variety, where, for example, one fertile sister 'gives' her infertile one a child, the product of her ovum and the infertile sister's husband's semen, the categorization might still stand. Note the language that has been used: we are talking of 'gifts' and 'products'.[142] The associations are more obvious when the model of commercial surrogacy is examined. The child then can be seen as the product of an expensive business transaction. Technically, the commissioning parents may be buying gestational services but they feel they are buying a baby. Furthermore, they want to feel that the child is at least half genetically theirs. That that half is the man's may itself cause problems but that is another question.

It was Mia Kellmer-Pringle who censured the attitude that children complete a family like any other consumer durable: she gave the example of a TV or fridge.[143] Is surrogacy encouraging a similar attitude? Just as you go to a shop to purchase video equipment, you go, so it is argued to the local surrogacy agency to purchase your child. And just as video

---

[139] *Re C (MA)* [1966] 1 All E.R. 838.

[140] On the slippery slope see David Lamb, *Down The Slippery Slope: Arguing In Applied Ethics* (London: Croom Helm, 1988).

[141] The Surrogacy Arrangements Act 1985 was designed to frustrate this.

[142] See Marcel Mauss, *The Gift* (1954). Gifts in the wide context of women's political inequality are discussed by Janice Raymond in 20(6) *Hastings Center Report* 7 (1990), and by Judith Lorber, 'Choice, Gift or Patriarchal Bargain?' in (eds.) H. B. Holmes and L. Purdy, *op. cit.* note 5, p. 169.

[143] *The Needs of Children* (London: Hutchinson, 1976).

equipment has to be of merchantable quality,[144] so too must the child. In the United States, in the notorious *Stiver-Mallahoff* case,[145] an unseemly battle was fought when the child was thought to be disabled.

The dangers in turning the baby into a market commodity are graphically portrayed by Margaret Jane Radin:

> If a capitalist baby industry were to come into being, with all of its accompanying paraphernalia, how could any of us, even those who did not produce infants for sale, avoid subconsciously measuring the dollar value of our children? How could our children avoid being preoccupied with measuring their own dollar value? This makes our discourse about ourselves (when we are children) and about our children (when we are parents) like our discourse about cars. In the worst case, market rhetoric could create a commodified self-conception in everyone, as a result of commodifying every attribute that differentiates us and that other people value in us, and could destroy personhood as we know it.[146]

That there is a potential danger cannot be denied. But it is both speculative and alarmist. It is premised on the basis of the emergence of a 'capitalist baby industry'. Whether this was nipped in the bud by the Surrogacy Arrangements Act of 1985 may be debatable, though the fears of 1985 certainly have not materialized. But even were surrogacy to flourish there is no reason why it should not be regulated and taken over by institutions like adoption agencies, and this would, I believe, surmount the sort of fears that Radin's language encapsulates.

Writing not long after the 'Baby Cotton' affair and the 1985 legislation it was argued that surrogacy posed a 'threat to our notion of childhood, certainly to an ideal of children for which the children's rights movement strives'.[147] This now looks unduly alarmist.

This is not to deny that children may encounter psychological problems. To have been bought and sold may well pose a threat to a child's sense of security. If it could happen once, why not again? There may also be burdens on the child to do well. As an 'investment', expectations must

---

[144] That this concept has now disappeared in English law (Sale and Supply of Goods Act 1994) does not detract from my point.

[145] Discussed in *op. cit.*, note 2, p. 118–119, "Imperfect" could also mean the wrong sex: in Taiwan in 1985 a man hired a surrogate to produce a boy; when she produced a girl he attempted to sue her (*The Guardian*, 23 January 1985).

[146] 'Market—Inalienability', 100 *Harvard Law Review* 1849, 1926 (1987).

[147] Michael Freeman, 'Is Surrogacy Exploitative?' in (ed.) Sheila A. M. McLean, *Legal Issues in Human Reproduction* (Aldershot: Gower, 1989) at p. 176.

be fulfilled. But these are not insuperable problems and establishing a right to identity may go a considerable way towards alleviating them.

If these problems are exaggerated in the context of surrogacy, *a fortiori* they should cause even less concern in other areas of assisted reproduction where the market imperative seems unlikely to penetrate.

Conclusion

Assisted reproduction has hitherto neglected a children's rights perspective—and it shows. There has been no systematic exploration of the questions it raises, which has put children, their interests and rights into the forefront. Too many of the conclusions and too much of the legislation have been hurried, often responding to scandal or panic. We owe the first generation of children of the reproduction revolution a better deal. I have outlined the approach I believe should be adopted if this is to happen.

CHAPTER 11

Can Children Divorce their Parents?

INTRODUCTION

It was the Gregory Kingsley case[1] in the United States which first evoked the image of the child divorcing his parents, though it was by no means the first case.[2] The use of the concept of 'divorce' is both emotive and inaccurate and it courts the misleading and sensational headline. Divorce is a licence to remarry and as such offers the opportunity to create a new relationship. The relationship of spouses is socially constructed: compared to the relationship of parent and child it is artificial. It requires state intervention both to create it and to dissolve it.[3] The parent-child relationship

---

[1] See *Kingsley v. Kingsley* 623 So. 2d 780 (Fla. Dist. Ct. App. 1993). Gregory Kingsley's case is different from the English cases discussed in this article. He was a foster child 'in limbo' in the Florida foster care system. He wanted to terminate relations with his biological parents and facilitate adoption by his foster parents. He was assisted in this by the fact that his wished-for adoptive father was a lawyer. The adoptive father has written on the case: see George H. Russ, 'Through the Eyes of a Child, "Gregory K.": A Child's Right To Be Heard', (1993) 27 *Family Law Quarterly* 365. Rather as with the English cases the 'media misconstrued a relatively ordinary case...as a pathbreaking legal event' (*per* Barbara B. Woodhouse, 'Hatching The Egg: A Child-Centred Perspective on Parents' Rights', 14 *Cardozo Law Review* 1836, 1836–1837 (1993)). Andrew Shapiro hailed Gregory Kingsley as the 'Rosa Parks of the movement to expand the rights of children against the traditional prerogatives of biological parents' ('Children in Court—The New Crusade', *The Nation*, September 27 1993, p 301). A good note on the case is Christina Dugger Sommer, 'Empowering Children: Granting Foster Children the Right to Initiate Parental Rights Termination Proceedings', 79 *Cornell Law Review* 1200 (1994). This article does not address the separate question of parents divorcing their children, in particular the concept of emancipation, found in a large number of US states. On this see Carol Sanger and Eleanor Willemsen, 'Minor Changes: Emancipating Children in Modern Times', (1992) 25 *University of Michigan Journal of Law Reform* 239.

[2] *Polovchak v. Meese* 774 F. 2d 731 (1985) is a celebrated earlier instance. Walter Polovchak is quoted 8 years later (when 20) to say 'As every day goes by I'm happier and happier I made the decision' (*International Herald Tribune*, April 11 1988, p. 3).

[3] Ironically the trend is towards making the former more regulated than the latter. Books on

by contrast as an incident of biology and genetics is absent this control (at least outside the context of assisted reproduction[4] and adoption[5]). Parenthood is not licensed.[6] Nor does it come to an end upon divorce, either when this takes place in its true sense or when children 'divorce' parents.

When we talk of a child 'divorcing' his parents, we really raise the question whether a child can choose where he lives and/or with whom. Not surprisingly, this raises controversy. To most, one of the characteristics of being a child is being deprived—and they would say rightly—of such choices. But we are witnessing a shift from children being seen as 'objects' to one where their subjectivity, their existence as individuals in their own right, is coming to be recognized. A generation ago children came to be seen as patients in the context of medical practice.[7] Twenty years ago it was recognized that children who were victimized by abuse deserved the role of litigant.[8] In other areas, but not education,[9] they have acquired the role of consumer. International documents, in particular the United Nations Convention on the Rights of the Child, accord children the status of rights-bearer.[10] Article 12 of this, recognizing the child's auton-

---

family law will soon have to devote more space to the mechanics of marriage than the process of divorce.

[4] A striking instance of which is *R* v. *Ethical Committee of St Mary's Hospital, Manchester exp. Harriott* [1988] 1 FLR 512. This was discussed by Catherine Steven, 'The Unnatural Selection of Suitable Parents', *The Independent*, 23 October 1987.

[5] The principle established in *A* v. *Liverpool C.C.* [1982] AC 363 applies to decisions taken by adoption agencies. See *Re W* [1990] 2 FLR 470. But see also *Re T* [1994] 1 FLR 632, particularly the remarks of Balcombe L.J. at p. 644.

[6] But see Hugh La Follette, 'Licensing Parents' (1980) 9 *Philosophy and Public Affairs* 182 (there is a reply by Lawrence E. Frisch (1982) 11 Philosophy and Public Affairs 173 and a reply to this by La Follette at p. 181). Also of value is John Harris, 'The Right To Found a Family' in (ed.) Geoffrey Scarre, *Children, Parents and Politics* (Cambridge: Cambridge University Press, 1989), p. 133.

[7] Family Law Reform Act 1969 s. 8(1) (consent at 16). See also s. 8(3) (interpreted by many—though not now the Court of Appeal—to mean that consent below the age of 16 not precluded). For the different attitude of the courts see *Gillick* v. *West Norfolk and Wisbech A.H.A* [1986] A.C. 112 and *Re R* [1992] 1 FLR 190 and *Re W* [1993] 1 FLR 1.

[8] The Colwell case of 1973–1974 catapulted this problem to public attention and the Children Act 1975.

[9] See Michael Freeman, 'Children's Rights as Protection and Autonomy: Education as a Test-Case' in (ed.) R. Davie, *Children's Rights and Children's Education* (London: Fulton Press, 1996).

[10] On which see Lawrence J. Le Blanc, *The Convention on the Rights of the Child* (Lincoln, Nebraska: University of Nebraska Press, 1995). More generally see Cynthia Price Cohen, 'The Developing Jurisprudence of the Rights of the Child', (1993) 6 *St Thomas Law Review* 1.

omy and granting participatory rights, is especially noteworthy.[11] And a significant strand[12] of the Children Act 1989 legitimates children as persons rather than objects of concern.[13] Yet the metaphor of divorce troubles. Perhaps this is because as a label, as a social construction, it comes with a ready-made package of associations.[14] And these, far from being associated with children, betray concerns with dysfunction and disintegration. The Lord Chancellor's paper 'Looking To The Future' encapsulated some of these concerns,[15] though, of course it did not address the issue of the child who wishes to sever links with his own family.

Children were 'divorcing' their parents long before the problem was so designated. The accentuated concern is associated with the concept of divorce. When the phenomenon did not attract the label, it did not evoke the critical responses it now does.[16] A generation ago an Indian girl,[17] close to her eighteenth birthday, fought her parents' attempt to remove her from voluntary care.[18] Their goal was an arranged marriage which she wished to resist. The Court of Appeal held that there was no 'absolute' obligation on the local authority to return her to her parents.[19] There is little doubt that this strained interpretation would have been applauded by many of those who criticize today's cases. Yet, of course, though no such label was used, the girl was to all intents and purposes divorcing her parents. Similarly, in the United States, the *Polovchak* case[20] was not characterized in terms of divorce but the issues involved were little different from those in contemporary cases. A 12-year-old had emigrated with his parents from the U.S.S.R. to the U.S.A., but his father had not liked America and decided that he and

---

[11] Said by Marta Santos Pais to make the child a 'principal' in the Convention (see 'The United Nations Convention on the Rights of the Child', 91/2 *Bulletin of Human Rights* 75, 76 (1992)).

[12] But only a strand. See Lorraine Fox-Harding, 'The Children Act 1989 in Context: Four Perspectives in Child Care Law and Policy', (1991) *Journal of Social Welfare and Family Law*, 179 and 285.

[13] The phrase may be traced to the Cleveland report, Cm. 412 (London: H.M.S.O., 1988).

[14] As 'mugging' did a generation ago. See Stuart Hall, *Policing The Crisis* (London: Macmillan, 1978).

[15] Cd. 2424 (London: H.M.S.O, 1993).

[16] Thus cases, when girls (often from the Indian sub-continent) warded themselves to leave, or stay away from, home were treated in a more subdued fashion.

[17] *Krishnan v. L.B. of Sutton* [1970] Ch. 181.

[18] What we would now call 'accommodation' (s. 20 of Children Act 1989).

[19] But *cf. Bawden v. Bawden* [1979] Q.B. 419.

[20] *Polovchak v. Meese* 774 F. 2d 731. See also *Schleiffer v. Meyers* 644 F. 2d 656.

his family should return to the Soviet Union. The 12-year-old, Walter, decided, however, that he liked America and wanted to stay. He accordingly ran away from home and refused to accompany his parents back to the Soviet Union. The case provoked enormous controversy with the American Civil Liberties Union, which had campaigned for children's rights, supporting the father's case. 'We believe', it said, 'kids have rights, but not that a 12-year-old has the right to choose where his family should live'.[21] But Walter was not claiming any such right: he was claiming the right to decide where he would live.[22]

The issue then is not new. The Children Act 1989 enables us to see it, however, in a new light.

THE 1989 ACT AND EMPOWERMENT

The 1989 Act is not about empowerment.[23] Indeed, it may be said that its principal aim, however flawed in execution, is to address and improve children's welfare. The paramountcy which this is accorded in the very first sub-section of the Act means that autonomy must often take a back seat. But the welfare checklist[24] nevertheless places the wishes and feelings of the child considered in the light of age and understanding first in the list of factors. To emphasize this *Working Together* in its post-Children Act form[25] urges the involvement of children in child protection conferences 'whenever [they] have sufficient understanding and are able to express their wishes and feelings and to participate in the process of investigation, assessment, planning and review…'.[26] In a number of situations the Act provides that children may initiate court actions. For example, s/he may challenge an emergency protection order,[27] seek contact when in care[28] and ask for a care order to be discharged,[29] and, as we shall see in detail, seek the court's leave to obtain an order (under section 8) making a

---

[21] *The Sunday Times*, 3 August 1980.
[22] An earlier case is *Re Snyder* 532 P. 2d 278 (1975). The court found 'the parent-child relationship had dissipated to the point where parental control [was] lost' (p. 281).
[23] David Hodgson is one to suggest it is.
[24] See s. 1(3).
[25] In contrast to the first edition in 1988.
[26] Para. 6. 13.
[27] Section 45(8).
[28] Section 34(2).
[29] Section 39(1).

decision as to where s/he is to live or with whom have contact.[30] It is usually a precondition that the child has sufficient understanding to make an application, but, surprisingly perhaps, this is not always so.[31] Since empowerment is often dependent upon representation, the more extensive use of guardians *ad litem* should also not be overlooked.[32] But nor should the disparity between such provision in the public law arena and in private law disputes be ignored.[33] The Children Act recognizes the autonomy of the child also in a number of provisions which give children when 'of sufficient understanding to make an informed decision' the right to refuse to submit to medical and psychiatric examinations and other assessments.[34] The impact of the *Gillick* case,[35] in particular of Lord Scarman's judgment,[36] is readily detectable in this language: indeed, it may be said to be one of the dominant influences on the Act.

COMPETENCE AND EMPOWERMENT

Lord Scarman, it will be recalled, tied in empowerment to competence. A competent child is one who 'achieves a sufficient understanding and intelligence to enable him or her to understand fully what is proposed' and also has 'sufficient discretion to enable him or her to make a wise choice in his or her own interests'.[37] In these terms competence incorporates understanding and knowledge with wisdom. There are dangers in conflating knowledge and wisdom, but this is commonly done. Few adults are *Gillick*-competent if competence hinges upon abilities to understand fully what is involved in a decision: many children who are well below the ages with which we tend to associate *Gillick*-competence are competent within Lord Scarman's test if 'wise choice' is genuinely situated within the child's personal experiential knowledge of his or her 'own interests'. The

---

[30] Section 10(2), (8).
[31] See section 34(2).
[32] See section 41.
[33] See J. Roche, 'Once A Parent Always A Parent', (1991) *Journal of Social Welfare and Family Law* 345.
[34] For example in section 38(6).
[35] *Gillick* v. *West Norfolk and Wisbech A.H.A.* [1986] A.C. 112.
[36] This has emerged as the *ratio*, though at the time Lord Fraser's judgment, which had more support, was thought to contain this. And he merely transferred authority to make decisions from parents to professionals.
[37] *Op. cit.*, note 35, p. 186.

courts in a series of recent cases[38] which have held that a child's right to consent to medical treatment does not extend to a right to refuse such treatment have failed to appreciate this. As Alderson and Goodwin have noted, 'professional, textbook knowledge is highly valued, personal experiential knowledge is discounted'.[39] This is what happened to the anorexic 17-year-old in *Re W*.[40] And once such 'wisdom' is ignored, the child is assumed to be ignorant, except insofar as he or she can recount medical or other professional information. It becomes easy then to discuss the contribution they can make to decision-making. Alderson and Goodwin argue that the non-competent child 'who figures in the legal imagination is treated as arational rather than irrational. When children are credited, at least, with a misguided rationality, the importance of explaining and correcting misunderstandings is accepted. If children are implicitly treated as arational, then enforced treatment without regard to the child's views is endorsed by the courts'.[41] This is what happened in *Re R*,[42] *Re W*[43] and the other less-publicized cases.[44] And it happens also outside the context of decisions about medical treatment.

Thus, for example, in *Re H*,[45] where in care proceedings it became clear that a 15-year-old and his guardian *ad litem* were giving conflicting instructions to a solicitor, the court had to interpret a Rule[46] which instructs solicitors to represent children in accordance with instructions received from the guardian *ad litem* 'unless the solicitor considers, having taken into account the views of the guardian *ad litem* and any direction of the court...that the child wishes to give instructions which conflict with those of the guardian *ad litem* and that he is able, *having regard to his understanding*,[47] to give such instructions on his own behalf, in which case he shall conduct the proceedings in accordance with the instructions received from the child'. The boy concerned is described as of 'above-average

---

[38] *Re R* [1992] 1 FLR 190; *Re W* [1993] 1 FLR 1; *Re S* [1994] 2 FLR 1065.
[39] 'Contradictions within Concepts of Children's Competence', 1 *International Journal of Children's Rights* 303, 305 (1993).
[40] [1993] 1 FLR 1.
[41] *Op. cit.*, note 39, p. 305.
[42] [1992] 1 FLR 190.
[43] [1993] 1 FLR 1.
[44] *Re K, W and H* [1993] 1 FLR 240; *South Glamorgan C.C.* v. *W and B* [1993] 1 FLR 574.
[45] [1993] 1 FLR 440.
[46] Family Proceedings Courts (Children Act 1989) Rules 1991 r. 12 (1)(a).
[47] My emphasis.

ability'[48] (he was in the 'A' stream of a grammar school), but emotionally disturbed. A number of the court's conclusions repay examination. Thus, for example, Thorpe J. held that 'the level of understanding that enables a child to make an informed decision whether to refuse to submit to a psychiatric examination is in all practical senses a much higher level than is required to enable him to give instructions to a solicitor on his own behalf'.[49] But why? Is the understanding and knowledge any greater or is it an underlying fear that the consequences of making an unwise decision in the former case are greater, more potentially deleterious to the child, than in the latter? Or is it once again a triumph of professional knowledge over personal, experiential insight?

It is also noteworthy that Thorpe J. dismissed H's counsel's argument 'almost any child of 15 years and 8 months must be taken to have sufficient understanding to instruct a solicitor' with the riposte 'Obviously a child suffering from a mental disability might not have such understanding. Obviously a child suffering from a psychiatric disorder might not have such a level of understanding'.[50] I pause for a moment to question whether it is indeed 'obvious'. Thorpe J. continues: 'But I cannot follow her to the conclusion that if a child is only suffering from some emotional disturbance then really there is little room to question his or her ability to instruct a solicitor. It seems to me that a child must have sufficient rationality within the understanding to instruct a solicitor. It may well be that the level of emotional disturbance is such as to remove the necessary degree of rationality that leads to coherent and consistent instruction.'[51] We do not question an emotionally-disturbed adult's ability to instruct a solicitor. Are we right to do so in the case of a child? Have the consequences of this sort of reasoning and the decisions it leads to been thought through? The removal of autonomy can lead to the destruction of identity, a feeling of being out of control can exacerbate disturbance.[52] Despite his emotional problems H probably[53] had the ability that Lord Scarman captured as 'wise choice', even if he may have

---

[48] *Op. cit.*, note 45, p. 443.
[49] *Ibid.*, p. 449.
[50] *Idem.*
[51] *Idem.*
[52] See M. D. A. Freeman, 'Removing Rights from Adolescents', 17(1) *Adoption and Fostering* 14 (1993); see also S. Melzac, 'Secrecy, Privacy, Survival, Repressive Régimes and Growing Up', 15 *Journal of the Anna Freud Centre* 205–224 (1992); W. Yule, 'Post-Traumatic Stress Disorders in Children', 4 *Current Opinion in Paediatrics* 4 (1992).
[53] It is impossible to come to a categorical conclusion on the facts available.

lacked the sort of professional knowledge that we associate with 'rationality'.[54]

CHILDREN AS PARTIES TO PROCEEDINGS

Re H was a public law case. Of greater relevance to the issue to the child who wishes to 'divorce' parents is the private law and the opportunities this presents for a child to participate in court proceedings.

Most media coverage of 'divorcing' cases has followed child-initiated actions. It is worth, however, first considering the status of the child in proceedings initiated by one of his parents. As Sir Thomas Bingham M.R. noted in *Re S*: 'the proposition that a boy of 11 should be accorded the full rights of a litigant to intervene in a dispute between his parents about the arrangements best suited to promote his welfare...may be surprising to some'.[55] In *Re S* there was an application made by S's father for residence and contact orders. S was made a party to the proceedings and the Official Solicitor[56] was appointed to act as his guardian *ad litem*. The Official Solicitor recommended that S should continue to live with his mother (he had done so since he was 5) and should see his father less frequently. It was the father's contention, supported by S, that S should live with him in North America. S contended from the outset of the proceedings that the Official Solicitor should not represent him and that he should be able to act independently through a solicitor. Under Rule 9.2A of the Family Proceedings Rules 1991 (as amended in 1992) a minor may 'begin, prosecute or defend' proceedings without a next friend or guardian *ad litem* with the leave of the court or where a solicitor considers the minor is able 'having regard to his understanding, to give instructions in relation to the proceedings' and has accepted instructions to act. The Rules also provide that a minor may apply to the court for the removal of a next friend or guardian *ad litem*. The Court of Appeal held that it would not grant leave for a minor to take part in proceedings without a next friend or guardian *ad litem* rules: the minor intended to be legally represented, in which case the issue

---

[54] On which see Judith Hughes's comment: 'If rational is what nineteenth-century gentlemen are, then children no less than women will come to grief in the rationality stakes' ('Thinking About Children' in (ed.) Geoffrey Scarre, *Children, Parents and Politics*, Cambridge: Cambridge University Press, 1989, 36–51, at p. 38).

[55] [1993] 2 FLR 437, 439.

[56] On the role of whom see David Venables, 'The Official Solicitor', (1990) 20 *Fam. Law* 53 and M. Hinchcliffe, 'The Role of the Official Solicitor in Child Abuse Cases' in Allan Levy (ed.), *Focus on Child Abuse* (London: Hawksmere 1989), p. 86.

would be whether the minor had sufficient understanding to give coherent instructions. It stressed that it was 'understanding',[57] not age, that underpinned the test. At least with children, so the Master of the Rolls believed, understanding increased with the passage of time. He noted that 'different children have differing levels of understanding at the same age. And understanding is not an absolute. It has to be assessed relatively to the issues in the proceedings'.[58] He concluded that 'where any sound judgment on these issues calls for insight and imagination which only maturity and experience can bring, both the court and the solicitor will be slow to conclude that the child's understanding is sufficient'.[59] The court concluded that it could not accede to S's request. Even were it to have done so, the Master of the Rolls believed, the continuing assistance of the Official Solicitor as *amicus curiae* would have been sought, 'so the gain to S might in any event have been small'.[60]

These last remarks were seized upon by Booth J. in *Re H*.[61] A 15-year-old boy was warded by his parents after the man with whom he was living was charged with sexual offences against other boys. He had been left in England when his parents moved to France. He now wished to stay in England and ran away each time he was taken to France. Like the previous case, *Re H* could be interpreted as one where a child wished to choose where he would live. The boy in *Re H* considered that the Official Solicitor who was representing him was not representing his views, and he applied to be allowed to continue to defend the proceedings without the Official Solicitor acting as his guardian *ad litem*, and for the removal of the Official Solicitor from that position. Booth J. was of the opinion that H had sufficient understanding to participate as a party in the proceedings and so should be permitted to do so. It was 'not for [the] court…to take into account what the court may or may not consider to be in the best interests of the child'.[62] As a result of this, the Official Solicitor's role as guardian *ad litem* ceased, but it thought it to be 'vital'[63] that he should continue in the capacity as *amicus*, 'an independent advisor to the court'.[64]

---

[57] *Op. cit.*, note 55, p. 444.
[58] *Idem.*
[59] *Idem.*
[60] *Ibid.*, p. 449.
[61] [1993] 2 FLR 552.
[62] *Ibid.*, p. 557.
[63] *Idem.*
[64] *Ibid.*, p. 578.

In *Re S* the Master of the Rolls had spoken of the need to strike a 'judicious balance' between recognizing the personality of children ('A child's wishes are not to be discounted or dismissed simply because he is a child. He should be free to express them and decision-makers should listen') and 'the fact that a child is, after all, a child ('children...are liable to be vulnerable and impressionable, lacking the maturity to weigh the longer-term against the shorter, lacking the insight to know how others will react and the imagination to know how they will react in certain situations, lacking the experience to measure the probable against the possible').[65] The solution hinted at in *Re S* and adopted in *Re H* reflects this balance: the child can dismiss the Official Solicitor, but the court retains him in a different, and, it has to be conceded, far from clear, capacity.

Neither in *Re S* (a residence application) nor in *Re H* (a wardship case) was the action initiated by the child. The Children Act, as indicated previously, does allow children in specified circumstances to initiate actions. It is the ability of children to seek residence orders which has given rise to the 'divorcing' parents phenomenon. To do so they must first obtain leave.

APPLYING FOR A RESIDENCE ORDER

A residence order settles the arrangements to be made as to the person with whom a child is to live.[66] It is governed by section 1 of the 1989 Act. Accordingly, the child's welfare is the paramount consideration[67] and the court is not to make the order 'unless it considers that doing so would be better for the child than making no order at all'.[68] If an application is contested, regard is to be had to the welfare checklist in section 1(3): a number of the factors including the ascertainable wishes and feelings of the child (which in 'divorcing parents' cases will be clear) and any harm the child is at risk of suffering[69] will be particularly pertinent.

---

[65] *Op. cit.*, note 55, p. 448. See also *Re CT* [1993] 2 FLR 278, 280 *per* Waite L.J.
[66] Section 8(1).
[67] Section 1(1).
[68] Section 1(5).
[69] A good illustration of which is *Re H* [1993] 2 FLR 552, where the possible alternative arrangement involved a suspected sex abuser.

A child cannot apply for a residence order as of right, as a parent or guardian can.[70] S/he must first apply for leave to make an application.[71] As a result of a Practice Direction, inspired no doubt by panic over a glut of well-publicized applications by children wishing to 'divorce' their parents, the application must be made to the High Court.[72] The court may only grant leave if it is satisfied that the child concerned has 'sufficient understanding' to make the proposed application.[73] Given that the child may well be eligible for legal aid in circumstances where the persons in whose favour the order is to vest are not, strategy may dictate that the child rather than the adults concerned make the application. There is no evidence that this factor is behind the number of cases brought by children, though it cannot be discounted.

Neither the Children Act nor the Rules nor for that matter the Guidance indicate what 'sufficient understanding' for the purpose of obtaining leave requires.[74] In one of the 'divorcing' parents cases (*Re CT*), Waite L.J.[75] quoted with approval remarks of Sir Thomas Bingham M.R. in *Re S* to the effect that: 'Where any sound judgment on these issues calls for insight and imagination which only maturity and experience can bring, both the court and the solicitor will be slow to conclude that the child's understanding is sufficient'.[76] That this approval is obiter needs to be stressed because, though Houghton-James perceives generosity[77] in the appeal court's interpretation in *Re CT*, it would be difficult so to interpret the import of this language. On Sir Thomas Bingham M.R.'s approved test who

---

[70] See Children Act s. 10(4). Parent includes an unmarried father.
[71] See s.10(8). This subsection (the 'sufficient understanding' provision) is the only mention of the child requiring leave.
[72] [1993] 1 FLR 668 and see *Re AD* [1993] 1 FCR 573.
[73] See s.10(8).
[74] See The Children Act 1989 Guidance and Regulations volume 1, *Court Orders* (London: H.M.S.O., 1991), para. 2.43 which merely paraphrases s. 10(8). Masson's annotation in *Current Law Statutes Annotated* notes that the test of understanding may be different according to the type of application (p. 29) but, other than quoting from Lord Scarman's judgment in *Gillick* v. *West Norfolk and Wisbech A.H.A.* [1986] AC 112, does not take the definition any further. Waite L.J. in *Re CT* [1993] 1 FLR 278, 281 also notes that the Act and the Rules do not further define 'sufficient understanding'.
[75] [1993] 2 FLR 278, 281–282.
[76] [1993] 2 FLR 437, 444.
[77] Hazel Houghton-James, 'Children Divorcing Their Parents' (1994) *Journal of Social Welfare and Family Law* 185, 197.

would have 'sufficient understanding'? Once again we can see how knowledge and understanding have trumped wisdom.[78]

Re CT[79] is unusual in that the child concerned, a girl of 13½, was in effect seeking to undo an adoption order.[80] She had re-established some contact with her biological father's relatives and wanted to live with an aunt and grandparents rather than with her adoptive parents. She consulted a solicitor who was satisfied that she was capable of giving instructions. She got leave from a county court[81] to apply for a residence order and then applied in her own right without the intervention of a next friend. The Court of Appeal disapproved of the High Court's attempt to require the girl to accept a guardian *ad litem* by means of wardship: wardship proceedings are family proceedings[82] and r.9.2A(1) applies equally in wardship as in private law cases, so that once the conditions are satisfied a child can bring and defend wardship proceedings without a next friend or guardian *ad litem*, and the court would have no power to impose one against her will. On the other hand, and despite what would appear to be clear language to the contrary,[83] the Court of Appeal ruled that it is the court itself, rather than the solicitor, which has the ultimate right to decide whether a child, who comes before it as a party without a next friend or guardian *ad litem*, has the necessary ability to instruct a solicitor. It followed that, if the court felt it necessary in order to protect the interests of the child, it could appoint a proper person to act as her next friend or guardian *ad litem*.

SEEKING LEAVE

The requirement to seek leave prior to making an application is intended to act as a filter process, as indeed it does. Unfortunately, we lack the statistical data which could enable us to gain an insight into the effectiveness of the leave procedure. But reported cases do assist us in discovering what some of the problems are and where the courts' concerns lie.

The courts are taking the applications seriously: certainly applications for leave to apply for a residence order are responded to with greater con-

---

[78] *Cf. ante*, 218. On the 'trumping' metaphor see R. Dworkin, *Taking Rights Seriously* (London: Duckworth, 1977).
[79] [1993] 2 FLR 278.
[80] That this cannot be done can be seen from the case of *Re B* [1995] 1 FLR 1.
[81] The case antedates *Re A D* and the *Practice Direction*. A similar case today would have to be transferred upwards to the High Court.
[82] See Children Act 1989 s. 8(3)(a).
[83] *Op. cit.*, note 79, pp. 288–289.

cern than similar applications by children for specific issue orders (if the contrasting approach of Johnson J. in *Re C*[84] can be generalized). Both Johnson J. in *Re C* and Booth J. in *Re SC*[85] have stressed that children have statutory rights to initiate to process, rights that should not be 'impeded'.[86] The argument was put in *Re SC* that the person in whom parental responsibility would vest under the residence order should make the application, not the child. Booth J., rightly I would argue, dismissed this argument. She said: 'Although the court will undoubtedly consider why it is that the person in whose favour a proposed residence order would be made is not applying, it would in my opinion be wrong to import into the Act any requirement that only he or she should make the application'.[87] The court 'should not fetter the statutory ability of the child to seek any s.8 order...if it is appropriate for such an application to be made'.[88]

Children are not the only persons who require leave prior to seeking a residence order. It is therefore pertinent to examine whether leave applications by children are dealt with similarly to such applications by other persons such as relatives or foster parents.[89] In *Re A and W*,[90] the Court of Appeal held that an application by a foster mother for leave to apply for a residence order did not raise any question regarding the upbringing of a child,[91] with the consequence that the child's welfare was not the paramount consideration of the court in exercising its discretion.[92] Balcombe L.J. said: 'In granting or refusing an application for leave to apply for a section 8 order, the court is not determining a question with respect to the upbringing of the child concerned. That question only arises when the court hears the substantive application'.[93] He followed *F* v. *S*[94] which related to the question

---

[84] [1994] 1 FLR 26.
[85] [1994] 1 FLR 96.
[86] *Op. cit.*, note 84, p. 27.
[87] *Op. cit.*, note 85, p. 100.
[88] *Idem.*
[89] Foster parents with whom a child has lived for 3 years do not need leave (see s. 10(5)(b)), but local authority foster parents may need the consent of the local authority to apply unless they are relatives or the child has lived with them for at least 3 years preceding the application (s. 9(3)).
[90] [1992] Fam. 182.
[91] See Children Act s. 1(1).
[92] So that the child's welfare did not determine the course to be followed (see Lord MacDermott in *J* v. *C* [1970] AC 668).
[93] *Op. cit.*, note 90, p. 191.
[94] [1973] Fam. 203. But it has been held that the grant of leave by the courts in applications

whether or not to grant leave for an adoption application to be made in respect of a ward of court.

This is not the only place where the courts have construed 'upbringing' narrowly.[95] The Lord Chancellor, in a debate on the Children Bill, did say it was 'a word of general scope' which includes 'education and social life while being reared'.[96] It is therefore easy to see why an application by a foster mother for leave should not be one relating to a child's upbringing. But, even if this conclusion is right, is it also right that where the application is by a child for leave that it should be similarly so characterized? Booth J., who was referred to *Re A and W* and *F v. S*, refused to distinguish the situations. She held that 'no distinction can be drawn between an application for leave made by a child and an application made by any other person. In neither case does the initial application fall within s. 1(1) of the Act'.[97] She also appeared to hold that the checklist in s. 1(3) was also irrelevant,[98] but, even if she is right as regards the upbringing/paramountcy point, this would not follow and cannot be right.[99] But I doubt whether she is right to refuse to distinguish an application by a child for leave from one by some other interested party. These applications are not made by happy children, but by troubled ones who are seeking help. To distinguish leave and the substantive application in such a way as to withdraw welfare paramountcy concerns from the former is not only artificial but fails, I believe, children who need these concerns to be addressed. If a parent faced with a child about to apply for a residence order were to ward the child,[100] the child's welfare would be the 'golden thread' running through the parent's application.[101] There is some support for my view in Johnson J.'s judgment in *Re C*.[102] His judgment was delivered two days before Booth J.'s and both are extempore. Having

---

for the removal of a child under Part III of the Adoption Act 1976 is governed by the welfare test in s. 6 of that Act. See *Re C* [1994] 2 FLR 513.

[95] Another (in my opinion) is *Richards* v. *Richards* [1984] AC 174 (ouster application by mother). And see, for confirmation that the Children Act has not altered this, *Gibson* v. *Austin* [1992] 2 FLR 437.

[96] *Hansard* H.L. vol. 502, col. 1168.

[97] *Op. cit.*, note 85, p. 99.

[98] The two arguments are seen as inextricably linked, so that if one is dismissed, so is the other (see *idem*).

[99] The court must have regard to the checklist in any contested s. 8 application: where the court is hearing an application for leave to apply for a s. 8 order it is surely 'considering whether to make...a section 8 order' (s. 1(4)(a)).

[100] *Cf.* the facts of *Re AD* [1993] 1 FCR 573.

[101] *Per* Dunn J. in *Re D* [1977] Fam. 158.

[102] *Op. cit.*, note 84.

decided that the considerations in s. 10(9) of the Children Act 1989 were inapplicable to applications by children (a question to which I will return), he deduced 'therefore, the principle that must guide my consideration...is that laid down by Parliament in s. 1(1) of the 1989 Act, namely that the child's welfare shall be my paramount consideration'.[103] He does not seem to have been referred to *Re A and W* or to *F* v. *S* (certainly neither is quoted in his judgment). It is difficult accordingly to vest his judgment on this point with much authority. Further, his reason for coming to this conclusion—the inapplicability of the s.10(9) considerations—does not have any force. And yet his conclusion does seem right. As the better reasoned judgment, however, it is likely that Booth J.'s will be followed, with the result that welfare will not determine whether the application proceeds or not.

The refusal to accept that an application for leave relates to upbringing means in one important respect applications by children are treated as applications by others. But there are other differences.

The Act itself is clear about two of these. Section 10(9) states:

Where the person applying for leave to make an application...is not the child concerned, the court shall, in deciding whether or not to grant leave, have particular regard to -

(a) the nature of the proposed application...;

(b) the applicant's connection with the child;

(c) any risk there might be of that proposed application disrupting the child's life to such an extent that he would be harmed by it; and

(d) where the child is being looked after by a local authority -

  (i) the authority's plans for the child's future; and

  (ii) the wishes and feelings of the child's parents.

This checklist of factors obviously does not apply where the application for leave is by a child, though it is not obvious why (a) and (c) (and (b) suitably adapted) should have been excluded. It was the exclusion of the guidelines for children's applications that led Johnson J. to conclude that he must seek guidance instead in s. 1(1).[104] A fallacy no doubt, but understandable in the circumstances. By listing factors as in s.10(9), the court is guided in the ex-

---

[103] *Ibid.*, p. 28.
[104] [1994] 1 FLR 26, 28.

ercise of its discretion. If neither s.10(9) nor the paramountcy principle applies, how is the court to exercise its discretion? Is it required to do more than be satisfied that the child has 'sufficient understanding'? Booth J. thinks so. She says: 'It does not...follow that the court is bound to grant leave once the test of s.10(8) is satisfied. The court still has a discretion whether or not to do so'.[105] But where does this discretion come from and how is it to be judicially exercised? If a child has satisfied the judge that s/he has sufficient understanding—as the 14-year-old in Re SC did—what other hurdles can s/he be expected to surmount? If leave is refused, it may be impossible for any court to decide matters relating to the child's welfare (this applies also, of course, if it is decided the child lacks sufficient understanding) for no one else may be prepared to bring the child's problems to the attention of a court (or to social services). It therefore seems wrong that leave may be refused for reasons outside the statutory framework.

The second difference is that only a child needs to establish s/he has sufficient understanding to make a section 8 application. A child who fails to establish this is left with no recourse to the courts: s/he may well be in the kind of distress that calls for an investigation of his or her circumstances and if the court is concerned it could order a section 37 investigation.[106] But, if it does not do this, or if the local authority, thus appraised of the concern of the court, does not pursue the matter any further,[107] the child can do no more. There is some irony in the fact that a child's cry for help may go unnoticed or be ignored because s/he does not meet a threshold of competence. And if, as is distinctly possible, the distressed and incompetent are also those where no one else is showing an interest, the problem is even greater.

SUFFICIENT UNDERSTANDING

What is meant by 'sufficient understanding'? The case law offers some guidance. Sir Thomas Bingham M.R.'s judgment in Re S has already been cited: the court recognized that children had 'individual minds and wills, views and emotions',[108] though they were nevertheless children and as such needed to be protected for example against their inability to distin-

---

[105] [1994] 1 FLR 96, 98.

[106] In Re CE (Section 37 Direction) [1995] 1 FLR 26, there was such a direction in a case where parents sought a residence order after a 14-year-old left home to live with her boyfriend's parents.

[107] This impotence is striking in Nottinghamshire County Council v. P [1994] Fam. 18.

[108] [1993] 2 FLR 437, 448.

guish short- and long-term interests. Since the test is understanding, too much should not hinge on the child's age.[109] In two unreported cases in 1992 children of 11 succeeded in their applications.[110] And in the unreported case of *Re H*,[111] Butler-Sloss L.J. said that 'rule 9.2A[112] would be extremely valuable for the older teenager and is most unlikely to be used in regard to younger children' (in this case they were 7 and 10). This does not take us very far.

There is an increasing amount of research in relation to a child's competence to participate in legal proceedings, and further guidance on a child's understanding may be sought in this.[113] One of the most enlightening of studies is that by Weithorn and Campbell.[114] They compared the response of 9, 14, 18 and 21-year-old participants to hypothetical problems of decision making about medical and psychological treatment. The 14-year-olds did not differ from the adult groups on any of the major standards of competency to consent: evidence of a choice; understanding of the facts; reasonable decision-making process; reasonable outcome of choice. Even the 9-year-olds were as competent as the average adult according to standards of evidence of a choice and reasonableness of choice. This is consistent with Lewis's finding that, when elementary school children were given essentially unlimited access to the school nurse for routine medical care, their health-care behaviour was very similar to adults with similar demographic characteristics.[115] These findings, Melton observes, present 'a conservative estimate of children's capacities'.[116] The reason for this is that where children have experience with, and overt permission for, participation in decision-making, their competence in rea-

---

[109] Note Sir Thomas Bingham M.R.'s comment that 'different children have differing levels of understanding at the same age' ([1993] 2 FLR 437, 444).

[110] See *The Independent*, 11 November 1992 and *The Independent*, 12 November 1992.

[111] Court of Appeal (Civil Division) Transcript No. 769, cited in *Re S* at p. 447.

[112] Inserted into the Rules by amendment in 1992.

[113] A good survey article is Elizabeth S. Scott, 'Judgment and Reasoning in Adolescent Decisionmaking', 37 *Villanova Law Review* 1607 (1992).

[114] 'The Competency of Children and Adolescents To Make Informed Treatment Decisions', (1982) 53 *Child Development* 1589.

[115] 'Decision Making Related To Health: When Could/Should Children Behave Responsibly?' in (eds.) G. Melton, G. Koocher and M. Saks, *Children's Competence To Consent* (New York: Plenum Press, 1983).

[116] 'Developmental Psychology and The Law: The State of the Art', (1983–1984) 22 *Journal of Family Law* 445, 464.

soning increases: the more autonomy children are given, the better they are to exercise autonomy.[117]

Research by Peterson-Badali and Abramovitch is also helpful, though both of their studies[118] are concerned with the criminal justice process. The first of these reports throws light on children's understanding of the role of lawyers. They found that 'a majority of even the youngest subjects [those between 9½ and 11¼] demonstrated an adequate understanding of the concept of defense counsel as an advocate in the criminal process'.[119] By contrast, even much older children, those of 14 and 15, showed substantial ignorance of the principle of lawyer-client confidentiality when probed regarding the lawyer's ability to reveal information to specific parties—but then so did young adults. The results of the second study revealed that 'a majority of even the 10-year-old subjects used legal rather than moral criteria in making their plea decisions'.[120] The author's comment: 'The actions of these children clearly indicate their ability to distinguish a legal domain, with its own set of rules and principles, from the domain of morality'.[121] They advocate extending research to include even younger children to explore the origins of children's legal reasoning ability.

Research has also been done on children's competence to participate in divorce custody decision-making.[122] It was found that 14-year-olds performed as well as 18-year-olds in stating a custodial preference. This finding is consistent with earlier work and comes as no surprise. But it was also found that 9- and 10-year-olds were as competent as the 14- and 18-year-olds according to the reasonableness of preference or the rationality of reasons standard—a conclusion which finds support in the Weithorn and Campbell research previously referred to. The Garrison work in particular is suggestive for the 'divorcing parents' context. But, as she warns, her study

---

[117] See R. W. Belter and T. Grisso, 'Children's Recognition of Rights Violations in Counseling', 15 *Professional Psychology: Research and Practice* 899 (1984); J. Tapp and G. Melton, 'Preparing Children for Decision Making: Implications of Legal Socialization Research' in *op. cit.*, note 115 at p. 215.

[118] 'Children's Knowledge of the Legal System: Are They Competent To Instruct Legal Counsel?', 34 *Canadian Journal of Criminology* 139 (1992) and 'Grade Related Changes in Young People's Reasoning About Plea Decisions', 17 *Law and Human Behavior* 537 (1993).

[119] 34 *Canadian Journal of Criminology* 139, 156 (1992).

[120] 17 *Law and Human Behavior* 537, 549 (1993).

[121] *Idem.* And see, for a consistent conclusion, E. Turiel, *The Development of Social Knowledge: Morality and Convention* (Cambridge: Cambridge University Press, 1983).

[122] Ellen Greenberg Garrison, 'Children's Competence To Participate in Divorce Custody Decision making', 20 *Journal of Clinical Child Psychology* 78 (1991).

'assessed competence rather than actual performance in custody decision-making'.[123] Real-life factors, such as stress, may adversely affect children's decision-making abilities. Melton also makes this point: 'that children have the *capacity* to perform competently and responsibly does not mean that they will exercise such maturity of judgment, particularly when the decision is made under circumstances of great stress or when social norms elicit undesirable behaviour'.[124]

It is increasingly obvious also that when sufficient understanding is tested the way questions are asked of the subjects will have an impact on the answers. For an adult, poorly worded questions may be simply a nuisance: for a child, they may be a potentially serious source of miscommunication. In an important recent study Anne Graffam Walker points to three sources of communicative mischief: (a) age-inappropriate vocabulary, (b) complex syntax, and (c) general ambiguity.[125] She is surely right to observe that 'the real question of children's linguistic competence in evidentiary settings belongs not to the children, but to the adults. It is our adult legal system that the children are caught up in, it is our adult language in which proceedings are conducted, it is our adult assumptions about both law and language upon which communication in the courts is based'.[126] It is her view, which recent English practice indubitably endorses, that 'we are not doing as well as we might in integrating children linguistically into a system not built for them'.[127] Those who construct our judicial process do not know enough about children's capabilities, cognitively and linguistically. And yet there is now research evidence into these cognitive and psychological issues if our judges, lawyers, guardians *ad litem* and others involved in eliciting evidence from children were prepared to examine it.[128]

---

[123] *Ibid.*, p. 85.

[124] *Op. cit.*, note 116, pp 465–466.

[125] 'Questioning Young Children in Court', 17 *Law and Human Behavior* 59 (1993).

[126] *Ibid.*, p. 78.

[127] *Idem*.

[128] In addition to work already cited, I would recommend S. J. Ceci, M. Toglia and D. F. Ross, *Children's Eyewitness Testimony* (New York: Springer-Verlag, 1987); S. J. Ceci, D. F. Ross and M. Toglia, *Perspectives on Children's Testimony* (New York: Springer-Verlag, 1989); A. G. Walker, 'Language at Work in The Law: The Customs, Conventions and Appellate Consequences of Court Reporting' in J. N. Levi and A. G. Walker (eds.), *Language in the Judicial Process* (New York: Plenum, 1990), pp. 203–44. Also useful as an overview is Gary B. Melton, *Reforming The Law: Impact of Child Development Research* (New York: Guilford Press, 1987).

In Whose Favour?

In *Re SC* it was made clear that a residence order cannot be made in favour of the child him or herself.[129] This is clear from the language of s. 8(1) of the Act which lays down that a residence order means 'an order setting the arrangements to be made as to the person with whom the child is to live'. It would be straining language to interpret 'person' to include the child him or herself. Further, as Booth J. notes in *Re SC*, a residence order vests parental responsibility in the persons in whose favour the order is made if that person is not the parent or guardian of the child.[130]

This is a legitimate interpretation of the statutory provision. But it has to be emphasized again that the legislature was not addressing the issue at the centre of this article. The question therefore must be raised, as a matter of policy, whether children should be able in effect to emancipate themselves. Clearly, the vesting of parental rights in themselves is a logical absurdity. But is there scope for children to 'divorce' parents without 'marrying' themselves to other adults? If children can, as is usually supposed, leave home at 16, is there a case for allowing them to ask a court to remove decision-making powers away from parents and to vest these same powers in the children? A child, after all, can marry at 16, with the permission of a court if parental consent is refused. The case for an emancipation statute is a strong one but I doubt if there would be any support for one in a society more concerned to control children than recognize their individuality or integrity. The spectre of the one-parent family and of juvenile crime would, it may be assumed, dominate the debate. The drafting of a statute to allow self-emancipation through a court order at 16 should, however, be seriously considered.

Conclusion—and Reform

The explosion of cases and news stories in 1992 and 1993 created an unnecessary moral panic. There is unlikely to be a large number of applications by children who wish—in the colourful language of our times—to 'divorce' their parents. The structure is, however, in place, though it may be doubted whether those who designed it thought it would be used in this way. An emancipation statute is in the future. It will, I think come, but not yet.

---

[129] *Op. cit.*, note 85, p. 100.
[130] *Idem.* See Children Act 1989 s. 12(2).

For the present it is worth pondering on the experience of the litigation discussed in this article, and on the lessons which we may learn from it. It has thrown up problems and suggested reforms.

Firstly, the leave requirement. This operates as a filter but unnecessarily duplicates work. Is there any reason why a child should not be able to apply as of right for a s.8 order? I can see none and would recommend the removal of the leave requirement.

Secondly, if the leave requirement is to be retained, there should be clarification as to the factors governing the exercise of the court's discretion. It is difficult to see how such an application cannot relate to the upbringing of a child. The parallel drawn in *Re SC* with an application for leave by a foster mother is illusory. The paramountcy test should apply and the welfare checklist in s.1(3) would also be relevant.

Thirdly, if leave is to continue to remain a first hurdle and neither the paramountcy test nor the welfare checklist is to be relevant, then it must follow that, once the court has determined that the child has 'sufficient understanding', it must grant leave for the application to be made. There are no other possible criteria for the exercise of discretion.

Fourthly, more sustained attention must be given to appreciating what is meant by 'sufficient understanding'. It must be realized that competence involves experiential knowledge as well as 'book work' learning: indeed, that the former is more relevant in this context than the latter. Courts should be made aware of the growth of empirical evidence on the development of children's capacities. If in other areas of law the courts are encouraging references to legal academic literature, let them have the courage to refer to and cite the research data of psychologists which offer greater insight into children's competence than the intuitive arguments the judges currently use and which were presented in the cases discussed in this article.

But, if 'sufficient understanding' is to remain the linchpin, do we need a judicial determination of this at all? Would it not be better for specially qualified guardians *ad litem* to determine this? The courts would still have to rule upon whether a residence order vesting parental responsibility in adults other than parents was in the child's best interests.

CHAPTER 12

The James Bulger Tragedy: Childish Innocence and the Construction of Guilt

The murder of toddler James Bulger by two 10-year-old boys in Merseyside in February 1993 came—depending upon how one looks at it—at just the right or the wrong time.

For the Right it was an instantaneously recognizable symbol for a wider malaise. 1992 had stood out as a year in which there was a sense of panic about youth crime. There was rioting on out-of-town council estates. Car theft and ram-raiding received considerable public exposure. In Manchester, on Moss Side, a 14-year-old boy was shot dead, it seems an innocent victim of so-called crack wars. In Manchester also, a 15-year-old girl was abducted, imprisoned and eventually tortured to death by her 'friends'. In South London, a 12-year-old boy was stabbed by another school child in his school playground. But concern turned to consternation and panic with the arrest of two 10-year-olds, revealed in photographs[1] after their trial and conviction, to look 'normal', even angelic, for the abduction and murder of a 2-year-old who strayed from his mother's attention in a shopping mall. The Home Secretary's immediate response was to say that persistent and serious offenders under 15 would, in future, be locked up. He urged MPs to 'catch up with the mood of the people', and he attacked 'laggard police authorities'. The Prime Minister called for a 'crusade against crime'. He blamed 'parents, the church and "opinion generally" for failing to disapprove of criminal behaviour'.[2] The Education Secretary proceeded, one week later, to announce a £10 million clampdown on truancy. 'Show me a persistent young truant; I will show you a potential young criminal', he said.[3]

As if not to be overtaken in sensing public mood, the Labour party (for these purposes ideologically part of the Right) responded with similarly

---

[1] These appeared in every daily newspaper on 25 November 1993.
[2] *The Sunday Times*, 21 February 1993.
[3] *The Sunday Times*, 28 February 1993.

fatuous sound bites. The Shadow Health Secretary demanded the reintroduction of national service and Tony Blair, then Shadow Home Secretary, demanded a régime of 'tough love'. The phrase was Bill Clinton's and embraces a régime in which secure containment is tempered with responsiveness to an offender's needs. By the summer of 1996 the Labour Party, still in opposition, was calling for the curfewing of children under 10, again an idea taken from the United States.[4]

In February 1993 the Bulger case could not have been more timely. A week after the murder *The Daily Telegraph* published its annual 'state of the nation' Gallup poll.[5] It oozes despair and despondency. More than a third of the population could think of nothing about Britain to be proud of and nearly half said they would emigrate if they could. A panic of such epidemic proportions demands, as Cohen reminds us,[6] a 'folk devil' and the juvenile delinquent—and now younger than ever—was on hand to fit the frame.

Only six months earlier the House of Commons Home Affairs Select Committee had examined the problem of persistent young offenders. It heard that, although the number of 10- to 18-year-olds convicted or cautioned by the police had fallen by 25 per cent between 1981 and 1991, recorded juvenile crime had risen by 54 per cent. There was, so the Association of Chief Police Officers argued, 'a small hard core who have absolutely no fears whatsoever of the criminal justice system'. What empirical or other evidence they had for this is into vouchsafed. Hagell and Newburn, however, have concluded, to the contrary, that most persistent juvenile offenders seldom commit serious crimes and that those who do commit serious crimes are seldom persistent offenders.[7] The Home Secretary was nevertheless convinced, as he told the public in a television interview, that 200 juveniles between 10 and 15 were responsible for 60 per cent of all juvenile crime. If this were true, each would have to commit about 16,000 offences a year or about 44 offences each day!

In a culture of panic, facts are of secondary importance. In a country 'in a state',[8] with deep fissures fracturing national life, with industry hav-

---

[4] *The Guardian*, 2 June 1996, criticized this in a leading article on 3 June 1996. The Shadow Home Secretary defended his curfew arguments in *The Guardian*, 4 June 1996. *The Times* wrote approvingly on 4 June 1996.

[5] *The Daily Telegraph* 22 February 1993.

[6] *Folk Devils and Moral Panics* (London: McGibbon and Kee, 1973).

[7] *Persistent Young Offenders* (1994).

[8] See Will Hutton, *The State We're In* (London: Jonathan Cape, 1995. A revised edition has been published in 1996).

ing disintegrated and one in three children growing up in poverty, in a society divided into 'us' and 'them' at least as great as in the days where class structure was clear, it is conventional to look for, find and blame victims.[9] Britain already imprisons more *per capita* of its population than any country in Western Europe. But adult penal policy, like almost every other policy pursued in Britain in the last decade and a half, has failed. Compared to the United States or many other countries, crime is actually a minor problem. So is illegal immigration. But, when discontented Conservatives were asked to explain a massacre of sitting Tories in recent local elections, they pinpointed both criminal activity and illegal immigration as areas of concern not addressed by 'their' government.

Moral panics feed on scandal. Whether fictionalized, such as that in Upton Sinclair's novel *The Jungle* which led to food and drugs legislation in the United States—but not, of course, to improvements in the working conditions of the labour of 'Packingtown'—or through the whistle being blown, eventually, on endemic social problems such as child abuse, often after a particular graphic episode, a Maria Colwell, a Dennis O'Neill, a Cleveland, action is often swiftly taken that otherwise might require lengthy deliberation over years. If the sad logo of Maria Colwell's face impressed itself upon the public imagination in 1973–1975, and as assuredly influenced the package of child care measures in the Children Act 1975, then the faces of Robert Thompson and Jon Venables, the 11-year-olds convicted of James Bulger's murder, have become identified, in the public's mind, with the problem of youth crime.

---

[9] *Cf.* W. Ryan, *Blaming The Victim* (New York: Vintage Books, 1976)

THE BULGER CASE

The *Bulger* case captured the world's headlines in February 1993 (when the murder occurred) and in November 1993 (when the case came to trial). Murders by children are thankfully rare. Charles Patrick Ewing, who has collected case studies of juvenile murder in America, notes that most juveniles who kill are 15, 16 or 17 years old. Fewer than one per cent of those arrested for murder or non-negligent manslaughter have been under the age of 15.[10] Britain had its Mary Bell case in 1968[11] and an interesting precedent in 1861—in fact a striking contrast as we shall see, but to find murderers as young as ten is rare. That the prelude to the awful crime was captured on video added to the public's disbelief: the boys looked (indeed were) ordinary, not demonic, and the site of the abduction, a modern shopping precinct, conveyed images of conventional normality. We don't televise our trials in England but in this case we almost went one better—televising over and over again the two boy-murderers leading the innocent child to his death.

The trial, which took place in an adult court before a judge and jury, some eight months after the murder, established very little. It lasted nearly three weeks, though nearly the whole trial consisted of prosecution evidence. The boys offered none and the defence case was condensed in the extreme. It cannot be said that the trial threw any insight into why the crime was perpetrated. It was not intended to do so. To describe the trial as a 'show trial', as a 'political trial' almost is hardly an exaggeration. The result was a foregone conclusion: the presence of the boys in the court a forensic irrelevance, though crucial in the construction of a demonology of deviance.

The boys were in detention (and separately detained) between their apprehension and trial. During this period they were examined by three leading psychiatrists, but their function was to establish that the boys were capable of distinguishing right from seriously wrong. There are two reasons for this. First, English law requires those who are aged between 10 and 14 to be *doli capax*, that is capable of understanding the difference

---

[10] *Kids Who Kill* (London: Mondo, 1993; originally published by Lexington Books in 1990). See also Kathleen M. Heide, *Why Kids Kill Parents* (Thousand Oaks: Sage, 1995).

[11] See Gitta Sereny, *The Case of Mary Bell* (London: Pimlico, 1995, originally published by Eyre Methuen in 1972).

between serious wrong and mere naughtiness or mischief.[12] And, secondly, because it was important to establish that they were mentally responsible for the acts at the time when they committed them. But English law forbids any therapeutic involvement by psychiatrists before the trial. The explanation for this denying ordinance is that it is said that intervention by psychiatrists that goes beyond these matters of criminal investigation towards therapy would adulterate the evidence.

The police officers involved in the case were deeply interested in the boys' backgrounds but it was not their job to excavate these. As far as the law is concerned, their primary function is to prepare the evidence for the prosecution. They must establish that there is a case to answer. It is not their job, however personally and seriously interested they may be in the question, to unravel the causes of the crime, to discover why the boys behaved in the way they did.

Both these limitations cast light on what the criminal justice system understands to be its function and on the narrow time-frame within which the criminal law operates. But Kelman[13] and others have commented upon this and it need not be pursued further here.

Again, because—so it was said—the trial had to take place in open court and because many of its facts were distressing and would have devastated James Bulger's family and offended anyone else listening to the case, there was an agreement between prosecution and defence to the effect that once there was sufficient forensic evidence to prove the case against the two boys beyond reasonable doubt, the audience—it was said the jury—would be spared some of the more unpleasant details. The result of this is that events which may have taken place and would go some way towards explaining why the murder happened were discreetly veiled from the public eye. It was considered that, whilst what was hidden would greatly interest an inquisitive press and prurient public, these facts raised issues which went beyond what was strictly necessary to establish the boys' guilt. But what results is a mismatch between forensic requirements and the need to 'know why'.

There can be little doubt that Thompson and Venables[14] were deeply disturbed. James Bulger was not just murdered but brutally murdered, even tortured. Even when the two boys had savagely beaten the small

---

[12] *C* v. *Director of Public Prosecutions* [1995] 1 FLR 933.

[13] 'Interpretive Construction in the Substantive Criminal Law', (1981) 33 *Stanford Law Review* 591.

[14] Their names were revealed upon conviction: they were previously know as 'Child A' and 'Child B'.

child to pulp, they left his body on a railway line to be cut in two by a passing train. Additionally, and very significantly, it has emerged since the case—a little only came out during the course of the trial—that serious sexual assaults were perpetrated on James Bulger. In the trial it emerged that the boys has removed James's underpants and played with his foreskin. It now also appears to be the case that the batteries the boys stole from the shopping centre shortly before they abducted James were used to force up the toddler's anus and to mutilate his mouth.

The question must therefore be asked as to whether these boys—or at least one of them—had himself experienced sexual abuse. That there is a cycle of abuse and that those who are abused frequently repeat this behaviour upon others is established beyond any doubt. It is all the more unfortunate that therapeutic intervention had to be delayed until after the trial.

Of the boys themselves we know a little. And what we know points to deep disturbance and to unstructured, disorganized lives. They were in a very real sense damaged children. Venables was a head banger. There was an incident at school when he had to be physically constrained from a savage attack upon another child. His was a broken home though, unlike Thompson, he did have contact with his father. Thompson came from a violent, disorganized home with other children of the family in local authority care. He was a truant and said to have a short temper. Neither boy was stupid: intelligence tests conducted before the trial by psychiatrists—allowed to establish that they were *doli capax*—showed Venables to be of average intelligence, and Thompson of 'good, at least average' intelligence.

It seemed to be assumed that they planned a killing on the fateful day in question (there had been a previous attempt at an abduction). But the pilfering of the batteries first, and the long, torturous route march before the attack suggests that if anything was planned it is not murder simpliciter. If they had murder in mind, there were unquestionably easier ways of perpetrating the act. They passed a canal on the way and there were dangerous roads and heavy traffic. If murder was their intention, plenty of opportunities presented themselves on the way—and they could have easily have covered their tracks. A small child could have fallen into a canal, or in front of traffic. It seems much more likely that, if anything, they, or one of them, planned a sexual attack. And, if this hypothesis is right—and it is certainly plausible—the decision to conduct the trial as involving a brutal murder, rather than a frenzied sexual attack, becomes particularly unfortunate.

It is doubtful whether an English Court would accept the defence of diminished responsibility (in the Homicide Act 1957 s.2)—if successful the plea would reduce the crime to manslaughter—because being traumatized by sexual abuse does not, it would be said, lead to an 'abnormality of mind' so as substantially to impair mental responsibility. However, it has to be accepted that the defence, like the concepts of responsibility generally, employ adult, and specifically adult male, concepts of responsibility.[15] Challenging one of the law's 'truths' is difficult at the best of times, but it was not even tried in this case.

The trial itself made no concessions to the age of the defendants. It was conducted in a traditional court room before a bewigged and robed judge and in the presence of a jury, though hardly one of the boys' peers. The trial proceeded according to adult norms of behaviour, expression, procedure and style. The boys sat in a dock (they were at least accompanied by two male social workers). It is clear that they had little or no understanding of what was going on in the three-week trial to which they were subjected. Both seemed bored and bewildered during much of the trial. The judge, who had wide experience of criminal trials, had not any of appearing in juvenile (youth) courts. At times he adopted the view that the boys in this case were Victorian urchins, so that they had to be addressed as one might those in *Oliver Twist*. He even at one point purported to put on a mock scouse accent, as if conceding that the language of the trial was alien to the boys.

Neither of the boys gave evidence, though what they might have been able to tell a less formally-constructed forum might well have been revealing. They did not do so because they were unable to do so. They were psychologically traumatized. Their minds were confused, their memories blurred, they were fantasizing in childish ways. One spoke (outside the trial) of James Bulger as a character in a chocolate factory and imagined that, as in some Disneyesque scenario, he might be brought back to life. The other also expressed the belief or hope—perhaps it is as well not to distinguish them—that James could be 'mended'.

This is not the world of Preston Crown Court, where counsel addressed 'significant others' about responsibility and action. The disjuncture between the boys' world and that of the world constructed by law and lawyers is such that they might have been inhabiting different planets. 'Jus-

---

[15] Thus see, for example, *R* v. *Tandy* [1989] 1 All E.R. 267. On women see Hilary Allen, *Justice Unbalanced: Gender, Psychiatry and Judicial Decisions* (Milton Keynes: Open University Press, 1987).

tice' demanded the presence of the boys—or so it was said. Their presence was important, just as the presence of the devil was important to the medieval mystery play. But it was politics also that demanded their presence. For Thompson and Venables were to become the visible representatives of the moral panic about crime and juvenile crime in particular. It wasn't necessary to reveal their names—they were known throughout the trial as 'A' and 'B'—but the judge allowed this to be done after conviction and a press, eager to catch the mood of the time, responded with the full glare of publicity. If the 'full' story was to be told, if the lessons to be learnt were to be used to justify new and harsher ways of dealing with criminal activity by children, it was imperative that the public could put names and faces to new 'folk devils', rather than having to talk of Liverpudlian urchins or murderers from Merseyside. That the new devils looks like cherubs (or at least ordinary school-kids in neat school uniforms) wasn't surprising. The devil always came in disguise, didn't he?

The press did, of course, hunt about for reasons to explain why the boys behaved as they did. In this they were 'assisted' by the judge who linked the boys' behaviour to the viewing of a particular 'video-nastie' ('Child's Play No. 3') and by statements by politicians and clergy which emphasized that both boys came from female-headed households (the implication being that the boys lacked role models or discipline or both) and that both perpetrated the murder when they should have been at school. Whether the boys had seen the video cannot be proved. Although it does show an incident which uncannily resembles acts perpetrated upon James Bulger, hundreds of thousands of other 10- and 11-year-olds will undoubtedly have seen the video. The male role models in Merseyside would almost certainly have been out of work and to have no prospects of work is hardly likely to encourage school attendance: the rate of youth unemployment on Merseyside is one of the highest in Britain, indeed in Western Europe. On the surface the boys' upbringing was little different from that of other working class boys. If there was sexual abuse this would, of course, go a long way towards explaining what happened on the railway line in Walton. But it would not provide the underpinning for new penal policies. Nor would accepting the murder as a 'one-off', rare, ghastly and unpredictable.

For the Bulger case to become a vehicle for a reconstruction of juvenile penal policy, the boys had to be evil and had to be representatives of a new phenomenon—violent, rootless, disorganized young thugs for whom tougher punishment was the only response. A government which was failing with its own constituency knew, or at least hoped, it could regain confidence by showing it was tougher on law and order and in particular on young, amoral or disrespectful, criminals. The *Bulger* case thus became a symbol for more repressive control measures against the young.

TURNING THE CLOCK BACK

There is some irony in this. The Criminal Justice Act 1991 ended the imprisonment of children under 15. (There had been a number of graphic and well-publicized suicides including Philip Knights in Swansea). This measure had been in operation only five months when, on 2 March 1993, a couple of weeks after the Bulger murder, the Home Secretary (Kenneth Clarke, a liberal in comparison with his successor Michael Howard), announced the introduction of a secure training order. This was aimed a 'that comparatively small group of very persistent juvenile offenders whose repeated offending makes them a menace to the community'.[16] These young people were to be 12- to 15-year-olds who had committed three imprisonable offences, and who proved unable or unwilling to comply with the requirements of supervision in the community.

Michael Howard, within weeks of becoming Home Secretary, decided that even this reformulation was insufficient. Newspapers in the summer of 1993 (before the Bulger trial) began to report, on the basis of a course of 'leaks', that Howard had ordered a rethink of secure training centres when it became clear that the scheme would be prohibitively expensive and would not tackle the explosion of youth crime. Thus, according to the *Daily Mail* (the mouthpiece of middle Conservative England): 'Ministers believe that hundreds more young things need to be locked up'. And by October he told the Tory party conference: 'Prison works, it ensures that we are protected from murderers, muggers and rapists—it makes many who are tempted to commit crime think twice. This may mean that many more people will go to prison. I do not flinch from that. We shall no longer judge the success of our system of justice by a fall in our prison population.'

The Tory press responded by finding just the stories upon which Howard could feed and in turn did his best to nourish them and *vox populi*. There were stories about juvenile delinquents being taken on 'overseas jaunts' by soft social workers. When checked the recipients of the 'holidays' were as often as not abused children rather than delinquent youth. But truth was not an important consideration. We were told that the pro-

---

[16] *The Independent*, 3 March 1993.

bation service—apparently staffed by young black women—had gone soft. Naturally, these jaunts were to be stopped and social work-trained probation officers were to be replaced with ex-soldiers and police officers.[17] A review in early 1995 was critical of the over-recruitment of ethnic minorities to the probation service: it proposed alternative routes for a new type of mature student. By March 1995, the Government published a Green Paper proposing the scrapping of the existing probation, community service and combination orders in favour of a 'community sentence', the detail of which would be specified by the magistrates.[18] The new two-pronged attack thus offered toughened teenage prison régimes and a more repressive rehabilitation system. Discipline had to be instilled into the sort of young, barbaric underclass that Thompson and Venables were thought to symbolize.

It is to be noticed that in all this there is no mention of the causes of crime. Any suggestion that it might have social or economic causes is discreetly overlooked. Crime is attributed rather to biological, psychological or intellectual deficiencies of individual offenders and/or to a lack of discipline. The former view derived its intellectual nourishment from the writings of James Q. Wilson[19] and Charles Murray.[20] Phrases like 'biologically predisposed man' and 'intellectually impaired man' were drawn from these authors, the latter from the notorious *Bell Curve*,[21] and used to support these reinvented penal policies. The latter view attributed blame to a loose network of counter-revolutionaries ranging from left-wing teachers to black probation officers and taking in for good measure on the way the Labour Party ('old Labour' as I suppose we must now call it).[22] Understanding a little less and condemning a little more became the bywords for this new policy.

Simultaneously with these developments—there is no need to believe in conspiracy theories to remark upon their coincidence—the Divisional

---

[17] Dewes and Wright, *A Review of Probation Officer Recruitment, Qualification and Training*, Home Office Probation Training Unit, 1994. Challenged as unlawful, judicial review was mounted but failed in February 1996.

[18] Home Office, *Strengthening Punishment in the Community—A Consultative Document* Cm. 2780 (London: H.M.S.O., 1995).

[19] *Thinking About Crime* (New York: Basic Books, 1975).

[20] 'The British Underclass', *The Public Interest*, No. 99, 4 (1990).

[21] See Charles Murray and Richard Herrnstein, *The Bell Curve* (New York: Simon and Schuster, 1994).

[22] But on the Labour Party's reactions to this see Angela McRobbie, 'Folk Devils Fight Back', 203 *New Left Review* 107 (1994).

Court purported to abolish the *doli incapax* presumption which has stood since at least the fourteenth century.[23] The House of Lords has since restored the presumption[24] but only because it believes that whether the presumption is retained or not should be a matter for Parliament rather than for judicial legislation. It is to be expected that Parliament will finally abolish the presumption at the earliest opportunity, perhaps as early as this year. To abolish the presumption will be to make ten the age of criminal responsibility without proof of more: only Ireland, Switzerland, Cyprus and Liechtenstein (seven), Scotland and Northern Ireland (eight) and Malta (nine) believe in a younger age of criminal responsibility than England. All other European countries have a higher age of responsibility: for example it is 13 in France, 14 in Germany, 15 in Sweden and 16 in Spain.[25]

Speaking on a BBC radio programme, which focused on *Crump's* case,[26] Susan Bailey, a forensic psychiatrist who gave evidence in the *Bulger* trial—she thought Thompson and Venables were *doli capax*—argued that most 10-year-old offenders have not reached moral maturity, and that there is a wide range between different children of the same age. She said: 'Between the age of 10 and 14, there is a tremendous range of developments within youngsters. They develop cognitively, emotionally and psychologically, and...one of the many elements is that during that time most youngsters develop the capacity to move from concrete thinking to abstract thinking. The ability to have abstract thoughts is associated with your ability to think through what the consequences of the action are when you're committing a crime. So it is a critical and central area'.[27] Somewhat uniquely the boy himself was interviewed on the radio programme. The following extract from what he said gives, I believe, considerable insight into the problem and suggests the cut-off is not as clear-cut as some of the judges think, and, we may suppose, Parliament will as well. The question was whether the boy (when 12) knew that it was wrong to damage a moped.

---

[23] *C* v. *D.P.P.* [1994] 3 W.L.R 888.

[24] See *op. cit.*, note 11. The Lords thought the presumption anomalous and absurd, but believed its abolition ought to be left to Parliament.

[25] And see J. Bourquin, 'The James Bulger Case Through The Eyes of the French Press', 1 *Social Work in Europe* 42 (1994).

[26] Known as 'C' in the law report.

[27] *The Independent*, 17 March 1995, p. 3.

Questioner:	Do you have an idea in your mind of what is right and wrong?
C:	Yeah.
Q:	What is right and wrong?
C:	Robbing cars is wrong.
Q:	Why is it wrong?
C:	It's taking somebody else's things.
Q:	When you were 12, there was this incident, do you know what was right and wrong?
C:	Yeah, and I never done nothing wrong. I was right, I was only looking. They (the police) said I had a crowbar. I never had a crowbar. They was telling lies through their teeth.
Q:	If you had been stealing or had been trying to take that motorbike would you have known that was wrong?
C:	Yeah, of course.
Q:	How would you have known that?
C:	I'm not stupid
Q:	Where do you think you learned what was right and wrong?
C:	In the infants, when I was younger.
Q:	Do you think that most young people of 12 would know what was right and wrong?
C:	I don't know. Some are thick. Some don't know the difference.
Q:	Who taught you what's right and wrong?
C:	My mum and dad, school, my nan, grandad.

Police told the BBC that he had been offending since he was 9. By 12, as part of a gang taking vehicles and stealing from shops, he had committed at least 20 offences of theft. Since 1992 (the apprehension in question) he had continued to offend. Boy C was again asked why he had offended when he knew it was wrong.

C:	Dunno, because everybody else was doing it. Its when you're there with all your mates and that, they're doing it, you do it.
Q:	Do you regret it now?
C:	Yeah, going to court and all that.

Listening to the broadcast or reading this transcript there is, to say the least, ambivalence in the boy's thinking and reasoning. He sees nothing wrong, it seems, in lying or in offending if the peer group is also doing this. Nor does he regret attempting to steal a motorbike, only 'going to court and all that'. Different children will appreciate what is right and wrong at different ages: there are class, gender and intellectual and social maturity differences. In England both case law (the well-known *Gillick* decision in 1985)[28] and legislation (in particular, the Children Act 1989) in the civil law area grade competence in terms of understanding (with, unfortunately, too great an emphasis on 'book work' information rather than experiential knowledge).[29] Thus, rather than saying that a child can consent to medical treatment at a certain age (below 16—at 16 all can do so)[30] or seek a residence order (in effect choosing where he or she shall live),[31] we grant such rights to those with sufficient understanding of what is involved. It may readily be conceded that competence is difficult to assess and that it is far from value-free. All the more reason then for not tying criminal responsibility to an inflexible standard. These arguments will not appeal to a government prepared to sacrifice children's interests to boost its flagging support. It knows its constituency and this does not consist of the (small) children's rights lobby.

Just how far these measures turn the clock back can be appreciated if we take a backward glance to the early 1980s, the early years of Thatcherism. Not that Thatcher and her supporters were soft upon crime.[32] The Police and Criminal Evidence Act 1984 increased police powers and the

---

[28] [1986] A.C. 112.

[29] See Priscilla Alderson and Mary Goodwin, 'Contradictions Within Concepts of Children's Competence', 1 *International Journal of Children's Rights* 303 (1993).

[30] Family Law Reform Act 1969 s. 8(1). But courts have now denied that they can *refuse* consent (see *Re R* [1992] Fam. 11 and *Re W* [1993] Fam. 64). On this see further ch. 15.

[31] On which see ch. 11.

[32] See Martin Kettle, 'The Drift To Law and Order' in (eds.) Stuart Hall and Martin Jacques, *The Politics of Thatcherism* (London: Lawrence and Wishart, 1983) p. 216.

government tried the so-called 'short, sharp shock'[33] as a way of dealing with juvenile delinquents. 'Short, sharp shocks' didn't work—perhaps they were not meant to. They pacified the Tory grass-roots who were given the feeling that something was being done to curb rising crime. But in reality it was only a holding measure. It bought time and gave the new Thatcher government political credibility.

The 1982 Criminal Justice Act was sold as a vindication of Thatcher's promise to make Britain's streets safe. But, actually, one of its aims was to limit the imprisonment of children and young people. In the light of the Bulger case it is worth remarking that part of the legacy the Conservatives inherited was an unfulfilled promise in the Children and Young Persons Act 1969 to raise the age of criminal responsibility to 14.[34] Of course, Labour, having failed to do this, it was not to be expected that the Conservatives would. But, had either government had the courage to do this, Thompson and Venables could not have been prosecuted.

The Conservatives inherited this commitment. They also inherited the incoherence of a welfare-oriented Act (the 1969 Act just referred to) and institutions such as borstals, detention centres and attendance centres which belonged to an earlier era and ideology.[35] It was this part of the system that was leading to more and more children and young persons being locked up. In the twelve years between 1965 and 1977 the number of young people aged between 15 and 17 sent to borstals by juvenile courts more than doubled. The detention centre population increased fourfold. But the number being supervised in the community (by social workers or probation officers) fell by more than a third.[36] An effect was a 'trickle up', with growing numbers of 17 to 21-year-olds filling adult prisons.

The 1982 Act was a failure but in 1983 the DHSS launched the Intermediate Treatment Initiative: £15 million was committed to providing 4,500 alternatives to custody over three years. This triggered the most extensive decarceration of the young this century: between 1981 and 1989 the number of juveniles incarcerated fell from 7,000 to 1,900 a year. This was accomplished by youth and welfare workers working together with police and magistrates. By the late 1980s there was a nation-wide structure

---

[33] See M. Freeman, 'Short, Sharp Shocks: a Comment', 130 *New Law Journal* 28 (1980).

[34] Allan Levy, *The Guardian*, 25 November 1994 criticized this in the aftermath of the Bulger Case.

[35] See M. D. A. Freeman, *The Rights and Wrongs of Children* (London: Frances Pinter, 1983).

[36] See John Pitts, *The Politics of Juvenile Crime* (London: Sage, 1989).

of multi-agency juvenile justice panels. These were composed of representatives from welfare agencies, the youth service, police and education departments. They tried, wherever possible, to divert children and young people from court. Police cautioning was used extensively to divert first offenders from prosecution. A system known a 'cautioning plus' evolved to deal with more persistent offenders. Such persons were offered the inducement of further cautions on condition that they participated in additional educational, recreational or therapeutic activities. The success of this persuaded the government by the late 1980s to attempt a similar strategy with over-18s in the adult system.[37] The policy of punishment in the community crystallized in the Criminal Justice Act of 1991.[38]

But Britain was already in economic recession. It can be no coincidence that recorded crime, which dropped by 5 per cent in 1988 (the apogee of economic boom), rose sharply from the end of 1989, climbing by 17 per cent in 1990 and a further 16 per cent in 1991. The government blamed police, probation officers, social workers, even the public (at the 1991 Tory party conference the Home Secretary, Kenneth Baker, accused victims of crime of not taking sufficient care of their property. He was vigorously booed). The Home Secretary's speech is frequently a thermometer to take the temperature of 'middle' Britain. This time it demonstrated that the policies of the 1980s had run their course. And not just the penal policies. Whatever economic success the few had enjoyed had not 'trickled down' to the many. There was economic, and increasingly social polarization, and growing crime and public disorder. In many senses the 'poll tax' riots symbolized the malaise. What began to be described, by Charles Murray and others, as an 'underclass', had emerged. In *The Public Interest* in 1990 he wrote of a Britain that 'has a growing population of working aged healthy people who live in a different world from other Britons, who are raising their children to live in it, and whose values are now contaminating the life of entire neighbourhoods'.[39] A rising tide of teenage barbarism was described.

---

[37] See Anthony Bottoms *et al*, *International Treatment and Juvenile Justice, Implications And Findings from A Survey of Intermediate Treatment Policy and Practice Evaluation Project*, Final Report (London H.M.S.O., 1990) See also John Pratt, 'Corporatism, The Third Model of Juvenile Justice', (1989) *British Journal of Criminology*.

[38] On the policy see Home Office, *Punishment In The Community* (London: H.M.S.O., 1989) and Home Office, *Crime, Justice and protecting The Public* (London: H.M.S.O., 1990).

[39] *Op. cit.*, note 19.

This offered an ideological underpinning for a government propelled back into an interventionist stance by a rising crime rate. If the 1980s' policies had drawn on James Q. Wilson's world[40] in which rational people act to maximize their pleasure and minimize their pain, now the 'insights' of Charles Murray were making their mark. A free market in morality was being distorted by a welfare system which rewarded young women for having children outside marriage by giving them local authority housing and welfare benefits.[41] An 'underclass' with separate moral values was being created. The language of Murray and Herrnstein's *Bell Curve*[42] with its talk of 'intellectually impaired man' synchronized with the feelings of a Conservative Party in Britain bent on reconstructing society, in creating a new social discipline.

Ironically, part of this was the rediscovery of rehabilitation. It was very different from the rehabilitative ideal we had become used to in the 1960s and 1970s with its use of 'psy' professionals to correct social and emotional difficulties. Now the goal was restoration of rationality, a reinjection of conformity, the teaching of discipline. Crime was attributed to intellectual deficiency and to lack of discipline. As so often rehabilitation went hand-in-hand with the urge to imprison and, as already described, the locking-up of the young became a key policy in the Howard era at the Home Office. Howard's decision to increase to 15 years the period for which Thompson and Venables are to be detained (the trial judge had recommended 8 years, the Lord Chief Justice 10) did not use the language of rehabilitation—he talked of public concern and the need to maintain public confidence in the criminal justice system.[43] But implicit in his directive is his belief that the murderers of James Bulger 'represent' a barbarism that needs to be tamed. They were to be made examples of to restore a new social discipline.

---

[40] Described in *Thinking About Crime*, *op. cit.*, note 18.

[41] On Peter Lilley's 'little list' of persons who would not be missed (*cf.* Gilbert and Sullivan's *The Mikado*) in his speech to the Tory party conference in October 1992. See also N. Dennis and G. Erdos, *Families Without Fatherhood* (London: Institute of Economic Affairs, 1992). More rational but similarly directed is Melanie Phillips, 'Rediscovering The Values of The Family', *The Guardian*, 26 February 1993.

[42] *Op. cit.*, note 20.

[43] This is being challenged at the European Court of Human Rights. See *The Independent On Sunday*, 22 May 1994: see also the leading article in *The Independent*, 'A Challenge to The Bulger Trial', 23 May 1994.

A VICTORIAN MURDER

That the Bulger trial did not have to be seen this way, that there and other ways of approaching crimes, even horrific crimes, by children is often remarked upon. Critics point justifiably to the recent Norwegian case which made headlines one day and disappeared the next as the children and their families were helped to come to terms with what was conceived as a tragedy.[44] But it is not necessary to point to contemporary parallels in other countries. Gitta Sereny, the author of the leading book on the Mary Bell[45] case and commentator on the Bulger trial,[46] has recently excavated evidence of a similar case in England in 1861, the interest of which lies in the approach taken.[47]

Two Stockport 8-year-olds, Peter Barratt and James Bradley, the age of criminal responsibility then being 7, were convicted of the manslaughter of a 2-year-old, George Burgess, a child they had—so far as is known, just as in the Bulger case—never laid eyes on before. Again, as in the Bulger case, it was a particularly brutal killing. Nor do the parallels end there. The boys had both been disruptive at school shortly before the murder (it was a Sunday school: as was common then children only attended school on Sundays). It seems, at least initially, that Barratt and Bradley, just as the children in Newcastle and Liverpool a century later, had no real concept of what they had done. The boys were charged with murder but convicted of manslaughter. The judge had told the jury that if they found that the boys did not understand the effect of the act they were committing, the presumption of malice would be rebutted and the crime reduced to manslaughter.

The similarities between the cases end with the verdict. James Bulger's killers were not given the opportunity of a manslaughter verdict and, whereas the judge in the Bulger trial seemed oblivious to the welfare of

---

[44] 5-year-old Silje Marie Redergard froze to death in a school playground after a 'game' with three boys (one aged 6, the other two are aged 5). A striking parallel is that the TV programme 'Power Rangers' was widely blamed in Norway and broadcasts of it were suspended. But the differences in social attitudes are also noteworthy: James Bulger's parents have campaigned for Thompson and Venables never to be released: Silje Redergard's mother is quoted as 'forgiving the ones who killed my daughter. It is not possible to hate small children'.

[45] *Op. cit.*, note 10.

[46] *The Independent on Sunday*, 13 and 20 February 1994 (reproduced as an appendix to the book referred to in the previous note).

[47] 'A Child Murdered By Children', *The Independent on Sunday*, 23 April 1995, pp. 8–12.

Thompson and Venables, in 1861 a judge could use this language: 'The prisoners will be sent to the Reformatory at Bradwall from whose excellent manager I received a letter stating that although the boys were younger than the generality of those under his care, under the peculiar circumstances of the case, he would have great pleasure in taking them and in looking after their future welfare'. In sentencing the boys, he said: 'I am afraid you have been very wicked, naughty boys, and I have no doubt that you have caused the death of this little boy by the brutal way to which you used him. I am going to send you to a place where you will have an opportunity of becoming good boys, for there you will have a chance of being brought up in a way you should be, and I doubt not but that in time, when you come to understand the nature of the crime you have committed, you will repent of what you have done. The sentence is that each of you be imprisoned and kept in gaol for one month, and at the expiration of that period you be sent to a Reformatory for five years.'

There was a leading article in *The Times*[48] on the case and what a striking contrast it makes with the 'op-ed' columns of to-day! It argued that children of the age of Bradley and Barratt could not be held legally accountable in the same way as adults. 'What is the reason then', it notes, 'why it should have been absurd and monstrous that these two children should have been treated like murderers?.... As far as it went [*i.e.* their conscience] was as sound and a genuine a conscience as that of a grown man: it told them that what they were doing was wrong.... [But] conscience, like other natural faculties, admits of degrees: it is weak, and has not arrived at its proper growth in children, though it has a real existence and a voice within them; it does not speak with that force and seriousness which justifies us in treating the child as a legally responsible being.'

Conclusion

But that is how Thompson and Venables were treated 132 years later. There was no psychology or psychiatry in 1861. In 1993 with psychiatry well-established it had to play a handmaiden's role to the masterful discipline of law.[49] It was the law which determined that Thompson and Venables could not be helped until after their trial. It was the law which decided that the role of the 'psy' sciences was to determine legal

---

[48] *The Times*, 10 August 1861.
[49] See, to like effect, Michael King, 'The James Bulger Murder Trial: Moral Dilemmas and Social Solutions' (1995) 3 *International Journal of Children's Rights* 167.

responsibility, but not to explain or excuse. From the perspective of the government this was as well. Had the child psychiatrists' evidence failed to establish that the boys were able to distinguish naughtiness from serious wrong or found that they lacked the mental capacity to stand trial, where would they have been? With no trial, with identities and biographies suppressed, the killing of James Bulger could not have been used as an object lesson for pontificating about evil, nor could it have used to symbolize the mischief that new government strategies were designed to tackle.[50]

---

[50] Nor as an atypical instance should it be. See, further, Stewart Asquith, 'When Children Kill Children', 3 *Childhood* 99 (1996), an article published too late for its valuable insights to be taken on board. Also valuable, but published after this article was written, is Colin Hay, 'Mobilization Through Interpretation: James Bulger, Juvenile Crime and the Construction of a Moral Panic', 4 *Social and Legal Studies* 197 (1995).

CHAPTER 13

Cleveland, Butler-Sloss and Beyond—
How are We to React to the Sexual Abuse of Children?

What should cause surprise is not that Cleveland happened, but that a Cleveland was so long in coming. The history books will record Middlesbrough as the place where the English conscience awakened to the sexual abuse of children. But they will also remember how the problem itself was clouded by revelations of ineptitude, of inter-professional rivalry, how Cleveland itself became the site for ideological conflict and the impetus for, and the battleground upon which, initiatives for reform were fought. Despite the media attention, despite a lengthy inquiry leading to the Butler-Sloss report,[1] we do not know even to-day how many of the children removed from parents in Cleveland were sexually abused.[2] We are unlikely, accordingly, ever to know whether the paediatricians, Marietta Higgs and Geoffrey Wyatt, were Midases who turned everything they touched into sexual abuse or, like many pioneers, were more sinned against than sinning. That they were single-minded and zealous, at times even obsessed with what they considered to be the truth, that at times they, and those, notably Sue Richardson, who worked with them in social services, paid insufficient attention to rights or legal proprieties cannot be denied. Politicians they certainly were not. In the immediate aftermath of Cleveland it is their actions which are remembered and some of them leave a sour taste. But, in the perspective of history, Cleveland will be remembered as the place where we first faced up to the iniquity of the sexual abuse of children.

---

[1] *Report of the Inquiry into Child Abuse in Cleveland 1987* (the Butler-Sloss report). London, H.M.S.O. Cm.412 (1988)

[2] A point commented upon (after publication) both by M. Phillips in *The Guardian* 8 July 1988, and S. Helm in *The Independent*, 5 September 1988. The issue erupted again in *The Guardian*, 18 February 1989 (a letter from 11 paediatricians claiming 90 per cent were abused).

Why is it that sexual abuse of children has for so long been kept under wraps? How are we to explain our reluctance to accept its existence? A hundred years ago we grudgingly accepted that children were physically abused.[3] A quarter of a century ago we awoke to the concept of the battered baby syndrome[4] and gradually became aware of non-accidental injury of children.[5] But revelations of sexual abuse continued to be greeted with disbelief. My book on *Violence In The Home*,[6] written in the mid-1970s, was to have contained a chapter on sexual abuse, but when the manuscript needed to be reduced, I readily acceded to the publisher's suggestion that the chapter to excise was the one on the sexual abuse of children. That chapter was separately published[7] but, I suspect, barely noticed. It was not that sexual abuse did not exist a decade ago: it was that we preferred to believe it did not exist. Why?

Professional interest in child sexual abuse can be traced to the publication of several incest histories in Krafft-Ebing's *Psychopathia Sexualis* in 1886.[8] But nothing seems to have come of this. The Kinsey reports in 1953[9] attracted a lot of interest but their revelations that many children had sexual experiences with adults seems to have caused little concern. Allegations of sexual abuse were dismissed as children's fantasies. In part we may attribute this response to the writings of Freud. He believed that an innate incest desire is evident in early childhood and that it continues throughout life in a repressed form.[10] Freud assumed that allegations of sexual abuse were primarily the result of a wish to have sex with a parent, usually the parent of

---

[3] See C. K. Behlmer, *Child Abuse and Moral Reform In England 1870–1908*, Stanford, Stanford Univ. Press, 1982; L. Gordon, *Heroes of Their Own Lives*, London, Virago, 1989.

[4] First revealed in C. H. Kempe *et al*'s 'The Battered-Child Syndrome', *Journal of the American Medical Association* 181, 17–24 (1962).

[5] On the history of this see N. Parton, *The Politics of Child Abuse*, London, Macmillan, 1985.

[6] M. D. A. Freeman, *Violence In The Home—A Socio-Legal Study*, Farnborough, Saxon House, 1979 (now Aldershot, Gower Press).

[7] M. D. A. Freeman, 'Sexual Abuse of Children', 8 *Family Law* 221–225 (1978).

[8] R. Krafft-Ebing, *Psychopathia Sexualis: A Medico-Forensic Study*, New York, Putnam, 1965 (Originally published in 1886).

[9] A. C. Kinsey, W. B. Pomeroy, C. E. Martin and P. H. Gebhard, *Sexual Behavior in the Human Female*. Philadelphia, Saunders, 1953.

[10] S. Freud, *The Complete Introductory Lectures on Psycho-analysis* (ed. and transl. by J. Strachey) New York, Norton (Originally published in 1933).

the opposite sex.[11] Although more recent clinical writings have also stressed the presence of a strong incest desire,[12] there is no doubt that oedipal fantasies are usually easily distinguished from allegations of sexual abuse. According to Kathleen Coulborn Faller, who gives good distinguishing examples, 'they are likely to be expressions of a general desire for closeness to one parent and exclusion of the other, and do not have explicit sexual content'.[13] In addition, she notes, 'the child perceives them as desired events and experiences'.[14] Freud's theories did not gel with anthropological evidence[15] or with that of historians of the family[16] or sociologists.[17] But it was, until recently, firmly entrenched as part of our cognition of sexuality.

Dating the breakthrough to a realization of the existence of child sexual abuse is not easy. The 'permissive' 1960s did not help advance the cause: too many professionals at the time were interested in liberalizing sexual mores and this may have led them to downplay the importance of abuse. In the United States the label 'child sexual abuse' first appeared in the federal Child Abuse Prevention and Treatment Act of 1974.[18] In the 1970s in the United States, and somewhat later in this country, advocates for children and feminist groups helped to acquaint both the public and professionals with the problem. They were the 'moral entrepreneurs' who, in Howard Becker's memorable phrase, 'blew the whistle'.[19] It was the sexual abuse of adult women, in particular rape, which in the end stimulated research and inquiry. It came to be recognized that rape was the most under-reported of crimes and to be clear that, although the reasons for this were complex and mani-

---

[11] See, further, R. Summit and J. Kryso, 'Sexual Abuse of Children: A Clinical Spectrum' *Amer. J. of Orthopsychiatry* vol. 48(2), 231 (1978); J. Herman, *Father-Daughter Incest*. Cambridge Mass. Harvard University Press, 1981; J. Masson, *The Assault on Truth*. New York, Farrar, Straus and Giroux, 1984; E. Ward, *Father-Daughter Rape*, London, Women's Press, 1984, pp. 100–117.

[12] For example, K. C. Meiselman, *Incest: A Psychological Study of Causes and Effects with Treatment Recommendations*. San Francisco, Jossey-Bass, 1978.

[13] *Child Sexual Abuse: An Interdisciplinary Manual for Diagnosis, Case Management and Treatment*. New York, Columbia Univ. Press, 1988, p. 133.

[14] *Idem*.

[15] B. Malinowski, *Sex and Repression in Savage Society*. London, RKP., 1927.

[16] E. Westermarck, *A Short History of Marriage*. London, Macmillan, 1926.

[17] J. R. Fox, 'Sibling Incest' *British J. of Sociology* 13, 128–50 (1962).

[18] D. K. Weisberg, 'The "Discovery" of Sexual Abuse: Experts' Role in Legal Policy Formation' *Univ. of California Davis Law Review* 18, 1–57 (1984).

[19] H. Becker, *Outsiders*. New York, Free Press, 1963.

fold, legal processes,[20] both at the level of forensic investigation and proof in court,[21] which 'blamed the victims',[22] were to a large part responsible. A television documentary in 1983, produced by Roger Graef, which revealed the bullying tactics of the Thames Valley police in investigating a rape allegation, shocked the nation. Judicial attitudes, in particular as regards sentencing, attracted a lot of adverse criticism at about the same time.[23] On both levels there was a reconsideration. Women got the right to request examinations by female officers and doctors, and some attempt was also made to ensure that sentences for rape reflected the seriousness of the offence.[24] More rapes began to be reported. Rape crisis centres became deluged not just with adult rape survivors but also with those who had experienced, or were experiencing, sexual abuse. In retrospect the explosion had to come and, as so often, as in the United States also, it took a scandal to ignite the fuse.[25] In the United States the issue of child sexual abuse was dramatically brought to the public's attention with the arrest in 1984 in Manhattan Beach, California, of Virginia McMartin and six of her employees for allegedly sexually abusing 125 children over a 10-year period at a day-care centre.[26] Shortly thereafter, indictments were brought against 24 adults and a juvenile (who included in their number a police officer and a deputy sheriff) for allegedly sexually abusing over 50 children in Jordan, Minnesota, a small town with a population of barely three thousand.[27] The *McMartin* case resulted in acquittals. The trial in the *Jordan* case collapsed after a convicted child molester, who had confessed to molesting more than a dozen Jordan children and had agreed to testify for the State, had his testimony struck from the record. This led to the acquittal of the Bentzes, whose 6-year-old

---

[20] On which see Jennifer Temkin's excellent *Rape and the Legal Process*. London, Sweet and Maxwell, 1987.

[21] See Z. Adler, *Rape On Trial*, London, RKP, 1987.

[22] On which see W. Ryan, *Blaming The Victim*, New York, Vintage, 1976.

[23] For example, Judge Bertram Richards' suggestion that hitch-hiking amounted to contributory negligence (*The Times*, 7 January 1982). This, and other examples, led to the Prime Minister announcing that only High Court or experienced Circuit Court judges would try rape cases.

[24] See *R* v. *Billam* [1986] 1 All E. R. 985; see also *R* v. *Roberts* [1982] 1 All E. R. 609 (see also *op. cit.*, note 20, pp. 16–25).

[25] See D. Hechler, *The Battle and the Backlash*, D. C. Heath, 1988.

[26] L. Coleman, *The Reign of Error: Psychiatry, Authority and Law*, Boston, Beacon Press, 1984. See also D. Hechler, *op. cit.*, note 25, ch. 8. Appendix 5 (an interview with a defence attorney in the case) is instructive.

[27] *Ibid.*, ch. 6. See also M. A. Tester, 'The Scott County Sexual Abuse Cases: A Closer Look at What Went Wrong', Dept. of Psychology, University of Virginia, 1986.

son had testified in court that they had sexually abused him, and to the dropping of all charges against the remaining defendants.[28] As in England, over Cleveland,[29] there were allegations of a witch-hunt.[30] Explicit parallels were drawn between Salem 1692 and Manhattan Beach 1985.[31] In the United States, as here, the battle to expose child sexual abuse has led to a backlash.[32] In Cleveland, as we shall see, there undoubtedly were injustices perpetrated. Some decisions were taken that were 'dictatorial, insensitive or prejudiced'.[33] Far too much emphasis was placed on the anal dilatation test. But out of Cleveland, the Butler-Sloss report and its aftermath has come a recognition that child sexual abuse is a real problem with which all of us concerned with the interests of children must grapple.

Before the facts and issues can be considered, and the Butler-Sloss report evaluated, some basic questions about the sexual abuse of children must be addressed. What is it? (the question of definition.) How much abuse exists? (the issue of dimension.) And, why does it occur? (the problem of understanding its causes.) It is to a brief consideration of these matters that I now turn.

WHAT IS CHILD SEXUAL ABUSE?

In *Violence In The Home* I wrote of physical abuse of children that the difficulties of definition depended 'on the purposes for which the definition is being sought'.[34] A definition for a reporting law (such as exists in the U.S.A.) or management guidance has, I noted, very different functions from one constructed for operational or sociological research. Another problem, as I saw it then, concerned 'the perspective from which the sub-

---

[28] E. R. Shipp, 'Children Testify Against Parents Over Abuse', *The New York Times*, 3 September, 1984. On the cases and the problem generally see also J. Crewdson, *By Silence Betrayed*. New York, Harper and Row, 1989.

[29] Notably by a local M.P., Stuart Bell, in his book *When Salem Came To the Boro*, London, Pan, 1988.

[30] In the United States, organizations like VOCAL and Men International have made such associations. (Hechler, *op. cit.*, note 25, discusses VOCAL at pp. 118–129).

[31] An advertisement published in various Southern California newspapers in the summer of 1985, drawing the parallel between Salem and Manhattan Beach, is reproduced in Hechler, *op. cit.*, note 25, p. 4.

[32] The most graphic and fullest description of which is in Hechler's book (*op. cit.*, note 25), chs. 6–9.

[33] *Per* Lord Oliver in *Re KD* [1988] A. C. 806, 813.

[34] *Op. cit.*, note 6, p. 11.

ject is approached.³⁵ How is one to emphasize the relative importance of the perpetrator's actions, the effects on the victim, the motivation behind the acts in question? Furthermore, solutions are often determined on the basis of problem definition.³⁶ Much, therefore, hinges on the definition accepted.

The definition of child sexual abuse is equally fraught with problems. The categories of sexual and physical abuse are, of course, not entirely separate categories. Some sexual abuse (certainly rape and arguably other forms) is gross physical abuse in addition to being sexual abuse. All sexual abuse is without question severe emotional abuse.³⁷ There has been a lot of discussion as to how much sexual abuse takes place. A figure commonly quoted in the press suggests that 10 per cent of adults were sexually abused when children.³⁸ This may have conveyed the impression that one in ten adults experienced intercourse with an adult when they themselves were children. With all the discussion of the anal dilatation test, some may have come to believe that buggery of children too was commonplace. But the definition of sexual abuse employed by the researchers, whose data provided the media with the 10 per cent figure, embraced a broad range of activities including exposure to pornographic material (including no doubt some of the very newspapers which reported the statistic) and talking about sexual things in an erotic way. There was similarly a lot of discussion at the height of the moral panic about the discoveries at Cleveland that fathers in particular would be reluctant to bath small daughters or show them physical affection for fear of such activities being interpreted as abuse. There may of course be borderline situations but it should not be difficult to distinguish sexual interference and affectionate physical contact. In many cases the distinguishing mark will be the feelings of the child: in others the presence or absence of genital involvement will serve as a sufficiently clear indicator. Too much has, I think, been made of this potential fear.

---

[35] *Idem.* See also J. Garbarino and G. Gilliam, *Understanding Abusive Families*, Lexington, Mass., Lexington Books, 1980 (see p. 5).

[36] N. Clapham and S. Nelson, 'On Being Useful: The Nature and Consequences of Psychological Research on Social Problems'. *American Psychologist,* 28, 199–211 (1973).

[37] See, for agreement, D. Glaser and S. Frosh, *Child Sexual Abuse.* Basingstoke, Macmillan, 1988, p. 9.

[38] This statistic, discussed further below, is based on a study by A. Baker and S. Duncan, 'Child Sexual Abuse: A Study of its Prevalence in Great Britain', *Child Abuse and Neglect* 9, 457–67 (1985).

How, then, are we to define sexual abuse? There is no universally accepted definition of what constitutes child sexual abuse. There are differences in how far 'sexual' extends: Finkelhor[39] defines 'sexual victimization' as 'sexual encounters' of children under 13 with persons at least 5 years older than themselves and encounters of children between 13 and 16 with persons at least 10 years older. 'Sexual encounters' are 'intercourse, anal-genital contact, fondling, or an encounter with an exhibitionist'. Others include within sexual abuse any activity that brings gratification to the perpetrator. Should an act be regarded as sexual abuse if it is not so seen by the child? Not every child will identify the same acts as sexual. Very young children will not be capable of labelling in this way even the most overt sexual acts. For these reasons the intention of the abuser is crucial, and the inclusion of anything that gives him sexual gratification within the definition of child sexual abuse is meaningful. It is crucial to stress this element for two reasons: first, there are actions (for example, voyeurism) of which the child is unaware and, secondly, by emphasizing what it does for the perpetrator, child sexual abuse can be seen as a wrong that reduces the child to a sexual object—her person is not the subject of 'equal respect and concern'.[40]

The age differential is also troubling. It is clearly postulated, by Finkelhor for example, to suggest coercion or undue influence. It is hardly satisfactory. It is not the age difference which is crucial but the ability to fend off advances and this is heavily dependent on development. Schechter and Roberge,[41] in a much-quoted definition, approved in the Butler-Sloss report,[42] take account of this. They define sexual abuse as:

> the involvement of dependent, developmentally immature children and adolescents in sexual activities that they do not fully comprehend and to which they are unable to give informed consent or that violate the social taboos of family roles.

---

[39] D. Finkelhor, *Child Sexual Abuse*. New York, Free Press, 1984, pp. 23–24.

[40] See R. Dworkin, *Taking Rights Seriously*. London, Duckworth, 1977, pp. 180–183. See also M. D. A. Freeman, 'Taking Children's Rights Seriously' in *Children and Society* 1(4), pp. 299–319 (1988), and ch. 2.

[41] 'Child Sexual Abuse' in R. Helfer and C. Kempe (eds.), *Child Abuse and Neglect: The Family and the Community,* Cambridge, Mass., Ballinger, 1976, p. 60.

[42] *Op. cit.*, note 1, p. 4, para. 4.

The concept of 'informed consent' is crucial. Victims of sexual abuse often do not object to participating in sexual activities but either lack knowledge of the social meanings and psychological impact of sexual encounters or because of the powerless and dependent position they occupy lack true free choice. It is impossible to say at what age children can give informed consent. A girl can consent to sexual intercourse at 16[43] and children of both sexes can consent to medical treatment at that age.[44] The American Psychological Association has argued that a 14-year-old is competent to consent to an abortion.[45] On one reading of the *Gillick* decision[46] a girl with sufficient maturity, knowledge and understanding should be able to consent to going on the pill before she attains the age of 16. This will, of course, depend on the individual girl but psychologists tell us that, in both moral and cognitive development, many children reach adult levels between 12 and 14.[47] But, given the relationship of dependency, would it not be wiser to assume that children cannot give informed consent to sexual relations with adults?

A fortiori this should be the case where the relationship is close, whether within or without the incest test (for example, a step-parent). The reason for this is not brought out in the Schechter-Roberge definition, save in the reference to dependency. Abuse is about the exploitation of power: abusers are always more powerful than their victims.[48] The sexual abuser manipulates his victim for his own gratification. Because of the position children occupy within a family it is difficult to see a sexual relationship with an adult family member on whom they are dependent as anything other than sexual abuse. Most sex abusers are men and most victims are female (facts often glossed over in the Cleveland debates[49]): in this sense child sexual abuse is but a microcosm of the abuse, ranging from domestic

---

[43] Sexual Offences Act 1956 s. 6.
[44] See Family Law Reform Act 1969 s. 8(1).
[45] See J. Bales 'Brief Stresses Competence of Minors,' *APA Monitor,* April 1987, p. 35.
[46] *Gillick* v. *West Norfolk and Wisbech Area Health Authority* [1986] A. C. 112.
[47] W. Damon, *The Social World of the Child*, San Francisco, Jossey-Bass, 1977; E. Douvan and J. Adelson, *The Adolescent Experience*, New York, Wiley, 1966.
[48] Recognized by the Standing Committee on Sexually Abused Children, *Definition of Child Sexual Abuse*, SCOSAC, 1984. See also B. Campbell, *Unofficial Secrets*, London, Virago, 1988.
[49] An attempt at a corrective is E. Welldon, *Mother, Madonna, Whore: The Idealization and Denigration of Motherhood*, London, Free Association Books, 1988.

violence,[50] through rape,[51] sexual harassment,[52] prostitution[53] and pornography[54] to which women are subjected.

Child sexual abuse takes many forms.[55] There is non-contact sexual abuse ('sexy talk', exposure and voyeurism). There is sexual contact, which includes any touching of the intimate body parts and frottage. There is oral-genital sex, involving the perpetrator's licking, kissing, sucking or biting the child's genitals or inducing the child orally to copulate with him. Fellatio is probably the most common example of this: the male perpetrator will insist on inserting his penis into a child victim's mouth. There is, fourthly, interfemoral intercourse in which the perpetrator's penis is placed between the child victim's thighs. With younger children this technique is employed where the vaginal opening is too small: with older girls it may be used to avoid the risk of pregnancy. There is sexual penetration which may be digital (sometimes as a prelude to genital intercourse), use objects (electric vibrators, crayons, a carrot, a cucumber), involve the penis entering the vagina or the anus. There are also forms of sexual exploitation. This has to be distinguished from abuse. It is often done for financial gain, not sexual gratification. It includes child pornography[56] and child prostitution,[57] particularly loathsome forms of exploitation.

It may be useful to conclude this section with a working definition at least of child sexual abuse. The most comprehensive is that put forward by the Standing Committee on Sexually Abused Children in 1984. I quote it in full.[58]

> Any child below the age of consent may be deemed to have been sexually abused when a sexually mature person has, by design or by neglect

---

[50] R. Dobash and R. Dobash, *Violence Against Wives*, New York, Free Press, 1979; E. Pizzey, *Scream Quietly Or The Neighbours Will Hear*, Harmondsworth, Penguin, 1974.

[51] J. Rowland, *Rape: The Ultimate Violation*, New York, Doubleday, 1985; S. Estrich, *Real Rape*, Cambridge, Mass., Harvard Univ. Press 1987; L. Clark and D. Lewis, *Rape: The Price of Coercive Sexuality*, Toronto, Women's Press, 1977.

[52] C. MacKinnon, *Sexual Harassment of Working Women*, New Haven, Conn., Yale U. P. 1979.

[53] See E. Wilson, *What's To Be Done About Violence Against Women?*, Harmondsworth, Penguin, 1983, ch. 5; L. Lederer, *Take Back The Night*, New York, Morrow, 1980.

[54] C, MacKinnon, *Only Words*, London, Fontana, 1993.

[55] *Op. cit.*, note 13, pp. 12–16. See also D. Finkelhor, *A Sourcebook on Child Sexual Abuse*, Beverley Hills, Calif., 1986, pp. 22–27.

[56] See F. Rush, ' Child Pornography' in (ed.) L. Lederer, *op. cit.*, note 53, pp. 71–81.

[57] See J. Ennew, *The Sexual Exploitation of Children*, Oxford, Polity Press, 1986.

[58] See *op. cit.*, note 48.

264 Chapter 13

of their usual societal or specific responsibilities in relation to the child, engaged or permitted the engagement of that child in any activity of a sexual nature which is intended to lead to the sexual gratification of the sexually mature person. This definition pertains whether or not this activity involves explicit coercion by any means, whether or not initiated by the child, or whether or not there is discernible harmful outcome in the short term.

HOW MUCH CHILD SEXUAL ABUSE IS THERE?

The simple, and only honest, answer to this question is that we do not know. The assumption has always been that it is rare and this despite the Kinsey revelations that 24 per cent of the women in their sample reported a sexual experience with an adult while they were children (though, when only sexual activity involving physical contact was considered, the rate fell to 9.2 per cent).[59] More recently in this country, in the United States[60] and in Canada,[61] attempts have been made to estimate the prevalence of sexual abuse. Many more cases are coming to light but this is a reflection of greater willingness to report and increased diagnoses, and not of greater occurrence. There was, almost certainly, more incest in Victorian Britain than there is to-day.

There are two types of information that assist us to estimate the frequency with which child sexual abuse occurs. There is data derived from studies of children referred to social services, doctors, police or therapeutic agencies. These suggest a low rate of abuse. For example, a survey by Mrazek, Lynch and Bentovim[62] of 1599 family doctors, police surgeons, paediatricians and child psychiatrists uncovered a total of 1072 cases seen in the year 1977–78. This would give an incidence figure of 1500 per year, or one child in every six thousand. Over the entire childhood period (up to the age of 15), this study estimated that three children in every thousand are recognized as sexually abused. But (i) the overall response rate from the professionals was low (39 per cent), (ii) the figures are, as ever in this

---

[59] *Op. cit.* note 9. The sample (of volunteers) was 4,444 adult women.

[60] See generally J. Haugaard and N. Reppucci, *The Sexual Abuse of Children*, San Francisco, Jossey Bass, 1988, ch. 3.

[61] Report of Committee on Sexual Offences Against Children Ottawa, Canadian Govt. Publishing Centre, 1984. In New Zealand the one in ten figure has been supported (see *The Independent*, 15 April 1988).

[62] 'Sexual Abuse of Children in the United Kingdom', *Child Abuse and Neglect* vol. 7, pp. 147–153 (1983).

kind of survey, a gross under-estimate because they only take account of the cases which have been identified and processed through the relevant agencies. The survey is interesting in that it reveals what incidence of abuse was coming to professional attention a decade ago. It does not, of course, uncover those cases which did not see the light of day because their victims were frightened, ashamed or confused, nor does it reveal anything about the cases that did not get beyond a disbelieving doctor.[63] With increased awareness of child sexual abuse, the number would be greater to-day. Thus, Wild[64] reports that referrals of child sexual abuse to paediatricians in Leeds increased from none in 1979 to 50 in 1984 and 161 in 1985. In 1984 in 60 per cent of the referrals abuse was confirmed or considered probable: in 1985 the equivalent percentage was over 65 per cent.[65]

Another approach is to survey adults on their sexual experiences as children. There have been many American studies of this type. One of the best known is Diana Russell's, based on a probability sample of households in San Francisco. She reported that 38 per cent of the women interviewed had experienced some form of sexual abuse involving physical contact before they were eighteen (28 per cent before they were 14).[66] The figures are 16 per cent and 12 per cent if only intra-familial abuse is counted. The fullest British investigation was conducted by Baker and Duncan.[67] It involved a detailed interview of 2019 women and men of 15 and over. It was a nationally representative sample. As indicated previously, it used a broad definition of sexual abuse. Respondents were asked if they had had experiences of sexual abuse (as defined) before the age of 16. 10 per cent said that they had, 77 per cent said that they had not: the remainder refused to answer the question. If those results can be generalized, it would mean that four and a half million adults in Great Britain were sexually abused as children. Other British studies suggest the number is even larger. West[68] found that 46 per cent of the 600 women he surveyed reported that they had been sexually

---

[63] As happened also with physical abuse. Doctors are now given guidance in DHSS, *Diagnosis of Child Sexual Abuse*, London, H.M.S.O. 1988.

[64] 'Sexual Abuse of Children in Leeds', British Medical Journal, vol. 292, pp. 1113–1116 (1986).

[65] The NSPCC has also experienced large increases in reported cases (90 per cent between 1984 and 1985).

[66] 'The Incidence and Prevalence of Intrafamilial and Extrafamilial Sexual Abuse of Female Children', *Child Abuse and Neglect*, vol. 7, pp. 133–146 (1933).

[67] *Op. cit.*, note 38.

[68] *Sexual Victimisation*, Farnborough, Gower, 1985.

abused as children and in Ruth Hall's sample of 1236 women 21 per cent remembered that they had been sexually abused as children (for one-third of these the experience had occurred more than once).[69] These statistics must be treated with caution: the Butler-Sloss report admitted as much.[70] But, however exaggerated, they reveal the existence of a major problem.

HOW IS CHILD SEXUAL ABUSE TO BE EXPLAINED?

Do we know why it occurs? A lot of research effort has gone into trying to explain the aetiology of physical abuse and different models of explanation have emerged: one emphasizing that abusers are 'sick' (the medical or psycho-pathological model),[71] another that abuse is located in stress produced by socio-environmental factors such as the multi-faceted correlates of poverty,[72] and a third that abuse is to be explained in cultural terms, as an inevitable consequence of the fact that children are treated as property rather than persons, as social problems rather than as participants in the social process.[73] There is no agreement. It may be that a multi-dimensional explanation is what is needed.[74] But in many ways physical abuse is easier to understand than sexual abuse: most of us can empathize with the parent who slashes out in anger but few can comprehend sexual interference with a small child or intercourse with an adolescent daughter. How can it be explained? Are the models constructed to comprehend physical abuse of any assistance?

Although we will see striking parallels, one factor in child sexual abuse stands out and separates the two phenomena. Most perpetrators of child

---

[69] *Ask Any Woman: A London Inquiry into Rape and Sexual Assault*, Bristol, Falling Wall Press, 1985. For a very different view see D. Aitchison, *The Guardian* 11 August 1988 (letter).

[70] *Op. cit.*, note 1, p. 5, para. 7. Sue Richardson is quoted as suggesting that 30 per cent of children may be abused (*The Independent*, 1 July 1987).

[71] See M. D. A. Freeman, *op. cit.*, note 6, pp. 21–27 and N. Parton, *op. cit.*, note 5, ch. 6 for critiques.

[72] See L. Pelton 'Child Abuse and Neglect: The Myth of Classlessness', *American Journal of Orthopsychiatry*, vol. 48, pp. 608–17 (1978) and see Freeman *op. cit.*, note 6, pp. 27–31 and Parton *op. cit.*, note 5, ch. 7.

[73] M. D. A. Freeman, 'The Rights of Children in the International Year of the Child', (1980) 33 *Current Legal Problems* 1–32.

[74] And see *op. cit.*, note 6. p. 32. And see D. Gil, *Violence Against Children*, Cambridge, Harvard Univ. Press, 1970. This was also recognized by the House of Commons Select Committee in its report on *Violence In The Family*, H.C. 329, 1977, para. 32.

sexual abuse are men[75] and most victims are female.[76] The general source of the abuse must, therefore, be located in masculine sexuality.[77] It is surprising (or is it?) that the gender of the perpetrator is so rarely made explicit. Discussion relating to Cleveland was invariably about 'parents'. The Baker-Duncan survey, referred to above, distinguishes 'intra-familial', 'extra-familial' and 'stranger' abuse but never mentions the gender of the perpetrator.[78] Many of those who discuss sex abuse to-day would like to think that women were abusers too, but the evidence just does not support this. For example, in Russell's sample of 930 women, only ten cases of incestuous abuse by women were reported, despite a wide definition of abuse.[79] Many of the early studies included women in the figures for perpetrators, not only when they had abused a child, but also when they had 'simply "allowed" sexual abuse to occur'.[80] It is common to find mother blaming in the orthodox literature on child sexual abuse.[81] Nelson notes that 'professionals cling to the collusive wife theory like drowning men grasping at flotsam.' 'Could it be', she asks most perceptively, 'because it is such a powerful defence against admitting the male abuse of power? And because without it family therapists might be like emperors without clothes? These are harsh questions which they owe it to their own integrity to ask.'[82] They, that is orthodox theorists, in particular exponents of family systems theory,[83] do not ask them, but we must. If the male dimen-

---

[75] All surveys save one (G. V. Hamilton, *A Research In Marriage*, New York, Albert and Charles Boni, 1929—generally thought suspect on methodological grounds—demonstrate this. See D. Finkelhor, *op. cit.*, note 55, pp. 61–64; D. Glaser and S. Frosh, *op. cit.*, note 37. pp. 12–15. Russell, *op. cit.*, note 66, found a very small proportion of female abusers (4 per cent where victims are girls. Finkelhor, *op. cit.*, note 39, found 20 per cent where the victims are boys.

[76] A useful summary is Finkelhor, *op. cit.*, note 55, pp. 20–21. He estimates (p. 62) that there are 2–5 women victims for every man (*i.e.* 71 per cent of victims are female).

[77] See, for agreement, B. Campbell, *op. cit.*, note 48 ('Abuse is an expression of a patriarchal sexual culture'), p. 62; D. Glaser and S. Frosh, *op. cit.*, note 37, p. 13.

[78] *Op. cit.*, note 38, p. 461.

[79] *The Secret Trauma: Incest in the Lives of Girls and Women*, New York, Basic Books, 1986, p. 297.

[80] D. E. H. Russell, *Sexual Exploitation: Rape, Child Sexual Abuse, Sexual Harassment* Beverley Hills, California, Sage, 1984, p. 219.

[81] For example, B. Justice and R. Justice, *The Broken Taboo—Sex in the Family*, London, Peter Owen, 1980; S. Forward and C. Buck, *Betrayal of Innocence: Incest and its Devastation*, Harmondsworth, Penguin, 1981; R. Kempe and C. H. Kempe, *Child Abuse*, London, Fontana, 1978.

[82] S. Nelson, *Incest: Fact and Myth*, Edinburgh, Stramullion, 1987 (revised ed.), p. 108.

[83] For example, CIBA, *Child Sexual Abuse Within The Family*, London, Tavistock, 1984; T.

sion in child sex abuse has been given such low profile, what is put in its place? How is sexually abusive behaviour explained in non-feminist literature?

As with the physical abuse of children, often it is individual factors in the abuser which are stressed. Some of the research findings can hardly be described as helpful.[84] Thus, abusers are described as being below average intelligence,[85] of average intelligence,[86] and of above average intelligence.[87] They have been defined as aggressive,[88] and as passive.[89] The mothers similarly have been seen in contradictory terms: thus to some researchers they are inadequate and dependent,[90] to others dominant.[91] The explanation for this variation may be that different factors are important in different cases but it should trouble those who subscribe to a pathological model that the variations should be so great.

Weinberg[92] has tried to categorize abusers in a scheme which has proved influential. He distinguishes between 'endogamic' abusers, who are oriented inwards towards their families, over whom they exercise a tightly possessive hold; 'psychopathic' abusers, who treat all people within their power as sexual possessions, and 'paedophic' abusers, whose psychological immaturity

---

Furniss, 'Conflict-Avoiding and Conflict-Regulating Patterns in Incest and Child Sexual Abuse', *Acta Paedopsychiat*, vol. 50, pp. 299–313 (1984).

[84] Good reviews of the literature are D. Finkelhor, *op. cit.*, note 55, ch. 3; R. Langevin, *Sexual Strands: Understanding and Treating Sexual Anomalies in Men*, Hillsdale, N. Y., Erlbaum, 1983; K. Howells, 'Adult Sexual Interest in Children: Considerations relevant to theories of Aetiology' in (eds.) M. Cook and K. Howells, *Adult Sexual Interest in Children*, New York, Academic Press, 1981.

[85] L. Bender and A. Blau, 'The Reaction of Children to Sexual Relations with Adults', *Amer. J. of Orthopsychiatry* vol. 7, pp. 500–518 (1937). It was Bender and Blau, however, who, in the same article, suggested that the child was the seducer rather than seduced.

[86] *Op. cit.*, note 12.

[87] A. Mayer, *Sexual Abuse*. Holmes Beech, Florida, Learning Publications 1985.

[88] A. N. Groth and H. J. Birnbaum, *Men Who Rape: The Psychology of the Offender*, New York, Plenum Press, 1979.

[89] B. Gottlieb, 'Incest: Therapeutic Intervention In a Unique form of Sexual Abuse' in (ed.) C.C. Warner, *Rape and Sexual Assault: Management and Intervention*, Germantown, Maryland, Aspen Publications, 1980.

[90] V. De Francis, *Protecting the Child Victim of Sexual Assault*, Denver, Colorado, American Humane Association, 1971; R. Sarles, 'Incest', *Pediatric Clinics of North America* vol. 22, p. 3 (1975).

[91] M-J. Stern and L. Meyer, 'Family and Couple Interaction Patterns In Cases of Father/Daughter Incest', in *Sexual Abuse of Children: Selected Readings*, Washington, D. C., Govt. Printing Office, 1980.

[92] S. K. Weinberg, *Incest Behavior*, New York, Citadel Press, 1955.

makes them fixate upon children as their sexual objects. Though not without interest, what the scheme implies is that children are abused only by sick or abnormal men. It is certainly convenient, even comforting, to think this: we would like to think of abusers as different, as a class apart.[93] But, when the characteristics of abusers are considered, they are found to be much like the rest of the male population, a diverse bunch whose range of sexual perceptions and responses are little different from 'normal' men. Rarely does the literature which hypothesises individual pathology use control groups. It points to such factors as a harsh or deprived childhood,[94] to such matters as parental marital discord,[95] multiple caretakers,[96] physical[97] or sexual abuse.[98] But why does this lead to these men becoming sexual abusers? If being sexually victimized pre-disposed to perpetrating sexual abuse, we would expect to find many more women committing sexual abuse. Those working within this paradigm do not explain why this does not happen: they content themselves with asserting that they marry abusing men and become pathological 'colluding' mothers. There is no research on men who were abused as children and do not abuse their children. Such men do not come to the attention of clinicians. If there were truly a link between being victimized as a child and becoming an abuser, we would find many more boy victims than we do—a matter not satisfactorily explained by those who espouse an individualistic interpretation of child sexual abuse.

Not all of those who work within an individual personality framework present such a crude analysis. Finkelhor,[99] for example, links the individual psychological and the socio-cultural in an attempt to construct a multi-dimensional explanation. He builds a theory of sexual abuse on a cluster of

---

[93] E. Zigler, 'Controlling Child Abuse in America: An Effort Doomed to Failure?; in R. Bourne and E. Newberger (eds.), *Critical Perspectives on Child Abuse*, Lexington, Mass., Lexington Books, 1979, pp. 171–213 (see particularly p. 176). See the example set out by K. C. Fuller, *op. cit.*, note 13, at pp. 101–103.

[94] See Groth and Birnbaum, *op. cit.*, note 88.

[95] K. Gruber and R. Jones, 'Identifying Determinants of Risk of Sexual Victimization of Youth', Child Abuse and Neglect vol. 7, 17–24 (1983). D. Finkelhor, *Child Sexual Abuse: New Theory and Research*, New York, Free Press 1984.

[96] See, *e.g.*, B. Justice and R. Justice, *The Broken Taboo*, New York, Human Sciences Press, 1979.

[97] M. De Young, *Sexual Victimization of Children*, Jefferson, North Carolina, McFarland, 1982; 'Approaching the Incestuous and Sexually Abusive Family', *Journal of Adolescence* vol. 6, pp. 229–246 (1983).

[98] H. Parker and S. Parker, 'Father-Daughter Sexual Abuse: An Emerging Perspective', *Amer. J. of Orthopsychiatry* vol. 56, pp. 531–549 (1986).

[99] See (with S. Araji) 'Abusers: A review of the Research' (ch. 3 of *op. cit.*, note 55).

factors: emotional congruence ('sexual abusers choose children for sexual partners because children have some especially compelling emotional meaning for them')[100]; sexual arousal to children, possibly produced by the effects of victimization; blockage of alternative avenues of gratification (Finkelhor quotes Storr who claims that 'a man...suffers from paedophilia...because he has been unable to find sexual satisfaction in an adult relationship. It is not from superfluity or lust, but rather because of a timid inability to make contact with contemporaries");[101] and disinhibitions of conventional social constraints (which includes explaining social and cultural elements that encourage or condone sexual behaviour directed toward children and thus weaken inhibitions—'anything that reinforces excuses for sexual abuse...acts to reduce inhibitions'.)[102] Finkelhor, then, is not attributing abuse to personality traits alone but is combining these and experiences, such as being abused in childhood, with internal characteristics, such as lack of relationship skills, situating the whole within a socio-cultural context which makes some attempt to explain the effect of socialization of men, the role of patriarchy in the denigration of women and children, the effect of pornography[103] and other disinhibiting factors. Of course, the feminist theories concentrate on the disinhibition factors. Finkelhor, by contrast, argues that these do not really offer full explanations of sexual abuse for they 'take for granted some prior motive in the abuser to interact sexually with a child'.[104] For Finkelhor they are, accordingly, a necessary but not a sufficient condition for abuse to occur. But, since the motive to indulge in a sexual relationship with a child hinges on man's sexuality or on social or cultural values, Finkelhor's thesis can be reconciled with a feminist interpretation of sexual abuse.

Again, as with physical abuse, the other dominant theory locates the source of sexual abuse in socio-environmental factors. The earliest writers[105] on sexual abuse hypothesized that it was an activity indulged in by the lowest social stratum. Thus Flugel in England (in 1926),[106] Sonden in Sweden in

---

[100] *Ibid.*, p. 94.

[101] The quotation (at p. 107) is from A. Storr, *Sexual Deviation*, London, Heinemann, 1965.

[102] *Op. cit.*, note 99, p. 113.

[103] *Ibid.*, pp. 105–106.

[104] *Ibid.*, p. 114.

[105] As far as physical abuse is concerned, many still subscribe to a strong association between it and low social class. *E.g.* L. H. Pelton, *The Social Context of Child Abuse and Neglect*, New York, Human Sciences Press, 1981.

[106] J. C. Flugel, *The Psychoanalytic Study of the Family*, London, Woolf, 1926.

1936 and Guttmacher in the United States (1951)[107] reported that incest behaviour was inversely related to socio-economic status. These studies can be readily dismissed: the cases were limited to deviants already successfully prosecuted or to victims hospitalized in mental institutions. The evidence is, in other words, grossly distorted by sampling biases.[108] Similar criticisms can be made about any conclusions based on cases of sexual abuse which come to the attention of child protection agencies and the police.[109] These involve the poor disproportionately, but their behaviour is more likely to come under professional scrutiny.

With physical abuse the debate continues to rage over whether it is to be found predominantly amongst the poor.[110] Much, of course, depends on how physical abuse is defined (is corporal chastisement abuse?),[111] on how the 'accident' in 'non accidental injury' is socially constructed.[112] As far as child sexual abuse is concerned, the evidence is overwhelming that it crosses the social class barriers. The evidence is American but there is no reason to believe it would not be replicated here. Thus Diana Russell's probability sample in San Francisco showed no association between sexual abuse and a father's education or occupation.[113] Peters' study of black and white women in Los Angeles could find no relationship between sexual abuse and either parental education or standard measures of social class.[114] And there are numerous other similar findings.[115] It could be that the middle classes are more open about abuse experiences when questioned by middle class interviewers and so report more abuse, but there is no evidence or inferential support for this conclusion.[116] It is impossible to draw conclusions from the families of

---

[107] T. Sonder, 'Incest Crimes in Sweden and Their Causes', *Acta Psychiatrica et Neurologica*, vol. 2, pp. 379–401 (1936); M. S. Guttmacher, *Sex Offences*, New York, Norton, 1951.

[108] I. B. Weiner, 'On Incest: A Survey', *Excerpta Criminologica*, vol. 4, p. 37 (1964).

[109] D. Walters, *Physical and Sexual Abuse of Children: Causes and Treatment*, Bloomington, Indiana Univ. Press, 1975. See also *op. cit.*, note 55, pp. 67–69.

[110] D. E. H. Russell, *The Secret Trauma: Incest in the Lives of Girls and Women*, New York, Basic Books, 1986 (no association between sexual abuse and measures of father's education or occupation). For agreement, see Finkelhor, *op. cit.*, note 95.

[111] *Cf.* M. D. A. Freeman, *The Rights and Wrongs of Children*, London, Frances Pinter, 1983, pp. 111–114.

[112] See M. D. A. Freeman, 'Child Welfare: Law and Control' in (eds.) J. Jowell and M. Partington, *Welfare Law and Policy*, London, Frances Pinter, 1979, pp. 223–231.

[113] *Op. cit.*, note 110.

[114] S. D. Peters' Doctoral Dissertation, quoted in *op. cit.*, note 55, p. 67.

[115] P. Miller's Doctoral Dissertation, also quoted *ibid.*, p. 67 and 69.

[116] See *ibid.*, p. 69.

Cleveland where abuse was diagnosed, but certainly there the impression was created of a problem found both in poorer working and unemployed families and in the middle-class, including professional families.

Even if poverty were linked with sexual abuse, it would still be necessary to demonstrate a causal relationship. What in poverty could be said to lead to abuse? Unemployment leading to greater access to the child (why then don't more women abuse children?), over-crowding and lack of privacy (but this may give the other parent greater opportunity to observe the abuse and to 'collude' or report it to the authorities, so that it would show up in the statistics), social isolation?

Social isolation is a commonly-cited cause of sexual abuse. Thus, the Kempes in *The Common Secret* assert that 'there are isolated communities or sub-cultures in which incest is accepted readily'.[117] Is there any evidence for this? Or does it just find its source in racist myths and class stereotypes? It is true that early researchers[118] did emphasize that incest rates were higher in rural than in urban environments and there is some anecdotal evidence[119] of concentrations of abusive families in rural areas. But the research studies, again American, do not associate abuse with isolated country communities:[120] indeed, the work of Miller[121] and Wyatt[122] suggests higher rates of abuse amongst women brought up in urban areas.

Studies do, however, confirm that sexual abuse victims appear to be isolated among their peers.[123] Those with fewer friends have been found to have more experiences of sexual abuse. But is this because they are looking for friendship and abusers take advantage of this, or is social isolation the 'result of having been victimized rather than a risk factor'?[124]

Other socio-environmental factors do correlate with abuse. A number of studies have found higher vulnerability to sexual abuse among women who

---

[117] R. S. Kempe and C. H. Kempe, *The Common Secret: Sexual Abuse of Children and Adolescents*, New York, Freeman, 1984, p. 51.

[118] *Op. cit.*, note 82, pp. 45–50 contains an insightful critique of the 'sub-culture' interpretation.

[119] See R. Summit and J. Kryso, *op. cit.*, note 11.

[120] Finkelhor, *op. cit.*, note 95, did find a significantly high rate (44 per cent) among college student women who had grown up on farms.

[121] Adolescents from farm communities reported the lowest rates (*op. cit.*, note 15).

[122] Higher rates in urban areas ('The Sexual Abuse of Afro-American and White American Women in Childhood', *Child Abuse and Neglect*, vol. 9, pp. 507–519, 1985).

[123] For example, Finkelhor (*op. cit.*, note 95) found that women with two or fewer friends at 12 had more experience of sexual abuse.

[124] *Op. cit.*, note 55, p. 72.

have lived without their biological fathers at some time during childhood,[125] though in several the finding is qualified.[126] There may also be a link between parental unavailability and abuse: girls who are victimized are more likely to have mothers who were employed outside the home, according to some studies;[127] they are more likely to have mothers who were disabled or ill[128] (but since the illnesses associated are alcoholism, depression and psychosis, one wonders which came first—the illness or the abuse?); they are more likely to witness conflict between their parents;[129] they are more likely to report a poor relationship with one of their parents.[130] Again, with these last two factors, there must be some doubt as to whether they are genuine risk factors rather than findings which result from abuse. A girl being abused by her father is likely to perceive there is conflict between her parents and/or perceive a poor relationship with her mother.

This leads us to the cultural interpretation of child sexual abuse. As with similar interpretations of other violence against women,[131] including domestic violence,[132] this is explicitly feminist. Such an interpretation is found in Florence Rush's *The Best Kept Secret*,[133] in Herman's study of father-daughter incest,[134] in the writings of Diana Russell,[135] of McIntyre,[136] Taubman[137] and Wattenberg,[138] in Sarah Nelson's important study[139] as well as in

---

[125] See Finkelhor, *op. cit.*, note 95; also S. D. Peters, *op. cit.*, note 114 (but only for white women).

[126] See *op. cit.*, note 55, p. 73.

[127] See Russell, *op. cit.*, note 110; J. Landis, 'Experiences of 500 Children with Adult Sexual Deviants', *Psychiatric Quarterly Supplement*, vol. 30, pp. 91–109 (1956).

[128] See J. Herman and L. Hischman, 'Families at Risk for Father-Daughter Incest'. *Amer. J. of Psychiatry* vol. 138, pp. 967–970 (1981); also D. Finkelhor, *op. cit.*, note 95.

[129] See J. Landis, *op. cit.*, note 127; D. Finkhelor, *op. cit.*, note 95.

[130] See J. Landis, *op. cit.*, note 127; D. Finkelhor, *op. cit.*, note 95; K. Gruber and R. Jones, *op. cit.*, note 95.

[131] J. Chapman and M. Gates (eds.), *The Victimization of Women*, Beverly Hills, Sage, 1978; J. Hanmer, *Women, Violence and Social Control*, London, Macmillan, 1987.

[132] K. Yllö and M. Bogard, *Feminist Perspectives on Wife Abuse*, Beverly Hills, Sage 1988.

[133] Englewood Cliffs, New Jersey, Prentice Hall, 1980.

[134] *Father-Daughter Incest*, Cambridge, Mass., Harvard Univ. Press, 1981.

[135] *Op. cit.*, note 110; also *Sexual Exploitation*, Beverly Hills, Sage, 1984.

[136] K. McIntyre, 'Role of Mothers In Father-Daughter Incest: A Feminist Analysis', *Social Work*, no. 81, pp. 462–46 (1981).

[137] S. Taubman, 'Incest In Context', *Social Work*, no. 29, pp. 35–40 (1984).

[138] E. Wattenberg, 'In a Different Light: A Feminist Perspective in the Role of Mothers in Father-Daughter Incest', *Child Welfare*, vol. 64, pp. 203–211 (1985).

[139] *Op. cit.*, note 82.

the post-Cleveland analysis of Bea Campbell[140] and those who put together the special *Feminist Review* number[141] entitled 'Family Secrets: Child Sexual Abuse'. Feminism not only offers a different interpretation of child sexual abuse but also challenges the responses of orthodoxy, in particular those of 'family systems' theory and family therapy.[142] It asks what is wrong with the functioning of the family and how can it be put back together again. It refuses to share responsibility or to blame victims. Its solutions are elsewhere, in cultural redefinitions to tackle the problem at societal level, and in excluding and punishing the perpetrator to deal with the individual case.

For feminists child sexual abuse is an example of the inequality between the sexes produced by a patriarchal social system. Says Wattenberg: 'The father rapes, abuses, brutalizes, and assaults the children and the mother, but somehow it is the mother's or child's fault'.[143] Men have been taught that they have the right to have their sexual urges satisfied. Belief that there was open access to wives led to the marital rape immunity surviving until 1991.[144] The extension to that other chattel, the daughter, seems quite logical, particularly if the wife for one reason or another is unavailable. And the structure of the family and society is such that both wife and children are trapped within dependency.[145]

An understanding of abuse requires an understanding of power. We have come to accept that rape is not so much a crime of sex, but a power trip.[146] In part sexual abuse has to be similarly understood. Herman, for example, documents the way in which the fathers of incest victims appear to those victims, when interviewed as adults, to have been dominating and authoritarian. These men exercise rigid and authoritarian control over wives and

---

[140] *Unofficial Secrets: Child Sexual Abuse—The Cleveland Case*, London, Virago, 1988.

[141] No. 28 (Spring 1988). In particular, see M. MacLeod and E. Saraga, 'Challenging the Orthodoxy: Towards a Feminist Theory', pp. 16–55. See also J. Hadley, 'Mum is Not The Word', *Community Care*, 5 November 1987, pp. 24–26.

[142] As in P. Mrazek and A. Bentovim 'Incest and the Dysfunctional Family Systems' in P. Mrazek and C. H. Kempe, *Sexually Abused Children and Their Families*, Oxford, Pergamon Press, 1981 or R. Porter, *Child Sexual Abuse Within The Family*, London, Tavistock, 1984.

[143] *Op. cit.*, note 138, p. 206.

[144] An extraordinary defence of this was offered by is B. Amiel as late as 1989. See her, 'An Unwanted Act', *The Times*, 24 March 1989.

[145] M. D. A. Freeman, 'Legal Ideologies, Patriarchal Precedents and Domestic Violence', in M. D. A. Freeman, *State, Law and the Family: Critical Perspectives*, London, Tavistock, 1984, pp. 51–78.

[146] J. and H. Schwendinger, 'Rape Myths', *Crime and Social Justice*, vol. 1, p. 18 (1974).

daughters, if necessary using force to impose their domination.[147] Jackson notes that 'child molesters and child rapists are almost invariably men who have learnt to express their sexuality through aggression, to seek power over others and to be attracted to the vulnerable'.[148] Is it possible to understand masculinity without seeing it in terms of aggression and violence?

There are those who respond by arguing that male sexuality is predetermined biologically, that it is produced by a biological drive, the function of which is the reproduction of the species. Men cannot help it: their sexuality is uncontrollable. To quote Ruth Porter's standard text: 'these men may misunderstand the adolescent's behaviour and be sexually aroused by it; or physical chastisement may lead the perpetrator to the excitement that blends into sexual activity'.[149] Clearly, these men are to be pitied! In one sense they are. They have not resisted or thrown off those definitions of masculine sexuality which most boys acquire during socialization. After all, most do. Most sexual abuse may be perpetrated by males, but most males are not sex abusers.

It becomes important, therefore, to understand the processes by which masculine sexuality is constructed. Stephen Frosh's attempt to do so is most thoughtful.[150] I quote it at length:

> Some theorists...draw attention to differential patterns of conscious and unconscious socialization for boys and girls which, together with wider social images of masculine sexuality, have the effect of constructing men as alienated from intimate relations and from our sexuality.... The characteristic patterns of masculinity, focusing on independence and "hardness" and turning away from intimacy and nurture, follow from this. In particular it produces a severely narrowed rendering of sexuality, operating primarily in two convergent ways. First, sex is one of the few means by which men aspire to closeness with others, and as such it becomes the carrier of all the unexpressed desires that men's emotional illiteracy produces. However, this same process makes sex dangerous to men whose identity is built on the denial of emotion; sex then becomes split off, limited to the activity of the penis, an act rather than an encounter. At the same time, sex becomes tied up with competition, separation and power—something used to bolster a

---

[147] *Op. cit.*, note 11, ch. 5.
[148] S. Jackson, *Childhood and Sexuality*, Oxford, Blackwell, 1982, p. 173.
[149] *Op. cit.*, note 141, p. 9.
[150] 'Issues For Men Working With Sexually Abused Children', *British Journal of Psychotherapy* vol. 3(4), pp. 332–339 (1987). See also *op. cit.*, note 37, p. 24.

man's sense of masculinity rather than to create a bond with another. The link between such a form of masculinity and sexual abuse is apparent: it is not just present, but *inherent* in a mode of personality organisation that rejects intimacy. Sex as defence and as triumph slides naturally into sex as rejection and degradation of the other.

As he acknowledges, there are also important questions relating to the processes whereby most men learn not to abuse children. He sees these as connected with the 'quality of their relationships in early life, internalization of moral constraints, and the development of capacities to form positive sexual and emotional relationships with adults'. But he adds: 'if there are systematic factors that make men more likely to sexually abuse children, then these factors will be present more or less strongly in all men'. Sex, dominance and abuse do not have to be linked: there is no biological inevitability. But in our culture they are and they produce the conditions in which the sexual abuse of children occurs, and excuses are proffered.

Much more work needs to be done but, in the light of our existing knowledge and our understanding of closely-related phenomena like rape and domestic violence, it is the cultural explanation of child-sexual abuse which most convinces. Armed with it, would we not look at orthodox solutions rather differently? With the kind of understanding it brings, would we not respond to Cleveland differently? How then are we to respond to the Cleveland crisis and its aftermath? What happened in Cleveland? What went wrong? Was sexual abuse properly managed? Were the resources of the legal system used efficiently, effectively and appropriately? What has emerged from Cleveland and the inquiry and litigation that it spawned? Are there lessons for the future? It is to these questions that we must now turn.

WHAT HAPPENED IN CLEVELAND?

Cleveland hit the headlines in June 1987.[151] The chronology of events leading up to the crisis has been told, variously, elsewhere.[152] No more

---

[151] Mainly in the *Daily Mail*. But see in particular F. Mount, 'Children Need Justice Not Moral Panic', *Daily Telegraph*, 3 July 1987, E. Rantzen, 'Listen To The Children's Cry', *Sunday Times*, 5 July 1987; M. Toner, 'Should a Father Be Afraid To Kiss His Daughter Goodnight?', *Sunday Express*, 28 July 1987; S. Weir, 'What If The State Kidnaps Your Child?', *London Daily News*, 23 July 1987. On the role of the press see M. Nava, 'Cleveland and the Press', *Feminist Review* no. 28, pp. 103–121.

[152] By Stuart Bell, *op. cit.*, note 29, and Bea Campbell, *op. cit.*, note 48.

than a brief summary is required. The events identified reveal how the historian perceives the 'crisis'. One could dig in the nineteenth century for insights and parallels;[153] one could look back to the events surrounding the discovery of the battered child where there are parallels too.[154] The more immediate background to Cleveland was the *Lancet* article of Hobbs and Wynne in 1986 with its assertion that anorectal abuse was more common than the battered-child syndrome ('More children are buggered than battered'),[155] the NSPCC's focus on sexual abuse,[156] the BBC *Childline* project which commenced in October 1986[157] and the Blom-Cooper reports *A Child In Trust*[158] and, more particularly, the results of the inquiry into the death of Kimberley Carlile, *A Child In Mind*.[159] The reports were highly critical of the 'rule of optimism'[160] that seemed to prevail in social services departments. They urged that greater emphasis be placed on the social control role of social workers and that, in particular, greater use should be made of the resource of law in tackling child abuse. Social workers in particular were castigated for not intervening swiftly enough or effectively.

The more immediate background to Cleveland itself was the declaration in 1986 by Cleveland County Council of child abuse as a priority and the appointment of a special child abuse consultant, Sue Richardson. Dr Marietta Higgs was appointed consultant paediatrician at Middlesbrough General Hospital in January 1987. Some six months before she had seen for the first time the phenomenon of 'reflex relaxation and anal dilatation'. She had recently learnt from Dr Wynne (the co-author of the *Lancet* article) that this is a sign found in children subject to anal abuse. The anal dilatation test is at the heart of the controversy surrounding Cleveland. Its

---

[153] See J. B. Twitchell, *Forbidden Partners*, New York, Columbia University Press, 1987.

[154] See B. Nelson, *Making An Issue of Child Abuse: Political Agenda Setting For Social Problems*, Chicago, Univ. of Chicago Press, 1984, and N. Parton, *op. cit.*, note 5.

[155] C. Hobbs and J. Wynne, 'Buggery In Childhood: A Common Syndrome of Child Abuse' *Lancet*, 2, pp. 792–796 (1986). Dr Wynne now says the test was 'given too much prominence' in the Cleveland affair (*The Independent*, 13 July 1988).

[156] See T. Simmons, *Child Sexual Abuse—An Assessment Process*, London, NSPCC, 1986 (Occasional Paper No. 1).

[157] Established by BBC TV on October 31 1986. On concern over how to handle cases brought to light by Childline see P. Hildrew, *The Guardian*, 28 November, 1987.

[158] The Jasmine Beckford report (published by L. B. of Brent, 1985).

[159] Published by L. B. of Greenwich in 1987.

[160] The phrase was coined by R. Dingwall *et al.* in *The Protection of Children*, Oxford, Basil Blackwell, 1983.

novelty, so often stressed during the last couple of years, lies in its application to detect the buggery of children: the diagnosis is well-known in forensic pathology.[161]

Using this aid to diagnosis, though not it alone,[162] Dr Higgs and a colleague, Dr Geoffrey Wyatt proceeded to diagnose a large number of cases in which, in their view, sexual abuse (in particular anal abuse) had occurred. In total 125 children in Cleveland were diagnosed as sexually abused between February and July 1987, 121 of them by Dr Higgs and Dr Wyatt. In wardship cases brought by the local authority 27 of the children were dewarded and went home with the proceedings dismissed; 24 went home on conditions which included supervision orders and conditions as to medical examination, and two of them went home on interim care orders. As at the time of the writing of the Butler-Sloss report (the spring of 1988), nine other children who were wards of court remained in the care of the County Council and away from their families. Of those children not made wards of court, a further 27 were the subject of place of safety orders. In all, again using evidence available at the time the Inquiry report was written, 21 children remain in care. Of the 121 children diagnosed by Drs Higgs and Wyatt as sexually abused, 98 are now at home.[163] The sheer weight of cases, the number of them in which judges subsequently concluded that sexual abuse had not occurred, the seemingly routinized way in which Drs Higgs and Wyatt used the anal dilatation test, the ways in which children were removed from families, the trampling upon parental rights—all these matters naturally gave, and continue to give, cause for concern.

We may never know exactly what happened in Cleveland. There is no doubt that the events of the first half of 1987 created a moral panic and that the folk devils[164] were the two paediatricians, Drs Higgs and Wyatt, and not those (in Cleveland and elsewhere) who were abusing young girls. There is a close parallel: in the aftermath of the Jasmine Beckford[165] and Kimberley Carlile[166] cases it was the social workers who, allegedly, had failed to pre-

---

[161] In this sense it is not a 'recent discovery' (and see *op. cit.*, note 1, para. 11. 26).

[162] *Op. cit.*, note 1, para. 8. 8. 73.

[163] This does not mean that some of these were not sexually abused. Further, we do not know how many of the fathers are also there.

[164] See S. Cohen, *Folk Devils and Moral Panics*, London, MacGibbon and Kee, 1972; S. Hall, *Policing The Crisis*, London, Macmillan, 1978; F. Fitzpatrick and D. Milligan, *The Truth About The Aids Panic*, London, Junius, 1987.

[165] As to which see *A Child In Trust*, London, L. B. of Brent, 1985.

[166] See *A Child In Mind*, London, L. B. of Greenwich, 1987. This point is made in the Butler-Sloss report also (*op. cit.*, note 1, p. 244, para. 15).

vent the deaths to whom opprobrium was attributed, not the men at whose hands the girls died. There is also a causal link: it was, in part, a response to the press social services departments had received when they failed to intervene in these well-publicized cases that Cleveland adopted, what appears in retrospect to have been, an over-interventionist policy.

Whilst not wishing to underestimate the importance of child sexual abuse, what Cleveland also reveals is abuse by the system. Cleveland was a battleground for personalities and social agencies. On one side were paediatricians and social workers who were too ready to diagnose sexual abuse. On the other were other doctors and the police who did not want to see signs of abuse. In the process, parents' rights were ignored and many children were unnecessarily damaged. Dr Higgs was right to believe that child sexual abuse had long gone undetected and right to believe that 'paediatricians had a responsibility to right this wrong.[167] But she had unswerving confidence in her diagnosis and this was wrong too often for us to repose any confidence in her. With Dr Higgs was Sue Richardson, the Cleveland child abuse consultant, who saw sex abuse as a 'unique constellation of trauma'[168] and never questioned a diagnosis. The techniques employed by the paediatricians (in particular the anal reflex dilatation test) and by the social workers and child psychiatrists (in particular the disclosure interview) are both suspect and neither is criticized as rigorously in the Butler-Sloss report as it should be. In the other camp were the police who failed to consider or understand the complexities of child sexual abuse. With them was the police surgeon Dr Alistair Irvine who adopted a position 'where his examination was unlikely to support an allegation or complaint'[169] and who 'rejected out of hand clinical symptoms and signs that other doctors considered significant'.[170] The report notes that his personal and emotional involvement compromised his professional position. In the middle of this battleground were the parents and the children. Parents like the Norths[171] whose 2-year-old, brought to Dr Higgs suffering from constipation, was diagnosed as having been anally abused. He had just had his first bowel movement in 17 days. This set in train a horrendous chain of events, with the other two children of the family

---

[167] *Op. cit.*, note 1, para. 8. 8. 71.

[168] *Ibid.*, para. 4. 187.

[169] *Ibid.*, para. 7. 39.

[170] *Idem.* See also B. Campbell, 'Heavy Hand of the Law Laid on Cleveland', *The Independent*, 26 September 1988.

[171] Neither the 'Norths' nor the 'Wests' are the real names. They were the ones used in an ITV programme transmitted on July 5, 1988 (the evening before the Butler-Sloss report was published).

280 *Chapter 13*

being similarly diagnosed, and the Norths only winning their children back after seven months. The social services withdrew at the wardship stage and the Norths were awarded costs, but the true costs to them and their children are inestimable. Or like the Wests, another example of constipation in a 2-year-old being diagnosed as anal abuse. Mrs West was 16 weeks pregnant at the time and was left in no doubt that once delivered of her baby it would be taken into care forthwith. They could not believe this could 'happen in England'. They describe themselves as 'members of the establishment' who believe in the system. At a case conference, to which they were not invited, it was decided that they could have one hour of access a week to their daughter. A second medical opinion diagnosed a mega-colon but not before the child had spent a month in care. And it was not just children taken to see a paediatrician with disorders which warranted anal examination who were given the anal dilatation test. Many with routine ailments like earache and asthma were subjected to this test,[172] which Dr Higgs had learnt at a half-day seminar in Leeds in June 1986.

The Butler-Sloss report apportions responsibility. All the agencies involved, save one, are shown, in one way or other, to be at fault. No one person is singled out for blame. The criticism is spread wide, highlighting a lack of proper understanding between social agencies, and a lack of communication. Dr Higgs and Dr Wyatt are criticized for 'the over-confidence with which they pursued the detection of sexual abuse in children referred to them'.[173] But, they were not solely nor indeed principally responsible for the subsequent management of the children concerned'.[174] Nevertheless, 'the certainty of their findings in relation to children diagnosed by them without prior complaint, posed particular problems for the Police and Social Services'.[175] The director of social services is also criticized. He is said to have 'reacted to events'[176] rather than controlled them, and to be at fault for not questioning the paediatric diagnoses and the need to take the children from

---

[172] There was no 'routine screening for sexual abuse' according to the Report (para. 9. 3. 22. 1a). The Report includes (*op. cit.*, note 1, para. 8. 8. 75) that 'she did not examine children for sexual abuse other than on occasions when in her professional judgment there were grounds to do so'. 'It was only rarely that she relied on R. A. D. as the 'only physical sign' (para. 8. 8. 73).

[173] *Op. cit.*, note 1, p. 243, para. 7. (see also para. 8. 8. 81). See also Judge Cohen in *Cleveland C. C. v. D* [1988] F. C. R. 615 (their concern to find sexual abuse 'paramount', so evidence not considered objectively).

[174] *Idem.*

[175] *Idem.*

[176] *Ibid.*, para. 4. 186. His own account of events is found in *Social Work Today*, 7 July 1988, pp. 12–13.

their homes. The police are criticized for allowing a rift to develop between themselves and social services, and for 'taking no effective steps to break the deadlock'.[177] The only agency not criticized are the magistrates. Since they appear to have granted every application for a place of safety order (without which authority none of the children could have been removed from home), the fact that they have got off virtually scot-free leaves one with a distinct feeling that those concerned with the administration of the law are immune from criticism. Could it be that Lady Justice Butler-Sloss would have felt embarrassment at subjecting legal personnel to criticism? The report describes the place of safety process as involving a 'discretionary judicial act'.[178] And so it should be, but in what did the discretion consist in Cleveland, and what judicial qualities were being exercised? The part played by magistrates and the place of safety process is a matter for concern. It, together with other of the problematic features of Cleveland, will be considered in the next section of this article.

PROTECTING ABUSED CHILDREN AND INNOCENT PARENTS

The central dilemma of the child sexual abuse process is how to protect abused children whilst at the same time protecting innocent parents.[179] In Cleveland they did not get the balance right. As a result a number (we will never know exactly how many) innocent parents and non-abused children suffered. We will never know either how many sick children were kept away from hospitals (and not just in Cleveland) because parents feared unfounded allegations of sexual abuse. We will never know the damage Cleveland has done to the credibility of a system, the aim of which was to protect abused children. What went wrong?

(i) The Reflex Anal Dilatation Test

So much of the criticism of what happened in Cleveland has centred on the reflex anal dilatation test that it is appropriate to begin with it. It is not the technique that is new but its application to tackle a form of child sex-

---

[177] *Ibid.*, p. 244, para. 9.

[178] *Ibid.*, para. 16. 5.

[179] *Cf.* D. J. Besharov, 'Introduction' to H. Wakefield and R. Underwager, *Accusations of Child Sexual Abuse*, Springfield, Illinois, C. C. Thomas, 1988, pp. 3–15. See also A. Neustatter, 'For the Sake of the Innocents', *The Guardian*, 5 July 1988.

ual abuse is.[180] What appeared to cause both astonishment and horror in Cleveland was that it was being used to uncover so much anal abuse. Is anal abuse (as opposed to other forms of sexual abuse) so prevalent? The incidence studies all appear to suggest that, amongst girls at least, it is rare.[181] The Hospital for Sick Children in Great Ormond Street, London appears to think that anal abuse accounts for only 1 per cent of that which it sees.[182] This could be explained by the fact that the test pioneered in Leeds was not being used. But it may also point to the unreliability of that test. The sign is as follows:

> When the buttocks are separated, the external sphincter and then the internal sphincter open so that the observer can see through the anal canal into the rectum. The anal sphincters are controlled in part automatically, in part by learned unconscious behaviour, and in part consciously; all in a very complex system not altogether understood by the experts. The controlling mechanism will change with age and will be influenced by levels of awareness and local sensations.... In many children subject to anal abuse, Hobbs and Wynne found that the canal opened on buttock separation. Sometimes it opened and shut, (winking); sometimes it opened and stayed open so that the observer could look into the rectum.[183]

At times the impression is created of some kind of magic sign, a sort of infallible litmus test. But this is far from the truth. The signal emitted by the test requires interpretation and there is no consensus on its meaning. As the Butler-Sloss report conceded: 'It is not known whether it occurs in normal individuals'.[184] But it almost certainly does. John McCann's research at the Valley Clinic in Fresno, California (not picked up in the Report) found signs of anal dilatation in 53 per cent of a random sample of

---

[180] *Op. cit.*, note 1, para. 11. 26.

[181] *Op. cit.*, note 45, p. 51. The Great Ormond Street book (ed. by A. Bentovim *et al*, *Child Sexual Abuse Within The Family*, London, Wright, 1988, barely mentions it (see pp. 67, 79).

[182] This figure was quoted in the ITV documentary on child sexual abuse, transmitted the night before the Butler-Sloss report was published.

[183] *Op. cit.*, note 1, para. 11. 26.

[184] *Ibid.*, para. 11. 28.

268 non-abused children.[185] Dr Graham Clayden,[186] a specialist in chronic bowel disorders at St Thomas's Hospital in London, who gave evidence to the Inquiry and who is quoted in the Report, certainly believes that anal dilatation is a normal response of all of us. Anxiety or fear might cause the opening, and many of the children subjected to the test had plenty of opportunity to express this. The Report states that it does not 'usually occur in normal children',[187] but this question-begs. Constipation, even chronic constipation, is not that abnormal in small children. The problem lies in drawing the conclusion that because anal dilatation is found in many children who have been anally abused that anal dilatation is a sign of sexual abuse when it may equally well be a symptom of other disorders or indeed a normal reaction. As the Butler-Sloss report notes: 'Although most experts agreed that anal dilatation may follow anal abuse, there was considerable disagreement as to the other circumstances in which it might occur'.[188]

The Report concludes that the sign of anal dilatation is 'abnormal and suspicious and requires further investigation'.[189] But 'it is not in itself evidence of anal abuse'.[190] However, Dr Higgs and Dr Wyatt did so interpret it and as a result of such interpretations children were removed from parents. The forensic examination did not, as Dr Hobbs and Dr Wynne indicate that it should, take place in the context of the whole child examination. Dr Higgs and Dr Wyatt, both of whom are relatively inexperienced, clearly often read too much into a complex sign and, as a result of simplistic thinking, initiated in a train of action which brought tragedy to a large number of families. The Report is, I think, too kind to Dr Higgs and Dr Wyatt and, it should be added, far too severe on Dr Raine Roberts,[191]

---

[185] This figure is somewhat higher than would be expected. But see now also A. Stanton and R. Sunderland, 'Prevalence of Reflex Anal Dilatation in 200 Children', *Brit. Med. Journal* vol. 298, pp. 802–803 (1989) who found such R.A.D. in 14 per cent of the normal child population. They conclude that it is a sign with poor discriminatory value in diagnosing anal abuse in children (p. 803).

[186] G. S. Clayden, 'Reflex Anal Dilatation Associated with Severe Chronic Constipation in Children', *Archives of Disease in Childhood* vol. 63, pp. 832–836 (1988).

[187] *Op. cit.*, note 1, para. 11. 26. In 'only 18 cases of 121' was R.A.D. the sole physical sign (para. 9. 3. 22. (b)).

[188] *Op. cit.*, note 1, para. 11. 28. DHSS, *Diagnosis of Child Sexual Abuse: Guidance for Doctors*, London, H.M.S.O., 1988, p. 20 recommends that children with R.A.D. 'be seen again at a later date for reassessment'.

[189] *Ibid.*, para. 11. 30.

[190] *Idem.*

[191] She is said to have been unable to provide the Inquiry with 'cool, detached and considered

whose experience of sexual abuse is wider than the Cleveland paediatricians and whose understanding of the issues and context far exceeds theirs.

(ii) The Use of Place of Safety

It is surprising how little attention has been given to place of safety procedures in the past. Their implications, the inter-relationship between the procedures in the 1933 and 1969 Children and Young Persons Acts and the draconian effect of an order have been little understood. In Cleveland, in the first seven months of 1987, 276 place of safety orders were applied for by social workers under powers laid down in section 28 of the 1969 Act. Children having been medically diagnosed as abused, this was, it seemed, the next logical step. It was thought that, armed with such an order, the social services department could consent to the child being medically examined and further medical examination did usually follow the anal dilatation test. If the Cleveland social services department had read the Blom-Cooper report *A Child In Mind* it would have known that a place of safety order does not confer this power (he recommended accordingly a new order, a 'child assessment order'). But this had clearly passed over its heads.[192]

The social services department operated 'a highly interventionist policy'[193] in the use of place of safety orders. A memorandum from the Director directed social workers to apply for them on receiving a diagnosis of sexual abuse from a paediatrician. To enable 'disclosure work' to be carried out, a decision was taken to reverse normal practice and request 28 day orders, the maximum period allowed by statute. Though most of the orders were granted during the day, most applications were also heard by a single magistrate at home and during the hours of court sittings. All but one application was *ex parte* and none was refused. Yet the Butler-Sloss Report persists, rather formalistically, in describing the granting of an order as a 'discretionary judicial act.'[194] There is no doubt that that is what it *ought* to be, just as applications for search warrants by the police and for

---

testimony' (*op. cit.*, note 1, para. 11. 66). But *cf.* Judge Hall in *Cleveland C.C.* v. *C* [1988] F. C. R. 607.

[192] *Op. cit.*, note 166, pp. 153–156. The pros and cons of this are debated in *Childright* no. 55 (April 1988) by A. Wilson (p. 12) and R. Osmond (p. 14).

[193] *Op. cit.*, note 1, para. 10. 7.

[194] *Ibid.*, para. 16. 5.

separate representation orders[195] ought to be judicial acts. But it cannot really be pretended that the granting of place of safety orders in Cleveland during the crisis of 1987 was cloaked with anything more than a veneer of either the judicial or the discretionary. It was a rubber-stamping exercise.

The Report is critical of much of the place of safety decision-making processes in Cleveland: the automatic assumption that the application should be *ex parte*; the lack of communication between magistrates granting orders and the clerk (is that why it appears that there were instances of more than one order on one child?); the use of the order to 'obtain repeat examinations for forensic purposes or for information gathering rather than for continuing treatment';[196] the use of the order and the concomitant denial of access to facilitate 'disclosure work', rightly condemned as an improper use of the legislation.[197] The Report is 'unhappy to see the acceptance of an automatic response by way of place of safety order to certain sets of facts'[198] and is especially critical of Sue Richardson's desire to use the place of safety mechanism 'by way of control as the first stage of intervention and management of the family in situations where there was no immediate danger to the child'[199] This is seen, quite rightly as a 'wholly unjustified use'[200] of the order, though, it has to be added, there is little unique in this reliance on the place of safety mechanism.[201] It should be added that the social services in Cleveland did also use 'voluntary' care, a practice which has been officially approved.[202]

The Butler-Sloss report followed other recent critics in challenging the use made of the 'place of safety' concept.[203] But it was already under sen-

---

[195] But see *R v. Plymouth Juvenile Court ex parte F and F* [1987] 1 F. L. R. 169.
[196] *Op. cit.*, note 1, para. 16. 10.
[197] *Ibid.*, para. 16. 12.
[198] *Ibid.*, para. 16. 14.
[199] *Idem.*
[200] *Idem* (See also p. 246). The views of Dr James Appleyard (reported in *The Independent*, 29 June 1987) that sexually abused children are not in immediate danger of death or serious injury and so can be left until proper proceedings can be gone through is worth noting.
[201] See J. Packman, *Who Needs Care? Social Work Decisions About Children*, Oxford, Blackwell, 1986.
[202] Nevertheless, 'child care practice traditionally relied heavily upon the use of statutory-based interventions and on place of safety orders' (para. 4. 27).
[203] See Packman, *op. cit.*, note 201, pp. 52–54; T. Norris and N. Parton 'The Administration of Place of Safety Orders,' *Journal of Social Welfare Law* pp. 1–16 (1987); Dartington Research Unit, *Place of Safety Orders*, 1985 (unpubl.).

286 *Chapter 13*

tence of death[204] and has now disappeared with the Children Act 1989, which replaces it with the better-designed and fairer emergency protection order.[205] This may account for the rather mild way in which the Report considers the place of safety provisions and, in particular, the role of magistrates and their clerks in the process. It is a virtue of the Report that it is even-handed and balanced, but the magistracy does get off rather lightly. It was carrying out a 'discretionary judicial act'. In what did its discretion consist? What judicial qualities were being exercised? If the magistrates exercised discretion, why were the orders invariably of 28 days' duration? This satisfied the administrative convenience of the social workers, but it is generally accepted that 28 days was too long and that orders of this length were not in the interests of the children or their parents. The new emergency protection orders last for 8 days only (with a possibility of extension by another 7 days in strictly defined circumstances).[206] If the magistrates exercised a judicial function, how much evidence testing was there? The absence of the clerk from the processes is likely to have limited the possibility of this. We do not know how much evidence was questioned, how long the average application took, what magistrates were told or what they asked. How many of the magistrates who granted orders were on the juvenile panel? It would have been appropriate for the Inquiry to have probed rather more deeply into the work of the Cleveland magistrates. There is no reason why legal actors (even when lay persons) should remain immune from critical scrutiny.

(iii) Medical Procedures and Consents

The Cleveland affair raises in acute form the question of who is capable of consenting to a medical examination. In many of the cases parents had taken the children to hospital for a paediatric examination. There can be little doubt that where this was, for example, for a bowel disorder that there was implied consent by the parents to an anal dilatation test. Parents complained, however, that this test was carried out when their child was brought to hospital with a complaint which could not possibly warrant an anal dilatation test. The Butler-Sloss inquiry found this did not happen.[207] That is not my interpretation of the facts but, whether it happened or not,

---

[204] See the Government White Paper, *Law on Child Care and Family Services* Cm. 62, London, H.M.S.O.
[205] See Children Act 1989 sections 44 and 45.
[206] See s. 45 (1), (5) and (6).
[207] *Op. cit.*, note 1, para. 8. 8. 75.

it is worth asking whether consent could be implied to such a test where a child suffering, for example, from ear-ache is taken to a doctor.

A letter from the Social Services Inspectorate,[208] dated February 1988 (that is long after the Cleveland storm), purports to rule that a doctor may conduct an examination to relieve distress, pain and suffering where this is 'immediately essential' for the child's welfare. But many anal dilatation tests were carried out for forensic purposes. It is difficult to see how these can have been 'immediately essential'. A parent could consent on behalf of his or her child: in certain circumstances the child herself can consent.[209] But, in default of such consents, the solution turned to by the local authority, *viz* assuming that a place of safety order gave it the authority to consent to a medical examination for forensic purposes, though understandable, is clearly unacceptable. A place of safety order did not terminate parental rights.[210] Social workers who held one had no more authority to consent to a medical examination on the child than they had prior to obtaining it.

This has changed with the emergency protection order which gives the applicant (in most cases the social services department) 'parental responsibility'[211] for the child, that is 'all the rights, duties, powers, responsibilities and authority which by law a parent of a child has in relation to the child and his property'.[212] Since the parent has the power to consent to medical treatment it will follow that a local authority vested with an emergency protection order will be in a similar position. But should any doubt remain the court, when making an emergency protection order, may give directions it considers appropriate regarding 'medical or psychiatric examination of the child'. It has, therefore, become the norm for a local authority to apply for such directions at the same time as seeking an emergency protection order.

(iv) Access to Children

A major ground of complaint by parents was the fact that they were denied access or given it in restrictive conditions. This caused 'great distress,

---

[208] DHSS Circular (88) 2 *(Medical Examination of a Child Subject To A Place of Safety Order)*.

[209] Family Law Reform Act 1969 s.8(1) (if over 16): *Gillick* v. *West Norfolk and Wisbech A.H.A.* [1986] A. C. 112 (if s/he understands what is involved). But courts may overrule a refusal to consent (see ch. 15).

[210] Part III of the Child Care Act 1980 does not apply (and see *op. cit.*, note 1, para. 16.9).

[211] Defined in section 3 of the Children Act 1989.

[212] A definition hardly more helpful than that in Children Act 1975 s. 85 (1).

much resentment and created great difficulties'.[213] The reason why access was refused or restricted was to enable 'disclosure work' with the child to take place to confirm the sexual abuse.

The Butler-Sloss report is rightly critical of this. It argues that the restriction or denial of access is 'not...within the authorisation of a place of safety order, save where the safety of the child required it, for example a violent parent or the likelihood of removal of the child from the place of safety'.[214] The Report also notes that 'there was for the parents no recourse to the courts either under the place of safety order or under the interim care order' [save under s. 12 B of the Child Care Act 1980].[215]

The contradictions found in these two statements must be noted. On the one hand we are told that the local authority could not by virtue of a place of safety order deny access (though this is qualified). On the other hand, the Report draws attention to the absence of legal redress, where access was denied. The problem is accentuated because place of safety and interim care orders are drawn together. They are hardly juridical equivalents and the Report rightly criticizes social workers in Cleveland for treating place of safety orders as if they were interim care orders.[216]

Were Cleveland social services able to deny parents access? The matter was little discussed, and yet the answer is clear: a place of safety order did not terminate parental rights and this included (under s.85 (l) of the Children Act 1975) a right of access. The Cleveland parents therefore had the right to unrestricted access to their children. Those who drafted the access provisions in 1983[217] realized that access could not be denied under a place of safety order: that is why they did not provide for parents denied access to apply to the juvenile court for an access order. Once an interim care order was made, such an application was allowed. Then why, one wonders, did Lady Justice Butler-Sloss suggest there was no recourse to the courts under an interim care order. This is clearly wrong. It follows from this analysis that a test case brought by a Cleveland parent for judicial review of the decision to refuse access where the local authority was retaining the child under a place of safety order should have succeeded. It may be added that the Code of Practice on Access to Children in Care was also ignored routinely in Cleveland.[218] The Report could have been more forthright in its condemna-

---

[213] *Op. cit.*, note 1, para. 10. 19.
[214] *Ibid.*, para. 16. 11.
[215] *Ibid.*, para. 10. 19.
[216] *Ibid.*, para. 4. 414.
[217] Health and Social Services and Social Security Adjudications Act 1983, Sch. 1.
[218] Described in *M* v. *Berkshire C.C.* [1985] FLR 257, 263, 'as an aid to construction' of the

tion of the Cleveland policies on access. It could also have been clearer in its analysis of the concepts involved.

(v) Disclosure Interviews

One of the most problematic features of the investigative process is the so-called 'disclosure interview'. Pioneered at the Great Ormond Street Hospital they are doubtless a valuable technique if used sensitively by trained professionals. But when they fall into the wrong hands they can become coercive, intrusive and an affront to the dignity of the child. A fundamental problem of the 'disclosure' approach is it implies there is always something to disclose. At its worst, a point often reached in Cleveland interviews, the assumption is that the child who does not disclose is 'in denial', that is to say cannot bring herself to accuse a parent. But, as Latey J put it, 'it would be helpful to the court if the questioners were alert to any indications of an innocent, as well as a sinister, interpretation and recorded them in their notes, reports and evidence'.[219] There is, in other words, a third possibility—the child has no sexual abuse to disclose. The danger is that this is not considered a viable, meaningful option. The premise is that abuse has occurred and that the child must be helped to reveal her awful secret. The wheel has come full circle: not so long ago a child who claimed she has been sexually abused would rarely be believed and now one who insists she has not is also sometimes disbelieved. Some of the Cleveland interviews were quite ghastly with children hectored and bullied into saying they were abused when they had insisted throughout they had not been. Sometimes they were threatened they would not see their parents until they admitted they had been abused.[220] Many were made to feel 'acutely uncomfortable'[221] as they were grilled by big, powerful adults and assured 'You can trust me, darling'.

---

statute but in *R* v. *Bolton M.B.C. ex p. B* [1985] FLR 343, 351 the Divisional Court refused to use the Code 'as a guide to the proper meaning of the words of the statutes'.

[219] *Re M* [1987] 1 F.L.R. 293, 296.

[220] Examples like this were shown in a number of TV programmes on the Cleveland affair, including that on ITV on 5 July 1988.

[221] *Per* Dr Elizabeth Tylden, as quoted in ITV programme on the Cleveland affair, 5 July 1988. According to Eastham J. in *Cleveland C.C.* v. *E* [1988] FCR 625 some children are left with 'psychiatric scars' as a result of 'relentless' questioning.

Questions have been raised as to the value as evidence of diagnostic interviews.[222] A series of cases, conveniently reported in one issue of *Family Law Reports*,[223] goes some way toward answering these questions. Thus, the court is unlikely to give weight to anything the child has said in response to leading questions.[224] The use of anatomically correct dolls as cues or prompts is said to be of limited value only and therefore must be treated cautiously.[225] The courts are unhappy to accept an interviewer's account and interpretation of the interview with the child unless a transcript and a videotaped recording are made available.[226] Further, the assistance that the recording can give is 'limited to enabling the court to catch the flavour of the interview, noting the length of pauses, the attitude of the child, the tone of voice of the interviewer, and so on'.[227] It could never be an acceptable substitute for the overall view which the court had to take of the evidence as a whole. There can be intervention (so that the child can be protected) even though the evidence does not indicate who has abused the child.[228] The court can conclude that a child has been abused on a balance of probabilities, that is on evidence short of what would be required to sustain a criminal conviction.[229] It has been said that a higher degree of probability is needed to satisfy a court that an individual has sexually abused a child than that required to establish that the child has been sexually abused. The Court of Appeal refused to express a view as to whether this dichotomy is generally correct, but held that where there is only one person who could be the abuser of the child, so that a finding of abuse inevitably leads to a finding on the identity of the perpetrator, the standard to be applied must be the higher standard.[230]

But the diagnostic interview raises many more questions than have been addressed in the cases or in the Butler-Sloss report. A few of them will be

---

[222] See G. Douglas and C. Willmore, 'Diagnostic Interviews as Evidence in Cases of Child Sexual Abuse', 17 *Family Law* 151–154 (1987).

[223] [1987] 1 F.L.R. 269–346.

[224] *Re E* [1987] 1 F.L.R. 269.

[225] *Re N* [1987] 1 F.L.R. 280.

[226] *Re M* [1987] 1 F.L.R. 293; *Re G (No. 2)* [1988] 1 F.L.R. 314.

[227] *Re W* [1987] 1 F.L.R. 297, 307.

[228] *Re J S* [1981] 2 F. L. R. 146.

[229] *Re W* [1987] 1 F. L. R. 297. A higher degree of probability is required to satisfy the court that a parent is guilty of sexual abuse than to satisfy it that the child has been abused by an unknown person (*Cleveland C. C.* v. *A & B* [1988] F. C. R. 593).

[230] See Sheldon J. in *Re G (No. 2)* [1988] 1 F. L. R. 314 and Balcombe L.J. in *Re W* [1994] 1 F. L. R. 419, 425.

raised here. Let us start with so-called 'anatomically correct' dolls. These are in widespread use.[231] Originally, they were used in therapy as toys and as aids to assist sexually abused children come to terms with their experience. Now they have come to be used as diagnostic tools in the investigation of suspected cases of sexual abuse. But, as Gabriel notes, many who work in the child protection field are untrained in play therapy. 'The result has been that material produced by children in this manner can appear to confirm suspicions of sexual abuse when it may actually be no more than a normal reaction to the dolls and the situation'.[232] King and Yuille point out that 'the dolls serve the function of a suggestive question with young children. The genitals and orifices of the dolls suggest a play pattern to children, and that play may be misinterpreted as evidence for abuse'.[233] Gabriel describes a study of 19 non-abused children who were observed with the dolls. They demonstrated behaviour which could have been interpreted as indicating likely sexual abuse. Many showed overt interest in the genitals and/or unusual interaction with them. He concludes that 'on the evidence of the dolls alone...the suspect will almost always be found "guilty", especially if the examiner is already biased in that direction'.[234]

A leading study which claims to demonstrate the value of using anatomically correct dolls is by White, Strom, Santilli and Halpin.[235] They report that their sample of non-sexually abused children interacted differently with the dolls than did the abused sample. But the article gives us no information on other differences which may have existed between the two groups, without which it is impossible to draw conclusions.[236] Even the editors of *Child Abuse and Neglect*, in which the article appears, preface it by stating that 'to date no data have been published which clearly delineate the responses to these interviews by children who have not been sexually abused. This study

---

[231] Discussed in the Cleveland report (*op. cit.*, note 1) at paras. 12. 54–12. 64. They are said to be 'highly undesirable as a routine prop in initial interviews' (para. 12. 64).

[232] R. M. Gabriel, 'Anatomically Correct Dolls in the Diagnosis of Sexual Abuse of Children', *The Journal of the Melanie Klein Society* vol. 3 (2), pp. 40–51 (1982) at p. 42.

[233] M. A. King and J. C. Yuille, 'Suggestibility and the Child Witness' in S. J. Ceci, M. P. Toglia and D. F. Ross (eds.), *Children's Eyewitness Memory*, New York, Springer-Verlag, pp. 24–35, at p. 31 (1987).

[234] *Op. cit.*, note 232, p. 49.

[235] J. White, G. S. Strom, G. Santilli and B. M. Halpin, 'Interviewing Young Sexual Abuse Victims with Anatomically Correct Dolls', *Child Abuse and Neglect* vol. 10, pp. 519–529 (1986).

[236] See, for agreement, H. Wakefield and R. Underwager, *op. cit.*, note 179, p. 205.

is necessary before the results of interviews of children who have been sexually exploited can be accurately interpreted'.[237]

One of the most interesting studies was conducted by Jensen, Realmuto and Wescoe.[238] Twelve children, aged 3 to 8, were interviewed by a single therapist. Three of them were known to have been sexually abused. Four had been referred for evaluation of other conditions (and were psychiatric controls). Five children were non-clinical controls. The interviews were videotaped and a panel, which included psychologists, then viewed the videotapes and rated the behaviours on a scale from 'not at all suspicious' to 'very suspicious'. No differences between groups were found. Some of the non-abused children got the highest rating of 'very suspicious' and some of the abused children got the lowest ratings of all. One of the psychologists identified none of the abused children, another rightly identified two but falsely identified a further three children.

The available data (none of which, incidentally, is picked up in the Butler-Sloss report) suggests that anatomically correct dolls cannot be used to distinguish abused from non-abused children.[239] No data supports the view that abused and non-abused children behave differently when dolls are used as diagnostic or assessment devices. Their use is likely to increase the rate of false positives, that is children said to have been abused when they have not.

Another questionable procedure is the use of children's drawings to diagnose sexual abuse. The assumption is that qualitative features of the drawings may be used as 'signs' that suggest that the child has experienced sexual abuse.[240] But the variability from drawing to drawing is such that particular features of any one drawing are too unreliable to draw any conclusions from them. Non-psychologists, including clerks and typists, have been reported to do as well as psychologists and psychiatrists in interpreting children's drawings.[241] Nevertheless, they continue to be used. Existing evidence

---

[237] *Child Abuse and Neglect* vol. 10, p. 519 (1986).

[238] J. B. Jensen, G. Realmuto and S. Wesloe, Paper To American Academy of Child Psychiatry, Washington, D. C., October 1986.

[239] W. McIver, H. Wakefield and R. Underwager, 'Behavior of Abused and Non-Abused Children in Interview with Anatomically-Correct Dolls', 1987 (unpublished manuscript, quoted *op. cit.*, note 179, pp. 206–208.).

[240] D. B. Harris, *Children's Drawing as Measures of Intellectual Maturity: A Revision and Extension of the Goodenough Draw A Man Test*, New York, Harcourt, Brace and World, 1963; H. B. Roback, 'Human Figure Drawings: Their Utility in the Clinical Psychologist Armanentarian for Personality Assessment', *Psychological Bulletin*, vol. 70, pp. 1–19 (1968).

[241] S. Fisher and R. Fisher, 'Test of Certain Assumptions Regarding Figure Drawing Analysis', Journal of Abnormal and Social Psychology vol. 45, pp. 727–732 (1950); E. Plaut

suggests that they can tell us very little and so should be used with the utmost caution, if at all.[242]

The so-called 'sexual abuse accommodation syndrome' also needs to be critically addressed. It is used by interviewers (and certainly was at Cleveland) to justify their questioning and interpretation of the responses of children during an interview. The concepts of the syndrome, described in an authoritative article by Ronald Summit,[243] are used to decide whether or not a child's statements about being sexually abused are valid or false. He proposes five categories of behaviour that constitute this syndrome: (i) secrecy; (ii) helplessness; (iii) entrapment and accommodation; (iv) delayed, conflicted and unconvincing disclosure; and (v) retraction. Abused children, so Summit argues, will demonstrate these behaviours when interrogated. The syndrome has never been validated; yet it is widely adopted by professionals involved with sexual abuse allegations. Thus, the concept of secrecy is used to support the tactic of continuing to question when a child denies abuse. This syndrome has been enormously influential in practice in this country, in Cleveland and elsewhere. It is therefore worth quoting in full the authoritative observations of Wakefield and Underwager, two leading American experts:

> The application of the sexual abuse accommodation syndrome to children's statements means that nothing they say, nothing they do, can count against the belief that abuse happened. If they deny initially, that's because they have to keep it secret and if you keep at them long enough they will finally admit the secret. If they admit and then deny, that's because they are helpless, confused, and it means they are abused. If they deny, admit, and then retract, that's evidence that they were abused. Everything is evidence that the child has been abused. Once an allegation hits a professional who holds the sexual abuse accommodation syndrome concept and the dogma that children must be believed at all costs, nothing can falsify it.[244]

---

and C. W. Crannell, 'The Ability of Clinical Psychologists To Discriminate Between Drawings of Deteriorated Schizophrenics and Drawings by Normal Subjects', *Psychological Reports*, vol. 1, pp. 153–158 (1955).

[242] C. G. Watson, 'Inter-judge Agreement of Draw-a-Person Diagnostic Impressions', *Journal of Projective Techniques and Personality Assessment* vol. 31, pp. 42–45 (1967).

[243] R. Summit, 'The Child Sexual Abuse Accommodation Syndrome', *Child Abuse and Neglect*, vol. 7, pp. 177–193 (1983).

[244] *Op. cit.*, note 179, p. 215.

Finally, some comments on the interviewing techniques employed are in order. The C.I.B.A. textbook advocates that an interview should begin something like this: 'You told your teacher/granny/foster-mother that Daddy put his hand in your pants/showed you his penis and that this was bothering you'.[245] But all of the research on memory and children as witnesses shows that the most reliable information from young children comes from a condition of free recall.[246] Closed or leading questions result in greater responses, but also greatly increase the risk that the children's answers will not be accurate.[247] The older the child is, the more he or she will be able to produce in free recall. But it is generally agreed that even the few statements produced by young children in free recall are likely to be accurate.[248] Thus, to begin an interview with a question inviting spontaneous, free recall ('Tell me, what happened?') is likely to be much more productive and reliable than the sort of question advocated in the C.I.B.A. publication and commonly found in practice.

It is also not uncommon for interviewers subtly to suggest events to children. A recent American study (by Ceci, Ross and Toglia) showed that young children in particular appear more likely to incorporate 'erroneous post-event information into their subsequent recollections than older children'.[249] It seems that their high level of suggestibility is related to their conformity to what they believe to be the expectation of the adult. Young children are, in other words, not just vulnerable to sexual abuse: they are also vulnerable to adult social influence. They conclude that if erroneous information is introduced in a diagnostic interview it may 'resurface in the form of the child's reconstruction of the events'.[250] Legrand and Underwager comment: 'In the light of their data and findings, it is difficult to locate the source of the optimistic belief that the majority of children's recollections are accurate'.[251] Again, whilst this seems to have the ring of truth to it, it is not research that has been picked up in English child sexual abuse

---

[245] (Ed.) R. Porter, *Child Sexual Abuse Within The Family*, London, Tavistock, 1984, p. 69.

[246] E. F. Loftus and G. M. Davies, 'Distortions In The Memory of Children', *Journal of Social Issues*, vol. 40(2), pp. 51–67 (1984).

[247] H. R. Dent and G. M. Stephenson, 'An Experimental Study of the Effectiveness of Different Techniques of Questioning Child Witnesses', *British Journal of Social and Clinical Psychology*, vol. 18, pp. 41–51 (1979; J. P. Lipton, 'On The Psychology of Eyewitness Testimony', *Journal of Applied Psychology* vol. 62, pp. 90–95 (1977).

[248] This was accepted by the Butler-Sloss inquiry (see *op. cit.*, note 1, para. 12. 34).

[249] S. J. Ceci, D. F. Ross and M. P. Toglia, 'Age Differences In Suggestibility: Narrowing The Uncertainties' in *op. cit.*, note 233, pp. 79–91, at p. 89.

[250] *Ibid.*, p. 90.

[251] *Op. cit.*, note 179, p. 79.

literature. It certainly was not brought to the attention of the Butler-Sloss Inquiry. And yet, of course, like so much of this data it is only an application of well-known and well-respected psychological research into eyewitness testimony that amongst well-informed opinion is taken for granted in examinations of the criminal justice system.[252] Why is it not penetrating the consciousness of those who work in the child sexual abuse area in this country? Is it that in an effort to tackle the acknowledged evil of sexual abuse anything which appears as an obstacle is cast aside or is it just plain ignorance? This question cannot be ignored for the civil liberties implications of misdiagnosis are profound and troubling.

WHERE DO WE GO FROM HERE?

Where do we go from here? How are we to get to grips with the evil of child sexual abuse whilst at the same time ensuring that intervention is properly targeted so that parents and children are not abused by the system. It is clear that the problem must be approached on two levels. Sexual abuse must be eradicated. This must be the primary goal for prevention is always better than cure. But whilst we must recognize this as an ultimate goal, an ideal to be striven for, we must also recognize that, short of a cultural revolution and even then, the problem will always be with us. And so efforts must also go into improving our responses, managerial, social work and legal, to sexual abuse when it occurs. If the responses are seen as the problem, as has happened in Cleveland, our attention becomes diverted from the abuse itself. Since Cleveland there has been major children's legislation[253] and other reforms, such as those in the Criminal Justice Act 1988. In this last section of this chapter I focus on these two dimensions and ask how do we stop sexual abuse of children and how do we tackle it when it occurs. In discussing the latter question some comments are offered on the new and proposed legislation.

---

[252] E. F. Loftus, *Eyewitness Testimony*, Cambridge, Mass., Harvard Univ. Press, 1979. See also M. S. Zaragoza, 'Memory, Suggestibility and Eyewitness Testimony in Children and Adults' in *op. cit.*, note 233, pp. 53–78.

[253] The Second reading debate of the Children Bill in the House of Lords, was contemporaneous with the lecture which is the basis of this chapter. See Hansard, H. L. vol. 502, col. 487–540.

(i) Eliminating Abuse

Child sexual abuse is essentially a problem of male sexuality. This is not pre-determined biologically but is socially constructed. The socialization processes which construct images of masculinity need to be re-examined. The role played by the legal system in these processes cannot be ignored. Can the law provide solutions to the problem of violence against women, of which the sexual abuse of girls is but a phenomenon, when it constitutes part of that problem?[254] It is not so long since a judge in London could say that a child sexual abuser had been driven to abuse his 12-year-old step-daughter, an epileptic with a mental age of 7, because his pregnant wife was not responding to his 'healthy' desires.[255] There were three assaults. The first described by the judge as 'not serious', the second involving manual contact with the girl's genitalia and the third the girl being induced to masturbate the man. On the third assault we are treated to the extraordinary comment: 'there were no threats or bribes and more significantly, there was no change in the behaviour or temperament of the young lady'. As so often, the mother is blamed and the inference drawn that the girl was at worst a 'Lolita', at best a willing participant.[256]

It is not only male sexuality that needs to be re-thought but also the position of children. Child sexual abuse cannot be explained only in terms of male-female power relationships, but needs to take account also of those between adults and children. For too long we have viewed them as property rather than persons.[257] Sometimes we have cloaked this in pseudo-scientific imagery by emphasizing the 'blood tie'.[258] We deny children rights. In one authoritative recent book, children are said to have one right

---

[254] See M. D. A. Freeman, 'Violence Against Women: Can the Legal System Offer a Solution When It Constitutes The Problem?' *British Journal of Law and Society* vol. 7. pp. 215–241 (1980).

[255] The judge was Sir Harold Cassell (see *The Times*, November 29, 1988).

[256] The judge concerned retired, on grounds of ill-health, the same week. His interpretation of events is far from unique. Judge Brian Gibbens opined that sex with a 7-year-old was 'one of the kind of accidents that could almost happen to anyone'. (*The Times*, 17 December, 1983).

[257] The Butler-Sloss report, in stressing that children are persons and not objects of concern (see *op. cit.*, note 1, p. 245), strikes a significant blow for children. See also P. Newell, 'Children's Rights After Cleveland', *Children and Society* vol. 2(3), pp. 199–206 (1988).

[258] Attacked by J. Howells, *Remember Maria*, London, Butterworths, 1974; see also *Re C (M A)* [1966] 1 All E. R. 838.

only—the right to autonomous parents.[259] Intervention in the family ('the smack of statism' according to one of my critics)[260] is deprecated to uphold freedom and dignity.[261] But whose freedom and dignity are being upheld when in its name children are allowed to suffer abuse and neglect? If we are to conquer the abuse of children, we must learn to 'take children's rights seriously',[262] we must accept their entitlement to 'equal concern and respect'.[263] But it is not just that children are reified. To understand sexual abuse we have to understand the ways in which the supposed sexuality of children is commodified. The commercialization of child sexuality is as prevalent as the use of female images to sell products. We have begun to object (though not to much effect) to the misuse of a half-naked woman to sell cars, but when 'the photograph of a pre-pubescent girl wrapped only in a towel, is used to advertise house insurance, there seems to be no objection'.[264] The apparent precocity of a group of young girls has been deliberately exploited also in the cinema in the last decades.[265]

As the campaigns in the past few years have emphasized, children must be taught to say 'no'. But they must also be taught more about what they are saying no to. The child's right to education is universally accepted but her right to a sex education is still questioned.[266] Is it not somewhat ironic that a government committed to stamping out sexual abuse should also subscribe to the moral right's backlash against sex education? If we really care about sexual abuse we will commit ourselves to teaching children what sex is all about.

---

[259] J. Goldstein, A. Freud and A. Solnit, *Before The Best Interests of the Child*, New York, Free Press, 1979, p. 9.

[260] B. Amiel, 'Smack of Statism', *The Times*, 21 October 1988.

[261] *Op. cit.*, note 259, p. 12.

[262] Per M. D. A. Freeman, 'Taking Children's Rights Seriously', *Children and Society* vol. 1 (4), pp. 299–319 (1988).

[263] Per R. Dworkin, *Taking Rights Seriously*, London, Duckworth, 1977, pp. 272–278.

[264] See J. Ennew, 'Selling Children's Sexuality', *New Society*, vol. 77, no. 1234 (22 August 1986), pp. 9–11, at p. 10. See further J. Ennew, *The Sexual Exploitation of Children*, Cambridge, Polity Press, 1986.

[265] Tatum O'Neal, Jodie Foster, Nastassja Kinski and Brook Shields are the best-known examples.

[266] *Cf.* R. Ives, 'Children's Sexual Rights', in B. Franklin, *The Rights of Children*, Oxford, Blackwell, 1986, pp. 143–162.

Improving the status of children requires many other things: an end to corporal punishment,[267] so clearly associated not least in the minds of some sex abusers, with sexual gratification and therefore abuse; a greater say in the decision-making processes which affect them,[268] better complaints procedures, an idea which is endorsed by the Children Act;[269] a fuller recognition of the implications of the *Gillick* decision,[270] particularly as found in Lord Scarman's reasoning; an understanding that the removal of a child from its home environment into care is no panacea;[271] the adoption of more child-centred policies.[272]

(ii) Dealing with Abuse

But sexual abuse will continue to occur. How are we to respond to it? First, we must examine existing approaches. As indicated, many of these are defective. By attributing the blame to the family system, they deflect it away from the perpetrator. We do not say burglars cannot help it or that people who go on holiday bear part of the responsibility for burglaries which take place in their absence. So, why do we respond to sexual abuse in this way? Sexual abuse is difficult to identify, but this does not excuse the development of techniques which lead to false positive identifications. Thus, the anal dilatation test must be used with the utmost caution and must never lead to a diagnosis of sexual abuse without more evidence. Those who carry out the interviewing of allegedly abused children must be better trained, must improve their techniques and must take on board the clear lessons of the psychological research to which reference has been made.

---

[267] See Michael Freeman, 'Time to Stop Hitting Children', *Childright* no. 51 (October 1988). An attempt to undermine this failed in the House of Lords on 24 January 1989; Hansard vol. 503, cols. 542–548.

[268] The original Children Bill removed automatic party status for children in care proceedings.

[269] See section 26 (3).

[270] [1986] A. C. 112.

[271] See section 1 (5) and revelations about sexual abuse in care (*e.g.* Devon, *The Independent*, 2 November 1987; Birmingham, *The Independent*, 1 September 1988. See also *The Guardian*, January 17, 1984: Liverpool). In 1996 a judicial enquiry was established, reluctantly it has to be said, to look into abuse in homes in Clwyd.

[272] See M. D. A. Freeman, *The Rights and Wrongs of Children*, London, Frances Pinter, 1983.

Interviewers[273] should (i) be aware of their biases (ii) minimize leading questions and ask open-ended ones; (iii) remain as objective and impartial as possible (this may require that the interviewer does not read background information prior to interviewing the child) (iv) be alert to the cognitive and moral developmental level of the child (for example, young children confuse the concepts 'know', 'remember', 'guess' and 'forget');[274] (v) minimize cues given to a child about what she is supposed to say; (vi) avoid pressure or coercion to give a desired response (an affirmation obtained under pressure is worthless); (vii) be calm and not show irritation when the child is not responding as desired; (viii) conduct the interview in a way that does not contribute to the emotional trauma of the child. There is reason to believe that many diagnostic interviews in England to-day fall well short of these optimal guidelines.[275] If it seems that a child has been abused, she must be protected. But this does not necessarily mean removal of that child from her home or cutting off or severely restricting contact with her family. Wherever possible, the least intrusive measure should be adopted.

The Children Act is in part a response to Cleveland. Had it been in operation during the Cleveland crisis would it have improved the processes and practices of the social agencies, would it have better protected the children involved, would it have safeguarded the rights of parents and children more fully? What differences would it have made?

The Act is in many ways an improvement on the law as it existed at the time of the Cleveland crisis. The emergency protection order[276] is a vast improvement on the place of safety order. It will last for a shorter period;[277] there will be a presumption of reasonable access[278] (or contact, as it is now to be called); the applicant (that is in most cases the local authority social services department) will have its powers and duties relatively clearly defined. But applications will still usually be *ex parte*. The granting of an E.P.O. will be a 'discretionary judicial act' (in theory): in practice its ad-

---

[273] A full account of the methods used in E. Vizard and M. Tranter, 'Helping Young Children to Describe Experiences of Child Sexual Abuse' in *op. cit.*, note 181, pp. 84–129.

[274] H. M. Wellman and C. N. Johnson, 'Understanding of Mental Processes: A Developmental Study of "Remember" and "Forget"', *Child Development* vol. 50 17 79–88 (1979) (children up to 6 years of age).

[275] See the cases reported in *Family Law Reports Special Issue* (note 223).

[276] See sections 44 and 45.

[277] Eight days (see s. 45(1)).

[278] See section 34.

ministration may not improve on that we associate with place of safety orders.

The whole process of care will be speeded up. A new provision requires a court hearing an application for a care order (or supervision order) to have regard to the general principle that 'any delay' is likely to prejudice the welfare of the child.[279] The courts now take a proactive role. Courts are required to draw up timetables.[280] There are now directions appointments and these are an integral part of the process to reduce delay by the efficient management of cases.[281] One consequence is that care proceedings will, in the future, nearly always take place before criminal proceedings (if they are brought). This may prejudice some parents[282] but if the child's welfare is to be prioritized this may be inevitable. It is anyway consonant with the decisions in the *Inner London*,[283] *Exeter*, and *Waltham Forest Juvenile Court*[284] cases.

The grounds for a care order have been remodelled. They are wider in scope (they cover for example prognosis of harm where none has yet occurred,[285] and thus make it easier to remove new-born babies).[286] The ground is also subject to the general principle in the Act that intrusion must be the least detrimental alternative[287] ('Where a court is considering whether or not to make one or more orders...it shall not make the order or any of the orders unless it considers that doing so would be better for the child than making no order').[288] Given the standard of some substitute care,[289] the importance of this principle cannot be underestimated. One consequence of the widening of the care ground is that local authorities' power to use wardship is severely

---

[279] See s. 1 (2) and also s. 32.

[280] See section 32.

[281] See F.P.R. 1991 s. 4. 14 (2).

[282] Who will be tried for a criminal offence *after* the determination of care proceedings. The Government says speed is 'vital' in prosecutions for child abuse (*The Times*, 19 February 1988).

[283] [1988] 2 F. L. R. 58.

[284] [1988] 2 F. L. R. 214.

[285] See section 31 (2) ('is likely to suffer significant harm').

[286] On the problems of which hitherto see M. D. A. Freeman, 10 *Fam. Law* 131–134 (1980).

[287] The phrase (not in the Act) was coined by J. Goldstein, A. Freud and A. Solnit, *Beyond The Best Interests of the Child*, New York, Free Press, 1973 p. 53.

[288] Section 1 (5).

[289] On foster care breakdowns, see D. Berridge and H. Cleaver, *Foster Home Breakdown*, Oxford, Blackwell, 1987. See also references in note 271.

restricted: a local authority which cannot acquire parental responsibility using a statutory ground is not able to use wardship as a safety valve.[290]

The law on access (what is now called 'contact') is also improved. There is a presumption of reasonable contact and,[291] for the first time, a child[292] may apply to be allowed contact with a parent, a sibling or other persons. As the law stood at the time of the Cleveland cases, a parent could only apply for an 'access order' where access was terminated[293] by a local authority or it refused to make arrangements for it.[294] Under the Children Act the decision rests with the court which is able to make an order authorizing the authority to refuse to allow the child contact, if it is necessary to do so to safeguard the child's welfare.[295] An authority's powers to refuse contact are most restricted: it may only do so in matters of urgency, for a maximum period of 7 days and then only if satisfied that it is necessary to do so to safeguard the child's welfare.[296] On the other hand, we must take seriously the concerns expressed that contact meetings can be detrimental to children. Even where sexual abuse of children is established, professionals, it is said, have 'showed a worrying tendency to encourage the father's contact and to dismiss concerns about the children's reluctance, thereby seemingly legitimizing further abuse'.[297]

There are important provisions also in the Criminal Justice Act 1988, which were not in operation at the time of Cleveland. Section 32 of this permits a child under 14 to give evidence through a live TV link at a trial or an appeal.[298] The two-way video link may assist the child to give evidence, but the dangers inherent in this process remain. What will a jury think when it observes that the defendant is not permitted to confront the child face to face like other witnesses? Does not the fact that he is compelled to be physi-

---

[290] See section 100. The authority will only be able to do so with leave (s. 100 (3)) and where the result the authority wishes to achieve cannot be achieved otherwise and there is reasonable cause to believe that if the court's inherent jurisdiction is not exercised the child will suffer 'significant harm' (s. 100 (4)).

[291] See section 34 (1).

[292] See section 34 (2).

[293] And not where it was merely restricted. For an example see *Re Y* [1988] 1 F. L. R. 299.

[294] And see *R v. Bolton M.B.C. ex parte B* [1985] F. L. R. 343.

[295] Section 34 (4).

[296] Section 34 (6).

[297] *Per* Marianne Hester *et al*, 'Domestic Violence and Child Contact' in (eds.) Audrey Mullender and Rebecca Morley, *Children Living With Domestic Violence*, London, Whiting and Birch, 1994, p. 107.

[298] But not in trials or committals in magistrates' courts or in appeals there from.

cally separated from the child create inferences of his guilt and dangerousness?[299] In an effort to assist the child to give evidence, may we not have undermined the civil liberties of the alleged perpetrator of the sexual abuse? Section 34 removes the requirement (in s.38 of the Children and Young Persons Act 1933) that the unsworn evidence of a child must be corroborated by some other material evidence to convict. Judges will no longer have to warn juries against convicting defendants on the uncorroborated evidence of a child. The rule of practice that juries must be warned that it is not safe to convict on the uncorroborated evidence of a complainant does, however, remain, though, of course, they may do so if satisfied that the child is telling the truth. The repeal of s.38 makes it imperative that those who examine and cross-examine children in court also take on board what has been said about interviewing techniques and their pitfalls.

At the time of Cleveland little attention had been given to the question as to whether the victims of abuse could sue the perpetrators. The problem is that they may only become aware of the abuse years later and fall foul of limitation laws. We have become more conscious of the possibility of recovered memory in the years since Cleveland.[300] In Canada[301] (where plaintiffs time-barred in tort have claimed breach of fiduciary duty) and California[302] (where statutes of limitations have been excepted by means of the doctrine of delayed discovery), victims have successfully sued. In England they have been less fortunate. Compensation from the Criminal Injuries Compensation Board has been denied[303] and actions in tort have failed.[304] Elementary justice dictates that we find a solution to this problem: of the two precedents amending legislation along the lines of the that in California would seem the most straightforward approach.

---

[299] G. B. Melton and R. A. Thompson, 'Getting Out of a Rut: Detours To Less Travelled Paths in Child-Witness Research' in *op. cit.*, note 233, pp. 209–229. See also G. Fontaine and R. Kiger, 'The Effects of Defendant Dress and Supervision in Judgments of Simulated Jurors', *Law and Human Behavior*, vol. 2, pp. 63–72 (1979).

[300] See E. F. Loftus, 'The Reality of Repressed Memories', *American Psychologist*, 48, 518 (1993); R. Fredrickson, *Repressed Memories*, New York, Simon and Schuster.

[301] *KM v. HM* [1992] 96 D.L.R. (4th) 289.

[302] *Doe v. Doe*, 216 Cal. App. 3d 285 (1989).

[303] *R v. Criminal Injuries Compensation Board ex parte P* [1993] 2 F.L.R. 600, upheld by the Court of Appeal at [1994] 1 F.L.R. 861.

[304] *Stubbings v. Webb* [1993] 1 F.L.R. 714.

CONCLUSION

Cleveland has come and gone but the shock waves it sent through the system continue to reverberate, even now nearly a decade later. It provoked passionate responses. There can be little doubt that in an attempt to rescue abused children, other children were wrongly diagnosed. Diagnostic errors could have been avoided and must be eliminated in the future. But the errors that were made, and they were grievous, must not divert our attention from the evil of child sexual abuse. We must find ways of protecting abused children whilst at the same time protecting innocent parents.

CHAPTER 14

In the Child's Best Interests? Reading the Children Act Critically

INTRODUCTION

The new Children Act is, as it has been described,[1] 'the most comprehensive and far reaching reform of child law...in living memory'. It sweeps much away and creates much that is new. Little of the existing corpus of child or child welfare law is left untouched.[2] Its changes are as cataclysmic for the family lawyer as the 1925 property legislation was for conveyancing practice. Gone are custody, care and control, access, 'voluntary care',[3] resolutions to assume parental rights, custodianship,[4] place of safety orders.[5] The use of wardship is restricted.[6] There are no more criminal care orders.[7] Children will no longer be able to be committed to care for truancy.[8] There will be no more section 41 'satisfaction hearings',[9] and s.41 itself is radically remodelled.[10]

---

[1] By Lord Mackay, *Hansard*, H.L. vol. 502, col. 488.

[2] The institution of adoption is the main exception. There are some amendments to adoption legislation too (s. 88; Schedule 10), notably the establishment of an Adoption Contact Register (Sch. 10, para. 21). The law of child support is also relatively untouched.

[3] 'A not wholly accurate term, but in common use' per Lord Scarman in *Lewisham L.B.C. v. Lewisham Juvenile Court Justices* [1980] A.C. 273.

[4] Only introduced in 1986, it took off slowly but there is evidence that it was being more used recently in the main by relatives to confirm the permanence of a placement. See, further, E. Bullard and E. Malos, *Caring For Other People's Children*, London, H.M.S.O., 1991. They suggest it should not be retained.

[5] It was the Cleveland affair in 1987 which brought the injustices to public attention for the first time, though it was already under 'sentence of death' by then.

[6] See s. 100, and *post* 337.

[7] See s. 90(1), (2).

[8] But there is the new education supervision order (s. 36). It is difficult to enthuse about this: the enforcement provisions are absurdly weak (see Sch. 3, pt III).

[9] Under attack for many years for serving little purpose (see G. Davis *et al.* (1983) 46 MLR 121).

[10] A 'minor amendment', according to the Act. See Sch. 12, para. 31.

The Act has a new philosophy (partnership,[11] a presumption of non-intervention);[12] new principles, largely contained in section 1,[13] new concepts, including 'parental responsibility' to replace parental rights and duties that were so redolent of the notion of children as property.[14] Children 'in need' is statutorily defined for the first time.[15] There are new orders (the residence order, the contact order, the specific issue order, the prohibited steps order—the so-called s.8 orders, as well as the family assistance order,[16] the education supervision orders,[17] the new emergency protection[18] and child assessment orders[19] and orders pending appeals,[20] an innovation of importance which will smooth the transition between care and home.)[21] The Act contains new restrictions[22] (and not just those on wardship).[23]

There is a new emphasis on the family.[24] There is a greater recognition of the child as a participant in the decision-making process affecting him or

---

[11] This is not referred to in the Act itself. But 'partnership with parents based on agreement so far as possible will be the guiding principle for the provision of services' *per* Lord Mackay, *Hansard*, H L vol. 502, col. 491. See also P. Smith, *Community Care*, 28 March 1991.

[12] See s. 1(5).

[13] See also D.H., *The Care of Children—Principles and Practice In Regulations and Guidance*, London, H.M.S.O., 1989 (42 principles of good child care practice).

[14] *Cf.* M. Kellmer-Pringle, *The Needs of Children*, London, Hutchinson, 1980 (2nd ed.), p. 156. See also the oft-cited 'the child is a person and not an object of concern' in the Cleveland report.

[15] See s. 17(10), (11).

[16] See s. 16. This replaces supervision orders in custody proceedings.

[17] See s. 36. The so-called 'Leeds system', under which care proceedings were started but repeatedly adjourned, is thus brought to an end.

[18] See s. 44.

[19] See s. 43. On assessment see D.H., *Protecting Children: A Guide To Social Workers Undertaking Comprehensive Assessment* (1988).

[20] See s. 40. There is a similar power to stay a decision approving the arrangements for a child in care to live abroad (Sch. 2, para. 19).

[21] Section 40(3) should enable all courts to achieve a phased return. This can also be achieved by a residence order with directions (see s. 11(7)).

[22] A significant one is the requirement that a local authority with a supervision order will need to go through the whole process of proof again should this prove unsatisfactory and a care order be needed. There is no more 'upgrading'.

[23] Or 'inherent jurisdiction' (see s. 100(2), (3). Further, *A v. Liverpool C.C.* [1982] A.C. 363 remains good law.

[24] 'The integrity and independence of the family' is said by the Lord Chancellor (Jackson Memorial Lecture in (1989) 139 NLJ 505, 508) to be 'the basic building block of a free and democratic society and the need to defend it should be clearly perceivable in the law'. See also *Hansard*, H.L. vol. 502, col. 493.

her,[25] with a concomitant move away from seeing the child as an object of intervention or as a social problem.[26] The *Gillick* decision[27] has left its mark. (It is, I suppose, one of history's ironies that Victoria Gillick will be remembered as an unwitting propagator of children's rights!). The status of the unmarried father, a growing category,[28] is enhanced (he is now a 'parent'[29] and the ways in which he can acquire parental responsibility have been augmented).[30] The position of grandparents and of relatives is strengthened. So is the status of the guardian *ad litem*[31] and children will be so represented more regularly than has been the case.[32]

The Act integrates and breaks down barriers. The distinction between the private law of children and the public (or welfare) law relating to them becomes a false dichotomy. Essentially private orders, such as residence orders, can be made on an application for care:[33] care orders can be made in 'any family proceedings'[34] (for example, where a wife applies for an ouster order).[35] The 'most valuable features of wardship' are incorporated into the statutory jurisdiction.[36] The ambit of the Act is wider than is conventional, embracing children in categories previously excluded from children's legis-

---

[25] As I have argued in M. D. A. Freeman, *The Rights and Wrongs of Children*, London: Frances Pinter, 1983.

[26] See S. Spitzer 22 Social Problems 638, 642 (1975).

[27] [1986] A.C. 112. As has the children's rights lobby (see N. Frost and M. Stein, (1990) *Childright* July/August 1990, p. 17).

[28] In 1990 28.3 per cent of births were outside marriage.

[29] Compare *Re M* [1955] 2 QB. 479.

[30] In addition to a court order (introduced by the Family Law Reform Act 1987 s. 4), this can now be achieved by a formal agreement with the mother (s. 4(1), as well as by residence order (s. 8, 12(1), or by being appointed the child's guardian (s. 5(1), (3), (8)). A court order does not confer enforceable parental responsibility when the child is in care (*D v. Hereford and Worcs C.C.* [1991] 1 FLR 205). The criteria to be considered are examined in this case (see particularly Ward J. at p. 212) and in *Re H* [1991] 1 FLR 214, 218 (*per* Balcombe L.J.).

[31] See s. 41 and 42 and also the Courts and Legal Services Act 1990, Sch. 16, para. 18.

[32] Lord Mackay anticipates an appointment in 'almost every case' (*Hansard*, H. L. vol. 503, col. 408). They will be used in emergency cases for the first time. It is envisaged that panels of 'duty' guardians will be required.

[33] Because they are 'family proceedings' (defined in s. 8(3), (4)).

[34] See s. 31(4).

[35] Under the Matrimonial Homes Act 1983 s. 1 or an eviction order under the Domestic Proceedings and Magistrates' Courts Act 1978 s. 16 or where the inherent jurisdiction of the High Court is invoked.

[36] *Per* Law Commission, No. 172, para. 4. 20. This is done by means of the prohibited steps order and specific issue order in s.8.

lation, such as children in long-stay hospitals,[37] the mentally handicapped[38] and children in independent schools.[39] Local authorities are given new responsibilities for the welfare of such children.[40]

There is a new court structure, but no Family Court as such,[41] with concurrent jurisdiction between the three tiers, and 'start' and 'transfer' rules which should ensure that cases find their right level.[42] More effort has been directed to training the judges and the magistrates than ever before—there are clear implications in this for future legislation.[43] The courts are to be more pro-active, a feature of the Act being not just the directions the courts, including the magisterial family proceedings courts, can make, but also the novel time tabling provisions.[44] There is too a new 'open door' policy of access to the courts.

---

[37] See s.85. Such children often have no contact with their families. See C. Hood (1976) 2 *Child Care, Health and Development* 239.

[38] See s. 86.

[39] See s. 87. And see N. Fielding, *Community Care*, 31 January 1991 and Fry, Social Work Today, 31 January 1991, p. 9.

[40] In addition to the duties in ss. 85–87, after-care must also be provided (see s. 24).

[41] Butler-Sloss L. J. referred to it as an 'embryo' Family Court in a Bentham Club lecture (see 42 C.L.P. 71, 80 (1989)).

[42] See The Children (Allocation of Proceedings) Order 1991. It is envisaged that the majority of public law cases will be heard in the family proceedings court. There is 'free choice' (within legal aid constraints) for private law matters.

[43] The Justice report, *The Judiciary*, 1972 which advocated greater training for judges ought to be looked at again.

[44] See sections 11 (in relation to s.8 orders) and s.32 (in relation to care and supervision). See also the *Official Introduction To The Children Act 1989*, paras. 1.47–1.50.

Consensus and Ideology

The Act has been welcomed, even by those not usually favourable to legislation passed by Conservative governments.[45] And, of course, it is true that the Act, the thinking behind which can be traced to a DHSS Review of Child Care Law,[46] Law Commission reports[47] as well as the reports of three child death inquiries,[48] is broadly based on consensus, itself a rare enough event in recent years. It is easy enough to state there was consensus (child assessment orders being the egregious exception)[49]: it is more difficult to explain it. In part the explanation lies in relief. Prior to the Act, as David Mellor put it without exaggeration, legislation for the welfare of children had been 'confusing, piecemeal, outdated, often unfair and, in important respects, ineffective',[50] like an ill-fitting 'patchwork quilt' was how I described it in 1980.[51] The powers it gave to social workers were too great: the rights it afforded children, their parents and their wider families too few.[52] The 'place of safety order', supposed to be a 'discretionary judicial act',[53] was over and inappropriately used.[54] The sanctioning of an administrative action to remove parental rights, a Poor Law legacy, was incompatible with perceived ideals of justice.[55] But the explanation is not as

---

[45] It is possible that the Children Act 1989 will become the most universally praised of all Acts passed between 1979 and 1997.

[46] Published in 1985. See also the White Paper, *The Law On Child Care and Family Services*, 1987, Cm. 62.

[47] See, in particular, *Review of Child Law: Guardianship and Custody*, Law Com. No. 172, 1988: see also *Wards of Court*, Working Paper no. 101, 1987.

[48] London Borough of Brent, *A Child in Trust*, 1985, (The Beckford case); London Borough of Greenwich, *A Child in Mind*, 1987 (the Carlile case); London Borough of Lambeth, *Whose Child? The Report of the Public Inquiry into the Death of Tyra Henry*, 1987.

[49] The pros and cons were debated in *Childright* no. 55 (April 1988) by A. Wilson (p. 12) and R. Osmond (p. 14).

[50] *Hansard*, H. L. vol. 158 col. 620.

[51] See M. D. A. Freeman, *The Child Care and Foster Children Acts 1980*, London, Sweet and Maxwell, p. v.

[52] See M. D. A. Freeman, 2 *Children and Society* 207 (1988).

[53] Per Butler-Sloss report, *Child Abuse In Cleveland 1987*, London H.M.S.O. Cm. 412, 1988, para. 16.5.

[54] See, *e.g.* J. Packman, *Who Needs Care? Social Work Decisions About Children*, Oxford, Blackwell, 1986; T. Norris and N. Parton (1987) *JSWL* 1; Dartington Research Unit, *Place of Safety Orders*, 1985 (unpublished).

[55] See S. Maidment in (eds.) H. Geach and E. Szwed, *Providing Civil Justice For Children*,

simple as this. For, although there is a dominant ideology, the Act is the product of a number of value positions.

Lorraine Fox Harding[56] has accurately pin-pointed these as:

 i) *laisser-faire* and patriarchy
 ii) State paternalism and child protection
 iii) defence of the birth family and parents' rights, and
 iv) children's rights and child liberation.

That each of these positions is taken in the Act seems to me uncontentious and illustrations of each can be readily given. The presumption of non-intervention in s.1(5), keeping compulsory intervention to a minimum within public and private law, is the clearest example of *laisser-faire*. Fox Harding is wrong to dismiss this as not a 'dominant motif'[57] in the Act. But, having thus dismissed it, it is not surprising that the patriarchal implications of non-intervention are glossed over.

But the Act not only strengthens the position of parents (by getting the state and local state off their backs),[58] it also strengthens the powers of local authorities to intervene. For example, the 'trigger' for care includes for the first time prognosis by social workers that the child is 'likely' to suffer 'significant harm'.[59] The new child assessment order, allowing removal of a child for investigative purposes, where there is suspicion but no hard evidence, is a further example. And yet, as Fox Harding indicates,[60] there is a pro-birth family perspective in the Act as well. The Lord Chancellor's Department's *Guide* to the Act encapsulates this philosophy well. The Act, we are told, 'rests on the belief that children are generally best looked after within the family with both parents playing a full part and without resort to legal proceedings'.[61] There is thus a new emphasis on prevention and on the provision of services to children and families 'in need'[62] and a greater emphasis on 'contact' between children and their

---

London, Edward Arnold, 1983, p. 71.

[56] *Perspectives In Child Care Policy*, London, Longman, 1991 and 'The Children Act 1989 in Context: Four Perspectives on Child Care Law and Policy', (1991) *JSWFL* 179, 285.

[57] (1991) *JSWFL* 179, 185.

[58] Not a lot of attention was focused on this during Parliamentary debates, or, I suppose, since. Ironically, lawyers and social workers, confronted by the revolution in the courts' role, may feel that the 'state' is now on their backs.

[59] See s.31(2).

[60] *Op. cit.*, note 565, p. 289.

[61] Lord Chancellor's Department, 1989, para. 1.3.

[62] See part III of the Act and Schedule 2. On 'in need' see s.17.

families where perforce they have had to be separated.[63] Parental responsibility, a key concept in the Act, is never lost, though its exercise may sometimes be suspended,[64] even when parents behave without parental responsibility. The fourth value position (children's rights) is not neglected either. The child may initiate court actions: for example, he or she may challenge an emergency protection order,[65] seek a contact order when in care,[66] ask for a care order to be discharged,[67] seek the court's leave to obtain a s.8 order making directions about where he or she is to live or with whom to have contact.[68] It is usually a pre-condition that the child is '*Gillick*-competent',[69] but not always.[70] It is perhaps a mark of how little this has been thought through that the institution of the 'next friend' has been forgotten.[71] There is also greater recognition of a child's wishes and feelings,[72] and more extensive use of separate representation of children by guardians *ad litem*.[73] It will not be necessary to establish a conflict of interest between parent and child, as previously,[74] before a guardian *ad litem* is appointed. Whether the Act has 'empowered' children, as one commentator[75] has observed, depends upon how 'empowerment' is understood. Certainly, their position has been strengthened and their identity recognized and this is a major advance.[76]

---

[63] See Schedule 2, para. 15.

[64] See s.33(3)(b) and (4). Even so a parent with 'care' may do what is reasonable to safeguard or promote the child's welfare during the existence of a care order (s.33(5)).

[65] Section 45(8)(a).

[66] Section 34(2). Contact as the right of the child can be traced back to *M* v. *M* [1973] 2 All E.R. 81. See further ch. 8.

[67] Section 34 (4).

[68] Section 10 (2)(b). The child must have 'sufficient understanding' (s.10(8)).

[69] This does not apply to applications for contact orders under s.34 or for such orders to be refused. A very young child could thus apply.

[70] Unless and until a guardian *ad litem* was appointed the solicitor approached would have to act in the child's best interests (see The Family Proceedings Courts (Children Act 1989) Rules 1991 r. 12(1)(c)).

[71] In the Family Proceedings Courts (Children Act 1989) Rules 1991, but this is where they are needed. The court may well appoint a guardian to act for the child, but how does the child get this far?

[72] They are at the top of the checklist in s.1(3).

[73] See s.41 for the specified proceedings (s.41(6)). It is anticipated that guardians will be appointed in 90 per cent of such cases (*per* D. Mellor, Standing Committee B, col. 255.

[74] Under s.32A(1) of the Children and Young Persons Act 1969.

[75] D. Hodgson (1990) 21 (44) *Social Work Today* 16 (July 12).

[76] But see P. Harris and M. Moss (1989) 747 *Community Care* 13 (January 26, 1989).

To Fox Harding 'the most important themes would appear to be paternalism on the one hand, and the defence of birth parents' rights on the other'.[77] The other two strands (*laisser-faire* and children's rights) are, she says, 'present to a lesser extent'.[78] This is not the way I interpret the Act, as will become clear further into this article. But, at this point, my goal is to explain why the Act is based on a consensus. Consensus can be engineered, created, forged (in both senses of that verb).[79] Legislation is a political act with political significance. It uses political language and political symbols.[80] It uses words like 'compromise' and 'balance' and it seeks to co-opt opposition. The Children Act appears to have done this successfully. Thus, the official *Guide* tells us that the Act 'strikes a new balance between the autonomy of the family and the protection of the children'.[81] But Acts do not 'strike' balances: they establish frameworks within which decisions (themselves political and taken moreover within political constraints) are made. If a balance is struck (and where) thus depends on social workers, on lawyers, on the police and on the courts. Much depends on the availability of resources,[82] on the acquisition of skills,[83] on the existence of enough trained personnel (to write welfare reports,[84] to represent children). Still, consensus has to be constructed and was, in this instance, by a projection of family values to which both sides could relate.

---

[77] *Op. cit.*, note 56, p. 299. She concedes that much depends on how the Act is interpreted and resourced. When these matters are taken into account, it seems to me that the *laisser-faire* of the Act will assume even greater prominence.

[78] *Idem.*

[79] Thus see Fox Harding's conclusion (*op. cit.*, note 56, p. 300). She seems to think that it is reasonable and not inconsistent to proceed in several directions at once to achieve 'effective balance'.

[80] See M. Edelman, *Political Language, Words That Succeed and Policies That Fail*, 1977.

[81] Department of Health, *An Introduction To The Children Act 1989*, para. 1.31.

[82] A constant theme in the social work journals. See *e.g. Community Care*, 14 March 1991.

[83] *Community Care* reported on 21 February 1991 that 12 per cent of social workers were not even aware of the existence of the Children Act!

[84] There should be more welfare reports: s.7 extends the court's power to call for a welfare report to 'any question' with respect to a child under the Act.

For the 'right'[85] the family is 'a haven in a heartless world'.[86] It is the quintessentially private space, 'a shelter for moral and spiritual values',[87] a 'utopian retreat'.[88] It is the place where 'Victorian values' reign,[89] a place of private security and closeness. It is gender-ordered, for, as Tennyson noted in 'The Princess', 'all else confusion'.[90] To the influential right-wing ideologue Ferdinant Mount, the family is the last defence of the individual against an increasingly tyrannical and interfering social and political system.[91] Whether this is myth or mystification, nostalgia or delusion, in the minds of the right the family functions according to prescription. Parents behave with parental responsibility, disagreements between parents or spouses are resolved amicably (if outside intervention is necessary it is conciliation,[92] not courts, on which attention focuses). Goldstein, Freud and Solnit explained the underlying philosophy as well as anyone when they wrote that a policy of minimum coercive intervention by the state accorded with their 'firm belief as citizens in individual freedom and human dignity'.[93] But, in a world of structured inequalities (gender, age, race etc.), we need to ask 'whose freedom' and 'what dignity' such a philosophy upholds.

---

[85] On the family and the right see M. David in (ed.) R. Levitas, *The Ideology of The New Right*, 1986. See also G. Douglas (1990) 17 *JLS* 411.

[86] *Per* C. Lasch, *Haven In a Heartless World. The Family Besieged*, New York: Basic Books, 1977. But *cf.* M. Barrett and M. McIntosh, *The Anti-social Family*, London: Verso, 1982, pp. 110–126.

[87] *Per* W. Houghton, *The Victorian Frame of Mind 1830–1870*, New Haven: Yale Univ. Press, 1957, p. 343.

[88] See K. Jeffrey in S. Teselle (ed.), *The Family, Communes and Utopian Societies*, 1972.

[89] See M. Thatcher's speech, reported in *The Daily Telegraph*, 16 April 1983.

[90] *The Poems of Tennyson* (ed. C. Ricks), p. 741.

[91] *The Subversive Family*, London, Jonathan Cape, 1982. I thought it highly significant that *The Times* leader on October 14 1991, fulsome in its praise of the Act, saw its 'laudable aim' as adapting law to take account of the 'latest metamorphoses of "the subversive family"'.

[92] For evidence that parents do not necessarily behave in this way see S. Maidment in (ed.) M. D. A. Freeman, *State, Law and Family*, London, Tavistock, 1984, p. 159. On conciliation as a filter rather than a resolver of disputes see G. Davis, *Partisans and Mediators: The Resolution of Divorce Disputes*, Oxford, Clarendon, 1988.

[93] *Before The Best Interests of The Child*, New York: Free Press, 1979, p. 12.

The new Act is a product of right-wing thinking but, conveniently, co-opts ideas drawn from the far left as well.[94] The target for most coercive intervention into the family has long been the working class. Children in care are concentrated in areas of high social deprivation. Poverty and its multi-faceted correlates (bad housing, unemployment, absence of child-care alternatives) does not 'cause' child abuse, but there is a statistically close association between them.[95] To the far left the image of the working class family comes not from Tennyson or Brooke ('And is there honey still for tea'?) but from the romantics. They idealize, almost idolize, the working class family. In their minds it has suffered from the 'slings and arrows' of state intervention, from the latest fads of social work practice, family therapy and so on. There has never been enough money to support such families. Of course, then, an Act which not only reduces coercive intervention and rids the statute book of such class-imbued concepts as being of 'such habits or mode of life as to be unfit to have care of [a] child',[96] but also emphasizes support, as the Children Act does in part III, is applauded by the left. There is enough in this Act for those who wish to see the problems of social work clients in materialistic, rather than individualistic, terms. As far as the left is concerned this is an Act which tells the local state to work with families ('partnership') and to provide support (day care,[97] family centres,[98] financial support)[99] so as to obviate the need to intervene against the wishes of parents.

Both the right and the left cherish the family: in both cases this is an ideal which does not exist. Both want it left alone. As all things to all people, it is hardly surprising that the Act was (and remains) broadly acceptable. The support of the left was solidified by part III and Schedule II of the Act (the provision of services for families). It is easy to look at this as a sop thrown by a Conservative government, which knew it had no intention of making resources available, in order to induce consensus. Even before the Act came into operation, we know that local authorities were re-defining their obliga-

---

[94] For example, Lasch (note 86) and J. Donzelot, *The Policing of Families*, London: Hutchinson, 1979.

[95] See L. H. Pelton (ed.), *The Social Context of Child Abuse and Neglect*, New York: Human Sciences Press, 1981 (as regards physical abuse). There does not seem to be the same association with sexual abuse (see D. Finkelhor, *A Source Book on Child Sexual Abuse*, Beverly Hills: Sage 1986).

[96] See Child Care Act 1980 s.3(1)(b)(iv). It dates back to 1899.

[97] See s.18.

[98] See Sch. 2, para. 9.

[99] See s.17(6). But, consonant with 'social fund' philosophy, cash assistance may be by way of a loan.

In the Child's Best Interests? Reading the Children Act Critically 315

tions under the Act or, as they prefer to put it (perhaps with judicial review in mind),[100] prioritizing 'children in need'.[101] It is clear that support for families will remain on the ideological level (that envisaged by the right). It is unlikely that the welfare support, sought by the left as a solution to the problems of working class families, will become a reality, at least in the immediate future.

NON-INTERVENTION

It is, accordingly, the *laisser-faire* strand in the Act which seems to me the key to understanding it. The law is in retreat from the private realm of family life.[102] This is not necessarily so elsewhere—note the increased interest of the state in domestic violence [103] and the creeping legalization of cohabitation outside marriage.[104] The Children Act does to a large extent privatize the family.[105] As such it can be seen in terms of the general thrust of recent Conservative legislation.[106] It is surprising that commentators as astute as Packman and Jordan[107] should not have noticed this.

The clearest enunciation of this ideology is in section 1(5). This states:

> Where a court is considering whether or not to make one or more orders under this Act with respect to a child, it shall not make the order or any of the orders unless it considers that doing so would be better for the child than making no order at all.

---

[100] Though on past performance the courts have evinced a reluctance to interfere with the ways local authorities carry out their duties under legislation. A good example is *R v. Tower Hamlets L.B.C. ex p Monaf* (1988) 20 HLR 529.

[101] See S. Barber, *Community Care* (15 December 1990). The Department of Health's response may be gauged from R. White, *New Law Journal*, 29 March 1991, p. 433. There are anyway enough 'designer loopholes' in the legislation (see R. Gardner, *Community Care* (22 November 1990)).

[102] See F. Olsen, 'The Family and The Market' (1983) 96 *Harvard Law Rev.* 1497.

[103] See M. D. A. Freeman (1989) 20 *Cambrian Law Review* 17, 20–26.

[104] See M. D. A. Freeman and C. Lyon, *Cohabitation Outside Marriage*, Aldershot: Gower, 1983.

[105] See also A. Bainham (1990) 53 *M.L.R.* 206.

[106] An example in an area close to, and having an impact upon, family policy is M. O'Higgins 55(2) *Political Quarterly* 129–39 (1984).

[107] (1991) 21 *Br. J. of Social Work* 315.

This creates a presumption against court action, and it has clear implications throughout the Act. It applies to orders in the private[108] and public[109] law areas. It will affect the work of solicitors, both their fact-gathering and their relations with clients who will need to be weaned away from beliefs that courts are about orders. It will make it easier for the Legal Aid Board to refuse applications. It will affect the work of social workers and lawyers working for local authorities: care is no panacea[110] and the court will need to be convinced that a care order is better for the child than no order. The court will also need to know why the order is being sought and what will be achieved by it.[111] The implications of the provision are far-reaching and not all have been given serious attention as yet. It seems to have been glossed over that financial provision for children is in the Act[112] so that consent orders relating to children are governed by s.1(5). But will consent orders now be made? What is their purpose? More significantly, in what way are they 'better' for children? What is the impact of the minimal intervention principle on housing authorities? Will they transfer a tenancy when no order has been applied for because the advice is that on a reading of s.1(5) it will not be granted? Or will residence orders be made to facilitate transfers on the basis that this is 'better' for the child than no order? And, how will foreign courts, confronted with a kidnapping, react when told that in England the presumption is that no order is made?

The impact of the new provision will be noticed first in the private law area, particularly in divorce. In 1988,[113] 11,920 custody orders were expressed to have been made by consent, 46,792 were 'unopposed but not expressly by consent' and 13,771 joint custody orders were made. It is difficult to see how the making of an order in any of these cases could be shown to be beneficial to the child. Joint custody orders,[114] as they were

---

[108] Not just s.8 orders but also for example parental responsibility orders under s.4 and financial provision orders under s.15 (and Schedule 1).

[109] Care, supervision, education supervision, interim orders, orders pending appeals, child assessment orders, emergency protection orders.

[110] Innumerable examples could be given of this: 'pin-down' is merely one of the best-documented (see A. Levy and B. Kahan, *The Pindown Experience and The Protection of Children*, Stafford, Staffs. C.C., 1991). See, more generally, W. Utting, *Children In The Public Care*, London: H.M.S.O., 1991.

[111] Emphasizing yet again the importance of planning.

[112] See s.15 and Schedule 1.

[113] Civil Judicial Statistics 1988, Table 5.8.

[114] These would now translate as joint parental responsibility orders. The practice was enormously variable (43 per cent in Oxford; 4 per cent in Romford) according to J. Priest and

called, would serve no purpose under the new régime anyway, since both parents retain parental responsibility after divorce,[115] irrespective of where the child is living. The number of post-divorce orders about children will decline considerably: concomitantly, the work of conciliators and counsellors will increase as those to be denied court resolutions seek the informal justice of agreements and settlements.[116] This may be attractive to some but, as I have agreed elsewhere,[117] one of the functions of law is to provide a measure of protection to the weak (in this case women as well as children) and the shift in the centre of gravity from adjudication to mediation may undermine this.

The significance of the minimal intervention principle will be felt even more forcibly in the public law area. It will apply not just to care and supervision orders, but to education supervision orders, contact orders, interim orders and orders pending appeals, as well as to emergency protection and child assessment orders. So, even if the local authority has successfully made out the threshold condition for a care order, no order should be made unless the authority can satisfy the court, in addition, that the making of an order would be better for the child than making no order. The court, in most cases a panel of lay magistrates[118] sitting as a Family Proceedings Court, will be asked to predict and to balance: to assess the child's future, to compare outcomes and to undertake a balancing exercise. There are likely to be more applications for care orders than there are at present (restrictions on wardship and the ease with which children can be removed from accommodation accounting for this).[119] How will magistrates react? What will be the attitude of the High Court to appeals? If the magistrates play safe, the number of care orders could go up. If care orders become difficult to get, there will be a glut of applications for leave to ward a child.[120] If these are treated sympathetically, part of the philosophy of the Act will be overturned. The prospect of a new breed of 'Rumpoles' with brief-cases bulging with newspaper cut-

---

J. Whybrow, *Custody Law and Practice in the Divorce and Domestic Courts* (Supplement to Working Paper No. 96 of Law Commission), London, H.M.S.O.

[115] See s.2. But the 'non-residential' parent cannot act incompatibly with any order (s.2(8). Nor can the 'residential' parent.

[116] See A. Bottomley and J. Roche in (ed.) R. Matthews, *Informal Justice?* Beverley Hills: Sage, 1988.

[117] In (ed.) J. Eekelaar and S. Katz, *The Resolution of Family Conflict*, Toronto: Butterworths, 1984, p. 7.

[118] See The Children (Allocation of Proceedings) Order 1991, Art. 3.

[119] See section 100 and section 20(8).

[120] See section 100(3).

tings about foster care breakdown,[121] sexual abuse in children's houses,[122] forcible feeding,[123] drugging[124] and so-called 'pin down'[125] hectoring magistrates into not making orders does not require too many leaps of imagination. The critical equation of care or home will often not be easy to solve. Whether social work resources will stretch to cope with the additional work that 'no order' may cause is also dubious. Whether children come out of this winners or losers is one of the many imponderables in this Act.

PARENTAL RESPONSIBILITY

'Parental responsibility', not surprisingly in view of what has been said so far, is the key concept of the Act. The shift from parental rights and duties (a property concept, almost) to parental responsibility, with parents as trustees for their children, the beneficiaries, has to be welcomed.[126] We clearly have to get away from the notion of children as consumer durables, completing a family after the C.D. player and video recorder.[127] But the innocuous phrase 'parental responsibility' secretes within it three messages. First, that parents are decision-makers rather than children. The decision in *Gillick* v. *West Norfolk and Wisbech Area Health Authority*[128] limited the power of parents to make decisions for their mature children. Despite assurances of Lord Mackay to the contrary,[129] the Act appears to have overturned this principle. This is surprising given the emphasis on children's rights elsewhere in the Act, but there is no procedure which

---

[121] See Department of Health, *Patterns and Outcomes in Child Placement*, London, H.M.S.O., 1991.

[122] For example, in West Yorkshire (see Community Care 21 March 1991, p. 3), in Nottinghamshire (where 26 out of 79 children placed in care because of sexual abuse were abused by other children whilst in care—see Social Work Today 25 October 1990, p. 7).

[123] As in a 1991 case in Lancashire.

[124] See M. D. A. Freeman, *The Rights and Wrongs of Children*, London, Frances Pinter, 1983, pp. 172–173.

[125] See *op. cit.* note 110. Community Care has started a 'Crisis in Care' campaign with a Campaign Hotline (see 870 *Community Care* 12, 4 July 1991).

[126] It can be traced back to a Justice committee report, *Parental Rights and Duties and Custody Suits*, London: Justice, 1975.

[127] See Mia Kellmer-Pringle's remarks in *The Needs of Children*, London: Hutchinson 2nd ed. 1980, p. 156.

[128] [1986] A.C. 112. But see now *Re R* [1991] 4 All E.R. 177.

[129] *Hansard*, H. L. vol. 502, col. 1351.

allows them to participate in decision-making where there is a dispute in court (for example, where one parent applies for a specific issue order).[130]

Secondly, the emphasis on responsibility as more important than rights is affirmed. Lord Fraser put this well in *Gillick*:

> parental rights to control a child does not exist for the benefit of the child and they are justified only in so far as they enable the parent to perform his duties towards the child, and towards other children in the family.[131]

This would have been contentious a hundred years ago,[132] but is today little more than a platitude.

It is the third message in the phrase to which attention must be drawn. It is that parents and not the state have responsibility for children. In an excellent article John Eekelaar[133] has shown how and why a shift has come about from an emphasis on responsibility rather than rights to one where what is emphasized is that parents have responsibility. This third message is consistent with other Government legislation: that making parents more criminally responsible for their children's crimes[134] and the new Child Support Act of 1991 re-iterating the maintenance obligations of the absent parent.[135] As Margaret Thatcher put it: 'parenthood is for life'.[136]

The consequences of this message need to be spelt out. Parents have responsibility in a normative sense even when in fact they act with complete disregard for that responsibility. So wedded is the Government to the ideology that individual parents, rather than 'Nanny State', must have responsibility that, short of adoption there is no way that a parent with parental responsibility can lose it or divest him or herself of it.[137] The child abuser, the

---

[130] The Act seems more conscious of the need to allow children to participate in the public law questions than the private law disputes, again an implicit regulation of the autonomy of parents.

[131] *Op. cit.*, note 128, p. 170. See also *Re KD* [1988] A.C. 806; *Re K* [1990] 2 FLR 64 and *F v. M.B. of Wirral* [1991] 2 FLR 114.

[132] *Re Agar-Ellis* (1883) 24 Ch.D. 317.

[133] (1991) *JSWFL* 37. See also his *Regulating Divorce*, Oxford: Clarendon Press 1991.

[134] Criminal Justice Act 1991, ss. 57 and 58.

[135] Child Support Act 1991, based on *Children Come First*, 1990 Cm. 1264. Section 1 states in statutory form for the first time the absent parent's duty to maintain (for the purposes of the 1991 Act).

[136] See *The Independent*, 19 July 1990.

[137] There is no method of voluntary surrender to the state (under the old law an assumption of parental rights amounted to this), nor is there a provision like the Guardianship Act 1973 s.1(2). Delegation is, however, allowed (see s.2(9)).

child neglecter, the child molester all retain parental responsibility, though they do not exercise it very responsibly. Even where the child is in care under a care order the parents still have parental responsibility vested in them.[138] True, the local authority is also vested with it[139] and can control the ways in which parents can exercise their parental responsibility.[140] In reality, all that a parent in such circumstances has is parental responsibility in some symbolic or ideological sense. If the hidden agenda is one of social engineering,[141] *viz.* that by encouraging parents to believe that they always have responsibility will mean that they will take their responsibility more seriously, the prospects of success must be slim.[142] There is no reason to believe that giving parents greater freedom will guarantee that the standard of care will improve. It was Bill Jordan who noted, many years ago, that when the case against intervention in family life was posited it often rested on 'the freedom of more powerful members (usually husbands in relation to wives and parents in relation to children) to exercise their power without restriction'.[143] There are restrictions on freedom here but are they enough to protect children? It is one of the ironies of this legislation that it imposes new and additional controls on others who look after children, child-minders,[144] those who run independent schools,[145] and it is right to do so. But it seems to take it for granted that parents will naturally behave with responsibility. This legislation would have been largely otiose if that were true.[146]

THE PROVISION OF ACCOMMODATION

One situation in which parents[147] retain parental responsibility to the exclusion of the local authority is where accommodation is provided for a child.[148] Under the Act such a child is not in care: being in care means

---

[138] See s.2(6).

[139] See s.33(3)(a).

[140] See s.33(3)(b).

[141] Empirical evidence suggests this does not work effectively in 'expressive areas'. See Y. Dror (1959) 33 *Tulane Law Rev.* 749.

[142] Though J. Packman and B. Jordan (21 *Br. J. of Soc. Work* 315, 326) are more optimistic.

[143] *Freedom and the Welfare State*, London: RKP, 1976, p. 60.

[144] See pt X of the Act.

[145] See s.87.

[146] See ss. 66–70 and Sch. 7.

[147] Where married. Where not, only the mother has parental responsibility (see s.2(2)).

[148] See s.20. There are important new duties in s.22.

subject to a care order.[149] The concept of a reception into care (or voluntary care, as it was often called) has been abolished.[150] The provision of accommodation, which replaces it, is to be arranged in voluntary partnership with parents. The original conception of this in the *Child Care Review* was for 'shared' care, a 'genuine and voluntary partnership' between the parents and the authority.[151] There would be requirements for consultation and the giving of notice before a child cared for for six months or more could be removed.[152] The rhetoric of partnership[153] remains but the sharing of responsibility and the concomitant restrictions have gone.

The Act does away with the distinction between short-term and long-term accommodation.[154] There is no need for parents to give written notice, or indeed any notice, of an intention to remove a child from accommodation.[155] And should the authority conclude that it is not going to be possible for the child to go home, so that a more permanent arrangement is required, parental rights cannot be assumed. The local authority and the child is thus in a more precarious position than before. If the child is over 16, he or she may insist on remaining in accommodation.[156] If under 16 and *Gillick*-competent, it is also arguable that he or she could prevent a removal,[157] but there is no statutory authority for this and it may be inconsistent with the emphasis on parental responsibility to which reference has been made.[158]

Two provisions in particular have provoked disquiet amongst child care organizations—and justifiably so. Section 20(7) states that a local authority may not provide accommodation under this section (it could therefore provide day care for a child 'in need' whatever the parental view)[159] if a person with parental responsibility is 'willing and able' to provide accommodation

---

[149] See s.105(1).

[150] The generic and unlegalistic expression 'looked after' embraces both provision of accommodation and care (see s.22(1)).

[151] See paras. 7–14, 31–32. This was still found in the 1987 White Paper (see paras. 5(b), 22, 23, 26).

[152] *Idem.*

[153] See D.H., *An Introduction To The Children Act 1989*, para. 56.

[154] Drawn at 6 months by the Children Act 1975, s.56.

[155] See s.20(8).

[156] See s.20(11).

[157] By analogy with *Krishnan* v. *L.B. of Sutton* [1970] Ch. 181.

[158] See *ante*.

[159] See s.18. And 'day care' means 'any form of care or supervised activity provided for children during the day' (s.18(4)).

or arrange it and 'objects'. The accommodation is not required to be satisfactory or even safe. The provision may make sense where the parent is a 'volunteer' (objection would be a contradiction in terms) but, as Packman's research found,[160] many clients of accommodation are likely to be 'victims' or even 'villains'. Section 20(8) states that 'any person who has parental responsibility for a child may at any time remove the child from accommodation provided by or on behalf of the local authority under this section'. Even, it may be noted, where that person cannot provide accommodation for the child. Although this is a return to the pre-1975 situation,[161] it has understandably caused concern and a search for options open to local authorities and carers where a parent exercises this right inappropriately (the example often cited is the drunken parent in the middle of the night).[162]

Of course, with the greater emphasis on written agreements[163] parents will agree (or rather be told) that they cannot do this. But this will provide no real defence against the irresponsible parent. What options then are open? Police protection may be invoked. Section 46 provides that where a constable has reasonable cause to believe that a child would otherwise be likely to suffer significant harm, he may remove the child to 'suitable accommodation'[164] or take such steps as are reasonable to ensure the child is not removed from where he or she is then being accommodated. The constable could ensure this by using the arrest powers in s.25 of the Police and Criminal Evidence Act 1984. The general arrest conditions[165] would be satisfied: it should not be difficult to establish 'reasonable grounds' for suspecting a criminal offence has been committed or attempted (at least in the 'drunken' example).

That such a response is extreme is, of course, true, but one of the consequences of this Act is that, by withdrawing the middle-range response, those concerned with the protection of children may be catapulted in over-coercive measures. Indeed, it is a fair bet that one result of loosening a local authority's control of accommodation will be the greater use of care orders.

---

[160] *Who Needs Care?* Oxford: Blackwell, 1986.

[161] And retains the existing situation where the child is in accommodation for under 6 months (see the *Lewisham* decision *op. cit.*, note 3, particularly Lord Salmon at p. 290 and Lord Keith at p. 301).

[162] See *Hansard*, H.L. vol. 503, col. 1412; vol. 505, col. 370.

[163] See D. Nelken (1987) 40 *CLP* 207 and Family Rights Group, *Using Written Agreements with Children and Families* (ed. J. Aldgate), London: FRG, 1989.

[164] No longer a 'place of safety'. The assumption is that this will be local authority accommodation or a refuge (s.51) (see s.46(3)(f)).

[165] See Police and Criminal Evidence Act 1984 s.25.

Removal may be thwarted in a number of other ways. An emergency protection order may be applied for. The trigger for this is 'significant harm' which will be easier to establish where the child has been in accommodation for a lengthy period. If an order is made it will create the sort of 'breathing space'[166] that existed with the 28 days' notice provision in the old law. The agreement can then be re-negotiated. If this is not possible or desirable, a care order may be sought and granted on the basis that the child is likely to suffer significant harm attributable to the quality of parental care falling below what would be reasonable to expect a parent to give—the assumption being that such a hypothetical parent would realize that uprooting a child who was well-settled would cause such harm.[167] The foster parent could seek a residence order (indeed, might be granted one on an application by the local authority for a care order) or even make the child a ward of court and seek care and control.[168] Advantage might also be taken of section 3(5),[169] though the inter-relationship of this and s.20(8) will need to be clarified in litigation. Section 3(5) empowers persons without parental responsibility who have the 'care'[170] of a child to do what is 'reasonable' to safeguard or promote the child's welfare, but this safety net is expressed to be 'subject to the provisions of this Act' and must therefore include s.20(8). The provision is wide[171] (it would enable a hospital to give a child a blood transfusion without consulting the Jehovah's Witness parents) but would it allow a foster parent[172] to refuse to hand over a child to a parent? And, if so, for how long? And in what circumstances? And what happens if the foster parent and local authority are in disagreement about whether the child should be returned?[173]

There are, it can be seen, numerous problems. Nor should it be forgotten that any person with parental responsibility may remove the child at any time. Where the parents are married (or were married), each may exercise

---

[166] *Per* Waterhouse J. in *Wheatley* v. *L.B. of Waltham Forest* [1979] 2 WLR 543.
[167] See D.H., *Introduction to the Children Act*, para. 1.3.6.
[168] But they would then cease to be local authority foster parents and this might have financial implications.
[169] Primarily designed to enable relatives and friends undertaking short-term care to take the necessary steps to look after the children.
[170] Not defined in the Act but meaning, presumably, the same as 'actual custody' did before.
[171] Or operate to save a baby's life against parental wishes (*cf. Re B* [1981] 1WLR 1421).
[172] Or child minder or school.
[173] It would seem the local authority would not need to take legal proceedings to recover the child (see *per* Goff, J. in *Krishnan* v. *L.B. of Sutton* [1970] Ch 181, 186). But the foster parent could ward the child (See *Re S* [1965] 1 All E.R. 865).

powers under s.20(8): one could accordingly place the child in accommodation and the other could remove the child. This could be done, for example, by a father with no contact or relationship with the child. This does not apply if the mother has a residence order,[174] for all those with residence orders must approve of the decision to remove the child. This illustrates one of the many imponderables which may be considered when deciding whether a residence order is 'better' for the child.[175]

There is a fear that local authorities could become dumping grounds, with children being placed in accommodation and removed at a parent's whim. This would exacerbate the fragility of the lives of the children concerned who are often already amongst the most disadvantaged and vulnerable of the population.

Another call on local authority accommodation is likely to come from homeless young people.[176] There has been a dramatic increase in the number of homeless young,[177] a problem heightened by the shortage of housing and hostel accommodation and by changes in social security rules removing entitlement for 16- and 17-year-olds and reducing it for other young people.[178] It should not be forgotten that the same Government which passed the Children Act presided over a decade in which child poverty and the number of homeless households more than doubled.[179] Housing authorities have evaded their responsibility: now the homeless young can exploit the Children Act as a new resource. Every local authority is now obligated to provide accommodation for any child in need over 16 whose welfare it considers is likely to be 'seriously prejudiced' if accommodation is not provided.[180] The help of the housing authority may be enlisted but it only has to comply with a re-

---

[174] See s.20(9).

[175] But if parents are divorcing and the child is thought to be at risk, for example from a violent father, the case for a residence order may be strong.

[176] See T. Lunn, *Social Work Today*, 21 February 1991, p. 21.

[177] See J. Gosling and Diarists, *One Day I'll Have a Place of My Own*, Central London Social Security Advisors' Forum and Shelter, 1989, estimating that over 150,000 experience homelessness every year as a result of leaving home or care and being unable to find or afford accommodation.

[178] See C. Craig and C. Glendinning, *The Impact of Social Security Changes: the Views of Families Using Barnardo's Pre-School Services*, London: Barnardo's Research and Development Section, 1990.

[179] See J. Bradshaw, *Child Poverty and Deprivation in the U.K.*, London National Children's Bureau, 1990; C. Oppenheim, *Poverty—The Facts*, C.P.A.G., 1990.

[180] Section 20(3). See also s.17(1) and note the relevance of s.24(2) if the young person is between 16 and 21 and was between the ages of 16 and 18 looked after by a local authority (not necessarily this one).

quest for help if it is 'compatible with [its] own statutory or other duties and obligations and does not unduly prejudice the discharge of any of [its] functions'.[181] Unless social services departments define 'in need' restrictively—perhaps to encompass abandoned children or children with disabilities only—they are likely to be inundated with demands for accommodation. This is a burden they did not expect and can ill-afford. It could also have an impact on the way accommodation is provided for younger children.

THE CARE ORDER[182]

The care order has been remodelled. Gone are the plethora of grounds and 'care or control' condition.[183] They are replaced by 'minimum threshold conditions'[184] set out in section 31(2). These have to be looked at in the context of s.1, including the injunction that the order must be better for the child.[185] The 'safety net' of wardship, which courts have encouraged local authorities to use,[186] has been revoked.[187] The care order is now the only route into care.

There are probably more interpretational problems in s.31(2) than any other sub-section of the Act. I have written about these elsewhere[188] and will, therefore, only comment on them briefly here. Section 31(2) states:

> A court may only make a care order or supervision order if it is satisfied -
>
> (a) that the child concerned is suffering, or is likely to suffer, significant harm; and
>
> (b) that the harm, or likelihood of harm, is attributable to -

---

[181] See s.27(2), (3)(a).

[182] I have written of this elsewhere. See 'Care After 1991' in (ed.) D. Freestone, *Children and the Law*, Hull University Press, 1990, p. 130.

[183] See Children and Young Persons Act 1969 s.1(2). But the 'grounds' and 'the condition' were often merged (see *Re S* [1978] Q.B. 120) or blurred. And see R. Dingwall *et al*, *The Protection of Children*, Oxford, Basil Blackwell, 1983, pp. 196–7.

[184] The Lord Chancellor has described them as the 'minimum circumstances' in his Joseph Jackson Memorial Lecture: (1989) 139 N.L.J. 505.

[185] See s.1(5).

[186] *Re D* [1977] Fam. 158, 166 *per* Dunn, J.; *Re R* [1987] 2 FLR 400.

[187] See s.100.

[188] See, *op. cit.*, note 182. A critique of some of the points in my article is A. Bainham (1991) *J. Child Law*, 99.

(i) the care given to the child, or likely to be given to him if the order were not made, not being what it would be reasonable to expect a parent to give him, or

(ii) the child's being beyond parental control.

The provision is forward-looking,[189] thus obviating much recourse to the wardship jurisdiction. Although the past is not specifically included, the admonition of Butler-Sloss J in *M* v. *Westminster C. C.* remains pertinent. 'A child's development is a continuing process. The present must be relevant in the context of what has happened in the past, and it becomes a matter of degree as to how far in the past you go'.[190] But whether the drug-addict mother case (*Re D*)[191] would be caught by the new provision is doubtful. It would have to be shown that the significant harm, which the baby in that case was undoubtedly suffering, was attributable to the care given her not being what it would be reasonable to expect a parent to give. Had the mother come off drugs she would have spontaneously aborted. Is this what a hypothetically reasonable woman would have done?[192]

The meaning of 'significant harm', the fulcrum upon which all coercive intervention in this Act rests,[193] will be tested and retested in years to come. 'Significant' suggests 'substantial'. As the *Review of Child Care Law* puts it, 'Minor shortcomings in the health and care provided or minor defects in physical, psychological or social development should not give rise to any compulsory intervention unless they are having, or likely to have, serious and lasting effects upon the child'.[194] Harm may be significant in a number of ways: in amount, in effect and in importance. Insignificant harm is not irrelevant for it may betoken risk of significant harm in the foreseeable future.[195] There is a spectrum of abuse and an index of harm.[196] The context is all-important: an act may lead to significant harm

---

[189] *Cf. Essex C.C.* v. *TLR and KBR* (1978) 9 Fam. Law 15. The *Review of Child Care Law* pointed to the burden of proof on the local authority and the difficulty of assessment (para. 15.17).

[190] [1985] FLR 325.

[191] [1987] A.C. 317.

[192] See E. Tylden, *MIMS*, June 1, 1983.

[193] The test is to be found in s.43, s.44, s.46, 47, and 25 as well. See also s.38(2) (interim orders).

[194] DHSS, *Review of Child Care Law*, para. 15(15).

[195] There are some good examples in S. Cretney and J. Masson, *Principles of Family Law*, London, Sweet and Maxwell, 1990, p. 615.

[196] See *Re B* [1990] 2 FLR 317.

in one context and not in another. Using the analogy of the old 'behaviour' fact in divorce, it is necessary to look at this child in this family and, arguably, in some cases in this culture.

Clearly, all forms of 'harm' are included; physical, emotional,[197] sexual. 'Harm' means 'ill-treatment or the impairment of health or development'; 'development' means 'physical, intellectual, emotional, social or behavioural development'; 'health' means 'physical or mental health', and 'ill-treatment' includes 'sexual abuse and forms of ill-treatment which are not physical'. 'Sexual abuse' is not defined,[198] but then only nine years earlier it was not included by the DHSS in the list of abuse of which local authorities should take cognizance.[199] Neglect is not specifically mentioned but is embraced by impairment of health'.[200] Where the question of whether harm suffered by a child is significant turns on the child's health or development, this is to be compared with that which could be reasonably expected of a 'similar child'. This is a child with similar physical attributes, not a child of similar parents.[201] In an Act which is broadly non-interventionist this is a surprising provision. It requires parents to provide the care children need, even though they lack the resources (whether these be economic, emotional or intellectual). It may protect the children of the poor but it also penalizes poor families.

The significant harm must be 'attributable' either to the quality of care or to the child's being beyond parental control. 'Attributable to' is, I believe, wider than 'caused by' and may allow for coercive intervention where the parent is not responsible for the harm (*e.g.* she is psychiatrically sick or is about to introduce a known abuser into the home).[202] The quality of care expected is what it is reasonable to expect of a parent, not this parent and not a parent in the position of this parent. The emphasis is on this child, given this child's needs.[203] These may be greater than the norm, if, for example, the

---

[197] Following *F* v. *Suffolk C.C.* [1981] 2 FLR 208.

[198] I discuss the problem of definition in (1989) 42 C.L.P. 85, 88–91. On whether 'vulgar and inappropriate horseplay' is sexual abuse see *C* v. *C* [1988] 1 FLR 462.

[199] LASSL (80), 4 August 1980: criticized at the time by BASPCAN, *Child Sexual Abuse*, 198).

[200] See, for agreement, J. Masson, *The Children Act*, London: Sweet and Maxwell, 1990, p. 71.

[201] See the Lord Chancellor's statement in *Hansard*, H.L. vol. 503, col. 354.

[202] *Cf.* A. Bainham, *Children—The New Law*, Bristol: Jordans, 1990, p. 101.

[203] See Lord Mackay, *Hansard*, H.L. vol. 512, col. 756.

child is asthmatic, has brittle bones,[204] or special needs.[205] A parent can be expected to cope with these additional problems: if this parent cannot he or she falls below the standard set. Like the provision just referred to, this does seem to be out of line with the general trend of the Act. But, since it is prone to penalize the poor, it is not altogether inconsistent with other government measures.

It is consistent, though, with the Act that the 'beyond parental control' ground from the earlier legislation[206] is retained, albeit in different form. Parents may be left alone to care for their children but clearly cannot be trusted to do so where they cannot control them. Law and order considerations also must not be ruled out in understanding why this provision is retained.[207] But it is now linked to significant harm: a beyond control child must be likely to suffer[208] significant harm before a care order can be contemplated. But parents cannot initiate an application,[209] despite the fact that other legislation[210] increases their own criminal responsibility for their children's actions when beyond control.

Since the 'minimum conditions' in s.31(2) are the pre-condition for intervention to protect children from abuse or neglect, it should be asked whether any gaps are created.[211] The inability of the local authority to assume parental rights and thus provide stability and planning for a child may mean that it will be impossible to prevent a parent who is capable of providing adequate facilities for a child from removing that child from a foster home where he or she has lived for a considerable time.[212] There may be no difficulty in proving that such a child would be likely to suffer significant harm: it may be rather more difficult to demonstrate that such harm is attributable to the care likely to be given to the child not being what it would be reasonable to expect a parent to give. Much will depend on how the courts interpret 'care given to the child'. A parent can give 'care' without day-to-day physical contact by showing love and affection, visiting, remembering

---

[204] See *Re Cullimore, The Times*, 24 March 1976; *Re P* [1988] 1 FLR 328.

[205] As to which see S. Curtis (ed.), *From Asthma to Thalassaemia*, London, BAAF, 1986.

[206] Children and Young Persons Act 1969 s.1(2)(d).

[207] See M. D. A. Freeman (1984) 37 *CLP* 175; I. Taylor (1987) *Socialist Register* 297.

[208] Not 'wreak' significant harm, as many beyond control children do.

[209] But they can request that the local authority provides accommodation for a child with whom they cannot cope (s.20).

[210] Criminal Justice Act 1991, ss.57 and 58.

[211] I consider this in more detail in (ed.) D. Freestone, *Children and The Law*, Hull: Hull University Press, 1990, p. 130 at pp. 158–171.

[212] See also S. Cretney in (ed.) D. Freestone *op. cit.*, note 211, p. 58 at p. 71.

birthdays and so on. If the courts interpret 'care' to include these manifestations, then a parent who, for whatever reason, fails to offer this 'parenting' may not surmount the hurdle of s.31(2). But interpreted more literally it could lead to children being removed by 'unimpeachable' parents where the trauma of removal from psychological parents to whom they are attached is likely to cause significant harm and where s.31(2) will not bite.

Of the remaining gaps the one which may expose children is the one created by the removal of the abandonment grounds in section 3 of the Child Care Act 1980, which necessarily disappear with the end of the parental rights resolution. In particular, there is concern that the Act lacks an equivalent to the concept of 'statutory abandonment',[213] which was deemed to occur if parents, with a child in 'voluntary care' did not notify their address to the local authority for twelve months. This may lead to children remaining in limbo with no prospects of rehabilitation and, in some cases, no way in which a permanent plan can be devised. It may be possible to argue that 'care' expected from a parent would include notification of change of address. Short of this, if a care order is not available, the foster parents will, after three years of caring for the child, be able to apply for a residence order,[214] which will give them parental responsibility.[215] The foster parents may also apply with the consent of the local authority without fulfilling the time requirement.[216] The court's leave will also be required and it is to have 'particular regard' to the authority's plans for the child's future and the wishes and feelings of the parents.[217] Given these hurdles, whether there is sufficient in the legislation to protect the child from 'drift'[218] will depend on how local authorities and courts interpret these provisions.

---

[213] See Child Care Act 1980 s.3(8).
[214] See s.10(5)(b). On the definition of 'three years' see s.10(10).
[215] See s.12(2).
[216] See s.9(3)(a) ('is or was at any time in last six months a local authority foster parent').
[217] See s.10(9)(d).
[218] *Cf.* J. Rowe and L. Lambert's thesis in a book which influenced the passing of the last major children's legislation, *Children Who Wait*, London: ABAA, 1973.

CARE AND PARENTAL RESPONSIBILITY

A care order vests parental responsibility in the local authority.[219] The White Paper[220] not surprisingly contemplated that parental powers and responsibilities would pass 'from the parents to the authority'. But the Law Commission, in its report on *Guardianship and Custody* took a different view: 'the parents remain the parents and it will be important in many cases to involve the parents in the child's care'. The Law Commission accepted that the care order would leave the parents little scope to exercise their responsibilities 'save to a limited extent while the child is with them, because the local authority will be in control of so much of the child's life'. But the Law Commission, nevertheless, concluded that 'parents should not be deprived of their very parenthood unless and until the child is adopted or freed for adoption'.[221] Note the word 'parenthood': the Law Commission did not say 'parental responsibility'.

These changes in thought and nuances of language are reflected in the mess (compromise, if you prefer it) of section 33. Parents retain parental responsibility[222] but local authorities acquire it also. As the Bill proceeded through Parliament it was realized that this was likely to cause conflict and, not just over contact which is separately provided for.[223] Accordingly, it is now laid down that, while a care order is in force, the local authority shall 'have the power...to determine the extent to which a parent...may meet his parental responsibility'.[224] The local authority may only do this if satisfied that it is necessary to do so to safeguard or promote the child's welfare.[225] The local authority will not have to satisfy anyone other than itself. There is no recourse to any court[226] for the aggrieved parent, unless,

---

[219] See s.33(3)(a).

[220] In para. 37.

[221] See para. 2.11.

[222] But they can only exercise it in accordance with s.2(8), which precludes action incompatible with a court order.

[223] Under s.34.

[224] See s.33(3)(b).

[225] See s.33(4).

[226] There is, however, a new complaints procedure (see s.26(3)).
But, given that 'parental responsibility' is a 'civil right' (Article 6 of European Convention on Human Rights), and the absence of a 'fair and public hearing...by an independent and impartial tribunal' (neither wardship nor a specific issue order is available) the route to Strasbourg seems clear.

as seems unlikely, the dispute fits within the categories of grounds[227] for judicial review.

It is difficult, therefore, to gauge the significance, beyond the ideological, of the parent retaining parental responsibility when there is a care order. The research[228] may indicate the value of incorporating parents into the decision-making processes relating to children in long-term care, but the Act and Regulations[229] since indicate the impracticability of so doing. Partnership breaks down where the child is in compulsory care and supervision and control take over. In practice that is inevitable (the parents have after all failed to act as parents should) and the Act should have recognized it by a transfer of parental responsibility on the making of a care order. What we get instead is a fudge, which may raise parental expectations and provoke fruitless litigation. It is hardly surprising that the Regulations should adopt a defensive position on 'home on trial',[230] conveying the impression that the relationship between the local authority and parents with a child in compulsory care is much as it was before the Act was passed—an admission, grudging perhaps, that the Government got it wrong.[231] Indeed, the latest research evidence suggests a high rate of breakdown of home on trial placements and as many as a quarter of such children being re-abused.[232]

---

[227] See the speech of Lord Diplock in *Council of Civil Service Unions* v. *Minister for the Civil Service* [1985] A.C. 374 (illegality, procedural impropriety and irrationality).

[228] For example, J. Rowe *et al*, *Long Term Foster Care*, London: Batsford, 1984, and S. Millham, *Lost In Care*, Aldershot: Gower, 1986.

[229] See, in particular, Consultation Paper No. 9 said to owe more to 'Beckford than the Children Act' *per* P. Smith, *Community Care*, 28 March 1991.

[230] Using it seems 'out of place middle-class notions' such as the need for two references: examples, it is said, of defensive social work (see Smith, *op. cit.*, note 229).

[231] Though more children will be in contact with their parents as a result of this Act, and rightly so, even where they are permanently placed. And such placements are less likely to break down where there is contact (see J. Fratter *et al*, *Permanent Family Placement; A Decade of Experience*, London: BAAF, 1991).

[232] See E. Farmer and R. A. Parker; *Trials and Tribulations: A Study of Children 'Home on Trial'*, London: H.M.S.O., 1991. Earlier research supports this (see B. Tizard, *Adoption: A Second Chance*, London: Open Books, 1977). But compare J. Trent, *Homeward Bound*, London: Barnardos, 1989.

332 Chapter 14

EMERGENCY PROTECTION

The law on emergency protection has, hitherto, been unsatisfactory in a number of ways.[233] Place of safety orders were frequently sought in situations short of emergency. They were often routinized ways of intervention and were granted routinely. There was no appeal[234] and no way of challenging a denial of access.[235] The evidence of the local authority was rarely challenged or even tested. Social workers were also criticized for not using the powers they had to protect children adequately.[236]

The new law is clearly an improvement, but problems remain. There is a new duty on local authorities laid down by s.47 to investigate cases of suspected harm and on other agencies (education, housing, health) to assist.[237] The place of safety order is abolished and two new orders (child assessment and emergency protection) are substituted for it. The new emergency protection order is both more explicit and more just than the place of safety order. It is also more complex and will place heavier demands on social workers and on courts. Guardians *ad litem*[238] will have a role to play for the first time so that the evidence of the local authority should be tested. Although most applications will, as with the place of safety order, be *ex parte* and the order is not subject to appeal, an application for discharge may be made after 72 hours provided the parent (or other person applying for the discharge) was not present when the application was made.[239] There is also a presumption of reasonable contact during the duration of[240] the order,[241] and this extends to a person 'acting

---

[233] The process of recognition of this was slow to unfold but the *Review of Child Care Law* (Ch. 13), the Cleveland report and the Carlile report (*op. cit.*, note 48) made reform inevitable. But 10 years ago it attracted barely a ripple of interest.

[234] And see *Nottinghamshire C.C.* v. *Q* [1982] 3 FLR 305; *Re E* [1983] 4 FLR 668.

[235] It was not covered by s.12A(1) of the Child Care Act 1980.

[236] Note in particular the L.B. of Greenwich report, *op. cit.* note 48 which is also the *fons et origo* of the C.A.O. (see pp. 153–156).

[237] This puts on a statutory footing the co-operation advocated as good practice by the DHSS in *Working Together*, 1988 (see also now the 2nd ed. of this published in October 1991).

[238] See s.41(6)(g).

[239] See s.45(8), (9), (11). There is some fear that parents may be inveigled into being present without fully understanding the implications of this.

[240] The maximum period is 15 days since one extension of 7 days is permissible (see s.45 (6)).

[241] See s.44(13). See also s.44(6): the court may make directions as it considers appropriate.

on behalf[242] of the parents so that an independent medical examination[243] may, for example, be arranged. The applicant (who may be anyone) acquires parental responsibility on the making of an E.P.O.,[244] but may only take such action in meeting this 'as is reasonably required to safeguard or promote the welfare of the child'.[245] Given the short duration of an E.P.O. (at maximum 15 days), and the fact that parents retain parental responsibility, and the power of the court to give directions[246] about medical and psychiatric examinations and other assessments, there are not many decisions the local authority is likely to be able to take. But, once again, if there is any disagreement between a local authority and parents, the scope for challenge is severely limited.

Emergency protection orders are intended as immediate, short-term protection in genuine emergencies. Protection relates to the future[247] so that present and past significant harm are only relevant to the extent that the child is likely to suffer again in the 'near' future.[248] There are three grounds. In the main ground (in section 44(1) (a)) the test is tightened by providing that it is the court which must be satisfied of the ground, and not as before the applicant. But this does not apply to the two other grounds for an E.P.O. with the consequence that it should be easier to establish these than it was the grounds for a place of safety order. Although the emphasis is on emergency, it is not envisaged that removal of the child will always take place and, even if removed, the child could be returned during the order, if, for example, the abuser were to leave.

The child assessment order is emphatically not for emergency situations.[249] It is intended for use where there is fear for a child's safety but no hard evidence. Only the local authority and NSPCC[250] may seek a C.A.O. The court has to be satisfied that the applicant has reasonable cause to suspect that the child is suffering, or is likely to suffer, significant harm, that

---

[242] See s.44(13)(f).

[243] An instructive case, though it did not concern emergency protection, is *R v. Hampshire C.C., ex p K and K* [1990] 2 WLR 649, where parents were denied the right to have their daughter independently examined.

[244] See s.44(4)(c).

[245] See s.44(5)(b).

[246] See s.44(6)(b).

[247] 'Is likely to suffer significant harm' (s.44(1)(a)).

[248] This was stressed in Consultation Paper No. 13 (see para. 36). See also D. Cooper, 22(11) *Social Work Today*, 8 November 1990, p. 20.

[249] See D.H. *Guidance and Regulations*, vol. 1, para. 44.

[250] It is the only 'authorized person' as yet (see s.31(9), 43(13)).

assessment is required to determine this, and that it is unlikely that there would be an assessment in the absence of an order.[251] The court is not to make a C.A.O. if satisfied that there are grounds for an E.P.O. and that it ought to make such an order rather than a C.A.O.[252] The intention of this provision is clear: where suspicions are aroused it should be possible to insist on a child, who may be at risk, being medically examined. But, if there are suspicions, the case should be investigated under s.47, and this provides that if access is refused in the course of such enquiries an E.P.O.[253] may be applied for. This casts doubt on the rationale or value of the C.A.O. Indeed, it may well be the case if an application for a C.A.O. is refused that an emergency will have been created to ground an application for an E.P.O. Further, an application for a C.A.O. is on notice.[254] The parents are to be involved and an order will presumably only be made if they are uncooperative. Even if an order is made, parents are to be able to express views about the 'who', 'where', 'when' and 'what' of assessment. The removal of children is a 'reserve provision':[255] it is envisaged that in some circumstances the parent will also be accommodated. Although the maximum period of the order is seven days, should a longer period be necessary it is possible that the provision of accommodation section could be used, provided the parent does not object.[256] The local authority could continue to authorize medical assessment, either as the parent's delegate under s.2(9) or under s.3(5), if it is reasonable to safeguard or promote the child's welfare, and it is not thought inconsistent with the child assessment provisions, though it may well be.

Despite this possibility of extending the order and the fact that the assessment need not begin immediately,[257] it may be thought that in practice the C.A.O. will be an unwieldy instrument of protection. If so, local authorities may find it easier to rely on the E.P.O. This does not require a full court hearing and is not subject to appeal. Furthermore, it gives the authority parental responsibility and lasts (with an extension) for 15 days as opposed to 7. In some circumstances local authorities may find it even easier to enlist the assistance of the police. The police may detain a child for up to 72 hours

---

[251] See s.43(1).

[252] See s.43(4).

[253] See s.47(6). There is a *duty* to apply for one of an E.P.O., C.A.O., care order or supervision order, unless satisfied that welfare can be satisfactorily safeguarded without doing so.

[254] See s.43(11) and D.H., *Guidance and Regulations* vol. 1, para. 4. 18.

[255] See Consultation Paper No. 13, paras 14–15.

[256] See s.20(7).

[257] See s.43(5).

and what contact they allow the child's parents is up to them.[258] The test is what, in the opinion of the designated officer, is both 'reasonable and in the child's best interest'. The width of these police powers seems largely to have escaped comment. More attention has been given to the question as to whether the police may authorize medical examinations to determine whether sexual abuse has occurred. There is no statutory provision directly on this but there is a provision parallel to s.3(5) mandating the designated officer to do what is reasonable to safeguard or promote the child's welfare. This is expressed as a duty and not, as in s.3(5) as a permission but, since specific regard is to be had to the length of time police protection will operate, it is difficult to see how anything beyond routine first aid or an X-ray can be justified. Whether the local authority has recourse to the E.P.O. or uses the assistance of the police, it is likely that in many cases they will be forced into applying for an interim care order.[259] If this is so, would it not have been preferable to have created a child assessment order that would run long enough to have enabled assessment to have taken place? If it is thought that this would have been too serious an intrusion on parental autonomy,[260] the consequences of not doing so may result in a series of decisions even more destructive of a parent-child relationship.

The balancing of the need to protect children and of the imperative to protect their rights[261] leads to a provision, repeated several times[262] in the Act to the effect that a *Gillick*-competent child 'may refuse to submit to a medical or psychiatric examination or other assessment'.[263] It is not, and could not be, clear of what the 14- or 15-year-old girl must have 'sufficient understanding to make an informed decision'. In the *Gillick* case itself Lord Scarman said of the decision to seek contraceptive services: 'It is not enough that she should understand the nature of the advice which is being given: she

---

[258] See s.46(6), (10). The wishes and feelings of the child are to be fully considered (D.H., *Guidance and Regulations*, vol. 1, para. 4.76). If a child is in police protection but in local authority accommodation (envisaged by s.46)(11)), the authority is, according to the *Guidance and Regulations*, 'required to afford such contact', that is as the 'designated officer'. But this is misleading, for the local authority's duties are governed by part III of the Act.

[259] Under s.38.

[260] The Government originally proposed that the child's removal should be permitted for up to 28 days to allow for comprehensive assessment (see Standing Committee B, cols. 276–329 in particular D. Mellor at col. 295).

[261] *Cf.* R. Farson, *Birthrights*, Harmondsworth: Penguin Books, 1978, p. 9.

[262] See sections 38(6), 43(8), 44(7) and Schedule 3, para. 4(4) and 5(5).

[263] It is doubtful whether refusal could be overcome by an order of the High Court in wardship (see J. Eekelaar (1986) 6 *Ox. J.L.S.* 161, 181).

must have sufficient maturity to understand what is involved. There are moral and family questions, especially her relationships with her parents; long term problems associated with the emotional impact of pregnancy and its termination and there are risks to health of sexual intercourse at her age, risks which contraception may diminish but cannot eliminate. It follows that a doctor will have to satisfy himself that she is able to appraise these factors before he can safely proceed on the basis that she has at law capacity to consent to contraceptive treatment'.[264] The question may well arise in the context of sexual abuse. It is one of the duties of the guardian *ad litem* to inform the court whether she thinks the under-16-year-old is *Gillick*-competent.[265] There are real possibilities of conflict if the girl and the guardian do not agree, and the girl purports to instruct her solicitor accordingly.[266] It is not clear how the issue would be tried,[267] nor how it would be resolved.

But the judgment of *Gillick*-competence will not be easy. It is well known that a sexually-abused girl may be so traumatized by her experience, which may go back many years, as to be incapable of making a rationally autonomous decision about whether she wishes to expose her father.[268] She may be intellectually capable of a level of decision-making which satisfies the *Gillick* test but at the same time be so emotionally dependent and confused as to be incapable of weighing up the considerations. We all make mistakes. If we are to take rights seriously, one of the rights we must accord to persons, including children, is the right to make the wrong decisions.[269] We should only interfere with the decision of a child of competence when the decision she wishes to take is irreparably harmful or in some way is likely to thwart her life choices.[270] In practice it will be difficult to reconcile these conflicts. However, if we believe in treating children's rights seriously,

---

[264] [1986] A.C. 112, 189.

[265] The Family Proceedings Courts (Children Act 1989) Rules 1991, r.11(4)(a).

[266] The solicitor is to take instructions from the guardian unless the solicitor considers that the child wishes to give instructions which conflict with those of the guardian and that he is able to give instructions, in which case the solicitor is to conduct the proceedings in accordance with the child's instructions (*op. cit.*, note 265, r.12(1)(a).

[267] The guardian might apply for an order terminating the solicitor's appointment. If the child is of sufficient understanding she is to be given an opportunity to make representations (see *op. cit.*, note 265, r.12(4)).

[268] The evidence on trauma is quite clear (see notably D. Finkelhor and A. Browne, (1985) 55 *Am. J. Orthopsychiatry* 530 and more generally, J. Haugaard and N. D. Reppucci, *The Sexual Abuse of Children*, San Francisco: Jossey Bass, 1988, Ch. 4). But there is no research evidence testing the assumption in the text.

[269] See R. Dworkin, *Taking Rights Seriously*, London, Duckworth, 1978, pp. 188–9.

[270] See M. D. A. Freeman, 1 *Children and Society* 299 (1988).

and this is an ideal embodied in the Act, their decisions must be given equal concern and respect.[271] How this problem is resolved will tell us much about the attitude of courts to children's rights and in particular to their right to autonomy. The Act gives very much less attention to the implications of a child's autonomy than it does to that of her parents.

WARDSHIP RESTRICTED

Though mooted in a Law Commission Working Paper,[272] it seems that the Government's decision to restrict wardship came late in the day.[273] The restrictions are controversial, but they are perfectly consistent with the pro-family ideology of the Act. It is right that state intervention into the lives of families should be circumscribed, and not left to depend on a judge's interpretation of welfare. But the fear is that some cases of abuse will slip through the net, cases which might be easier to substantiate in wardship than in care proceedings.[274] It is also significant that, in a number of the recent cases of 'ritualistic' or 'organized' abuse, other forms of abuse have emerged in the course of wardship hearings.[275] That may not be an adequate defence of wardship before the Act; but it does suggest that under the new law some abuse will go undetected.

The Act restricts the local authority's recourse to wardship in four ways. First, the High Court's powers to commit a child to care in s.7 of the Family Law Reform Act 1969 are abolished.[276] Secondly, the inherent jurisdiction[277] of the High Court cannot be exercised to require a child to be

---

[271] See *op. cit.*, note 269, chs. 7–9, 11, 13.

[272] No. 101, *Wards of Court*, but this came to no firm conclusions.

[273] See Lord Mackay's Jackson Memorial Lecture (1989) 139 *N.L.J.* 505, 507.

[274] For example see *Re P* [1987] 2 FLR 467, where wardship was used where there was suspected child sexual abuse which it was difficult to prove. See also Somerset Area Health Authority, *Inquiry into Wayne Brewer*, 1977.

[275] See 23(5) *Social Work Today*, 26 September 1991, reporting on evidence from the Official Solicitor. The first reported case on 'ritualistic' abuse is *Rochdale B.C.* v. *A* [1991] 2 FLR 192.

[276] Section 100(1). The High Court will still be able to make a care order but only if the minimum conditions in s.31(2) are substantiated. If a wardship court thinks a care order is appropriate it can make a s.37 direction but whether an application is then made depends on the local authority.

[277] 'Wardship is only one use of the High Court's inherent *parens patriae* jurisdiction...it is open to the High Court to make orders under its inherent jurisdiction in respect of children other than through wardship' *per* Lord Mackay (1989) 139 *NLJ* at 507. On inherent jurisdiction generally see Jacob (1970) 23 *CLP* 23.

placed in care, supervised by a local authority, or accommodated by or on behalf of a local authority.[278] Thirdly, if the local authority wishes to apply to the court for an order under inherent jurisdiction it must obtain leave[279] and satisfy conditions.[280] The court must be satisfied that the result could not be achieved by the local authority applying for an order other than by exercise of the court's inherent jurisdiction, and there is 'reasonable cause' to believe that the child will suffer significant harm if the jurisdiction is not exercised. 'Reasonable cause to believe' suggests a lower standard of intervention than that required for a care order but I doubt if it will be so interpreted. The result is that in practice it is likely the local authority will have to satisfy the same test as for care, even though it does not wish to acquire parental responsibility. There was surely a strong case for arguing that a lower standard should need to be satisfied for intervention on a single issue of upbringing. This would not have undermined the general philosophy of the Government, and may well have served the interests of children better.[281]

The inherent jurisdiction of the High Court will remain available to local authorities but in circumstances yet to be defined. It is possible that leave will be granted liberally. This would be against the spirit, if not the letter, of the Act. But it would not be altogether surprising for the judges may feel their wings have been rather clipped by the restrictions. Matters which could well legitimately fall within the High Court's inherent jurisdiction include sterilization of the mentally handicapped[282] and the intractable problem of the defective neonate.[283] But on this it is worth comparing two leading cases. In 'Baby Alexandra',[284] the Court of Appeal ruled that a life-saving operation to remove an intestinal blockage on a Down's Syndrome baby should be performed. It upheld the right of life where it could not be shown that such life was demonstrably awful. It seems the criteria for leave are easily satisfied: if the court's inherent jurisdiction had not been exercised Alexan-

---

[278] Section 100(2).

[279] See s.100(3).

[280] These are in s.100(4).

[281] For agreement see A. Bainham, *Children—The New Law*, Bristol: Jordans, 1990, p. 202, and J. Eekelaar and R. Dingwall (1989) 139 *NLJ* 217.

[282] See *Re D* [1989] A.C. 189, particularly Lord Templeman's *dictum* at p. 205 and *Re D* [1976] Fam. 185.

[283] See M. D. A. Freeman, *The Rights and Wrongs of Children*, London: Frances Pinter, 1983, pp. 259–63.

[284] *Re B* [1981] 1 WLR 1421.

dra would have died. In *Re C*[285] the child was 'terminally ill, even before she was born'.[286] The Court of Appeal agreed with the first instance judge who held that life-prolonging treatment should be withheld. It is difficult to see how the 'significant harm' criterion would be met in such a case, though much would depend on how 'harm' was interpreted. It would be unfortunate if decisions like that in *Re C* were to be taken without the public scrutiny of a judicial hearing. The public interest requires this, or some other method of, accountable review.[287] Lord Mackay acknowledged that there were 'difficult borderline cases where at present wardship...would offer a remedy'.[288] This is clearly one. Others, such as the unruly 17-year-old,[289] who is outside the remit of care, but was susceptible to wardship are of less concern. The invocation of wardship in such a case seems an inappropriate use of welfare legislation.

There is one final restriction on a local authority's recourse to the High Court's inherent jurisdiction. This prevents the High Court from exercising its inherent jurisdiction 'for the purpose of conferring on any local authority power to determine any question...in connection with any aspect of parental responsibility for a child'.[290] This provision is far from clear. *Prima facie* it would seem to push or encourage local authorities into applying for care orders (they cannot use prohibited steps or specific issue orders)[291] when they do not want full parental responsibility, but merely seek the court's guidance on a particular matter.

A good illustration is the recent case of *Re B*,[292] a pregnant 12-year-old living with her grandparents. Her mother objected to an abortion. The girl, said to be of 'normal intelligence and understanding', wanted her pregnancy terminated. The local authority was brought in by the GP, wardship proceedings were initiated and a termination was authorized. Under the Act the grandparents could apply for a residence order, but would then share parental responsibility with (in this case, the child being illegitimate) the mother and the further dispute would have to be resolved—all, of course, within a

---

[285] [1990] 1 FLR 252.

[286] *Ibid.*, p. 254.

[287] 'The court's decision and the reasons for it should be open to public scrutiny' (*ibid.*, p. 260). And see further I. Kennedy and A. Grubb, *Medical Law*, London: Butterworths, 1989, pp. 498–528.

[288] In the Jackson Memorial Lecture at p. 507.

[289] *Re SW* [1986] 1 FLR 24.

[290] Section 100(2)(d).

[291] See s.9(5)(b).

[292] *The Independent*, 22 May 1991.

short time limit. A specific issue order would not be available to them.[293] If the GP were now to bring in the local authority, the only option open to it would be to commence care proceedings, and to seek to acquire in the process more parental responsibility than it would want or require.[294] For an Act which prides itself on its flexibility, this is a strange consequence. Furthermore, if the girl were already in care, since the local authority would have parental responsibility, it could not invoke the inherent jurisdiction. If, therefore, there was a disagreement between the local authority and the girl's parents, the matter could not be referred to a court for resolution.[295] If the girl is being 'accommodated', the local authority may do what is reasonable to safeguard her welfare,[296] but whether consenting to an abortion comes within the 'reasonableness' criterion must be doubted.

The decision to restrict wardship has been taken precipitately. Given the interpretational problems in this Act it ought to have been retained as a safety net. It is a flexible institution and one which has responded to social and moral changes in the past. It has been less cumbersome than legislative frameworks. It has the facility to respond to novel problems. Its demise is not in the interests of children or of those concerned with child welfare. A decade, or more, of experience with the consequences of *A v. Liverpool City Council*,[297] an earlier restriction on wardship jurisdiction, bears this out. It should not cause surprise if, very soon, there are as many calls to reverse the Act's initiative on wardship as there currently are the House of Lord's decision in *A v. Liverpool C.C.* and its consequences.[298] It is one of the ironies or contradictions[299] of the Act that, in strengthening the position of the parents, the logical step was not taken of restoring to them the challenge of local authority decision-making by wardship.[300] Could it be that logic falters when cost is counted?

---

[293] They would need leave to apply (a 'filter against unwarranted interference' *per* Law Commission No. 172, para. 4.41).

[294] And it would share parental responsibility with the mother with all the problems attendant on this. If the local authority authorized the abortion and the mother disagreed with its decision, there is no way the conflict could be resolved in court.

[295] See *ante*, 330.

[296] See s.3(5).

[297] [1982] A.C. 363.

[298] Wardship has been denied to parents even where there has been an abuse of power by local authorities. See *Re DM* [1986] 2 FLR 122, *Re S* [1987] 1 FLR 479, *Re RM and LM* [1986] 2 FLR 205, *Re Y* [1988] 1 FLR 299.

[299] The continued use of wardship was supported by Butler-Sloss J in the Cleveland report (para. 16. 37) and the injustice of *A v. Liverpool C.C.* attacked (para. 16.65).

[300] Their position is even weaker after the Act because the local authority cannot now waive

DIVORCE AND CHILDREN

The implications of this Act for the children of divorce has provoked much less comment than it deserves.[301] It tends to be forgotten that many more children are involved in their parents' divorce than in decisions taken by child welfare authorities. The stance of the Act towards these children is, in line with the philosophy of the Act, broadly non-interventionist. After divorce their parents retain parental responsibility. Although the Act allows for joint parenting arrangements,[302] it may be assumed that, as before, the majority of children will live with their mothers and one-third or more of them have decreasing contact with the fathers. It may be easier to enforce[303] a contact order than it was access, but the end of marriage will spell the end of parenthood for many fathers.

But it will not mean the end of their parental responsibility.[304] It is argued that because parental responsibility is retained by both parents there will be fewer disputes. The court cannot take parental responsibility away from a parent; so, the argument goes, there should be fewer unseemly court fights, and, because conflict will be reduced, children will benefit. All the court can do is make a Section 8 order, but this merely settles the living arrangements of the child and does not touch the issue of parental responsibility. The norm will be no order[305] because it is assumed that parents, with or without the assistance of conciliation services, will be able to agree for themselves what arrangements to make for their children. Not surprisingly, the new statement of arrangements is now a substantial document and, if possible,[306] the respondent is expected to append his signature as an indication that he is agreeable to the arrangements.[307] This

---

objection to a wardship application (as in *A and B* v. *Hereford and Worcs C.C.* [1986] 1 FLR 289). They were sometimes encouraged to do this (see *R* v. *L.B. of Newham* [1988] 1 FLR 416.

[301] S. Cretney comments on it briefly in (ed.) D. Freestone, *Children and the Law*, Hull: Hull University Press, 1990, 58, 60–62.

[302] See s.11(4), effectively overruling *Riley* v. *Riley* [1986] 2 FLR 429.

[303] Note it is an order requiring 'the person with whom the child lives to allow the child to visit or stay with the person named in the order...'.

[304] See s.2(5), (7). Under the old law the position was not clear (see *Dipper* v. *Dipper* [1981] Fam. 31). The Act is at odds with the view expressed initially by the Law Commission that parental responsibility should 'run with the child' (Working Paper No. 96, para. 4. 53).

[305] See s.1(5).

[306] See The Family Proceedings Rules 1991, r. 2.2.2.

[307] It should be stressed that agreement does not preclude the court making an order where it would be 'better' for the child.

provision in the Rules is understandably causing concern amongst practitioners.

It will cause consternation amongst primary carers too when the message, as yet I suspect well-disguised, gets to them that it is their job and not the courts to sort out, what they will still call, custody. Conciliators may believe, as Piper found, that 'the court process is...bad for children and good responsible parents do not use courts'.[308] But this ignores the large number of irresponsible parents, and in particular those for whom 'parental responsibility' may be a new weapon for meddling, interfering and undermining. The Act, by insisting that the non-caring parent retains equal parental responsibility, has put the primary carer in a worse position than she occupied previously, and, since the welfare of the child is inextricably bound up with the well-being of the caring parent, has as a consequence deleteriously affected the lives of many children. This is not about children's rights at all but is a charter of fathers' rights. The family is a site of power: continuing parental responsibility one way in which that power can be exercised.[309] This means that mothers will never be able to take decisions without the possibility that they will be challenged.[310] One result will be many more applications for specific issue orders and, as the courts come to see applicants as vindictive or harassing, orders will be made that no further applications without leave be permitted.[311] It would have been easier and better for the child had the parental responsibility of the primary caretaker been recognized.[312]

The other important change, tucked away in a Schedule headed 'Minor Amendments' (it is gratifying to know that Parliament is not entirely without humour!) is the radical restructuring of s.41 of the Matrimonial Causes Act 1973. It alters the whole function of the divorce court as regards children. It abolishes the requirement that before a decree of divorce can be made absolute the court must be satisfied that the arrangements for the welfare of any child of the family are satisfactory, or the best that can be devised in the circumstances, or that it is impracticable for the party or parties appearing before the court to make any such arrangements. The 'satisfaction hearing'

---

[308] 16 *Int. J. Soc. Law* 477, 490 (1988).

[309] See C. Smart in (eds.) C. Smart and S. Sevenhuijsen, *Child Custody and the Politics of Gender*, London: Routledge, 1989. Articles by J. Brophy and M. Fineman in this collection are also very useful.

[310] Whether imposing a duty of consultation, as Bainham advocates (1990) 53 MLR 206, 211), would be of value is dubious.

[311] See s.91(14).

[312] On this concept see M. Fineman, *op. cit.*, note 309, and (1988) 101 *Harvard Law Rev.* 727.

has been criticized as 'paternalistic',[313] and for failing to achieve its objective of protecting children.[314] Under the new provision the court must consider whether there are any children of the family to whom the section applies and, whether, in the light of the arrangements which have been, or are proposed to be, made for their upbringing and welfare, it should exercise any of its powers under the Children Act with respect to any of them. A decree absolute can still be delayed but in the normal case the statement of arrangements will not be subjected to any judicial scrutiny.

But where is the child in all this? Provided the statement of proposed arrangements is not outrageous, whatever the parents have agreed will be rubber-stamped. Will the much-vaunted 'wishes and feelings of the child'[315] get a look in? The child will not be independently represented: the new emphasis on the guardian *ad litem* in public law[316] has been quietly forgotten in private law disputes but the child may need independent representation as much when his or her parents are at war as when there is some conflict between them and the local authority. There is, it seems, no voice for the child in divorce.[317] The opportunity to strengthen s.41 and convert the high-sounding language of s.1 from rhetoric to reality has been missed. When it comes to divorce this is parent-centred, not child-centred legislation.

CONCLUSION

The Children Act can be, and has been, viewed in a number of ways: as an Act to protect children better or protect their families more; as a manifesto of children's rights or an Act which sacrifices them to their rights; as an Act which is pro-children, pro-the birth family or just pro-fathers; as a lawyer's paradise or a social worker's nightmare—perhaps not surprising in view of its attempt to deal both with the perceived intrusive coercion of Cleveland[318] and the ham-fisted ineffectiveness documented in the Beckford, Carlile and Henry tragedies.[319] Clearly, a number of strands can be detected, even though they cannot always be detected clearly. But domi-

---

[313] By the Booth Committee, *Report of the Matrimonial Causes Procedure*, 1985, para. 2. 24. 727. A good critique is S. Boyd (1990) 7 *CFLQ* 1.
[314] See G. Davis *et al.* (1983) 46 *MLR* 121.
[315] See s.1(3)(a).
[316] See s.41.
[317] The court welfare service cannot be expected to provide this.
[318] *Op. cit.*, note 53.
[319] *Op. cit.*, note 48.

nant is the prevailing image of the family. And it is an image. It is found on the front of corn-flake packets and, we are told, was how it was in Victoria's day. Propagators of this myth are not strong on history. In this construction the family is a cosy, conflict-free environment. There are no power differentials. Questions of economic dependency are neatly glossed over. Parents know what is best for children, as husbands do for wives. It is the image which dominates this Act, which enables it to emphasize parental responsibility and autonomy, which views a court's intervention with suspicion. Whether it is a better instrument to protect children from abuse and neglect may be doubted. It is an Act which, its protagonists would say, sites the welfare of the child under the protective umbrella of his or her family. It is an Act which, I fear, may situate the welfare of the child in the shadow of the welfare of the family.

CHAPTER 15

Removing Rights from Adolescents

The last quarter of a century has seen a growth in awareness of the personality and integrity of children and an increased recognition of their autonomy,[1] both in this country[2] and at international level. In England the courts led the way.[3] The ruling in *Gillick*[4] in 1985 that parental rights yielded to the child's right to make his or her own decision when of 'sufficient understanding and intelligence' seemed to usher in a new age. The trend was affirmed by the Children Act of 1989[5] and by the passing of the United Nations Convention on the Rights of the Child the same year.[6] But the new cases of *Re R*[7] and *Re W*[8] suggest we may have been witnessing a false dawn.

Children's rights issues arise in many areas. In *Gillick*, the question raised, about access to contraceptive advice and treatment without parental consent, was hypothetical.[9] In *R* and *W* the dilemmas were real. In *R* a 15-year-old girl was refusing psychotic medication: in *W* a 16-year-old suffering from anorexia nervosa was refusing medical treatment for this condition and there was a danger that she would starve herself to death.

---

[1] M. D. A. Freeman, *The Rights and Wrongs of Children*, Pinter, London, 1983; B. Franklin, *The Rights of Children*, Blackwell, Oxford, 1986; J. Eekelaar, 'The Emergence of Children's Rights', *Oxford Journal of Legal Studies*, 6, 161.

[2] To a greater extent in Scotland. See Scot. Law Com. No. 135, *Report on Family Law*, 1992.

[3] An early example was *M* v. *M* [1973] 2 All E.R. 81 (access as a child's right).

[4] [1986] A.C. 112. The work of Priscilla Alderson (see *Children's Consent to Surgery*, Open University Press, Buckingham, 1993) is strong support for the *Gillick* ruling.

[5] M. D. A. Freeman, *Children, Their Families and the Law*, Macmillan, Basingstoke, 1992.

[6] See, in particular, Article 12.

[7] [1992] 1 F.L.R. 190.

[8] [1992] 4 All E.R. 627.

[9] The action was a challenge to a Circular: none of Mrs Gillick's daughters was then seeking contraceptive advice or treatment.

Gillick had decided that a child under 16 could, when competent[10] so to do, agree to medical treatment. For reasons which will become apparent shortly, it was taken for granted that 16-year-olds could so do whether they were competent in a *Gillick* sense or not. But *Re R* and *Re W* have cast doubt on the scope of the *Gillick* decision and on what was thought to be the very clear status of 16 and 17-year-olds. Whether *Gillick*-competent 15-year-olds and 16-year-olds, whatever their level of intellectual maturity, can now say 'no' to medical treatment must, as a result of the two new Court of Appeal decisions, be in doubt. An understanding of the current state of the law requires an examination of the stages through which it has passed.

THE FAMILY LAW REFORM ACT 1969

The 1969 Act lowered the age of majority from 21 to 18. It also in s.8(1) provided in unambiguous language that 'the consent of a minor who has attained the age of sixteen...shall be as effective as it would be if he were of full age'. But Lord Donaldson M.R. believes this language is ambiguous. He states (in *Re W*):

> The argument that W, or any other 16- or 17-year-old, can by refusing to consent to treatment veto the treatment notwithstanding that the doctor has the consent of someone who has parental responsibilities involves the proposition that s.8 has the further effect of depriving such a person of the power to consent. It certainly does not say so.[11]

In *Re R* he had argued that, although the 16-year-old had the right to consent, 'if he or she refuses, consent can be given by someone else who has parental rights or responsibilities'.[12]

It is true that s.8(1) does only refer to the power to give a consent and not to a refusal so to do. In other words, there is nothing in s.8(1) which creates the power of veto in favour of the 16-year-old. But it is wrong to draw the conclusion that Lord Donaldson does for two reasons. First, Parliament did not consider and reject the power of veto and may have been assumed to believe that consent embraced refusal. Secondly, in coming to his conclusion Lord Donaldson is overlooking s.8(3). The meaning of this is far from clear, and it has long puzzled commentators. It states:

---

[10] Though the judgments give very little attention to what amounts to 'competence'.
[11] [1992] 4 All E.R. 627, 634.
[12] [1992] 1 FLR 190, 199.

Nothing in this section shall be construed as making ineffective any consent which would have been effective if this section had not been enacted.

This sub-section is concerned with the preservation of pre-existing rights. My own view at the time was that the subsection was intended to preserve the right of a child under 16 to continue to be able to provide a valid consent. This interpretation has the support of Hoggett[13] and Bromley.[14] The question was addressed in *Gillick* but no firm conclusion reached.[15] Lord Donaldson in the two new cases can be taken to be upholding a different interpretation of s.8(3): namely that the pre-existing right upheld by s.8(3) are the rights of those with parental responsibilities. But Lord Donaldson is wrong because, if s.8(3) is referring to parental rights at common law, these are rights which have 'dwindled'[16] to the point of 'yielding' to the child's right to make his own decisions when of 'sufficient understanding and intelligence'.[17] Lord Scarman's language in *Gillick* could not be clearer:

> ...the parental right to determine whether or not their minor child below the age of 16 will have medical treatment terminates if and when the child achieves a sufficient understanding and intelligence to enable him or her to understand fully what is proposed.[18]

It does suggest that the refusal of a child below 16 who is *Gillick*-competent is 'determinative'[19] and, despite what Lord Donaldson says,[20] it is a view endorsed by the majority in the Lords in *Gillick*, and not just the opinion of Lord Scarman, as he insinuates. Further, if Lord Donaldson were right (and counsel for Mrs Gillick argued similarly) until the passing of the 1969 Act any treatment of anyone under 21 without parental consent must have been unlawful—a conclusion so utterly preposterous that it

---

[13] *Parents and Children*, Sweet and Maxwell, London, 1981, p. 12.

[14] *Family Law*, Butterworth, London, 1987, p. 275.

[15] Lord Scarman thought s.8(3) clarified the law without conveying any indication as to what it was before: Lord Fraser that it left open the question whether consent by a minor under 16 would have been effective if the section had not been enacted.

[16] See Lord Denning M.R. in *Hewer v. Bryant* [1969] 3 All E.R. 578, 582.

[17] Lord Scarman's words in *Gillick v. West Norfolk and Wisbech A.H.A.* [1985] AC. 112, 186.

[18] [1986] AC 112, 188–189. According to Alderson, above, note 4, children as young as 8 (in some cases younger) may be able to consent to surgery.

[19] See Lord Scarman in *Gillick* at p. 186.

[20] [1992] 1 FLR 190, 197–198.

is difficult to imagine anyone contemplating it (though Lord Donaldson himself comes close to so doing).[21]

THE CHILDREN ACT 1989

The Children Act 1989 was not in operation at the time Re R was decided, but was in force when the courts came to consider Re W. The Act in this context is significant for a number of reasons. First, following the *Gillick* precedent, there are five provisions[22] in the Act which give a child of sufficient understanding to make an informed decision the power to refuse to submit to medical and psychiatric examinations and other assessments (and in one provision only[23] psychiatric and medical treatment). Whilst none of the provisions was directly relevant in Re W and whilst, with the exception mentioned, all deal with examinations and assessments and not treatment, the general philosophy favours empowering the *Gillick*-competent child and vesting in him and her the power specifically of veto. Neither of the two judges who addresses these provisions does so other than cursorily. Lord Donaldson notes that the provisions 'do not impinge upon the jurisdiction of the court to make prohibited steps or specific issue orders'[24] (where there is no power of veto). But neither of these orders was anyway relevant here. And Balcombe L.J. sees the provisions merely as an application of the test (in s.1(1) of the Act) that the welfare of the child is the paramount consideration.[25] If by this he means that the power of veto is entrenched as a principle in the Act even where it is not specifically enunciated, I would endorse his sentiment. But it is much more likely that this interpretation is intended to be used to assess whether the child has made an informed decision—and, so used, it will conflate protecting a child's rights with protecting the child.[26]

---

[21] And see M. Jones, 'Consent To Medical Treatment by Minors After *Gillick*'. *Professional Negligence*, 2, 41.

[22] They are in s.38(6) (interim care or interim supervision order), s.43(8) (child assessment order), s.44(7) (emergency protection order), and paras 4(4)(a) and s.(5)(a) of Schedule 3 (supervision order). One of the provisions has already been interpreted—contrary to the meaning of the words used and parliamentary intention—in accordance with the authority of *re R* and *Re W*. See *South Glamorgan C.C. v. W and B* [1993] 1 FLR 574.

[23] Para. 5(5)(a) of Schedule 3.

[24] *Re W* [1992] 4 All E.R. 627, 638.

[25] *Ibid.*, p. 643.

[26] An important dichotomy noted by R. Farson, *Birthrights*, Penguin, Harmondsworth, 1978, p. 12.

Secondly, W was in the care of the local authority. It, accordingly, had parental responsibility.[27] It would seem to follow from *Re R*[28] that it could have consented to W's treatment on her behalf. But it applied to the court for a direction that it be at liberty to place W in the hospital specializing in the treatment of eating disorders and that she be given medical treatment without her consent if necessary. Section 100 of the 1989 Act is designed to circumscribe the extent to which a local authority may seek to invoke the inherent jurisdiction of the Court.[29] Inherent jurisdiction cannot be invoked to make a child who is the subject of a care order a ward of court.[30] But leave may be sought and granted if, *inter alia*, 'there is reasonable cause to believe that if the court's inherent jurisdiction is not exercised with respect to the child he is likely to suffer significant harm'.[31] It may be argued that in granting leave and in making the directions sought the judges have evinced a reluctance to accept one of the clear goals of the Children Act—to leave decisions to parents and their substitutes.[32] In doing so they have left us with a number of concerns. If the local authority had, despite W's protestations to the contrary, consented to treatment, it would have been flouting s.22 of the Children Act. This requires the views of the child to be ascertained and 'due consideration' to be given to them in making a decision with respect to the child.[33] If the local authority were not able to invoke the court's assistance it would risk a challenge by way of judicial review if it ignored a competent child's protestations.[34] The child would also have a legitimate cause for complaint under the representation procedure.[35] By transferring responsibility from its shoulders to those of the court it avoids both challenge and opprobrium. The court's decision may be appealed but there is no other recourse—and, there is in children's cases, a reluctance to second-guess a trial judge.[36]

---

[27] Under s.33(3) of the Children Act 1989.
[28] [1992] 1 FLR 190.
[29] S. Cretney, 'Defining the limits of State Intervention: The Child and the Courts', in D. Freestone, *Children and The Law*, Hull University Press, Hull, 1990, pp. 58–74.
[30] See s.100(1).
[31] Section 100(3), 4(b).
[32] See Lord Mackay, 'Joseph Jackson Memorial Lecture', *New Law Journal*, 139, 505–508 (1989).
[33] Section 22(4)(a), (5)(a).
[34] H. W. Wade, *Administrative Law*, Clarendon Press, Oxford.
[35] See Children Act 1989 s.26(3).
[36] *G* v. *G* [1985] 2 All E.R. 225.

The Children Act may be of significance for a third reason. The 'checklist' in s.1(3) lists among the circumstances that courts are to have regard 'the ascertainable wishes and feelings of the child concerned (considered in the light of his age and understanding)'. The checklist only applies to contested s.8 applications and to part IV orders.[37] Thorpe J, at first instance in *Re W*,[38] accordingly held it to have no application to W's case. He added *obiter* that if it applied we would not have been under any compulsion to prioritize W's wishes over the other circumstances in the checklist.[39] In the Court of Appeal Nolan L.J. expressed the opinion that 'it is...common ground that [the checklist] may be treated as having general application'.[40] Whilst there is nothing to stop a court using the criteria in s.1(3),[41] it is surely wrong to assert the checklist has general application. Indeed, there is a clear rule of statutory construction that where legislation specifically enunciates the scope of a provision it at the same time excludes situations it does not list.[42] But Nolan L.J., having held that W's wishes ('the first of the factors to which the court must have regard')[43] were of importance, considered that 'the determination must always be that of the court'.[44]

THE DECISIONS IN *RE R* AND *RE W*

Re R and *Re W* have much in common, but the fact that R. was 15 and W. 16, if nothing else, makes it necessary to discuss the reasoning in the two cases separately.

R, a 15-year-old, was refusing to give her consent to the administration of medication. The unit caring for her made it clear that, if she were to remain there, they required a free hand to administer drugs to her, against her will if necessary. The local authority who had care[45] of her was reluctant to authorize the administration of drugs to her against her will and

---

[37] See s.1(4) of the Children Act 1989.
[38] It is then reported as *Re J*. See *The Times*, 14 May 1992.
[39] *Idem*.
[40] [1992] 4 All E.R. 627, 647.
[41] See, for agreement, R. White, P. Carr and N. Lowe, *A Guide To The Children Act 1989*, Butterworths, London, 1990, para. 1. 18.
[42] Known as *expressio unius, exclusio alterius*.
[43] [1992] 4 All E.R. 627, 648.
[44] *Idem*.
[45] Her status is not entirely clear. She had originally been received into care (Lord Donaldson comically describes this as a voluntary care order). An interim care order was made subsequently but it does not appear that a care order was ever made.

thus had recourse to wardship proceedings.[46] The issue was thus whether the court had the power to override a refusal by a ward to undergo medical treatment to control her mental condition. The Court of Appeal considered that she was not *Gillick* competent because she had neither the ability to understand the nature of the proposed treatment, nor a full understanding and appreciation of the consequences both of the treatment in terms of the intended and possible side effects, and the anticipated consequences of a failure to treat.[47]

Staughton L.J. considered that it was not necessary on the facts to decide whether *Gillick* provided authority for the proposition that the parent of a competent child has the power to override the child's decision because the powers of the wardship judge include the power to consent to medical treatment when the ward has not been asked or has declined.[48] *Gillick* was not a wardship case. The wardship court had, it was held, the power to override the decisions of a *Gillick* competent child (whether saying 'yes' or 'no' to treatment) and his or her parents. The court conceded that this meant that the powers of the court over the child could be greater than the powers of his or her parents.

Lord Donaldson went beyond what was necessary to decide the case before him and commented *obiter* on the question of a conflict between the child's wishes and the parents. Motivated primarily by the need to protect the doctor against what otherwise might be unlawful treatment, he constructed the 'keyholder' metaphor.[49] He considered that there are a number of people who can give their consent to the treatment of a child under 16, so that the doctor does not commit a battery. Only if all these people withhold their consent will the treatment be prevented. He sees consent as 'a key which unlocks a door'.[50] A *Gillick* competent child has that key but so do his or her parents. They have a several as well as a joint right 'to turn the key and unlock the door'.[51] And referring to Lord Scarman's judgment in *Gillick*,[52] he argues:

---

[46] Which it could then do (this was several months before the Children Act came into operation).
[47] See Lord Donaldson [1992] 1 FLR 190, 200.
[48] [1992] 1 FLR 190, 202.
[49] [1992] 1 FLR 190, 196. He rejected this in *Re W* (see below).
[50] *Idem.*
[51] *Idem.*
[52] See above, p. 347.

...Lord Scarman was discussing the parents' right to *determine* whether or not their minor child below the age of 16 will have medical treatment and this is "parental right" to which he was referring in the latter passage. A right of determination is wider than a right to consent. The parents can only have the right of determination if *either* the child has no right to consent, *i.e.* is not a keyholder, *or* the parents hold a master key which could nullify the child's consent.

I do not understand Lord Scarman to be saying that, if a child was "*Gillick*-competent"...the parents ceased to have an independent right of consent as contrasted with ceasing to have a right of determination, *i.e.* a veto. In a case in which the "*Gillick*-competent" child refuses treatment, but the parents consent, that consent *enables* treatment to be undertaken lawfully, but in no way determines that the child shall be so treated. In a case in which the positions are reversed, it is the child's consent which is the enabling factor and again the parents' refusal of consent is not determinative.[53]

So, in Lord Donaldson's view a *Gillick*-competent child could have treatment forced upon her against her will. In effect this would remove autonomy and self-determination from children at an age when more responsibility and self-direction is expected of them. Many will find the implications of Lord Donaldson's judgment offensive: a Gillick competent girl of 15 cannot object to a male doctor touching her, if one of her parents gives consent. Further, once the child is a ward of court the court's 'well-established task'[54] is to have regard to the welfare of the ward as the first and paramount consideration.[55] In other words, the wishes of a 17-year-old and her parents could be overridden if, in the court's opinion, this was in the ward's best interests. *A fortiori*, the wishes of a *Gillick*-competent 15-year-old and her parents could also be overridden applying this criterion.

W was 16 (and thus within the scope of s.8 of the Family Law Reform Act 1969), an orphan with whom 'fate has dealt harshly'.[56] She was in the care of the local authority which invoked the inherent jurisdiction of the High Court when W, who was suffering with anorexia nervosa, refused treatment for her eating disorder. Balcombe, L.J., following the line of

---

[53] *Ibid.*, pp. 197–198.
[54] *Ibid.*, p. 206, in *Re D* [1977] Fam. 158 Dunn, J referred to the welfare of the child as 'the golden thread' running through wardship.
[55] Now 'the paramount consideration' (Children Act 1989 s.1(1)).
[56] [1992] 4 All E.R. 627, 629 *per* Lord Donaldson M.R.

Farquharson, L.J. in *Re R*,⁵⁷ holds that, in exercising inherent jurisdiction, 'the child's welfare is the court's paramount consideration'.⁵⁸ He agrees that respecting the wishes of the child may be one way of giving paramount consideration to the welfare of the child:

> ...the older the child concerned the greater the weight the court should give to its wishes, certainly in the field of medical treatment. In a sense this is merely one aspect of the application of the test that the welfare of the child is the paramount consideration. It will normally be in the best interests of a child of sufficient age and understanding to make an informed decision that the court should respect its integrity as a human being and not lightly override its decision on such a personal matter as medical treatment, all the more so if that treatment is invasive.⁵⁹

According to Balcombe L.J., the court must ascertain the wishes of the child and approach the decision with a strong predilection to give effect to those wishes, since this will often be in the child's best interests. But where, in the court's view, it is not, those wishes may be overridden. As already indicated,⁶⁰ Nolan L.J. to a large extent agrees. He draws on s.1 of the 1989 Act including the reference in the checklist to the child's wishes and feelings.

The courts have allowed rights to be trumped by their view of the best interests of a minor before.⁶¹ The views of Farquharson, L.J. in *Re R*, and Balcombe and Nolan, L.JJ. in *Re W* are consistent with authorities like the notorious sterilization decision of 1987.⁶² But R. was 15 and not adjudged to be Gillick competent and 'Jeanette' in the sterilization case was mentally handicapped. W., on the other hand, was 16 (and were it relevant, which it is not, seemed to satisfy the law's competency tests). The Court of Appeal could have limited itself to considering the rights of the court in exercising its inherent jurisdiction. But it did not do so and examined, as in *Re R*, the rights of parents (somewhat ironically because W does not have any). Much of the analysis in *Re R* is *obiter*, given that R. was not

---

⁵⁷ [1992] 1 FLR 190, 206.
⁵⁸ [1992] 4 All E.R. 627, 641.
⁵⁹ *Ibid.*, p. 643.
⁶⁰ Above, p. 350.
⁶¹ See M. D. A. Freeman, 'Sterilising the Mentally Handicapped' in M. D. A. Freeman, *Medicine, Ethics and the Law*, Stevens, London, 1988, 55–84, and see ch. 16.
⁶² *Re B* [1988] AC 199.

Gillick-competent, and not within s.8 of the 1969 Act. *Re W* is thus an authority of greater significance.

Lord Donaldson, aware of the criticism[63] that his judgment in *Re R* attracted, restates what he believes the law to be. He rejects his unfortunate keyholder metaphor and substitutes for it the analogy of the 'legal "flak jacket"'.

> [This] protects the doctor from claims by the litigious whether he acquires it from his patient, who may be a minor over the age of 16 or a "*Gillick*-competent" child under that age, or from another person having parental responsibilities which include a right to consent to treatment of the minor. Anyone who gives him a flak jacket (*i.e.* consent) may take it back, but the doctor only needs one and so long as he continues to have one he has the legal right to proceed.[64]

To forestall the criticism that a 17-year-old could be forced to undergo an abortion against her will (he admits it is a hair-raising possibility), he dons himself the flak-jacket of medical ethics. Doctors would not let it happen 'unless the abortion was truly in the best interests of the child'.[65] But it concedes it could happen and cites the famous 'Sotos Syndrome' case[66] where chance intervention by an educational psychologist financed by the NCCL prevented an unnecessary sterilization of an 11-year-old.[67]

It will be noted that again Lord Donaldson's concern is not with the rights of adolescents but in protecting doctors from the 'litigious'. What he fails to see, or address, is how removing legitimate expectations from rights-conscious adolescents is likely to provoke litigation. Extending his reasoning to 16-year-olds, a generation after the passing of the 1969 Act and in an age more conscious of the importance of taking children's rights seriously[68] is thoroughly objectionable and, indeed, unprincipled. By extending his reasoning to parental rights, quite unnecessarily on the facts

---

[63] He cites several of which I would pick out A. Bainham, 'The Judge and The Competent Minor', *Law Quarterly Review*, 108, 194 (1992) and L. R. Thornton, 'Multiple Keyholders—Wardship and Consent to Medical Treatment', *Cambridge Law Journal*, 34.

[64] [1992] 4 All E.R. 627, 635.

[65] *Ibid.*, p. 635–636. See also Balcombe L.J. at 644–645.

[66] *Re D* [1976] Fam. 185.

[67] What the judges fail to appreciate is that until the whistle is blown gross infringements of human rights are routine. No one knows how many involuntary sterilizations preceded *Re D* or, for example, how many defective newborns were allowed to die on a parent's say-so before *Re B* [1981] 1 WLR 1421.

[68] See M. D. A. Freeman, 'Taking Children's Rights More Seriously' *International Journal of Law and The Family*, 6, (1992), and ch. 2.

before the court, he has created a situation where a plethora of parties can by their acts foist treatment on a unwilling adolescent. In his summary Lord Donaldson states this conclusion succinctly:

> No minor of whatever age has power by refusing consent to treatment to override a consent to treatment by someone who has parental responsibility for the minor and *a fortiori* a consent by the court. Nevertheless, such a refusal is a very important consideration in making clinical judgments and for parents and the court in deciding whether themselves to give consent. Its importance increases with the age and maturity of the minor.[69]

How significant the concession that an adolescent's refusal is a 'very important' factor in clinical decision-making becomes cannot be judged in advance. But in a climate which is pro-clinical judgment[70] and pro-treatment it is difficult to imagine any but the bravest standing up successfully to parents and doctors.

There is an understanding of adolescence in Lord Donaldson's judgment. It is a pity that his understanding of anorexia nervosa is not greater for the dilemma posed in W's case constitutes a paradigm for those who want to understand the importance of children's rights. The anorexic is typically lacking in self-confidence. She may suffer, what Hilda Bruch discussing one case, calls 'the basic delusion of not having an identity,..., of not even owning their body and its sensations'.[71] The causes of anorexia differ but what unites them is 'the urgent need to be in control of their own lives and have a sense of identity'.[72] We know that W wanted control over her life: she wanted to stay in the adolescent psychiatric unit and decide when she would eat. The ability to make these decisions were taken from her. Her life may have been saved, but at the price of further undermining her identity and integrity. Indirectly, decisions like those in *Re W* will create more anorexics, more disturbed adolescents.

---

[69] [1992] 4 All E.R. 627, 639–640.
[70] Even now countenancing forcing an adult competent woman to undergo a Caesarean (*Re S* [1993] 1 FLR 26 and *Tameside and Glossop Acute Services Trust v. CH* [1996] 1 FLR 762). See, generally, *Re J* [1992] 2 FLR 165.
[71] *Eating Disorders*, Routledge, Kegan Paul, London, 1974. p. 50.
[72] *Ibid.*, p. 88.

Conclusion

It was Balcombe, L.J. who, in *Re W*, admitted that 'in logic there can be no difference between an ability to consent to treatment and an ability to refuse treatment'[73] *Re R* and *Re W* have created an illogical distinction. The rulings are a backlash against *Gillick*, against the Family Law Reform Act 1969, against the latest Children Act, against the new international Convention. That a 17-year-old could be forced to undergo an abortion against her wishes, but that that 17-year-old, if she has the child, has more control over decisions relating to her child than over her own body, points to the mess that is now the English law on consent by children. Nor is it instructive to be told that medical ethics will sort it out. Why should lawyers expect doctors to dig them out of the holes they have created? Most cases, of course, will not go to courts and we will not hear the discussions that take place in consultation rooms. But we can expect a few brave adolescents to challenge the system and case law to burgeon. Ultimately, the decisions we come to will depend on our philosophy of childhood. And if we denigrate and undermine we cannot expect responsibility in return.

---

[73] [1992] 4 All E.R. 627, 643.

CHAPTER 16

Sterilizing the Mentally Handicapped

The legal year has seen England's judges wading through a moral quagmire as novel ethical questions have been paraded before them: surrogacy issues,[1] the "rights" of a father to stop his girlfriend having an abortion,[2] the extent to which account should be taken of harm suffered by the child of a heroin addict before birth[3], the freedom of an IVF clinic to deny treatment to an ex-prostitute[4] and, or course, the plight of Jeanette.[5] All these decisions received wide media coverage and were subjected to criticism, not all of it well-focused and some of it ill-informed. The then Lord Chancellor, Lord Hailsham, was forthright in his condemnation of, what he considered to be, intemperate criticism.[6] I was one of the critics, the one, indeed, whose remark on the *Today* programme[7] that the Court of Appeal decision in the Jeanette case was "Nazi-like" (the proposition put to me was it was "Orwellian") reverberated round the globe. I do not consider this comment intemperate or unfounded, but it was a snap reaction at 7.20 (or thereabouts) and it was made without the benefit (if that is the right word) of the Court of Appeal judgments. I return to *Re B* now with the wise words of the editor of the *Journal of Medical Ethics* in my mind. He wrote in a leading article that: "We must be even more than usually meticulous about subjecting our gut 'response' to the searchlight of critical moral reasoning."[8] There can be few better test-beds of the need to in-

---

[1] *Re Adoption Application* 212/86 [1987] 2 F.L.R. 291; *Re P.* [1978] 2F.L.R. 421.
[2] *C v. S* [1987] 1 All E.R 1230.
[3] *D v. Berkshire C.C.* [1987] 1 All E.R. 20.
[4] *R v. Ethical Committee of St Mary's Hospital, Manchester, ex parte. Harriott,* [1988] 1 FLR 512.
[5] *Re B* [1987] 2 All E.R. 206.
[6] *The Daily Telegraph*, 16 April 1987.
[7] 17 March 1987.
[8] Raanan Gillon, 'On Sterilising Severely Mentally Handicapped People', (1987) 13 *J. Med. Ethics* 59 at 61.

ject critical moral thinking into questions of law and medicine than the Jeanette saga.[9]

But, whatever the fact of *Re B.*, and Lord Bridge in the House of Lords was right to say that in many quarters there had been an "erroneous appreciation of the facts,"[10] it is necessary to put the sterilization issue into its wider historical and cultural context. Only then can the sense of moral outrage which greeted the Jeanette decision be appreciated. The remark of La Forest J. in *Re Eve* (Canada's recent counterpart to *Re B*) that "social history clouds our vision"[11] is all too true.

STERILIZATION: THE HISTORICAL CONTEXT

I will start with a quotation from a reform school administrator in the United States. "Many people", he said, "are 'put off' by what Hitler did in Germany; but again, you have to be practical."[12] I find this remark utterly distasteful but it is essentially what the courts were saying in *Re B*. But sterilization for eugenic or other social control purposes neither begins nor ends in Nazi Germany. As an ideology eugenics can be traced back to 1869 and, whisper it not too loudly, to the portals of that bastion of liberalism, University College London.[13] The first attempt to pass a law mandating involuntary sterilization was made in Michigan in 1897.[14] It failed. But vasectomies were already being used at an Indiana state reformatory (they started in about 1890). A Dr Sharpe employed this procedure on 600 to 700 boys.[15]

In 1907 Indiana became the first American state to pass a compulsory sterilization statute. Similar statutes were soon enacted in Washington, California and Connecticut and, by the time the eugenics movement

---

[9] Another good illustration is the *Arthur* case which Raanan Gillon uses as the theme of his *Philosophical Medical Ethics*, Wiley, 1986.

[10] *Op. cit.*, note 5, p. 213.

[11] (1986) 31 D.L.R. (4th ed.) 1, 29.

[12] Quoted in Moya Woodside, *Sterilisation in North Carolina*, Univ. of N. Carolina Press, 1950, p 81. See also E.S. Gosney and P. Popenol, *Sterilisation for Human Betterment*, Macmillan, 1930.

[13] The founder of the eugenics movement was Sir Francis Galton. As an undergraduate at U.C.L. most of my lectures took place in the Eugenics Theatre. The term was coined in the 1880s.

[14] Another failed in Pennsylvania in 1904. It passed the legislature but was vetoed by the Governor.

[15] See (eds.) R. Macklin and W. Gaylin, *Mental Retardation and Sterilisation*, Plenum Press, 1981, pp. 64–65.

reached its peak in the 1920s, 28 states in the U.S.A. had passed involuntary sterilization laws. A number of them were declared unconstitutional: some were impugned as "cruel and unusual" punishment; others fell foul of "due process" or "equal protection under the law" clauses. But in 1927 the Supreme Court decided *Buck* v. *Bell*.[16]

Carrie Buck was, in the language of the day, "feeble-minded", the daughter of a mother alleged to be feeble-minded and the mother herself, research has shown, of a daughter of above average intelligence (though in the law report she is described as an "illegitimate feeble minded child"). Her proposed sterilization under a Virginia statute was challenged on "due process" and "cruel and unusual" punishment grounds. The court's response was it was not done as a punishment, and that in fact sterilizing her enabled her to be released to the community—an argument often still heard today, the reverberations of which also echo in *Re B*. Due process and equal protection arguments were also rejected. The sterilization statute was upheld as constitutional. The only opinion was given by Justice Holmes. His judgment is not good news for the "bad women".[17] He noted that the attack was "not upon the procedure but upon the substantive law". However, he argued:

> We have seen more than once that the public welfare may call upon the best citizens for their lives. It would be strange if it could not call upon those who already sap the strength of the State to make lesser sacrifices, often not felt to be such by those concerned. In order to prevent our being swamped with incompetents, it is better for all the world if instead of waiting to execute degenerate offspring for crime or to let them starve for their imbecility, society can prevent those who are manifestly unfit from continuing their kind. The principle that sustains compulsory vaccination is broad enough to cover cutting the fallopian tubes. Three generations of imbeciles are enough.[18]

Those familiar with Lord Denning's remarks in *Bravery* v. *Bravery*[19] may wonder what it is about sterilization that brings out the worst in great judges.

---

[16] 274 U.S. 200 (1927).

[17] Holmes, as a jurist, viewed law from the "standpoint" of the "bad man" ('The Path of the Law' (1897) 10 *Harv. L. Rev.* 457–478).

[18] *Op. cit.*, note 16, p. 207. An interesting postscript on the case is S.J. Gould, *The Mismeasure of Man*, Penguin, 1984, pp. 335–336.

[19] [1954] 3 All E.R. 59. See in my comment in *Lord Denning: The Judge and the Law* (eds. J. L. Jowell and J. P. W. B. McAuslan), Sweet and Maxwell, 1984, pp. 111–112.

Justice Holmes' opinion has been castigated so often that anything I might say about it is otiose. A couple of points, however, should be made if only to guide us through the thickets of the Jeanette case. First, Holmes' analysis, in particular his analogies, is weak (the temptation is to describe it as "sub-standard" whatever the implications of this might be!) His language is intemperate and value-laden. The war analogy is fatuous: the enemy who kills our soldiers is in no way comparable to the progeny of a mentally handicapped person who may require state support. The principle behind compulsory vaccination (a policy, incidentally, opposed by the very Social Darwinists who advocated eugenics)[20] cannot encompass involuntary sterilization, any more than it would the cutting off of the hands of habitual thieves: the quality of the intrusion is totally different. Secondly, it needs to be said that Holmes was far too readily convinced that due process had been observed. It surely behoves any judge sanctioning the deprivation of a basic human right to invoke higher standards of scrutiny than in the ordinary case.

There have been a number of significant cases in the U.S.A. since *Buck v. Bell*.[21] There have been attempts to reverse the decision. That this has not happened is in part attributable to the fact that the line of argument has changed. Eugenics (or rather "negative"[22] eugenics) is out of fashion: instead, the appeal is grounded on the burden placed on society by the need to care for the handicapped. The most interesting of the recent cases is *North Carolina Association for Retarded Children v. State of North Carolina* in 1976.[23] The statute challenged authorized both voluntary and involuntary sterilizations. There was a duty to institute sterilization proceedings when the relevant official felt it was either in (i) the best interests of the retarded person or (ii) the public at large or (iii) where the retarded person would be likely, unless sterilized, to procreate children with a tendency to

---

[20] Herbert Spencer in *Social Statics* (1850) argued that the individual should be allowed to make avoidable fatal mistakes because in this way the inefficient and the stupid would be eliminated and the human species improved.

[21] *Skinner v. Oklahoma* 316 U.S. 535 (9142); *Relf v. Weinberger* 372 F. Supp. 1196 (1974); *Cook v. State* 495 P. 2d. 768 (1972); *North Carolina Assn. for Retarded Children v. North Carolina* 420 F. Supp. 451 (1976). See, further, M. Bayles in *op. cit.*, note 15, Ch. 11, and J. H. Landman, *Human Sterilisation*, Macmillan, 1932 (useful especially for the laws and legal decisions, as well as the history generally).

[22] "Positive" eugenics has, however, come into fashion among the "Moral Right", see for example, the proposals in R. K. Graham, *The Future of Man*, Foundation for the Advancement of Man, 1981. An excellent critique in G. Corea, *The Mother Machine*, Harper and Row, 1985, Ch. 1.

[23] 420 F. Supp. 451 (1976).

serious physical, mental or nervous disease or deficiency or would be unable to care for the child or (iv) when the next of kin or legal guardian of the retarded person "requests" that he file the petition. The court found (iv) irrational and irreconcilable with (i), (ii) and (iii). But it thought the first three provisions made out "a complete and sensible scheme".[24] The fourth, however, granted to the retarded person's next of kin or legal guardian "the power of a tyrant".[25] The scheme was thus found constitutional with the exception of the fourth provision. The language and ideology of Holmes' "incantation" was rejected. "Medical and genetical experts," the Court noted, "are no longer sold on sterilization to the benefit of either retarded patients or the future of the Republic".[26] The case is also significant for containing a number of general propositions about the origins of mental retardation, about expression of sexuality, about the ability of the handicapped to use contraceptive methods. Finally, the opinion holds that in rare unusual cases it can be medically determined that involuntary sterilization is in the best interests of either the mentally retarded persons, or the state, or both.

A lot of people have been sterilized in the U.S.A. pursuant upon the compulsory programmes depicted here. By 1964, by which time the programmes had long passed their peak, 63,678 such sterilizations had taken place.[27] Those sterilized were mainly young women and for the large part they were poor and came from socio-economically and culturally deprived environments. Whether it was, as Gonzales indicates,[28] a popular way of controlling reproduction, it certainly was a convenient method for controlling the reproductive urges of the populace. Given the population concerned and the imperfections of classification, the dangers of labelling with sterilization merely an incident of stigmatization were difficult to overcome. The evidence suggests they were not surmounted.[29]

In the light of all this, it is somewhat surprising that forced sterilization policies should be associated with Nazi Germany. But the reputation is

---

[24] Ibid., p. 455.
[25] Ibid., p. 456.
[26] Ibid., p. 454.
[27] This figure is quoted in D. Meyers, *The Human Body and the Law*, (1971) Edinburgh University Press, p. 29. Of these 27,917 were sterilized on grounds of mental illness and 32,374 on grounds of mental deficiency.
[28] 'Voluntary Sterilization: Counseling and Informed Consent' in *Proceedings of the 5th World Congress on Medical Law*, 1979, p. 64.
[29] See Jane Mercer, *Labeling the Mentally Retarded*, (1973) Univ. of California Press. On the psychological impact see P. Roos (1975) *Law and Psychology Review* 45–56.

deserved for no political system has pursued the policy with greater vigour or ruthlessness.[30] The Nazi compulsory sterilization law dates from 1933, the very outset of the Third Reich and long before the Nuremberg Laws. The 1933 law created "hereditary health courts" made up of a district judge and his physicians to supplement, what was called, the "law on the Prevention of Hereditary Diseases in Future Generations". A variety of diagnoses could lead to forced sterilizations including hereditary blindness or deafness, epilepsy, Huntington's disease and alcoholism. Many others designated "anti-social", such as Gypsies or, what were called "Rhineland bastards" (children conceived after the First World War by French North African troops) were also sterilized. A gradual shift towards measures aimed at racial elimination is evident here, as it became all too evident later.[31] The U.S.A. and Nazi Germany are but two of the countries in which involuntary sterilization policies have been pursued.[32] Most recently, under Indira Gandhi, Indian governments have used sterilization as a method of population control; in theory persons agreed to be sterilized (some, I seem to remember in return for gifts of transistor radios) but in practice there is no doubt that forced sterilization was carried out on a wide scale.

In England there has been surprisingly little discussion of sterilization. The "Sotos Syndrome" case in 1975 (*Re D*)[33] commanded a lot of public attention and Heilbron J.'s decision was generally acclaimed. But the Sheffield girl in *Re D* was not the first English victim, or even the first in Sheffield. The chance intervention by an educational psychologist and the financial support of the NCCL for once converted a private matter into a public concern. Just how many young persons have been sterilized in Britain is something that will never be known. Dr. David Owen in 1975 said the Ministry of Health kept no comprehensive statistics. He quoted figures from 2 out of 14 regional health authorities.[34] According to *The Sun* in September 1975 the DHSS believed that in 1973 and 1974 11 girls and 4 boys under 16 had been sterilized and 29 girls and 34 boys between 16 and 18.[35] Figures in The *Journal of Medical Ethics* do not tally with these. It is indicated there (by Sir George Porter) that at least 14 sterilizations were performed in this period on under 16-year-olds and another 22 on

---

[30] It is estimated that there were 300,000 victims.
[31] See F. Pfafflin and J. Gross (1982) *Int. J. of Law and Psychiatry* 419–423.
[32] Another recent example is El Salvador.
[33] [1976] 1 All E.R. 326.
[34] *Hansard*, H.C. vol. 894, col. 629, 635, (25 June 1975).
[35] 1 September 1975.

those in the age range 16 to 18.[36] According to the *Birmingham Evening Mail* (in January 1976) one West Midlands leading child psychiatrist had himself recommended twelve adolescents under 16 for sterilization.[37] In *Re D* there is reference to two sterilizations having been carried out in Sheffield.[38] Figures released by the Department of Health in March 1987 indicate that about 90 sterilizations are performed a year in England on females under 19. The Department is unable to break the figures down into those aged under 18, and those who have reached the age of majority, nor to give the reasons for the sterilizations.[39]

Re D. provoked "an outrage about human rights"[40] (how many have slipped through the protective net that saved D?). It also provoked the DHSS into formulating a Discussion Paper "Sterilisation of Children under 16 years of age" which, so far as I can tell, has now sunk without trace. It should have led to an agreed Code of Practice. It may be that interest in formulating such a code will have been re-activated by the *Jeanette* case. Without such a code, the only guidance will remain the legal decisions in *Re B* and *Re D*.

The question of sterilization has rarely claimed public attention. Was anyone really interested before the Sheffield case or between it and *Re B*? It is very significant that Mason and McCall Smith, whose second edition of *Law and Medical Ethics* was published in the same year as *Re B*, devote barely two pages to the subject and, though they call sterilization "a minefield of powerful objection",[41] were able in 1987 to describe abortion as the law's only "major incursion into reproductive practices".[42] It is also, I think, worth observing that Lord Oliver in *Re B.* thought Jeanette's case raised "no general issue of public policy".[43]

I turn now to look at *Re B*, and in doing so take a backward glances to the "Sotos Syndrome" case, as well as envious looks across the Atlantic to Canada where the Supreme Court handed down last year a decision (*Re Eve*), which is in striking contrast to the Lords' ruling and reasoning.

---

[36] (1975) 1. *J. Med. Ethics*, 161.
[37] 14 January 1976.
[38] *Op. cit.*, note 33, p. 333.
[39] *The Independent*, 21 March 1987.
[40] See (1975) 1 *J. Med. Ethics*, 163.
[41] 2nd ed., 1987, p. 62.
[42] *Idem*.
[43] *Op. cit.*, note 5, p. 219.

JEANETTE: HOW THE COURTS REASONED

The facts of Jeanette's case are now well known. Her chronological age was 17, her mental age 5 or 6. She was exhibiting the normal sexual drive and inclinations for someone her age. She is described as severely mentally handicapped and epileptic. It was said that she had no understanding of the connection between sex, pregnancy and birth; that she would not be able to cope with birth or care for a child. There was expert evidence that it was vital that she should not be permitted to become pregnant and that certain contraceptive drugs would react with drugs administered to control her mental instability and epilepsy. There was further evidence that it would be difficult, if not impossible, to place her on a course of oral contraceptive pills. The local authority, in whose care she was, applied for her to be made a ward of court and for leave for her to undergo a sterilization operation. Her mother supported the application. So did Bush J., the Court of Appeal and the House of Lords. Why?

In reading the judgments (and speeches) there is a natural break between Bush J. and the Court of Appeal on the one hand the House of Lords on the other. Though Dillon L.J in the Court of Appeal can describe it as an "anxious case",[44] the public policy issues only emerge in the speeches of the Lords after the Court of Appeal's decision was subjected to critical attention in the media. But in terms of what is decided, there is essential continuity between all three courts. This was a wardship application and it is clear law that only one criterion should govern such applications: *viz.*: that the minor's welfare is the first and paramount consideration.[45] It is, it has been said, "the golden thread" which runs through the wardship jurisdiction: welfare is considered "first, last and all the time".[46] All three courts rightly identified Jeanette's welfare as their only concern. This is most forcibly stated in the Lords, doubtless to counter criticism made of the earlier decisions, but it is clearly also Bush J.'s concern. "Welfare" assumes less profile in Dillon L.J.'s judgement (the only relatively full judgment in the Court of Appeal) but it clearly is at the root of his thoughts. The Lords use the expression "welfare", "best interests" and "benefit" interchangeably: although these are not identical conceptions, this is not something with which I will quibble. The Lords accordingly

---

[44] *Ibid.*, p. 209.
[45] Guardianship of Minors Act 1971, s.1 and *J* v. *C* [1970] A.C. 668 at 710 *per* Lord MacDermott. Wardship (or inherent jurisdiction) is now governed by the paramountcy standard in the Children Act 1989 s.1(1).
[46] *Per* Dunn J. in *Re D* [1977] Fam. 158 at 163.

held that where it was for the welfare and in the best interests of the ward that she be sterilized the Court had jurisdiction to authorize the operation. On the facts, they held it was. To Lord Hailsham the welfare of the ward in this case was the "only" consideration (there are, of course, cases where it is not,[47] but Lord Hailsham is not casting doubt on the exceptions). Similarly, for Lord Oliver the appeal was concerned "with one primary consideration and one alone, namely the welfare and best interest of this young woman".[48]

In *Re D* Heilbron J.'s refusal to authorize the sterilization of an 11-year-old had been premised on its irreversible nature and the deprivation of "a basic human right," namely the right of a woman to reproduce.[49] None of the judges found any difficulty in distinguishing *Re D* and, it is true, there are material differences. Lord Hailsham, indeed, contented himself in the belief that Heilbron J. would decide *Re B.* as he was now deciding it. As far as the "basic human right" is concerned, Bush J. expressed the reaction of all the judges: "one is in effect depriving her of nothing because she will never desire the basic human right to reproduce".[50] For Lord Hailsham: "To talk of the 'basic right' to reproduce of an individual who is not capable of knowing the causal connection between intercourse and childbirth, the nature of pregnancy, what is involved in delivery, unable to form maternal instincts or to care for a child appears…wholly to part company with reality".[51] In Dillon L.J's opinion the loss of the right would mean "nothing to her."[52] For Lord Oliver the right to reproduce "is of value only if accompanied by the ability to make a choice or indeed to appreciate the need to make one".[53] Is this, one wonders, to be the judicial criterion for the exercise of *all* rights or just the right to reproduce? Generalized, Lord Oliver's reasoning would have some very strange consequences, to which reference will be made subsequently.

That sterilization was a recourse of "last resort" was stressed both in the Court of Appeal (by Dillon and Stephen Brown L.JJ.) and in the

---

[47] For example, *Re X* [1975] Fam. 47; *S* v. *McC* [1972] A.C. 24. Lord Hailsham's own reasoning in *Richards* v. *Richards* [1984] A.C. 174 (not a wardship case) should also be ignored.

[48] *Op. cit.*, note 5, p. 215.

[49] *Op. cit.*, note 33, p. 332.

[50] *Op. cit.*, note 5, p. 208.

[51] *Ibid.*, p. 213.

[52] *Ibid.*, p. 210.

[53] *Ibid.*, p. 219.

House of Lords, most especially in Lord Oliver's speech. The fact that a sterilization operation is irreversible concerned them but they saw it as the "least detrimental alternative".[54] Lord Oliver stressed that the "necessity for the course proposed ha[d] been exhaustively considered by the Official Solicitor on the minor's behalf".[55] The only alternative was the administration daily in pill form of progestogen. Lord Oliver compared the two courses of action. "Of the two possible courses, the one proposed [*i.e.* sterilization] is safe, certain but irreversible, the other speculative, possibly damaging and requiring discipline over a period of many years from one of the most limited intellectual capacity."[56] His Lordship saw only one way out of this dilemma. "The danger to which she is exposed and the speculative nature of the alternative proposed are such that, on any footing, the risk is not one which should properly be taken by the court."

The Lords were also at pains to point out that their authorization of a sterilization was motivated solely by consideration for her welfare and not by any ulterior purposes. She was being treated, in other words, as a person and not as a means to other persons' ends. Thus Lord Hailsham turned roundly on critics who asserted that there might be other considerations when he said: "There is no issue of public policy…which can conceivably be taken into account, least of all…any question of eugenics".[57] Lord Oliver was equally forthright and both he and Lord Bridge were insistent that the convenience of Jeanette's carers played no part in their decision-making process.

The Lords were also critical of attempts to draw a distinction between therapeutic and non-therapeutic reasons (or presumably medical treatment more generally). The distinction was first drawn by Heilbron J. in *Re D* in 1975. The learned judge ruled that a decision to carry out a sterilization for non-therapeutic sterilizations (or presumably medical treatment more generally) was not solely within a doctor's clinical judgment.[58] If this meant that the decision to sterilize a child for therapeutic purposes did lie within exclusive clinical competence, it is a statement that cannot be accepted and, after *Re B*, for reasons that will become apparent, can no longer represent the law (if it ever did). Heilbron J.'s statement also left open the whole question as to how the therapeutic and non-therapeutic

---

[54] The term (in another context) belongs to Goldstein, Freud and Solnit, *Beyond the Best of the Child*, Free Press, 1973, pp. 53–64.

[55] *Op. cit.*, note 5, p. 217.

[56] *Ibid.*, p. 218.

[57] *Ibid.*, p. 212.

[58] *Op. cit.*, note 33, p. 335. *Cf.* Wood J. in *T* v. *T* (*post*, p. 370).

were to be distinguished: on what side of the line did vaccination fall, particularly in controversial cases such as whooping cough? Is male circumcision therapeutic or non-therapeutic? The questions are endless.[59]

The distinction assumed importance once again with the judgment in the Canadian Supreme Court of La Forest J. On the facts the learned judge found that "there is no evidence to indicate that failure to perform the operation would have any detrimental effect on Eve's physical or mental health. The purposes of the operation...are to protect her from possible trauma in giving birth and from the assumed difficulties she would have in fulfilling her duties as a parent...(and) to relieve her of the hygienic tasks associated with menstruation."[60] The judge noted that "the justifications advanced are the ones commonly proposed in support of non-therapeutic sterilization".[61] After examining these justifications (using data culled from the Canadian Law Reform Commission report on Sterilisation) he concluded: "The grave intrusion on a person's rights and the certain physical damage that ensues from non-therapeutic sterilization without consent, when compared to the highly questionable advantages that can result from it, have persuaded me that it can never safely be determined that such a procedure is for the benefit of that person. Accordingly, the procedure should never be authorised for non-therapeutic purposes under *parens patriae* jurisdiction."[62]

Lord Hailsham found La Forest J.'s conclusion "totally unconvincing and in startling contradiction to the welfare principle."[63] The distinction between "therapeutic" and "non-therapeutic" (in the context of this operation) he castigated as "totally meaningless, and, if meaningful, quite irrelevant to the correct application of the welfare principle."[64] Lord Bridge also thought the distinction diverted "attention from the true issue: namely what was best for Jeanette."[65] He had no intention of indulging in "arid semantic debate" as to where the line was to be drawn between "therapeutic" and "non-therapeutic." But judges indulge in semantic debates all the time and much can hinge on which side of the line the facts of a case are

---

[59] See N. Lowe and R. White, *Wards of Court* (2nd ed., 1986), Barry Rose, pp. 88–89.
[60] *Op. cit.*, note. 11, pp. 30–31.
[61] *Ibid.*, p. 31.
[62] *Ibid.*, p. 32.
[63] *Op. cit.*, note 5, p. 213.
[64] *Idem.*
[65] *Ibid.*, p. 214.

deemed to fall.⁶⁶ Are the debates "arid" only where the judges are unprepared to participate in them? Lord Oliver thought the description of the proposed operation in *Re D* as "non-therapeutic" "apt enough in that case"⁶⁷ but nevertheless rejected the distinction in the context of the case he was deciding. It seemed to him 'entirely immaterial whether measures undertaken for the protection against future and foreseeable injury are properly described as "therapeutic."⁶⁸ The real reason, he insisted, was only whether they were for Jeanette's welfare and benefit.

Perhaps the most positive thing to emerge from this sad litigation is to be found in the judgment of Dillon L.J. and in Lord Templeman's speech. Dillon L.J. ruled that neither parents nor a local authority with parental rights could consent to a sterilization of a minor and that the leave of the Court in wardship proceedings was an essential pre-condition to such an operation taking place.⁶⁹ Lord Templeman agreed and added that a doctor performing a sterilization operation "with the consent of the parents might still be liable in criminal, civil or professional proceedings."⁷⁰ His reason was the absence of "a more satisfactory tribunal or a more satisfactory method of reaching a decision."⁷¹ Neither Dillon L.J. nor Lord Templeman said anything to suggest that this ruling applied only to non-therapeutic sterilizations. It must, therefore, be taken to apply to all sterilizations of minors. It is perhaps a pity that the other law lords did not give their express support to Lord Templeman's remarks.⁷²

The reason for the rather unseemly haste with which the Jeanette litigation was rushed to a conclusion was the proximity of it to her eighteenth birthday. This raises the question of involuntary sterilizations of mentally handicapped adults. Clearly, they cannot give informed consent,⁷³ but can anyone give consent on their behalf? This was not a matter upon which the

---

⁶⁶ A point made especially well by Glanville Williams, 'Language and the Law' (1945) 61 *L.Q.R.* 183–185.

⁶⁷ *Op. cit.*, note. 5, p. 219.

⁶⁸ *Idem.*

⁶⁹ *Ibid.*, pp. 210–211. The concept of parental rights has now been replaced by that of parental responsibility (see Children Act 1989 s.2).

⁷⁰ *Ibid.*, p. 214.

⁷¹ *Ibid.*, p. 214.

⁷² Particularly, in the light of Wood J.'s judgment in *T v. T* ([1988] 2 W.L.R. 189) that, where *an adult* was concerned, "a medical adviser is justified in taking such steps as good medical practice demands". (p. 204).

⁷³ A useful article (on U.S. law) is G.S. Neuwirth *et al*, 'Capacity, Competence, Current: Voluntary Sterilization of the Mentally Retarded' (1975) 6 *Columbia Human Rights R.* 451.

courts in *Re B* had to pronounce and, of course, anything said by them in the course of the Jeanette litigation is strictly *obiter dictum*. Nevertheless, two of the law lords did direct their attention to the question. Lord Hailsham contented himself with referring to the contrast of views in Hoggett[74] and Halsbury[75] and concluded that "whether residual *parens patriae* jurisdiction remains in the High Court after majority"[76] is in doubt. He added that "in twelve months time it would be doubtful…what legal courses would be open".[77] Lord Oliver was "prepared to assume" that the *parens patriae* jurisdiction did not come to an end when the mentally handicapped person reached the age of majority. He was not, however, prepared to give a ruling in the absence of the much fuller argument which might have been available had a final ruling not been deemed urgent. This reluctance to express and opinion, though predictable, is somewhat unfortunate. It was inevitable that the issue would have to be raised in further litigation and this has, indeed already happened. Not once, but three times.[78]

---

[74] *Mental Health Law*, 2nd ed. 1984, p. 203.
[75] *Laws of England* vol. 8, 4th ed. 1974, para. 901, note 6.
[76] *Op. cit.,* note 5, p. 212.
[77] *Ibid.*, p. 218.
[78] The first (by Latey J. on 14 May 1987) is unreported; the second (*Re X*), a decision of Reeve J. is reported in *The Times*, 4 June 1987. For the third see below note 80.

I will make a few remarks only about one of these cases.[79] *T* v. *T*[80] concerned the sterilization of (and an abortion on) a severely mentally handicapped adult. Her mother asked Wood J. for a declaration that the relevant operations without the patient's consent would not constitute an illegal act. T's mental age was even less than Jeanette's. There was no doubt that the abortion sought would satisfy the test in section 1 of the Abortion Act 1967, it being necessary to protect the health of the mother. Was there anyone who could consent on her behalf? It was held that, in the absence of any residual power of *parens patriae* in the court, there was no one who could consent on her behalf. Wood J. concluded that where there is no one who can (or ever will be able to) give consent, a medical adviser is justified in taking such steps as good medical practice demands. He accordingly declared that the operations sought would not be tortious acts merely because of the absence of consent.[81] There is some irony in this ruling for, if it is correct, it becomes easier to sterilize a mentally handicapped adult than a mentally handicapped child: the former rests upon good medical practice, whereas the latter requires judicial intervention. In other words, the haste in Jeanette's case was unnecessary, for upon majority she could have been sterilized without any litigation at all. It is surprising the *T* v. *T* has been subjected to almost no criticism at all.

The issues in *T* v. *T* call to mind both the notorious *Sparkman* case in the United States[82] and *Re Eve.* in *Sparkman* v. *McFarlin* the judge who authorized the sterilization of a 15-year-old girl, said by her mother to be "somewhat retarded", and the doctors who carried out the operation, were sued some years later by the girl and her husband. The US Court of Appeals for the Seventh Circuit held that the action of the judge had no basis in either law (the Indiana statute not being applicable) or equity, and was therefore taken without jurisdiction. The facts of the case defy belief: not only were the girl's interests not independently represented, but she was

---

[79] See, further, Brenda Hoggett, 'The Royal Prerogative in Relation To The Mentally Disabled: Resurrection, Resuscitation or Rejection' in (ed.) M. D. A. Freeman, *Medicine, Ethics and the Law*, Stevens, 1988, p. 55.

[80] [1988] 2 W.L.R. 189 and see now *Re F* [1990] 2 AC 1 where Lord Griffiths said "I would myself declare that on grounds of public interest an operation to sterilise a woman incapable of giving consent on grounds of either age or mental incapacity is unlawful if performed without the consent of the High Court". Nevertheless, the Lords held that the court's consent to the sterilization of a 36-year-old woman was unnecessary, though all of their Lordships urged the wisdom of making an application to the court. See further now the Official Solicitor's "Practice Note" reported at [1993] 3 All E.R. 222.

[81] Of course, he did not (and could not) declare that they would not be criminal acts.

[82] 532 F. 2d 172 (1977), reversed in *Stump* v. *Sparkman*. (1978) 435 U.S. 349.

told the operation was to remove her appendix. The Supreme Court in *Stump* v. *Sparkman* reversed the ruling that the judge had forfeited his immunity. One result of this was that courts subsequently found their jurisdiction to authorize sterilizations in equity, when they could not ground it in a statutory scheme. "Equity" is the functional equivalent of *parens patriae* jurisdiction. The closest we get to a statute is our mental health legislation. But this does not cover the situations envisaged either in Jeanette's case or *T* v. *T*: the compulsory procedures in the Mental Health Act 1983 do not apply.[83] *Parens patriae* jurisdiction over mentally handicapped adults does not seem to have survived the Mental Health Act of 1959, though clearly it could be revived by prerogative action. The question therefore arises as to whether Wood J. (or the judges involved in the other cases) had jurisdiction to make a declaration. They almost certainly had none in law (the Mental Health Act) and, despite Lord Oliver's remarks in *Re B*, probably none in "equity" (*parens patriae*). In other words, Wood J. almost certainly lacked the jurisdiction to give the declarations as, of course, did the judges in the other two cases. The implications of this are intriguing, raising as they do the authority of a declaration seemingly *ultra vires* and the liability of a judge for the consequences of an act so authorized. But since the judges are undoubtedly immune from actions taken in a judicial capacity,[84] a more serious question to which to direct attention is: how is the gap in the law to be plugged?

The choice is between resurrecting the prerogative power of the Crown and giving the Family Division (or a Family Court) *parens patriae* jurisdiction over the lives ("the custody of the body," as Sir Edward Coke put it in *Beverley's* case[85]) of mentally handicapped adults along the lines of wardship (though as *parens patriae* jurisdiction the case of the mentally handicapped long antedates that of children) and a new statutory formula. I think the latter preferable in the light of the Jeanette saga but it needs to be said that the Canadian Supreme Court copes perfectly adequately with *parens patriae* in *Re Eve*, where the Court held that wardship cases were a "solid guide"[86] to the exercise of *parens patriae* power even in the case of adults. That such power is still vested in Canadian courts when it does not

---

[83] The 1983 Act framework embraces only medical treatment for mental disorders; it does not apply to treatment for physical disorders, or operations of a non-therapeutic nature such as vasectomy or an abortion.
[84] *Scott* v. *Stansfield* (1868) L.R. 3 Ex. 220, 223.
[85] (1603) 4 Co. Rep. 123b, at 126a, 126b (76 E.R. 1118, 1124).
[86] *Op. cit.*, note 11, p. 14.

in those in England is the result of differences in statutory law in the last hundred years.

"JEANETTE": AN ASSESSMENT

Any assessment of *Re B* must use the Canadian Supreme Court decision of *Re Eve* as a critical guide. *Re Eve* was not picked up by those involved in *Re B* until after the furore caused by the Court of Appeal decision, and insufficient attention was given to it by the House of Lords. Of course, the facts of the two cases are different. Jeanette is severely mentally handicapped, whereas Eve is described as "at least mildly to moderately retarded".[87] We are not (wisely) told her mental age. She is said to suffer from extreme expressive aphasia and to be attracted to, and attractive to, men. Though thought to be able to carry out mechanical duties of a mother, she was said to be incapable of being a mother in any other sense. The Canadian Supreme Court refused to authorize Eve's sterilization. Its reasons for doing so are set out in one, very full, well-argued and well-documented judgment. It contains copious reference to periodical literature and, with the assistance of the Canadian Law Reform Commission, an awareness of the research results of those who have studied mental retardation. The court was helped in its deliberations by the participation of several *amici curiae*, who presented the view of interested third parties, enabling it to benefit from the widest range of arguments. It also spent 16 months pondering its judgment. By contrast the House of Lords barely reserved judgment. There were, of course, no *amici curiae*. The speeches are thin. The only judge with Family Division experience declined to give a judgment.[88] The Supreme Court in Canada was honest enough to acknowledge that "judges are generally ill-informed about many of the factors relevant to a wise decision in this difficult area...."[89] *A fortiori*, we can only assume such ignorance in our judiciary, though there is no similar acknowledgement.

The Canadian Supreme Court's decision can best be summarized in one short passage from La Forest J.'s judgment, which has already been quoted.[90] It will remembered that what he rejected was non-therapeutic sterilization. The Court, however, agreed that sterilization might some-

---

[87] *Ibid.*, p. 4 *per* McQuaid J. (in lower court).
[88] Lord Brandon of Oakbrook.
[89] *Op. cit.*, note 11, p. 14.
[90] *Ante*, p. 63.

times be necessary and lawful as "treatment of a serious malady".[91] But in the view of the Canadian Supreme Court it was difficult "to imagine a case in which non-therapeutic sterilization could possibly be of benefit to the person on behalf of whom a court purports to act, let alone one in which that procedure is necessary in his or her best interest".[92] La Forest J. was also concerned that any error could not be corrected subsequently. He was aware of the contingency that "nature or the advances of science"[93] might ameliorate Eve's situation. He concluded: "The irreversible and serious intrusion on the basic rights of the individual is simply too great to allow a court to act on the basis of possible advantages which, from the standpoint of the individual, are highly debatable".[94]

It is difficult not to be impressed by both the scholarship and humanity of La Forest J.'s judgment. By contrast the Lords' speeches are shoddy and their compassion unconvincing. I believe the Lords' reasoning was wrong and its conclusion dubious. Why?

(a) "Best interests" reconsidered

The core of their decision is that it was for Jeanette's welfare and in her best interests that she be sterilized. To the question what is meant by "best interest", the Lords give only a partial answer. They lay down no guidelines, thus leaving considerable latitude to lower courts and ultimately doctors and others concerned with the care of the mentally handicapped. This is unfortunate because the concept itself is indeterminate, speculative and value-laden. That we have used it, often unthinkingly, in other areas, does not excuse the Lords. We can probably never determine what is a child's best interest,[95] but this should not obstruct us from trying. First, we need information. Secondly, we need predictive ability, to be able to assess the probability of various outcomes and evaluate the advantages and disadvantages of each. Thirdly, we have to admit that our choice will be informed by values: we must be clear what these values are and be prepared to justify our choice of them.

Of these problems the first is the easiest to surmount. We must assume that the Lords were in possession of most of the facts about Jeanette, un-

---

[91] *Op. cit.*, note 11, p. 34.
[92] *Ibid.*, p. 32.
[93] *Idem.*
[94] *Idem.*
[95] On indeterminacy see R. Mnookin, *In the Interest of Children*, W. H. Freeman, 1985 particularly pp. 16–24.

like, for example, the US Supreme Court when it considered Carrie Buck. She was independently represented and the case against sterilization and in favour of alternative contraceptive measures was put. It is true that alternative forms of contraception have limitations, including some not mentioned in the Lords' speeches (for example with the IUD that of pelvic infection and the risk of expulsion and thus pregnancy). But the assumption was that Jeanette was fertile: the majority of those with severe mental handicaps do not have effective fertility.[96] Pregnancy amongst the severely mentally handicapped is extremely rare. According to a letter in the *British Medical Journal* in 1980, perhaps only a score of women with Down's Syndrome had had babies (and only one of these was under 16).[97] How many sterilizations are we prepared to tolerate to save one mentally handicapped woman becoming pregnant? It may be necessary to carry out hundreds of sterilizations to avoid one pregnancy.

If it was really unlikely that Jeanette would become pregnant, was sterilization the right answer? If she understood as little as the law report seems to indicate, she certainly needed (and needs) protection, in particular from exploitation. It is noticeable how many parents of mentally handicapped daughters complain about their daughters being "raped" by employees of institutions, for example, drivers employed to take them back and forth.[98] One right that the mentally handicapped undoubtedly have is the right not to be sexually abused.[99] Sterilization does nothing to protect them from sexual exploitation. Saner employment policies (for example the employment of female drivers) and better sex education[100] might achieve rather more.

Once in possession of the "facts", the decision-maker has still got to predict what the probable results of alternative outcomes are. The problem is, as Mnookin observed,[101] that "present-day knowledge about human behaviour provides no basis for the kind of individualized predictions required by the best-interests standard." There are competing theories of human behaviour related to different conceptions of human nature and, of

---

[96] See the letters by D. Chakrabanti and B. Kirman in 281 *British Medical Journal I 1281–1282 (1980)*.

[97] By B. Kirman (see note 96), and also in Symposium on 'Child Sterilisation' in (1975) 1 *J. Med. Ethics* 163–167.

[98] This point was forcefully made on the BBC TV 'Kilroy' programme.

[99] See J. Ennew, *The Sexual Exploitation of Children*, Polity Press. 1986.

[100] See in R. Ives in B. Franklin (ed.), *The Rights of Children*, Blackwell, 1986, ch. 7.

[101] 'Child-Custody Adjudication: Judicial Functions in the Face of Indeterminacy', (1975) 39 *Law and Contemporary Problems* 226 at 258.

course, no consensus as to which, if any, of these views is the correct one. Even if there were a right answer, it is difficult to see how it could be a reliable guide to predict what is likely to happen to a particular child. But if this applies to "normal" persons, how much more so is it pertinent to the mentally handicapped? We cannot even agree on what constitutes mental retardation. A common interpretation uses a below 70 Intelligence Quotient as a cut-off point but this would put over two per cent. of the population (or one million people) in the broad category of mental handicap. There are any number of different models of mental retardation and explanations as to its aetiology.[102] Much therefore depends on interpretation so that prediction itself is heavily dependent on the model adopted. This must be kept in mind when decisions to remove a mentally handicapped person's rights are under consideration. Diana Meyers puts this well. She writes: "Because diagnostic procedures are notoriously fallible and because the mistaken denial of a person's inalienable rights can be catastrophic, it is necessary to adopt a conservative policy requiring irrefragable proof of irremediable moral incompetence before an individual's inalienable rights can be denied".[103] Thus, she indicates, "the protection of inalienable rights extends to many humans who may never engage in moral relations".[104] And she add that "though it is only accidental if all humans qualify for inalienable rights, few humans will ever be rightfully deprived of the protection these rights afford".[105] Meyers is not referring to the right to reproduce (to which right I will return) but her remarks about diagnostic procedures are very apposite to Jeanette's case. How can we be certain that Jeanette will not develop? To what extent is her lack of development due to her total life history? Why is it, as Zigler points out, that "in the case of the retarded individual, we seem all too ready to believe that a cognitive deficiency makes one impervious to those environmental events known to be central in the genesis of the personality of individuals of normal intellect"?[106] We know that Jeanette has a mental age of 5 or 6 (whatever that might mean) but do we know what her mental age would be if she had not had such a depriving and atypical social history? What has been the effect on her intelligence of constant experiences of failure? It is

---

[102] There are over 200 known causes of mental retardation. A good account is R. W. Conley, *The Economics of Mental Retardation*, The Johns Hopkins Press, 1973, chs. II and III.

[103] *Inalienable Rights: A Defence*, Columbia U.P. 1985, p. 141.

[104] *Idem.*

[105] *Idem.*

[106] 'The Retarded Child As A Whole Person' in (ed.) D. R. Routh. *The Experimental Psychology of Mental Retardation*, Aldine, 1973, p. 231 at 237.

possible to improve the behaviour of the retarded through manipulation of the environmental events. The danger with decisions like that in Jeanette is that it is so much easier to avert the supposed danger by sterilizing than to put time, effort and commitment into education, training, counselling and assistance of the mentally handicapped. Their sexual needs and their sexual rights can easily be steamrollered in the name of convenience. Whatever the Lords may say, it was convenient (or "practical" in the language of the reform school administrator) to sterilize Jeanette. It was only in her best interests in so far as these coincided with the best interests of those whose task it was to care for her.

This leads me to the question of values. Much has already been said about this. But a few more remarks are in order. How is utility to be determined? Should best interests be looked at from a long-term or a short-term perspective? How high in the scale of values does physical integrity come? Are we concerned with Jeanette's welfare now or when she is 25 or 50? Supposing Jeanette (or someone in her position) were to be capable of improvement: should the judge in some Rawlsian way decide as the matured handicapped person looking back would have wanted?[107] And what aspect of "welfare" are we emphasizing? Is Jeanette better off now? Can we actually answer that question? Can a judge, or five elderly male judges, answer it? It may well be that if sterilization decisions are to be taken (and I do not rule them out completely) that a court is the most appropriate place to go (thought not necessarily one as presently constituted). But more thought than is currently given should be devoted to how such cases are prepared. The details of this lie beyond the scope of this article, but the idea of an inter-disciplinary Ethics Committee as part of reproductive health clinic for persons with mental handicap, as described by Elkins *et al.* in a recent *Hastings Center Report*, is both patient-centred and reflects an awareness of informed societal views.[108] It would be valuable to see such an initiative pursued in this country.

(b) A right to reproduce?

It was Heilbron J. in *Re D* who said that sterilization (in that case) would deprive a woman of a basic human right, the right to reproduce. In *Re B*, the judges did not deny that the right to reproduce existed, but they held

---

[107] On Rawls see *A Theory of Justice*, Harvard University Press 1971. See also M. D. A. Freeman 'Taking Children's Rights Seriously' in *Children and Society* vol. 1 no. 4, p. 299 (1988).

[108] (1986) *Hastings Center Report* vol. 16 (3), pp. 20–22.

that it meant "nothing" to Jeanette (Bush J., Dillon L.J.) or she couldn't exercise it (Lord Bridge) or the right was of value only if accompanied by the ability to make a choice, of which in Jeanette's case there was no question (Lord Oliver). Discussion of the right to reproduce raises a number of questions.

First, does the right to reproduce exist? Two published articles on the question come to different conclusions. Kingdom,[109] who tells us that "appealing to the right to reproduce is a liability in feminist politics and an obstacle to the development of social policy", concludes there is no right as such to reproduce. She reaches her conclusion after analysing *Re D* "If," she says, "the possibility of a right to reproduce is dependent on a judgment about the presence or absence of medical grounds for sterilisation" (as it would be if the therapeutic/non-therapeutic distinction is accepted), "then there is no clear basis for ascribing this right to an individual".[110] McLean, on the other hand, believes there is a right to reproduce, though, with both its extent and exercise limited, she has to conclude it is not a "general" right.[111] Gillon's view is similar: he writes of a general *prima facie* right "not to be stopped."[112] Wald,[113] who like Kingdom and McLean quotes the United States Supreme Court in *Eisenstadt* v. *Baird*,[114] asserts that the right to bear children is a "basic civil right of man" *(sic)*. Carby-Hall,[115] in a thoughtful unpublished paper, also assumes the existence of a right to reproduce, though as we shall see, holds that Jeanette for one did not possess it.

What none of these thinkers do is attempt to answer the question *why* we have (or do not have) the right in question. Both Kingdom and McLean make the mistake of examining the positive law and drawing their conclusions (which happen to be different) from their interpretation of legal

---

[109] 'The Right to Reproduce' in (ed.) M. Ockleton, *Medicine, Ethics and Law*, p. 54.

[110] *Ibid.*, p. 57.

[111] 'The Right to Reproduce' in T. Campbell *et al*, *Human Rights*, Blackwell, 1986, p. 99, 112.

[112] *Op. cit.*, note 8, p. 60.

[113] 'Basic Personal and Civil Rights' in (ed.) M. Kindred *et al.*, *The Mentally Retarded Citizen and the Law*, Free Press, 1976, p. 3 at 11.

[114] 405 U.S. 438 (1972). "If the right to privacy means anything, it is the right of the individual, married or single, to be free from unwarranted governmental intrusion into matters so fundamentally affecting a person as the decision whether to beget or bear a child." (p. 453).

[115] 'The Right to Reproduce'. I am grateful to Felicity Carby-Hall, a former Ph.D. student of mine, for giving me the permission to comment upon her work in this way, somewhat exceeding normal tutorial licence.

codes. This is a misleading approach. Even if they were to find the right to reproduce embodied in a legal system (or even in all legal systems), it would not follow that a normatively necessary moral requirement had been established. Whether the right to reproduce exists is independent of what Heilbron J. said *Re D* or the House of Lords in *Re B*. It depends on moral argument.

The other thinkers, to which reference has been made, tend to assume the existence of the right in some form or other. This is not surprising. It is all too common to do this. Thus, Nozick asserts peremptorily in the Preface to *Anarchy, State and Utopia*: "individuals have rights".[116] Neither he nor Dworkin[117] tried to explain why we have the rights we do. Nor, for that matter, has either of them explained why they have not tried to explain this.

It is not, however, difficult to explain why rights are important. A society without rights would be morally impoverished. Rights are important because they "enable us to stand with dignity, if necessary to demand what is our due without having to grovel, plead or beg or to express gratitude when we are given our due…".[118] In Joel Feinberg's words: "A world with claim-rights is one which all persons, as actual or potential claimants, are dignified objects of respect.… No amount of love or compassion, or obedience to higher authority, or *noblesse oblige*, can substitute for those values."[119] Given the social history of this century it is not surprising that we should wish to construct a right to reproduce, or that the United Nations Declaration on Human Rights should talk of "the right to marry and found a family".[120]

But we still need a justifying principle. Why do we have the rights we have including the right to reproduce? One common answer links rights with interests. Such a view was implicit in Bentham and Ihering and is found in such contemporary writers as Feinberg[121] and McCloskey.[122] Thus, Feinberg writes that "the sort of beings who can have rights are pre-

---

[116] Basic Books, 1974, p. ix.

[117] In *Taking Rights Seriously*, Duckworth, 1978 (revised.).

[118] See B. Bandman 'Do Children Have Any Natural Rights?' (1973) *Proceedings of 29th Annual Meeting of Philosophy of Education Society*, p. 234 at 236.

[119] 'Duties, Rights and Claims' (1966) 3 *Amer. Phil. Q.* 137.

[120] Art. 16 (1).

[121] 'The Nature and Value of Rights' (1970) *Journal of Value Inquiry* 243–260.

[122] 'Rights' (1965) 15 Phil. Q. 115–127. In a later article he holds that persons have a *prima facie* right to the satisfaction of needs: See (1976) 13 *Amer. Phil. Q.* 9.

cisely those who have (or can have) interests".[123] It is an argument often employed by those who believe that animals have rights.[124] It is also one of the arguments employed by Carby-Hall to demonstrate that Jeanette did not have the right to reproduce. She writes: "A being can truly be said to have an interest in x, the subject of a potential right, if and only if, x will benefit him in the sense of furthering some or all of his present or future desires".[125] She argues that a necessary condition of possession of a right is at least the capacity to possess the relevant concepts and a desire for that right. Jeanette clearly lacked the former and almost certainly the latter. But is this association of rights and interests justifiable? I think not. What this does not answer is how the having of interests establishes the grounds for having rights. Animals have interests. I have an interest in Middlesex winning the County Cricket Championship. In neither would it make sense to talk of rights. Human beings do not have the same interests. Surely this does not justify an unequal distribution of human rights. I agree with Alan White that "no valid argument can be given either for including or for excluding children, imbeciles (*inter alia*)...as holders of rights on the ground that being capable of having something in one's interest or of being interested in something". Hence, he concludes, "the question whether animals etc. can or cannot have interests either in the sense of something being in their interest or in the sense of their being interested in something, is irrelevant to the question whether they can have rights...".[126]

Before we pursue the justifying principle any further it may be as well to ponder the Carby-Hall claim. Can it be right that a necessary condition for the possession of a right is the capacity to possess relevant concepts and a desire for the right in question? Carby-Hall is far from being alone in thinking that it is. In *Causing Death and Saving Lives*, Glover puts the case as follows: "Desires do not presuppose words, but they do presuppose concepts. A baby can want to be fed, or changed, or go to his mother, although he does not speak. Innumerable signs of recognition and pleasure show us that he has these concepts. But a baby cannot want to escape from death any more than he can want to escape the fate of being a chartered accountant when grown up. He has no idea of either."[127] Glover goes on to

---

[123] *Rights, Justice and the Bounds of Liberty* (1980), Princeton U.P., p. 167.
[124] For example, J. Feinberg (see 'The Rights of Animals and Unborn Generations' in W. Blacstone (ed.), *Philosophy and Environment Crisis*, (1974). See also M. A. Warren; 'Do Potential People have Moral Rights?' (1977) VII *Canadian J. of Phil.* 275–89.
[125] *Op. cit.*, note 115, p. 18.
[126] *Rights*, Clarendon Press, 1984, p. 82.
[127] Penguin Books, 1977, p. 158.

argue that the autonomy argument is no objection to infanticide. "In killing a baby, someone is overriding the baby's autonomy to no greater extent than he would be if he prevented the mother from coming home that day."[128] Or, in the language of *Re B*: "In sterilising Jeanette, we are overriding her autonomy to no greater extent than we would be if we prevented her seeing her boyfriend this evening (by, for example, arranging for him to be elsewhere)". I do not find this very convincing. The fact that a baby has no awareness of, or desire for, life cannot mean that it does not have a right to life. It may be difficult, if not impossible, to exercise a right if one is unaware of its existence or one lacks the concepts of the desire, but this cannot mean that one lacks the right in question. If the Carby-Hall-Glover line is correct, what are we to do with the comatose patient, why do we strive to keep alive the potential suicide who has ingested an overdose? Surely, White is right when he argues that it is a "misfortune, not a tautology"[129] that certain persons cannot exercise or enjoy, claim or waive their rights.

In what other ways, then, can rights be grounded? There are any number of justifications. I will consider only a few, and only briefly. There is the intuitionist answer found in thinkers ranging from Jefferson[130] to Nozick.[131] But it offers no argument at all and therefore is unlikely to convince those whose intuitions tell them otherwise. It certainly offers little to resolve the sterilization dilemma.

There are purely formal answers: the argument that all persons ought to be treated alike unless there is a good reasons for treating them differently, that, in other words, persons have the right to equal treatment.[132] But what is a "good reason" for treating persons differently? Gender and colour have now been almost universally accepted as indefensible distinctions: age and intelligence have not. The principle looks egalitarian but potentially could undermine egalitarianism. Those who support the Lords' decision in *Re B* will find differences between Jeanette and the "normal" woman (lesser intelligence and competence, inability to defer gratification, the ease with which she might be led astray) and those who criticize

---

[128] *Idem*.

[129] *Op. cit.*, note 116, p. 90.

[130] Who held it to be "self-evident" that all humans equally have certain rights. A good account is C. D. Brown, *Miracle at Philadelphia*, Little Brown, 1966.

[131] *Anarchy, State and Utopia*, Basic Books, 1974.

[132] Ch. Perelman, *The Idea of Justice and the Problem of Argument*, (1963), RKP pp. 15–16; H. L. A. Hart, *The Concept of Law*, (1961) Clarendon Press, p. 158. *Cf.* R. Dworkin, *op. cit.*, note 117 at 227.

the decision as unwarranted discrimination will argue that she has more in common with "normal" women than separates her from them (similar feelings, drives, desires and so on). Ironically, if this line of argument is pursued, it becomes relatively easy to defend discrimination by the gifted against those of ordinary intelligence.[133]

An appealing argument was put by William Frankena in an important article in 1962.[134] He argued that humans are "capable of enjoying a good life in the sense in which other animals are not...it is the fact that all men are similarly capable of enjoying a good life in this sense that justifies the *prima facie* requirement that they be treated as equals".[135] Though superficially attractive, there are a number of problems with this. It question-begs. Are all persons capable of enjoying a good life? Those who support the decision to sterilize Jeanette will say she was not, so that the *prima facie* requirement is removed. Frankena's argument also derives an "ought" from an "is" and fails to show how factual similarity justifies the normative obligation which he supports. Nor is it entirely clear why factual similarity should lead to egalitarian treatment: it would be possible to agree that two persons were similar whilst supporting unequal treatment on the grounds that the value of one person's happiness is greater than that of other persons.[136]

Amongst many other arguments those put forward by Hart in his classic article "Are There Any Natural Rights?"[137] and Rawls in *A Theory of Justice* are too well known (as are their faults) to merit any discussion here. But we cannot ignore the argument contained in the United Nations Universal Declaration of Human Rights, because it is commonly invoked in the sterilization debate. The first article states: "All human beings are born free and equal in dignity and rights." It is not clear what is meant by "dignity" here or whether it adds anything to "rights". But if "dignity" is identified with respect for persons which leads to their being accorded dignity and hence equality of treatment so far as rights are concerned, the argument is advanced considerably.

---

[133] See the arguments of Daniel Wikler, 'Paternalism and the Mildly Retarded' (1979) 8 *Phil. and Public Affairs* pp. 377–392.
[134] 'The Concept of Social Justice' in R. Brandt, *Social Justice*, (1962), Prentice-Hall, p. 1.
[135] *Ibid.*, p. 19.
[136] *Cf.* G. Vlastos, "Justice and Equality" in *op. cit.*, note 134, pp. 52–53 (note 45).
[137] (1955) 64 Phil. Review 175.

I believe it is possible to argue, as Melden[138] does, that we have the rights we do because of our status as moral agents, and that we cannot explain what it is to be a moral agent without eventual reference to our rights. But here we come up against the arguments of Neville.[139] He has two arguments in favour of sterilizing the mentally handicapped. One (he calls it the "humble" argument) maintains that sterilization is in their best interests. His arguments here add little to what has already been said and need no further elaboration or comment. He calls his second argument "philosophical". It is an attempt to defend the policy of sterilization against the Kantian objection that it is wrong because it denies the subjects their proper place in the moral community, treating them as means only and not ends in themselves, and also against the objection that it is wrong for community representatives to carry out a policy of doing violence to particular subjects. Neville tries to answer both of these objections. He attempts to neutralize the fears of the objectors. Far from treating persons as things, rather than as responsible agents, Neville claims, he admits somewhat paradoxically, that "to refrain from sterilisation is to do them the violence of preventing them from participating in the moral community in one of the most important respects of which they are capable".[140] The characteristics of the moral community he sets out as follows: (i) membership is relative to the capacity for taking moral responsibility; (ii) most capacities for taking moral responsibility need to be developed: "ordinary socialisation" develops most of them; (iii) a "general moral imperative for any community is that its structures and practices foster the development of the capacities for responsible behaviour whenever possible, and avoid hindering that development".[141] He agrees that the idea of a moral community is "an ideal that exists in pure form only in the imagination".[142] He accepts partial membership for children. But as far as the mildly retarded are concerned (and it should be stressed that he is justifying involuntary sterilization of the mildly retarded), they, unlike children, do not develop in such a way that "emotional maturity" is achieved at the same time as "bodily maturity". The example he gives could come straight from *Re B*. "For instance, the emotional and intellectual capacities to manage conventional birth control methods, to adjust to pregnancy, or to

---

[138] *Rights and Persons*, O.U.P., 1977.

[139] 'Sterilising the Mildly Mentally Retarded Without Their Consent: The Philosophical Arguments' in (eds.) R. Macklin and W. Gaylin, *op. cit.*, note 15, pp. 181–193.

[140] *Ibid.*, pp. 190–191.

[141] *Ibid.*, p. 186.

[142] *Idem*.

raise children do not develop by the time their physical development and their social peers among unretarded people are ready for sexual activity."[143]

Neville is prepared to admit mildly mentally retarded people as members of the moral community on condition that they meet certain restrictions, the only one of which he mentions is involuntary sterilization. What kind of "moral" community is it that can only admit sterilized members of the class of the mildly mentally handicapped? Neville gropes for an analogy and comes up with an "imperfect" one. "Just as people with bad eyesight may be licensed to drive with the restriction that they wear glasses, so mildly mentally retarded people may be required to meet certain restrictions in order to be members of the moral community."[144] The analogy is "imperfect," he believes, because "a person cannot choose to be in or out of the moral community; one is either in the position to be held responsible or one is not."[145] I believe it is imperfect because it is quite fatuous.

Neville does not spell out his reasons for believing the mildly mentally retarded to be irresponsible. I suspect what he has in mind is the supposed inability to care for any children parented, with the burden accordingly falling on the state. But fundamental rights cannot justifiably be abrogated merely because respecting them involves the community in expense. Furthermore, the evidence on parenting competence is shaky. Can incompetence be tested objectively? "Normal" parents may also be deficient. There is "clear injustice" when a parent "adjudged 'normal' is sometimes able to 'get away' with 'a number of defects in parenting capacity, whereas the retarded person, simply because he or she is labelled retarded, is liable to the instigation of sterilization procedures".[146] Our social control apparatus may not reach as intrusively as the American, but we saw how in the same year as the Jeanette case the battle waged between Wolverhampton Social Services and a mentally handicapped couple over the question as to whether they could keep their child.[147] To indulge in "slippery slope" arguments is dangerous, but so are slippery slopes.

But we must return to moral agency before we re-climb the slope and examine how slippery it is. How fair are we being to the mentally handi-

---

[143] *Ibid.*, p. 187.
[144] *Ibid.*, p. 189.
[145] *Idem.*
[146] *Op. cit.*, note 15, p. 96.
[147] *The Guardian*, 2 July 1987.

capped? The distinction between "normal" persons and the handicapped is often drawn too starkly. How many of us achieve the ideal of "personhood"? It was Dennett[148] who remarked wisely that few humans are persons in the sense that Kant and Rawls seem to require. We can insist on autonomy not because we are "persons" in the ideal sense of being maximally rational reflective agents, but because, as Wikler put it, "with respect to the challenges [we] have fashioned for [our]selves, [we] are nearly on a par with persons".[149] Very few of us, if any, achieve perfect moral insight.

The rights we have we have simply by virtue of being human. The right to reproduce is one of these rights. Involuntary sterilization, save where it is carried out for exclusively medical reasons, denies an aspect of humanity. Adequate moral systems must recognize these rights and must do all that is feasible to sustain moral agency. Faced with a choice of changing the world or denying the less able (those who have not achieved and who may never achieve moral agency) access to it, Neville goes for the latter solution. It will be clear that I choose the former solution. If this prioritizes the civil liberties of all, including the mentally handicapped, in the name of equal liberty for all at the costs of the general welfare, so be it. But the general welfare should not suffer for it is "a public good...that [society] is infused with a sense of respect for human beings".[150] A good criterion for judging a society is the way it treats its weaker members.[151]

It may be objected at this point that rights are subject to limitations. How we look at this is heavily dependent upon which conception of rights we adopt.[152] We could adopt a conception of rights as a very important interest, weighted as against other calculations. As such it could be knocked off its pedestal by a goal of special urgency: for example, the right to strike may be forfeited during a war-time emergency.[153] We could also give rights (in Rawls' expression) lexical priority.[154] This would promote them above all other considerations and mean that they clearly prevailed over

---

[148] 'Conditions of Personhood' in A. Rorty (ed.), *The Identities of Persons*, (1976), Univ. of California Press, pp. 175–196.

[149] *Ibid.*

[150] *Per* J. Raz, 'Right-Based Moralities' in R. S. Frey (ed.), *Utility and Rights*, (1985) Blackwell, p. 42 at 46–47. See also now *The Morality of Freedom*, (1986) O.U.P., ch. 8.

[151] *Cf.* Urie Bronfenbrenner, *Two Worlds of Childhood,* (1970) Russell Sage, or B. Blatt, *Exodus from Pandemonium.* (1970), Allyn and Bacon.

[152] See J. Waldron, *Theories of Rights* (1984), O.U.P.

[153] See L. J. MacFarlane, *The Rights to Strike* (1981) Penguin, pp. 127–132.

[154] A *Theory of Justice*, (1971) Harvard University Press, pp. 42–45.

considerations of utility. This model accepts that rights may conflict with each other, in which case the preferred solution is one which maximizes the fulfilment of rights and minimizes their violations. A third approach defends the notion of absolute rights: it sees rights as the reason for constraints on action by others.[155] There can be few absolute rights.[156] The right not to be sterilized must come close to being one of them. The main objection to absolute rights is that any right must be overridden if the consequences of fulfilling it are sufficiently disastrous, what Nozick calls "catastrophic moral horror".[157] By accepting, as I have done, that involuntary sterilization can be defended when it is in the mentally handicapped patient's best medical interests, clearly a lesser test than disaster or horror, I am committing myself to the *second* view of rights. On this view, and returning to Jeanette, it was her rights, and not her welfare, which should have been given first and paramount consideration. Only a compelling reason would justify interference and only then if all less restrictive alternatives had been considered and rejected. In my opinion the House of Lords was too easily convinced that a compelling reason existed in Jeanette's case.

(c) The Slippery Slope

I have left the "slippery slope" argument deliberately to last. It assumed an over-weighty profile in the public debates surrounding the sterilization of Jeanette. It, rather than an appeal to rights, is an argument (or scenario) with which the public can readily identify. This is not surprising given the social history, to which reference has already been made. Nor should the public's fears be ignored. It is all too easy, as an American court indicated, to drift into policies with unfathomed implications.[158] In a "law-and-order" society with more and more intrusive social control,[159] with bio-technology improving" reproduction all the time,[160] with Nobel prize-winners calling

---

[155] See *op. cit.*, note 131, at p. 29.
[156] See Alan Gewirth, *Human Rights,* (1982) Univ. of Chicago Press, ch. 9.
[157] In *Op. cit.*, note 131, at p. 29.
[158] *Relf v. Weinberger* (1974) 372 F. Supp. 1196.
[159] For historical and theoretical insights see S. Cohen and A. Scull, *Social Control and the State*, (1983) Martin Robertson. On contemporary issues see S. Cohen, *Visions of Social Control*, (1985), Polity Press.
[160] M. Stanworth, *Reproductive Technologies*, (1987) Polity Press. G. Corea, *The Mother Machine,* (1985), Harper and Row; R. Arditti (ed.), *Test-Tube Woman*, (1985), Pandora Press.

for licensing of parenthood[161] and favouring temporary sterilization by means of a time-capsule contraceptive reversed upon government approval,[162] it is as well to be wary.

Slippery slope arguments appeal to the dangerous consequences that can flow from the adoption of particular policies. But slippery slope arguments are themselves dangerous if not structured and carefully though through. The *logical* implications of a decision must be distinguished from their supposed *empirical* consequences.[163] There is no reason to suppose a logical slippery slope unless it is genuinely feared that courts will permit sterilization when they do not think it is in the interests of the person concerned. This cannot be foreseen as a danger, but, on the other hand, we cannot predict what will come under the umbrella of "best interests". The shift from *Re D* to *Re B* shows how easily "best medical interests" have become "best interests" with the obliteration of the therapeutic/non-therapeutic distinction. It should not be forgotten that a leading gynaecologist wrote in the *Journal of Medical Ethics* in 1975 that "from society's point of view it is rational to encourage sterilisation not only of the mentally abnormal but other groups of disadvantaged individuals". He saw this as "the logical endpoint of genetic counselling".[164] But the logical slippery slope should not become a reality if we ensure that the test remains in the best interests of the mentally handicapped person and provides adequate mechanisms to defend those interests.

The problem with the empirical slippery slope argument is, as Gillon indicates, that "it can be used against *any* proposal that is capable of misuse".[165] On the other hand, we will know that sterilization has been used for social control purposes and not just in the Third Reich. Some of us fear the implications for civil liberties of current law and order policies.[166]

---

[161] William Shockley, winner of Nobel Prize for making transistors. See the discussions of his ideas in Corea, *op. cit.*, note 160, pp. 25–27.

[162] These views of Shockley are traced in C. Djerassi, *The Politics of Contraception*, (1979), W. W. Norton, p. 180. Francis Crick (co-discoverer of the cell's DNA structure) expressed similar views at a CIBA conference in 1963 and reported in G. Wolstenholme (ed.), *Man and His Future*, 1963, Churchill.

[163] And see R. Gillon, *op. cit.*, note 8, p. 61.

[164] *Per* M. Brudenell, (1975) 1 J. Med. Ethics 263, 164.

[165] *Op. cit.*, note 8 (1st series), p. 61. On "slippery slopes" generally see B. Williams 'Which Slopes are Slippery?' in (ed.) M. Lockwood, *Moral Dilemmas in Modern Medicine*, (1986) Oxford, pp. 126–137.

[166] See M. D. A. Freeman, 'Law and Order in 1984' (1984) 37 *Current Legal Problems* 175–231. The Police and Criminal Evidence Act 1984, the Public Order Act 1986, further attacks on the jury and on the press (note the use of civil law injunctions rather than the dis-

And a few of us even remember Sir Keith Joseph's speech in 1972.[167] It would be a wise person who could declare for certainty that there is no danger of sterilization policies being pursued beyond the range intended by the Lords in Jeanette's case. The case for an empirical slippery slope is unproven and unprovable, but I would not rule it out. At the very least the Lords' decision helps to foster an ideology which denies human rights and, in doing so, denies the humanity of an already disadvantaged group of people.

---

credited Official Secrets Act prosecution, where there is a good chance of a jury acquitting), all provide further ammunition for the thesis presented there.

[167] 'The Cycle of Deprivation' in (eds.) E. Butterworth and R. Holman, *Social Welfare in Modern Britain*, (1975) Fontana, pp. 387–93 (somewhat retracted in an article on Social Class in *The Guardian*, July 18, 1979).

CONCLUSION

I have criticized the House of Lords for (i) putting what they conceived to be Jeannette's best interests before her rights; for (ii) the way they identified those interests, in particular their refusal to accept that best interests means in this context "best medical interests" and for (iii) giving too little consideration to Jeanette's rights, and not taking them seriously. Further, on best interests they offer little guidance, thus creating enormous latitude for subsequent decision-makers. The only positive things to emerge from this sad litigation are the rejection (once again) of parental rights and clinical freedom (in particular in Lord Templeman's speech) and, most importantly, the opportunity the saga offers us to rethink the rights of the mentally handicapped.[168] If something positive comes out of rethink, then Jeanette will not have suffered in vain.

---

[168] See W. Kempton, 'Sexual Rights and Responsibilities of the Retarded Person' in *The Social Welfare Forum* 1976, (1977), Columbia U.P., pp. 206–220; B. Gray, 'Whose Handicap?' in (ed.) D. Carson, *The Law and the Sexuality of People with a Mental Handicap*, (1987), University of Southampton, pp. 7–12.

CHAPTER 17

Afterword

Children's rights, at least the rhetoric of children's rights, have come a long way in the recent past. When I wrote *The Rights and Wrongs of Children* in the early 1980s there was no expectation of an international convention or a World Summit or that interest in children's rights would be ignited in Africa or the Council of Europe.[1] The upheavals in the world could not have been anticipated, nor would we have expected that newly emergent countries, like South Africa, would encode children's rights within their constitutions.[2] All this, and much more, has happened, and yet the plight of children world-wide has not got better but worse. That there is heightened concern for this condition—given the world's response to the United Nations Convention it could hardly be otherwise—may constitute the light at the end of the tunnel. But, as yet, this remains a glimmer.

A glance at events and news items in Britain in the last twelve months is revealing. A third of children in Britain now live in poverty (it was 10 per cent in 1979)[3] At least 5,000 children under the age of 16 are used for prostitution in Britain (an article in *The Guardian* reported on girls aged 12 being 'fed to paedophiles').[4] An estimated 1.5 million children work illegally in Britain, often in dangerous conditions (a survey among 7000 10–16-year-olds in Edinburgh, Glasgow, Birmingham and London discovered that 88 per cent were working illegal hours, in jobs forbidden for

---

[1] In addition to the Convention, discussed in chapter 3, there is also a European Strategy for Children (see EREC 1286, 1996). See also CDPS CP (96) 'Children's Rights and Childhood Policies in Europe: New Approaches?' Conclusions from Leipzig Conference of Council of Europe, 30 May–1 June 1996.

[2] See Julia Sloth-Nielsen, 'The Contribution of Children's Rights To The Reconstruction of Society' (1996) 4 The International Journal of Children's Rights 323.

[3] See Ruth Cohen *et al.*, *Hardship Britain: Being Poor in the 1990s* (London: Child Poverty Action Group, 1992).

[4] *The Guardian*, 21 August 1996, reporting on a study in Bradford.

their age group and without the necessary permits).[5] Every 12 days, on average, a baby less than a year old is killed in Britain: infants are four to five times more likely to be killed than people of any other age.[6] Details of a child sex abuse scandal in Clwyd's children's homes were suppressed, it seems because insurers threatened that negligence cover could be revoked (more than 100 children were sexually abused over a period of 20 years of whom 12 subsequently died, a number of which were recorded as suicides).[7] Poor children, it was revealed in May 1996, were being denied a summer holiday because of child abuse fears: 'the age of innocence is dead, killed by suspicion', proclaimed *The Independent*.[8] In September 1996 Britain's most advanced children's hospital, the first to be built in Britain this century, was opened in Derbyshire—but, at the opening ceremony, they talked of its closure because of budget cuts.[9] In August 1996 the world took its first step to halt the sexual exploitation of children, 'To abuse children is to abuse our future', said the Swedish Prime Minister. 'We must go from words to deeds by developing strategies to fight these intolerable acts.'[10] Britain responded the following week by gaoling a senior diplomat for smuggling obscene child pornography videos into Britain[11]: in Belgium it seems, where bodies of children have been dug up, the cancer goes higher and deeper.[12]

And if we look to policies about children we find it remains the most intensively governed sector of personal existence. The 'Left' would curfew the under 10s[13]: the Right favour the 'naming'[14] and the caning[15] of juvenile offenders. The *Daily Telegraph* has recently called for the reintroduction of corporal punishment in state schools though it qualifies this somewhat dis-

---

[5] See *The Independent*, 16 June 1996.

[6] See *The Independent*, 12 July 1996.

[7] See *The Independent*'s leading article (13 April 1996) ('Our Worst Child Abuse Scandal Must Not Be Hushed Up'). On the deaths see *The Independent*, 29 March 1996. See also Bea Campbell, 'Too Little, Too Late', *The Guardian*, 14 June 1996.

[8] See article by Polly Toynbee, *The Independent*, 1 May 1996.

[9] See *The Guardian*, 3 September 1996.

[10] *The Independent*, 28 August 1996.

[11] *The Independent*, 5 September 1996.

[12] News of the deaths and disappearance of children there surfaced in mid-August 1996.

[13] See *The Independent*, 3 June 1996.

[14] See *The Independent*, 2 September 1996. The 'Left' is also in favour, but its proposal is limited to those aged between 16 and 18.

[15] The Corporal Punishment (Reintroduction) Bill moved by Warren Hawksley MP would have introduced 12 strokes of the cane as a punishment to those between 10 and 18. It was lost by 153 votes to 58 (see *The Independent*, 7 June 1996).

ingenuously by recommending that 'teachers cannot simply be allowed to cane pupils at will'.[16] Children in Britain are to be tested at the age of 4:[17] at the same age, it is now reported,[18] children are having counselling at school. And, though there have been some improvements notably in the Family Law Act 1996,[19] it remains the fact that children's opportunities for participation remain limited. Objects of intervention they certainly are: social actors rarely so. The case for children's rights remains as strong as ever, perhaps stronger but there has been a backlash against rights, and children's rights have taken its share of this onslaught. An early critic was Onora O'Neill, whose views are discussed in chapter 2.[20]

Today the attack on rights, 'rights-talk' as it is often called,[21] comes from the Left, from the Right and from communitarianism. As an example of the Left, the American Critical Legal Studies movement may be cited.[22] Mark Tushnet is representative of this school.[23] Rights, he argues, mask the ugly realities behind the law, such as oppression, greed, the pursuit of self-interest. Those who wield power can manipulate the meaning of 'rights' as they wish because the concept is vague and interdeterminate. The 'régime of rights' oppresses society. Rights are a smoke-screen: the language of rights undermines efforts to accomplish genuine social change by diverting attention from the real abuses, the imbalance of power, economic disparities, social oppression, and focusing instead on symbolic abstractions. Of course, there is some truth in this and even some relevancy to children's rights. The indeterminacy of legal rights does allow for judges to insert their personal and cultural biases into the law.[24] Rights-talk may well at times foster excessive individualism that harms relationships and can lead to the neglect of

---

[16] 20 September 1996.

[17] *The Sunday Telegraph*, 10 September 1996.

[18] *The Daily Telegraph*, 30 September 1996.

[19] See, in particular, section 64, responding to a concern expressed amongst others by myself (see 'Looking Away from the Child's Future' (1996) 9 *Representing Children* 42).

[20] See pp. 25–29.

[21] See Mary Ann Glendon, *Rights Talk* (New York: Free Press, 1991).

[22] On this generally see Lloyd and Freeman, *Introduction To Jurisprudence* (London: Sweet & Maxwell, 1994), Ch. 12.

[23] See his 'An Essay on Rights', 62 *Texas Law Review* 1363 (1984) and 'The Critique of Rights', 47 *Southern Methodist University Law Review* 23 (1992).

[24] And see Wendy Fitzgerald, 'Maturity, Difference and Mystery: Children's Perspective and the Law', 36 *Arizona Law Review* 11 (1994).

responsibilities.²⁵ But Barbara Woodhouse is surely wrong to note that 'rights talk by definition seems to exclude children because not all children can talk'.²⁶ Nor can many adults—at least in a way which will enable them meaningfully to participate. And Martha Minow is equally wrong, as I note in chapter 1,²⁷ to call for the revision of the current language of rights talk because, so she thinks, 'something [is] terribly lacking in rights for children that speak only of autonomy rather than need, especially the central need for relationships with adults who are themselves enabled to create settings where children can thrive'.²⁸ Too many children realistically cannot rely on this. But the Left's castigation of rights is ultimately wrong and this is now recognized by many of its leading exponents. In chapter 1 I quote from E. P. Thompson, Alan Hunt and Kimberlé Crenshaw.²⁹ Here, and in the context of children it is especially pertinent, it is only necessary to reiterate that a régime of rights is one of the weak's greatest resources. We can debate over which rights it is best to have, not, I think, over whether rights are 'pernicious' merely by virtue of being rights.³⁰

The attack from the Right and from communitarianism cannot always by distinguished. For both there are 'too many rights' and 'too few responsibilities'.³¹ I will distinguish them by focusing initially on the Right's critique of rights for it is particularly prominent when the role of law in children's lives in explicated. Goldstein, Freud and Solnit were early critics of children's rights.³² I criticized their arguments in *The Rights and Wrongs of Children*.³³ The only right that Goldstein, Freud and Solnit appear ready to concede to children is the 'entitlement to autonomous parents'.³⁴ They are anti-intervention: state 'intrusion' can shake a child's belief that his parents

---

[25] See Roberto Unger, *The Critical Legal Studies Movement* (Cambridge, Mass: Harvard University Press, 1986).

[26] '"Are You My Mother?"': Conceptualizing Children's Identity Rights in Transracial Adoptions', 2 *Duke Journal of Gender, Law and Policy* 107 (1995).

[27] See p. 11.

[28] *Making All The Difference: Inclusion, Exclusion and American Law* (Ithaca, New York: Cornell University Press, 1990), p. 306.

[29] See p. 15. And do again in (1997) *Int. J. of Law, Policy and Family* (fothcoming).

[30] See Cass R. Sunstein, 'Rights and Their Critics', 70 *Notre Dame Law Review* 727, 729 (1995).

[31] See Amitai Etzioni, *The Spirit of Community* (New York: Simon and Schuster, 1993), p. 161.

[32] Both in *Beyond The Best Interests of The Child* (New York: Free Press, 1973) and *Before the Best Interests of The Child* (New York: Free Press, 1979).

[33] See ch. 7.

[34] See *Before*, p. 9.

are 'omniscient' and all-powerful'.[35] A policy of minimum coercive intervention by the state accords with their 'firm belief as citizens in individual freedom and human dignity'.[36] Unfortunately, they fail to address the obvious question of whose freedom and dignity is to be upheld. It is, of course, that of the parents and not that of the children that this ideology upholds.[37] This position is simplistic—it does not question autonomy long since taken away[38]—and dangerous as the case studies in *Before The Best Interests of The Child* illustrate.[39]

More recently the attack on children's rights has come from Lynn Wardle.[40] He alleges that children's rights advocates are undervaluing marriage and parenting and overvaluing the capacity of children's rights 'to make things right'.[41] Children's rights advocates are said to 'manifest the lingering hubris of the belief in the infinite and invincible capacity of the law to do good. They see law as a secular Messiah, a care-all for every social ill, a big yellow social bulldozer that can shove away the old problems and build new temples of goodness.'[42] Wardle believes that 'defining parent-child relationships in terms of rights misses the point and undermines the real needs of the parties themselves'.[43] 'The point' of course is not further explained or developed. It is taken for granted that we all know what 'it' is. Just as it is assumed we all agree that the 'parties' define 'needs' in the same way. A dangerous and false consensus lurks in the shadows. One only has to substitute 'husband-wife' for 'parent-child' in the sentence just quoted to realize how untenable is Wardle's position. The importance of relationship and needs should not lead us to belittle the importance of rights as a resource in structuring and constraining relationships.

---

[35] See *Beyond*, p. 9.
[36] See *Before*, p. 12.
[37] And see Bill Jordan, *Freedom and The Welfare State* (London: R.K.P., 1976), p. 60.
[38] For example, education decisions. See, *op. cit.*, note 33, p. 248.
[39] See *op. cit.* note 33, pp. 259–267 for a critique of some of these.
[40] 'The Use and Abuse of Rights Rhetoric: The Constitutional Rights of Children' 27 *Loyola University Chicago Law Journal* 321 (1996).
[41] *Ibid.*, p. 326.
[42] *Ibid.*, p. 332.
[43] *Idem.*

The onslaught on rights has also come from within communitarianism. This is a critique which alleges that many societal ills can be attributed to an emphasis on rights and a concomitant neglect of responsibilities. It is associated with Mary Ann Glendon's *Rights Talk: The Impoverishment of Political Discourse*[44] and with various publications produced by members of the American Responsive Communitarian movement, Etzioni,[45] Bellah,[46] Galston,[47] and Sandel[48] being prominent academic spokespersons. The communitarian discontent with rights and its questing for responsibility offer opportunities for exploring important questions about rights and their relationships to responsibility and irresponsibility. What is it about rights that triggers the irresponsibility critique? Do legal rights include a right to be irresponsible: if so, are such rights defensible? Does the structure of legal rights discourage or even preclude individual, community, or societal reflection on right conduct and efforts to encourage responsible behaviour? How much of what in at issue in charges of irresponsibility is about rights at all, as distinguished from behaviour that is already subject to sanctions?[49]

To Glendon rights have a strident and absolutist character: for this reason they impoverish political discourse.[50] They are unduly individualistic and associated with highly undesirable characteristics, including selfishness and indifference to others. Right miss, she claims, the 'dimension of sociality'[51]: they posit selfish, isolated individuals who assert what is theirs, rather than participating in communal life. Rights neglect the moral and social dimensions of important problems. She is concerned about the effects of rights on responsibilities.[52] She is critical of the view upheld by the U.S. Supreme Court[53] that the constitution imposes no affirmative duties on government—and so she should be. She fears that judicial decisions like *De Shaney*,[54] that

---

[44] *Op. cit.*, note 21.

[45] *Op. cit.*, note 31.

[46] *The Good Society* (New York: Vintage Books, 1991).

[47] *Liberal Purposes* (Berkeley: Univ. of California Press, 1991).

[48] *Liberalism and The Limits of Justice* (Cambridge: Cambridge University Press, 1982). Communitarianism has influenced President Clinton's administration: it seems likely it will influence also Blair's in Britain.

[49] And see Linda C. McClain, 'Rights and Irresponsibility', 43 *Duke Law Journal* 989 (1994).

[50] *Op. cit.*, note 21, pp. 45–46.

[51] *Ibid.*, pp. 109–144.

[52] *Ibid.*, pp. 76–108.

[53] *De Shaney v. Winnebago County Dept. of Social Services* 489 U.S. 189, 196 (1989).

[54] An English equivalent is *X v. Bedfordshire County Council* [1995] 2 FLR 276.

fail to recognize for example the duty of social workers to protect children from violence at home, harm public discourse and social understandings.

There are truths in a lot of this. But it remains difficult to see why attaching importance to rights should necessarily diminish commitment to duty and responsibility. Of course, there are situations where it may be very wrong to exercise one's rights. It would be wrong to deny women the right to abortion,[55] but remains right nevertheless to insist that this is a right which ought not to be exercised or to have to be exercised very often. It is part of the pathology of a culture of rights that people think that because they have a right to do x, they cannot be criticized or blamed for doing it.

It would be difficult to recognize this as a critique of children's rights. Though many criticize 'irresponsible' youth, in particular what they perceive to be a culture of anti-social activity, delinquency, drug abuse and sexual promiscuity, it is difficult to see the relationship between this and an increased recognition of children's rights. It is common to assert links between the end of corporal punishment in schools and dysfunctional behaviour of a sort which lends to exclusion from school.[56] It is however clear that an increase in the latter antedates the removal of this sanction by some years. Nor can cases like the James Bulger murder[57] be attributed to any increase in our awareness of the importance of children's rights. The irresponsibility critique does not establish a strong case against rights, though it clearly provides an opportunity to reflect on a range of social problems.

The case against children's rights has not been made out. The case for recognizing the moral status of children and recognizing their rights remains as strong as ever. This book has emphasized a range of children's rights, rights to protection, to welfare, to autonomy and participation. Some new rights, the right to sever relationships with a parent,[58] the right of the artificially-procreated to knowledge of their identity,[59] the right in certain circumstances not to be born[60] have been explored. The U.N. Convention represents a breakthrough, but it also represents a challenge. A challenge to

---

[55] In England they do not have such a right. The right vests in medical practitioners. On the U.S. position see *Roe* v. *Wale* 410 U.S. 113 (1973) and *Planned Parenthood* v. *Casey* 112 S. Ct 2791 (1992). See also Cass R. Sunstein, 'Rights and Their Critics', 70 *Notre Dame Law Review* 727 (1995).

[56] See, further, Carl Parsons, 'Permanent Exclusions from Schools in England in the 1990s: Trends, Causes and Responses', 10 *Children and Society* 177 (1996).

[57] On which see ch. 12.

[58] See ch. 11.

[59] See ch. 10.

[60] See ch. 9.

encode its standards in the lives of children. And a challenge also to go beyond it: to make children a priority in resource allocation. If we are not to rest on our laurels, we (that is the world) need an action plan for children. The Convention is but a beginning.

Index

Abortion, 112
Abramovitch, R., 230
Abuse and neglegt, 115-117, 181
   sexual, 159-162, 255-303
Accommodation, Children Act and, 320-325
Accommodation, syndrome, 293
Adoption, 107, 122-124, 190, 209-210
   and artifical reproduction, 191-194
   inter-country, 123-124
   step-parent, 194
Albania, 22
Alderson, P., 218
Alexandra, Baby, 171, 172, 184, 338-339
Alston, P., 154
Argentina, 198
Ariès, P., 25, 75
Arras, G., 182
Artificially procreated child, rights of
   and adoption, 191
   and marriage, 198
   and secrecy, 198-201
   and status, 206-209
   identity, 198
   material interests, 189
   medical history, 189, 190
   to have father, 206
Association, freedom of, 28-29, 40, 46, 120-121
Asquith, S., 255
Australia, 204
Austria, 116. 199
Autonomy,
   limits of, 37-39, 95-98
   rights and, 37, 51-53, 153-156

Bandman, B., 83, 188
Barratt and Bradley case, 251-252
Bedau, H., 32
Bentham, J., 137

Benedict, R., 138
Bentovim, A., 264
Bergh, H., 48
Berlin, L., 25
Binet, A., 101
Bok, S., 202
Bowen, J., 13
Bowling, A., 124
Brandt, R., 39, 175
Brazil, 20, 21, 81, 85
Brock, D., 169
Brooke, R., 314
Bruch, H., 355
Buchanan, A., 169
Buck v. *Bell*, 359, 374
Bulger case, 6, 28, 108-109, 235-253, 395
   and Home Secretary, 249
   and penal policy, 237, 242-243
   and sexual abuse, 240
   and trial, 238-239, 241-242
   and videos, 242
Butler-Sloss, E., 8, 59, 106
Butler-Sloss Report, 255, 259, 278, 280, 282, 285, 288, 290, 292

California, 302
Cambodia, 48
Campbell, 229, 230
Campion, M.J., 173
Canada, 152-153, 302
Carby Hall, F., 377, 379, 380
Ceci, S., 294, 296
Certificate, birth right to see, 190
Childhood,
   correct, 9
   culture and, 8
   disappearance of, 5-10
   golden age, as, 4, 24
   myths of, 84-86

social construction, as, 7, 8, 25, 75, 86
Child In Mind, 277, 278, 284
Child In Trust, 277, 278
Child labour, 133-134, 141-142
Child-saving movement, 48, 84
Child Support Act, 108, 179, 180, 208
Cigarette advertising, 125-126
Children Act 1989, 51, 57, 74, 85, 105, 107, 110, 115, 117, 120, 180, 181, 211
   care and parental responsibility, 330-331
   care order, 325-329
   consensus and ideology, 309-315
   divorce and children, 341-343
   emergency protection, 332-337
   gaps, 328-329
   introduction to, 305-308
   non-intervention and, 306, 315-318
   rights of children and, 310-312
   parental responsibility, 318-320, 330-331
   wardship, 307, 337-342
   contact and, 301
Children in need, 315
Children's Rights,
   adoption and, 55,
   African Charter and, 54
   alternative home environment, 51
   armed conflict, 67
   association, 28, 40, 66
   capacity and, 10-13
   capital punishment, 67
   child liberation movement and, 51-53
   challenging education to, 13, 50, 51
   conscience, freedom of, 28, 53, 56, 66, 68, 119
   culttural values and, 54-55, 129-147
   divorced parents, 49, 213, 214, 215-216
   drive, to, 50
   drugs, to, 52
   early history, 49-50
   education, to, 40, 48, 67
   enforcement of, 69-71
   European Convention and, 57-59
   expression, freedom of, 56
   female circumcison and, 54
   fight, to, 67
   food, to, 67
   health and, 66-67
   hit, not to be, 14, 72
   identity, to, 66, 67, 68
   indigenous children, 67
   information, to, 51
   justice, to, 52
   medical services, 50
   minority children of, 67
   name and nationality, 50, 66
   neglect and cruelty, to be free of, 50
   non-discrimination, to, 50
   participation, to, 3, 4, 40, 56, 64, 111-114
   political power, to, 52
   pre-history of, 47-48
   privacy, to, 66
   refuse medical treatment, to, 53
   religion, freedom of, to, 54, 56
   responsible parents, to, 13
   responsive design, 52
   rest and leisure, to, 67
   Sharia and, 65-66-
   self-determination, to, 51-52, 53
   sex, and, 51
   slogan, as, 47
   social security, to, 40, 50
   take more seriously, why, 31-37
   Ten Commandments and, 47
   thought, freedom of, 40, 53, 56
   traditional practices and, 54, 65
   travel, to, 52
   unborn, 53
   vote, to, 52, 81-82
   work, to, 52
Children's studies, 1
Claydan, G., 283
Cleveland Affair, 8, 255-303, 343
Clwyd scandal, 390

Commodities, children as, 209-212
Convention, U.N., 3, 4, 8, 19, 22, 40, 53-57, 64-71, 72, 99, 100, 102-103, 133-135, 196, 197, 214-215, 345
Contact,
  Australia, in, 152
  Canada, in, 152-153
  child right, as, 149-163
  Cleveland and, 287-289
  commodification and, 163
  England, in, 151
  Goldstein, Freud and Solnit and, 150
  parent's rights, as, 150
  recalcitrant child and, 156-158
  recalcitrant parent and, 158
  sexual abuse, after, 159-162
  support and, 162-163
  U.N. Convention and, 149
  United States, in, 149-150, 156-158
Cook, J., 140-141
Corporal punishment, 4, 14, 23, 48, 52, 72, 106, 116-117, 131-132, 142, 271, 390-391
Cohen, H., 21, 27, 190
Colwell, Maria, 83
Committee on Rights of Child, U.N., 69-71
Costa Rica, 19, 77
Cotton, Baby, 211
Grenshaw, K., 15, 392
Criminal responsibility, age of, 106, 238-239, 240, 244-245
Cultural pluralism
  and monism, 137, 141-142
  and relativism, 137-140
  theory of, 136-137, 142-147
Curfews, 3-4, 390
Cyprus, 116, 245
Czanpanskij, K., 162-163
Czechoslovakia, 201

Daniels, K., 201, 204
Decency, rights and, 13
Deech, R., 130-131

Defective Neonates, 166
Denmark, 187
Dennett, D., 384
Decisions, at home, 113-114
Dependency, child's, 26-27, 73-74
Derrivierre decisions, 131-132
Dickens, B., 80
Dignity, rights and, 87-88
Disclosure interviews, 289-295
Divorce, 51, 113, 341-343
Divorcing parents, 213, 214, 215-216
Doli capax, 238-239, 240, 244-245
Dolls, anatomically correct, 291
Domination, 74-75
Donor Insemination (D.I.), 195-196
Duane, M., 39, 67
Dunblane, 4
Duncan, 265, 267
Dwork, D., 64
Dworkin, G., 39, 98
Dworkin, R., 17, 22, 23, 31-34, 35, 38, 87-88, 89-90, 97, 261, 378

Education, 40, 50, 67, 109-110, 114, 214
Eekelaar, J., 13, 14, 33, 52, 180, 319
Elkins, 376
Emancipation, 232
Emergency protection order, 286, 299
Empowerment, 72-76
  and Children Act, 216-217
  and competence, 217-220
Ennew, J., 9
Equality, rights and, 33-34
Eve, Re, 358-363, 367, 370, 371-373
Ewing, C., 238
Environmental pollution, 125
Ethiopia, 187
Etzioni, A, 181
Expression, freedom of, 56, 117-118

Faller, K., 159-160, 257
Family Court, 308
Family Law Act 1996, 112, 113, 127
Family Law Reform Act 1969, 346

Farson, R., 37, 39, 49, 51, 52, 94, 153
Federle, K.H., 10-12
　and birhtrights, 167-168, 170, 172, 183
Female circumcision, 54, 126, 141, 142-146
Feminism, 73, 74, 273-274
Finkelhor, D., 261, 269-270
Finnis, J., 180
Finland, 57, 114, 116
Flekkøy, M., 78
Floyd, 179
Flugel, J., 270
Foucalt, M., 25, 75, 86
Fox Harding, L., 310-312
France, 48, 125, 135, 245
Frankena, W., 33, 381
Frankfurt, H., 35
Franklin, B., 187
Friedman, 73
Freud, S., 256-257
Frosh, S., 275

Gabriel, 291
Garrison, E.G., 230-231
Geithner, 203
Germany, 198-199, 200-201, 245, 247
Gillick decision, 19, 35, 53, 56, 69, 81, 99, 111, 112, 120, 153, 205, 262, 318, 319, 321, 335, 336, 345, 346, 351-352, 354, 356
Gilligan, C., 73
Glendon, M-A., 394, 395, 396-397
Glover, J., 379
Goldstein, J., Freud, A., and Solnit, A., 24, 85, 150, 171, 313, 392-393
Golombok, S., 199-200
Goodwin, M., 218
Gordon, R., 14
Graef, R., 258
Gramsci, A., 14
Great Ormond Street Hospital, 289
Guatemala, 4, 20, 85
Guttmacher, 271
Gutmann, A., 139

Haderka, J., 201
Hafen, B., 37, 93
Haimes, E., 192-193, 202
Hall, 266
Hardman, C., 3
Harris, J., 167-168, 173-174, 179
Hart, H.L.A., 189, 381
Hatch, 137
Hawes, J., 45, 46
Haworth, L., 35, 52
Held, V., 74
Helmholz, R., 47
Herodutus, 136
Herman, J., 273
Herskovits, M., 138
Higgs, M., 255, 277, 278, 279, 280, 283
HIV Infection, 181-183
Hobbes, T., 23
Hockey, 9
Holocaust, 63-64
Holt, J., 5-6, 39, 49, 51, 52, 94, 153
Holmes, O. W., 21
Home environment, alternative, right to, 51
Homosexuality, 117-118
Hough, J., 59
Housing Legislation and children, 110
Hoyles, M., 93
Human Fetilisation and Embryology Act 1990, 197, 206-209
Hume, D., 136
Hungtington's Chorea, 183
Hunt, A., 15-16, 392

Identity, right to, 55, 66, 68, 186, 189, 196-205, 212
Illegal work, 391
Illich, I., 25
ILO, 133-134
India, 134, 362
Iraq, 49, 187
Irigaray, L., 12
Israel, 19, 49
Italy, 49, 125

Incest, 76
International Year of The Child, 2
Indigenous children, rights of, 67
Information, right to, 51
IQ Test, 30, 101
Illegitimate children, 49
Impact statement, child, 77-78, 127
'In need', children, 110
Interests, and rights, 188-191

J case, 171-172, 183
James, A., 8, 9, 25, 75
James, S., 139
Jeanette decision, 353, 364-387
Jenks, C., 7, 9
Jordan, B., 315, 320
Jordan, Minnesota, 258-260
Juvenile Court, 30, 94, 101
Juss, S., 112

Kant, I., 35, 90, 141, 384
Karsten, I., 131
Kelman, M., 239
Kellmer-Pringle, M., 210
Kempe, C., 272
Kennedy, D., 15
King, M., 252
Kingdom, E., 377
Kingsley, Gregory, 213
Kinsey Report, 256, 264
Kitch, A., 162
Kleinig, J., 23, 24, 36, 87, 188
Knitzer, 79
Korczak, J., 48, 49
Kotlowicz, A., 63
Kraft-Ebing, 256

Lacey, N., 12
La Fontaine, J., 159
Lawyering for the Child, 79-80
Learning disabilities, sterilization and, 357-387
Le Blanc, L., 53
Legitimacy, 206
Lewis, S., 229

Liberal paternalism, theory of, 40, 68, 96-98
Liberating children, rights and, 93-95
Lindley, R., 35-36, 52
Lindsay, M., 102
Lomasky, L., 36
Lowe, N., 112
Lucas case, 158
Luff decision, 123, 124
Lynch, M., 264, 266

Mackie, J., 32, 88
Majority, age of, 91
Male circumcision, 119, 126
Malta, 245
Mandatory reporting of child abuse, 9, 95
Manhattan Beach case, 260
Margolin, C., 37
Marriage, arranged, 215
Massachusetts Body of Liberties, 48
Matsuda, M., 15
Max, L., 22, 63
McCann, 282-283
McCormick, N., 188-189
McLean, S., 377-378
McMarting case, 258
Marshall and Nussbaum decision, 157
Mause, L. de, 2, 105
Mediation, 58
Medical services, right to, 50
Medical traetment, consent to, 112-113
Melden, A., 382
Melton, G., 38, 229, 231
Menkel-Meadow, C., 16
Meyer, P., 50
Meyers, D., 375
Militant concept, rights as, 21, 188
Mill, J. S., 26, 139, 141, 166-167
Miller, A., 36
Minow, M., 11, 15, 17, 394
Ministry for Children, 77
Mistakes, rights and, 97
Mitchell, 200-202

Mnookin, R., 374
Mohamed v. *Knott*, 129-131, 146-147
Montaige, 136
Montesquieu, 136
Mount, F., 313
Muntarbhorn, V., 53
Murray, C., 244, 250
Muslim children, 119
Mrazek, 264

Narveson, J., 32, 88-89
NAYPIC, 120-121
Nelson, S., 269, 273
Netherlands, 63
Neville, R., 382-383
Newell, P., 77
New Zeeland, 3, 19, 63, 77
Newson, J. and E., 116
Nigeria, 129-131
Northern Ireland, 106
Norway, 19, 59, 77, 116, 127
Nozick, R., 32, 89, 378, 380, 385

O'Donovan, K., 189, 191-192, 203
Ollendorf, R., 51
Olsen, F., 72
O'Neill, O., 25-29, 52, 180, 391
Ombudswork for Children, 19, 59, 74-79, 127

Packman, J., 317
Paedophilia, 391
Pais, M. S., 54, 111, 153
Panor, 203
Parent,
  autonomy and, 166-167
  responsibility and, 166, 178-184
  right to be, 165-166
Parfit, D., 39, 174-176, 181
Participation in Englisch Law, 111-114
Party to proceedings, child as, 220-222
Paulsen, M., 30, 101
Peters, 271
Peterson-Badali, M., 230

Phillipines, 75
Pin down, 318
Pluralism, cultural, 129-147
Poland, 49, 53, 57
Polovchak case, 213, 215-216
Pomerantz, 179
Pornography, 51
Porter, R., 275
Postman, N., 5, 6-8
Poverty, child, 19-20, 86, 106
Practices, traditional, 134-135
Pregnancy, control of, 181-182
Privacy, protection of, 121
Prostitution, child, 20-21
Prout, A., 8, 25, 75
Punishment, corporal, 4, 13, 23, 48, 52, 72, 106, 116-117, 131-132, 142, 271, 390-391
Purdie, 204

R case, 345-356
Radin, M., 163, 211
Raves, 121
Rape, 257-258, 274
Rawls, J., 31, 34, 37, 38, 87, 96, 381, 383, 384
Raz, J., 137
Renteln, A., 140
Representation, 113, 307, 370
Responsible parents, right to, 166-167
Richardson, S., 255, 277, 279, 287
Rights,
  autonomy and, 34-36, 37-39, 51-53
  beign, of, 12
  best interests and, 57, 107-111
  capacity and, 10-13
  decency and, 13
  dignity and, 87-88
  double standards and, 91-93
  equality and, 33-34
  from where? 88-91
  importance of children, 23-25, 84-87
  limits of, 29-30
  militant concept, as, 21, 188

mistakes and, 97
obligations and, 25-29
paternalism and, 37-39, 68
resources and, 30
tokenism and, 29
values, other, and, 23
why? 13-17, 21-23
will and interest theories of, 27
women's, 12
Roberge, 261, 262
Robertson, J., 169
Rodham, H., 47, 186
Rogers, C., 37
Romania, 22, 123
Rosenbaum, M., 78
Rowland, 204
Rush, F., 273

Sants, H., 203
Scarre, G., 92-93
Schechter, 261, 262
School uniforms, 118
Self-determination, child's rights to, 51-52
Senegal, 54, 135
Sex, child's right to, 51
Sex tourism, 4
Sexual abuse, 23, 255-303
  definition, 259-264
  explanations of, 266-276
  form, 263
  male sexuality and, 296
  models of, 266
  quantifying amount, 264-266
  socio-economic conditions and, 271
  rest, and dilatation, and, 277-278, 282-284
  victims sue for, 302
Sharia, 65-66
Skolnick, J., 30, 101
Slack, A., 142-143
Snowden, R., 199, 200-201
Sotos Syndrome case, 354
South Africa, 3, 13, 25, 48, 86, 91, 389
Spain, 245

Steinbock, B., 169-170, 175
Sterilization,
  Buck v. *Bell*, 359, 373
  England, in, 362-363
  Eve, Re, 358-363, 367, 370, 371-372
  India, in, 362
  Jeanette case, 363, 364-369, 372-389
  Nazi Germany, in 358, 361, 362, 386
  United States, in, 358-361
  University College London and, 358

Tayler, C., 138
Tay-Sachs, 170, 176, 182-183
Tenneyson, A., 315, 316
Thailand, 75
Thompson, E. P., 15, 392
Thought, freedom of, 40, 53, 55, 119-120
Traditional practices, 126, 134-135
Treatment,
  consent to, 346-348
  refusal to consent to, 350-356
Tribunals and best interests, 109
Turner, 7
Tushnet, M., 391

Ukraine, 20
United Kingdom and U.N. Convention, 19, 99-100, 105-128
Underwager, R., 293, 294
United Nations Convention on Rights of Child, 3, 4, 8, 19, 22, 40, 53-57, 59, 64-71, 72, 99, 100, 102-103, 133-135, 196-197, 214-215, 345, 347
United Nations Declaration on Rights of Child, 50
Utilitarianism, 34

Vallès, J., 48, 84
Veerman, P., 54-55
Venezuela, 123

Vico, 136
Videos, *Bulger* case and, 242
Vietnam, 132

W case, 345-346
Wakefield, 293
Wald, P., 377
Walker, A. G., 231
Walzer, M., 139
Wardle, L., 393
Wardship, 305-306, 337-340
Warnock, M., 202
Warnock Report, 190, 204-205, 207
Wasserstrom, R., 72, 83, 98, 188
Weithorn, L., 229, 230
West, 265-266
West Indies, 131-132

Wild, 265
Wiggin, K. D., 48
Wilkerson, 47
Wilson, C., 244, 250
Woodhouse, M. B., 392
World Summit on Children, 19, 64
Wrightsman, C., 37
Wrongful Life Actions, 176-178, 186
 in England, 177
 in Israel, 177
 in United States, 176-178
Wyatt, G., 255, 278, 280, 283

Yoruba, 126

Zigler, E., 375
Zulu case, 13